The New Death

School for Advanced Research
Advanced Seminar Series
Michael F. Brown
General Editor

Since 1970 the School for Advanced Research (formerly the School of American Research) and SAR Press have published over one hundred volumes in the Advanced Seminar series. These volumes arise from seminars held on SAR's Santa Fe campus that bring together small groups of experts to explore a single issue. Participants assess recent innovations in theory and methods, appraise ongoing research, and share data relevant to problems of significance in anthropology and related disciplines. The resulting volumes reflect SAR's commitment to the development of new ideas and to scholarship of the highest caliber. The complete Advanced Seminar series can be found at www.sarweb.org.

Also available in the School for Advanced Research Advanced Seminar Series:

Designs and Anthropologies: Frictions and Affinities edited by Keith M. Murphy and Eitan Y. Wilf
Trumpism, Mexican America, and the Struggle for Latinx Citizenship edited by Phillip B. Gonzales, Renato Rosaldo, and Mary Louise Pratt
Archaeologies of Empire: Local Participants and Imperial Trajectories edited by Anna L. Boozer, Bleda S. Düring, and Bradley J. Parker
Walling In and Walling Out: Why Are We Building New Barriers to Divide Us? edited by Laura McAtackney and Randall H. McGuire
How Nature Works: Rethinking Labor on a Troubled Planet edited by Sarah Besky and Alex Blanchette
The Psychology of Women under Patriarchy edited by Holly F. Mathews and Adriana M. Manago
Governing Gifts: Faith, Charity, and the Security State edited by Erica Caple James
Negotiating Structural Vulnerability in Cancer Control: Contemporary Challenges for Applied Anthropology edited by Julie Armin, Nancy Burke, and Laura Eichelberger
Puebloan Societies: Homology and Heterogeneity in Time and Space edited by Peter Whiteley
New Geospatial Approaches to the Anthropological Sciences edited by Robert L. Anemone and Glenn C. Conroy

For additional titles in the School for Advanced Research Advanced Seminar Series, please visit unmpress.com.

The
New
Death

MORTALITY AND
DEATH CARE IN
THE TWENTY-FIRST
CENTURY

Edited by Shannon Lee Dawdy and Tamara Kneese

SCHOOL FOR ADVANCED RESEARCH PRESS • SANTA FE

UNIVERSITY OF NEW MEXICO PRESS • ALBUQUERQUE

Library of Congress Cataloging-in-Publication
data is on file with the Library of Congress.

ISBN 978-0-8263-6345-9 (paper)
ISBN 978-0-8263-6346-6 (e-book)

Founded in 1889, the University of New
Mexico sits on the traditional homelands of the
Pueblo of Sandia. The original peoples of New
Mexico—Pueblo, Navajo, and Apache—since
time immemorial have deep connections to the
land and have made significant contributions
to the broader community statewide. We honor
the land itself and those who remain stewards
of this land throughout the generations and
also acknowledge our committed relationship
to indigenous peoples. We gratefully recognize
our history.

Cover illustration: courtesy of Donovan Fannon
Composed in Minion Pro 10/14

The seminar from which this book resulted was
made possible by the generous support of the
Annenberg Conversations Endowment.

A note to the reader: Some of the photographs
included in the text depict deceased individuals.
They have been included here with the
permission of the bereaved, who wanted to share
these images with the public. Changing attitudes
about photographing the dead is one of the
topics addressed in this book.

Part II. Death Care

On Endings

This book would never have happened without the generous support of the School for Advanced Research. We send out some special appreciation to Leslie Shipman, Carla Tozcano, and the rest of the kitchen staff for keeping us well nourished and outright pampered during our week-long stay in Santa Fe. Through the consumption of nutritious quiches, soups, and salads, we not only found the stamina to work through the most grueling aspects of the human condition but experienced real pleasure in the process. Deep thanks goes to Maria Spray for coordinating our visit and keeping us on task. We are also grateful to Nancy Owen Lewis, Paul Ryer, Michael Brown, and everyone else who took the time to meet with us while we were on the beautiful SAR campus (given our macabre interests, the tour of the dog cemetery was a highlight). We thank the SAR fellows and affiliates, along with the members of the public, who attended our public forum during the seminar and offered their thoughts and questions. We would also like to thank Sarah Soliz and everyone else at SAR Press and University of New Mexico Press, along with our anonymous reviewers, for their attention to, and care for, our manuscript.

Along with all the seminar participants and the authors who later contributed chapters to the volume, the editors would like to thank all our interview subjects as well as our wider circles of friends, loved ones, colleagues, and pets, the networks of collaborators that make any academic work possible.

.

Introduction

SHANNON LEE DAWDY AND TAMARA KNEESE

One of the most sensationalist titles for an academic article ever published may be sociologist Geoffrey Gorer's "The Pornography of Death" (1955a), all the more eyebrow raising because it was published in the relatively prudish 1950s. Gorer's thesis was simple: pornography should be understood as a genre of media consumption intended to stimulate private, and often unrealistic, fantasies of a subject matter that was publicly taboo. Using this definition, he says that the roles of sex and death have, pornographically speaking, switched places since the Victorian era among British and American audiences. Remarkably, Gorer predicts that as the personal experience of death and its social mediation through shared rituals declined, media fantasies of death would rise. The plausibility of his claim became only stronger over the second half of the twentieth century: "While natural death became more and more smothered in prudery, violent death has played an ever-growing part in the fantasies offered to mass audiences-detective stories, thrillers, westerns, war stories, spy stories, science fiction, and eventually horror comics" (Gorer 1955a, 51). Today, it is difficult to turn on a television and avoid graphic, bloody, and forensically exquisite representations of human death and decay. But this proliferation raises a different problem with Gorer's thesis: the absence of censorship. If it isn't censored, is it pornography? Whatever one labels it, he correctly identified an essential interrelationship between experience, taboo, and mediation. Having reached a saturation point, today the death taboo in daily life appears to be dying in the context of all this mediatized gore.

One has to wonder if this overexposure through virtual death is diluting the uncanny qualities of the corpse. If it has become so familiar, can it still be strange? It is difficult to write about death without touching on Freud, not just because of his peculiar notion of the "death drive" (that we all live with an instinct for self-destruction) but because he was an early and prolific thinker on both taboo and the uncanny (Freud 1899, 1913, 1916, 1920). And perhaps nothing, cross-culturally, is as subject to elaborate taboos as the corpse, precisely to contain its uncanny qualities as both familiar and strange, both subject and object. In Freud's central theory of the unconscious, dreams, jokes, and so-called Freudian slips are mechanisms of parapraxis that reveal suppressed thoughts, those that we don't allow ourselves to think consciously because they are terrifying, taboo, or both. Maybe here, then, lies the secret to gallows humor.

This book is not about gallows humor, although that book does need to be written, but it did originate in a meeting of the minds that one of our contributors (Jenny Huberman) jokingly referred to as "death camp," a summer camp for adults on the beautiful Santa Fe campus of the School for Advanced Research (SAR) that took place in September of 2018 with the seminar topic of contemporary death. Of course, this was funny, because who in their right mind would voluntarily attend a death camp? The joke is on us; it is hard to avoid the social pollution that comes with studying death. Most of us have probably gotten a whiff of disapproval from colleagues insinuating that our research interests amount to overindulging goth tendencies or a cry for help. Or, even if our motivations are not questioned, most assume that depression must be a hazard of the work. In reality, at death camp we enjoyed ourselves quite a lot. There was an intensity to our discussions but also a lot of wonder and laughter. The SAR staff said we were one of the liveliest groups to stop by in a while.

We, the editors, also served as the organizers of that advanced seminar, motivated by a desire to discuss our own research but, more fundamentally, to understand why and how our very subject of study seemed to be shifting beneath our feet. A glossier way to put it is that we are studying "emergent" phenomena. We wanted to bring together other scholars who were similarly intrigued and perplexed by the ways in which death practices and attitudes have been undergoing rapid change in the last two decades. The questions we proposed for the seminar are still relevant for the collection of essays that it produced: How is the experience of death and mourning changing under conditions of growing religious plurality and secularization, technological mediation, and globalization? Cultures throughout history have deployed different media and objects to communicate with, and to remember, the dead. In the first two decades of the twenty-first century, this assemblage is undergoing profound and rapid change. New (and revived) ways of treating the body and memorializing the dead are proliferating across global cities. What are the beliefs, values, and ontologies entwined with these emergent death practices? Are they indicative of new cosmologies and ideologies? What are their historical genealogies and continuities? Are we witnessing a shifting relationship between the living and the dead?

Empirically, the contributors, including authors who joined the project after the initial seminar, share a focus on new attitudes toward mortality and/or new funeral practices, from the possibilities of technologically enhanced afterlives to industrialized "necro-waste," the ethics of care, the meaning of secular rituals, and the political economy of death. They observe and attempt to interpret new behaviors and attitudes about the dead and dead matter. They work in the fields of anthropology, history, media studies, science and technology studies, and comparative religion.

This collection of chapters rides a rising tide of both scholarly and popular interest in death. As we will address below, both contexts are necessary to trace the path of our own efforts as researchers, practitioners, and writers. Death scholars utilize a combination of more familiar forms of ethnography, including attention to treatment of the corpse itself and related mourning practices, along with a close examination of the relationship between technology and culture. The latter includes new methods for corpse disposal, digitized funeral rituals, and dreams of technological life extension as a means of mitigating death itself. While there have been several recent works on digital death practices (Arnold et al. 2018; Moreman and Lewis 2014) and several updated readers on death topics worldwide (Boreț, Long, and Kan 2017; Cann 2018; Das and Chan 2016; Garces-Foley 2006; Hockey, Komaromy, and Woodthrope 2010; Jacobsen 2017; Newby and Toulson 2018; Robben 2018; Walter 2020), this volume uses ethnographic description to support the proposition that death itself is changing, at least in the bourgeois bosom of cosmopolitan centers.

While scholarly volumes and conversations at academic conferences tend to stick either to digital death and technoscience or to mortuary practices and funerary rites, this volume explicitly brings these two divergent threads in death studies together. Death has become a popular subject of study in a variety of disciplines, but panels regarding death are often spread across large conferences, rarely putting many approaches to death studies together in one place. In this volume, we convene scholars who are on the cutting edge of death scholarship in their respective fields, providing an opportunity for them to think across disciplinary boundaries while maintaining an ethnographic spirit. For the authors included in this volume, ethnography might be historically oriented or it might be digital or even speculative, based on interactions with different kinds of death-care providers and mourners in a variety of spaces, online or in other mediated places and in family homes, funeral homes, professional conventions, and at memorial services. Discussions of death practices tend to be siloed by region or type of ritual. Often, digital death practices are completely left out of discussions of green burial and DIY mortuary rituals, while digital death volumes often focus on online memorials in the Anglophone world while leaving out the richness of materiality that also comes with death-care practices, whether digital or physical. What are these new forms of death, what is their genealogy, and how do they relate to other social, economic, political, and cultural currents? As we will address below, the chapters generally cluster around two poles, one about mortality and one about death care. These headings themselves suggest a shifting cultural terrain.

There is perhaps no realm of cultural behavior that more overtly exposes the shape-shifting of populist ontologies than funeral practices. What do these new styles of death tell us about what sort of beings we are when we are alive and what we think happens to us after we die? What is the status of the subject/object divide in daily life? What is a "person" before and after death? What persists of them, and what is lost? What is a secular afterlife? Is a (new) type of spirit ontology being expressed through these practices? What is the nature of the relationship between the living and the dead, and how might it be changing? Inevitably, questions arising from death are as big as life itself. In this volume, we address these questions through ethnographic inquiry. Together, the following chapters coalesce around the argument that the "new death" is in many ways a remaking, re-mediation, and reimagining of older forms of mortuary care and relationships to mortality. Pushing back against the folklorization endemic to anthropological studies of death practices and the whiteness of death studies as a field, the following chapters override divisions between the Global South and Anglophone world, focusing instead on syncretization, globalization, and magic within the mundane.

Context

Prominent anthropologists such as João Biehl, Katherine Verdery, Nancy Scheper-Hughes, and Alexei Yurchak have in recent years offered important studies on death and dying (Biehl 2005; Scheper-Hughes 1993; Verdery 1999; Yurchak 2015), from the institutionalization of terminal illness and social death to describing the political lives of corpses and the commodification of the body. However, none has focused explicitly on new conceptions of mortality or emergent funeral practices shared across globalized urban contexts. We focus not on the gerund *modern dying* but on the substantive *contemporary death*.

In a recent review of the anthropology of death, Matthew Engelke (2019) identifies deep continuities in the literature regarding how death is used to regenerate life through ritual and memorialization, as well as through a persistent concern with the materiality of the corpse even as the boundaries of purity and danger keep shifting. Although much critiqued and reworked, Engelke recognizes the enduring relevance of Robert Hertz's pioneering work on death rituals. Hertz was the first to recognize that in many cultures, biological, social, and spiritual death do not all arrive at the same moment (Hertz [1900] 1960). Finding common threads in recent publications, Engelke demonstrates that recent work has moved the anthropology of death beyond what Johannes Fabian called its "folklorization" ([1973] 2004) and a stagnation in conceptual approaches to death and dying that might have characterized the last decades of the twentieth century. Still, the field continues to exhibit a general tendency to deny the dead as significant social actors in globalized (once glossed "Westernized") societies. Robben's observation that most scholars seem to view Western death culture as "ordinary, shallow, secular" (2004, 1) remains relevant. Modern death has been presumed to be boring and profane, perhaps an academic attitude that is itself an iteration of the "denial of death" that the Annales historian Philippe Ariès (1974a) argued arose with the development of the post-Enlightenment self. While evidence supporting the denial-of-death thesis has always been a bit murky, today the argument is wholly untenable. Contemporary death culture might be confusing in its innovations and pluralism, but it cannot be said to be boring or evasive. You can mix your loved one's ashes into a vinyl record that plays a recording of their voice. You can live on through a software program timed to send messages to your family from the beyond. You can have your body frozen, incinerated, scattered in a redwood grove, plastinated, dissected for science, or dissolved in chemicals. Soon you will be able to be composted in a steaming pile of wood chips on an urban lot. Your family can use your processed remains to fertilize their garden or incorporate them into jewelry, artificial reefs, or paperweights.

Anthropology has had a particularly strong influence on comparative studies of death, explicitly or implicitly serving as a foundation for many of the chapters in this volume. Peter Metcalf and Richard Huntington's *Celebrations of Death: The Anthropology of Mortuary Ritual* ([1979] 1991) provides a cross-cultural comparison of burial practices, drawing on classic ethnographies by Evans-Pritchard, Radcliffe-Brown, and Durkheim. In the final section of the volume, titled "American Deathways," they turn their ethnographic attention to funerary rites in the modern United States, including the rise of commercial funeral homes. At the time of their 1991 revision, they noted that a gap in the field persisted: while "American death rites are probably the most elaborate in the industrialized West" (23), "we have more descriptive material about funerals in Indonesia than in America" (193). One of the major contributions of this volume is to offer a belated corrective to that characterization, while refusing to isolate the United States from its global connections.

Although studies of mortuary practices generally languished in the post-structural, post-symbolic era of American anthropology of the 1990s through early 2000s, studies of *dying* were vibrant throughout this period, particularly through the lenses of medical anthropology and psychology. These studies grew in tandem with an aging population and an expanding hospice system. European studies of funeral cultures, by contrast, have been a relatively steady effort through the UK-based interdisciplinary journal *Mortality* and related conferences, although still strongly weighted toward historical, ethical, and health perspectives. There is a rich tradition of British death studies, including foundational works like Tony Walter's *The Revival of Death* (1994) and Elizabeth Hallam and Jenny Hockey's *Death, Memory and Material Culture* (2001). Walter (1994) argued that while British culture tended to repress discussions of death, it was important for people to start talking about it openly. Hallam and Hockey (2001) focused on the ways that various materials, from human hair to stone and jet, are integrated into mourning rituals, both historically and in the present day. Everyday objects like kitchen spoons can become sacred mementos after people die. In this volume, the authors address the materiality of mourning and temporality of death-care rituals in a globalized world.

One finding of our own effort is the realization that ethnographers need to catch up with fast-changing global phenomena. Although we had intended to provide a global comparison of contemporary and emergent practices, we found that there are still many gaps on the map, particularly Latin America, where few people are working on this topic. Jason De León (2015) describes the necropolitics of the US-Mexico borderlands but focuses on the politics of migrant death, not the rituals around death care. De León notes that migrant bodies are a common sight, almost normalized as part of the landscape, and that they are covered in blankets rather than being treated as sacred, ritualized objects. This volume differs from earlier collections in that we focus on emergent phenomena rather than on traditions. Additionally, although the volume is weighted toward documenting North American death practices, we include several chapters that bring in Asian, African, and British counterparts. In a globalized world of mass media, pat generalizations of local cultures (aka "folklorization") would be foolhardy. Instead, the reader will find common themes across diverse regions and some evidence for mutual exchange and influence (see especially chapters by Dawdy, Olson, Liu, and Toulson).

Although we are interested in facilitating comparisons and tracking flows across spaces, the extremes of the American death story sketch the outlines of the profound changes we are witnessing. Jessica Mitford's classic exposé *The American Way of Death* ([1963] 2000) documented the ways in which the American funeral industry standardized this important life ritual and professionalized what used to be a form of family care. Central to this transition at the beginning of the twentieth century was the development of embalming and viewing of the body (Dawdy, this volume). Despite Mitford's critique of the profit drive behind many practices, for decades, little changed in American funeral practices. But between 2000 and 2015, the cremation rate doubled, and now half of all Americans choose this disposition of the body with rates projected to reach 70 percent by 2030. The reasons for this change are debated, but reduced cost, the decline of organized religion, and a highly mobile society in which family members are less likely to live near multigenerational cemetery plots are the pushes most often cited by funeral directors in the United States. The United Kingdom has already reached this rate. An additional reason cited for that and other island nations such as Singapore is a shortage of available land for perpetual care. Cremation is also growing quickly in China, France, and Scandinavia. Cremation is having huge impacts on mortuary and mourning rituals and the business of death (Engelke, this volume; Howie, this volume).

Changes in burial practices reflect larger structural shifts. As historian Vincent Brown (2008) argues in his book on mortuary rituals connected to the transatlantic slave trade, *The Reaper's Garden*, how death is handled reveals power relations: Who is buried? Where and how? What rituals are performed for and by some groups and not others? Often these distinctions conform to gendered, class-based, and racialized hierarchies, all of which continue to inform contemporary burial rites. Or, as Schiavenato's poignant piece in this volume makes clear, according to age and shifting conceptions of personhood.

Thomas Laqueur's substantial *The Work of the Dead* (2015) looks at physical remains as cultural agents across historical periods and cultures. Despite secularization, caring for the dead continues to be an important aspect of modern life. The dead remain social beings and change agents, potentially doing the work of disrupting the existing social order. In *Is the Cemetery Dead?* (2018), David Charles Sloane examines the present cultural turn away from institution-alized death care as people seek ethical, green, and more sustainable versions of established burial practices. Sloane argues that skyrocketing real estate and consumer reluctance to pay for prime grave locations mean people are turn-ing to alternative means of disposition, and many cemeteries are in financial trouble, falling prey to vandalism and into disrepair. To attract the living, some cemeteries are trying to return the cemetery to its former role as public park space, attempting to attract the attention of younger clientele and redefine what a cemetery is by featuring jazz concerts and movie nights along with historically oriented tours. Sloane argues that the graveyard is also a museum. Cemeteries are attempting to (once again) become places for families to gather not just to mourn and remember the dead but to enjoy life by picnicking, walking dogs, pushing babies in strollers, or jogging. Cemeteries may also encourage more personalized gravestones, incorporating murals, images, and other symbols. If not redefined, cemeteries are in danger of becoming obsolete, as consumers turn toward cremation and newer disposal methods, from designer mushroom suits that facilitate the rapid decomposition of flesh into bioavailable matter to the clinical process of alkaline hydrolysis, in which human remains are liquefied and poured down the drain. Whether interred in the churchyard or scattered in a forest, human remains reflect changing social facts.

Cemeteries are not monolithic, and they are often shaped by racist institu-tions and prejudices of their place and time. A recent edited volume examines North American cemeteries for immigrants, marginalized groups, and religious minorities (Amanik and Fletcher 2020). In a more activist vein, the Collective for Radical Death Studies has pushed for a decolonization of death studies, examining mourning rituals in relationship to queer studies, colonialism, capi-talism, and ethnicity.[1] Our own volume is sympathetic to this agenda while developing a line of continuity to an older anthropology of death. Some past studies (like Gorer's mentioned in the opening paragraph) were radical in ways that remain quite relevant.

Just as death practices are influenced by social norms and hierarchies, death ethnography, too, is connected to flows of power (Golomski, this volume). What does it mean to be present for a family or community's funeral services or to be engaged in the handling of a corpse as part of ethnographic research (Schiavenato, this volume; Toulson, this volume)? Following anthropologists versed in science and technology studies who have started "studying up" as a way of pushing back against old ethnographic power differentials, several chapters in this book take on the powerful elites of Silicon Valley, treating them as subjects of ethnographic inquiry in their own right (see chapters by Farman, Huberman, and Kneese).

Indeed, by expanding ethnographies of death to include the integration of new technologies into mortuary practices, this volume documents how the new death is a globalized phenomenon. Through Zoom and social media interactions, mourners can virtually attend funerals halfway around the world. Corporate platforms with a global reach, including Facebook, Snapchat, and Instagram, along with digital infrastructures like hashtags, now organize memorialization and mourning. During the COVID-19 pandemic, such mediated forms of mourning were often the only options available, as people said goodbye to loved ones over FaceTime when they could not visit them in the hospital or engaged in other mortuary rituals through streaming services when they could not travel to gravesites. Digital platforms are also entangled with mortuary practices, as in the case of crowdfunded funerals and life insurance start-ups that cover burial costs (Kneese, this volume). Crowdfunding for burial costs intensified as a practice during the pandemic, becoming part of mutual aid practices for marginalized communities most affected by the pandemic.

In addition to facilitating mourning rituals and mortuary care, technology is affecting people's relationship to mortality itself. Even within seemingly secular spaces, from a humanist funeral service (Engelke, this volume) to tech tycoons' attempts at reengineering the human life span (chapters by Farman, Huberman, and Kneese, this volume), there are transcendent or spiritual elements. Indeed, the internet facilitates the latest in a wave of electronically mediated communication with the dead and immortality through new technologies. Crucially, not only are bodies being treated differently, but people are sidestepping the traditional funeral and inventing rituals of their own. Religious traditions long governed the disposition of the dead, but many faiths have become more open to variation in funeral rites while individuals may now define their beliefs about the human spirit in a highly idiosyncratic way. It has also opened the door for new subcultures and rituals to form around mortuary practices.

In a 2013 *Atlantic* article titled "Death Is Having a Moment," journalist Erika Hayasaki argues that while the denial of death has been a part of American culture for the past hundred years or so, social networking has catapulted death back into the mainstream. She describes the endeavors of the first death salon, held in Los Angeles in 2013. The Death Salon is a now-regular gathering where "deathlings," in the words of cofounder Megan Rosenbloom, come together to celebrate death as an essential part of life. Many of the attendees wear what can be considered goth clothing; nearly everyone is wearing black and there are steampunk elements like lace gloves, corsets, black parasols, dark crimson lipstick shades, and white pancake makeup. To contextualize the scene, Hayasaki directly invokes a classic work on death avoidance, anthropologist Ernest Becker's *The Denial of Death* (1973). Becker connects the fundamental human fear of mortality with the desire to build up one's self-esteem and legacy as a hero. Humans create identities in order to protect themselves against the knowledge that they will one day die, which may help to explain the markers of identity used in different subcultures, even goths. In this view, everything we say and do, including all the material possessions we accumulate and all our attempts at self-expression or community belonging, insulates us from acknowledging our impending deaths. In Hayasaki's article, Caitlin Doughty, a major figure in the death DIY movement in the United States who is colloquially known as a "hipster mortician," discusses her appreciation of Becker's work: "What is the fundamental root of human behavior? . . . I think it's death. I agree with Becker. I think about what I'm doing every day working to bring awareness of death into the culture'" (Hayasaki 2013). Becker applied his post-Freudian arguments universally to all humans (albeit with a largely unquestioned Western male subject serving as the generic). Doughty's views fall better within the genealogy of cultural critics like Evelyn Waugh and Jessica Mitford, who believed that death denial is a pathology peculiar to American life.

Doughty first became famous for her YouTube series "Ask a Mortician," where she frankly discusses the aspects of death care that many people may wish to ignore. She has since created a veritable media empire out of making death visible and accessible to the masses. She is an organizer of the Death Salon and the founder of the Order of the Good Death, initiated in 2011, which advocates for DIY funeral care, advising mourners to wash, prepare, and bury their own loved ones' bodies rather than outsourcing that labor to corporate funeral homes. She has also written two trade books hyped as *New York Times* bestsellers (Doughty 2014, 2017). The Order is predicated on the notion of "making death a part of your life," and members include macabre bakers, death midwives, co-op funeral directors, start-up undertakers, and an "international corpse explorer." Order members envision their project as overtly anti-capitalist, feminist, and queer in nature. They align themselves both with the DIY ethos of hacker and maker spaces and with the Riot Grrrl movement of the 1990s. Doughty takes the position that facing death will make individuals more ethical subjects as they become aware of their own mortality and try to live the best lives possible (Kneese 2016). Deathlings, in their embrace of hands-on death care and attempts at reclaiming folk knowledge from medicalized death, position themselves in direct opposition to transhumanists.

Megan Rosenbloom has explicitly stated that those affiliated with the Death Salon and Order of the Good Death view transhumanists, or those who seek radical life extension through technology or, in some cases, computational immortality through mind uploading, as mortal enemies of their mission (Kneese 2016). Many DIY death-care activists are young women who wish to embrace the body and its flaws, including decay, whereas transhumanists are primarily older white men who want to escape their own fleshly existence (Farman, this volume; Huberman, this volume). The new death reflects this tension. Death midwives and doulas, green and DIY burial, and other manifestations of the new death center around reclaiming and remaking older or traditional ways of knowing, reimagining them for a new, more diverse generation. As Phil Olson makes clear in his contribution to the volume, Doughty and company should be understood as millennial popularizers of a broader and older movement with roots in second wave feminism. Instead of removing death from public life in cosmopolitan settings, they advocate making it part of normal everyday interactions once again. As with the earlier home-birth movement, they focus on bringing death care back into the home rather than outsourcing it to the hospital or funeral home, at the same time marking a movement away from embalming to more natural forms of disposal.

While these new manners of death and disposal are gaining followings, thanks in part to the social media savviness of groups like The Order of the Good Death, privately, people have long found material, intimate ways of preparing and remembering the dead. Through his ethnographic fieldwork in twentieth-century rural Pennsylvania, anthropologist Jay Ruby (1995) uncovered a surprising amount of postmortem photography practices in the twentieth-century United States. Because of the stigma associated with postmortem photography, however, most of his subjects expressed their desire to keep such photographs private or secret. Victorians displayed postmortem photographs in family parlors or in personal lockets, but the people Ruby encountered hid the images from view and were sometimes ashamed of having them in the first place. Unlike the arduous photographic process of the Victorian period, which could require living subjects to sit disciplined by metal rods to keep them from blurring in the finished image, smartphones and digital photography allow images to be taken quickly or surreptitiously. Thanks to new technologies, rather than calling on a professional photographer's cumbersome equipment, grieving family members can use their own devices to secure the shadows of dead loved ones. More and more, these images are publicly viewable on Instagram and other social media platforms. The embalmed feet of Aretha Franklin were broadcast around the world in the media coverage of her very public funeral in 2018, suggesting that public comfort with postmortem photography is on the cusp of a revival; the general idea was acceptable, but the uncanny details of her forever-resting face were a risk to decorum and only visible to those who attended the live event. As Howie (this volume) argues, Black funeral directors often insist on difference in death. Black American culture has long been a source of inspiration and mimicry in global culture, now accelerated by various forms of media, so it would not be surprising if it becomes a source for the spread of new death practices as well (see also Dawdy, this volume).

In this volume, authors foreground the gendered and embodied work of caring for the dead, as well as the similarly gendered and embodied work of grappling with mortality (chapters by Golomski, Howie, Kneese, Olson, Schiavenato, and Toulson in this volume). The cultural logics of DIY death-care activists versus those of transhumanists who are attempting to reengineer the human lifespan (Farman, this volume; Huberman, this volume) reveal divergent ways of handling mortality in twenty-first century North America, but they also speak to contemporary issues surrounding gender, embodiment, sexual and social reproduction, and social inequality in the context of late capitalism. Schiavenato's chapter captures a particularly transformative moment in death care—witnessing how the corpses of babies are going from unthinkable to embraceable in ways that question the perfectibility of scientific medicine, as well as presumptions we might make about secular personhood. Relatedly, celebrating the decaying body through green burials or Katrina Spade's new "human composting" start-up (Quirk 2017) may offer radical interventions in a globalized system of technocapitalism, where invisible labor and rationalization drive so much "innovation." While ailing bodies and fresh corpses can, of course, be monetized, in many of the cases studied here, the line between biology and person is blurred in such a way that commodification is, at the very least, complicated. While digital avatars might offer more of a possibility for profiting from death, any mildly sophisticated user can create an online postmortem presence for themselves or a loved one free of cost. This is not to say that the new death is summarily anti-capitalist (quite the contrary, many entrepreneurs see the new openness around death as a business opportunity), but it is certainly redefining regimes of value that affect not only the quality of life and the experience of mourning but the nature of the afterlife.

Popular death movements like the Order of the Good Death and the Death Salon are just one manifestation of death's current cachet. There are new spaces for research on death in academic contexts as well. The Death Online Research Symposium, sponsored by the Death Online Research Network, which was founded in Copenhagen in 2013, is a regularly occurring international conference that links academic interests with the practical concerns of palliative and mortuary care alongside digital posterity. The International Conference on the Social Context of Death, Dying, and Disposal (DDD) is another well-established and ongoing meeting (the journal *Mortality* stems from the first DDD conference). Both conferences attract researchers and scholars along with practitioners, grief counselors, funeral industry representatives, tech designers, artists, and privacy, intellectual property, and estate planning lawyers.

As Arnold et al. describe in *Death and Digital Media* (2018), stodgy-seeming organizations like the National Funeral Directors Association are trying to become savvier with regard to digital mourning methods, worrying about how to keep the industry relevant. Mourners and death-care practitioners alike are combining new technologies with burial practices, even carrying out funerary rites in virtual spaces like Second Life or World of Warcraft. Funeral selfies are another contemporary manifestation of the incorporation of digital media into funerary practices, as young people pose next to caskets and use hashtags to call attention to their public acts of mourning.

Digital media can work to collapse the distance between corpses and mourners, or between mourners in disparate locations. QR codes on headstones maintain links between web pages with information about the dead with the physical location of the corpse. In China, families celebrate the dead through tomb sweeping during the Qingming Festival (Liu, this volume). Mourners can watch graveyard keepers sweep and clean their ancestors' burial plots while adding bouquets to grave sites. They can also livestream the event through WeChat, the largest Chinese social media app. In China and Japan, many gravestones and shrines also have QR codes, which allow for more interactive experiences between graveyard visitors and gravesites (*BBC News* 2017). La Paz, a Jewish cemetery in Uruguay, uses QR codes on every headstone to link visitors to information about specific graves. Thanks to the codes, every tombstone's location is known, and the curious can even view the cemetery remotely (Kneese 2014). The new death is governed by commercial platforms and new infrastructures, from hashtags to QR codes, that intervene in both burial and mourning practices. While some of the same technologies are available in many parts of the world, their uses reflect their specific contexts.

The affective register of speculative data is made clear in the fantasy of postmortem chatbots, showcased in popular TV series such as *Black Mirror* and reflected in new start-up ventures like Replika, a company that mines text conversations, photographs, and social media profiles to create a convincing avatar of a person (Newton 2017). But these more fanciful examples aside, digital death practices often intersect with mortuary rituals. Dead Social, yet another death-care-related start-up company, combines end-of-life and funeral planning with digital account preservation. Its CEO and founder, James Norris, lost his father at a young age and was thus inspired to start the company, which encourages people to be mindful in considering their own mortality, putting their awareness of death into action:

> As a society we are generally very bad at preparing for death in the physical world, mentally and in the digital world. By thinking about and making plans for what we would like to happen toward the end of our lives, once we die and at our funeral we are able to make the logistics easier on ourselves and those who are left behind. By spending a very little amount of time stating and documenting our end of life *wishes we can help to significantly reduce the grieving process and heartache* caused upon our death [emphasis in the original].[2]

Dead Social claims that we are currently in the largest period of change since the Industrial Revolution and that death care must keep pace with economic and technological transformations. The company started as a way of managing people's social media accounts after death but quickly added other components, including will-writing aids and burial plans.

At its most extreme, the new death employs technology to radically extend life or to avoid death altogether. As demonstrated by several chapters in this volume (by Farman, Huberman, and Kneese), there is substantive overlap between Silicon Valley technoculture and transhumanism—supplements, Soylent, and biohacking to name a few. The technologists who build platform infrastructures ultimately control digital posterity; mind uploading and less spectacular forms of technological life extension through self-optimization regimens are intended for an elite group, not the masses. Keeping Vincent Brown's conception of "mortuary politics" in mind while seeing the cultural work of the dead, changes in views of mortality and death-care practices are tied to larger social hierarchies and political inequalities.

Against this backdrop of rapid changes in technology and popular culture, we collectively address two fundamental questions: In the early twenty-first century, how do people make sense of mortality, and how do they treat the dead?

Mortality and Death Care

Part 1 is titled "Mortality." We mean mortality not in the sense of a health statistic but in the philosophical sense of how thoughts about death affect life as intentionally lived, a type of temporal consciousness that Heidegger proposed as a uniquely human capacity at the root of all philosophical speculation ([1927] 1962). Where we differ with Heidegger is that there are many different kinds of death, not a singular, universal one, and thus just as many ways to live. And this plurality is changing, not just under a drift from organized religion and its overconfident figurations of the afterlife but under the influence of science, technology, and a recent resurgence of interest in psychoactive drugs (Sessa 2017). Definitions of death—medical, legal, social—are not stable, and thus nor are the ways in which we live our way toward them. Different forms of imagined death arc back and shape different kinds of life. It is this arc that we call "mortality."

The next section is an interlude in which we hear from two ethnographers writing from the field in the midst of their dissertation research. While these studies do not yet have settled conclusions, the writers reveal in real time how quickly death is changing, even in the more established settings of hospitals and funeral homes.

Part 2 is titled "Death Care." This phrase, and many of the practices the reader will find described in this section, comes from the individuals engaged in transferring, preparing, and disposing of the corpse, as well as from those assisting in the rituals of mourning and necessities of grief. In the United States, the language of death professionals has closely indexed changes in training, organization, and personnel. The shift from "undertaker" to "mortician" to "funeral director" tracks the transition from cabinetmakers and draymen to sanitation professionals to full-service providers. Recently, those in the professional sector have been insisting on the phrase *death care* rather than *funeral industry* to signal that what they do cannot be reduced to a profit margin. Inadvertently, perhaps, the phrase *death care* is a sweeping one that includes the "nonprofessionals"—death doulas and home-funeral assistants—who are encouraging a move away from the expertise of the licensed funeral home and the arcane skills of the embalmer.

Mortality

In this section, contributors write about different ways of coping with the fact of physiological death. While informed by empirical research, these chapters deal more with ideation—with thoughts, beliefs, mediation, and epistemes affecting, or affected by, death. Fears and fantasies regarding finitude and decay impact the treatment of corpses. But how do people make sense of death in the first place? Authors in this section take seriously the fringes of technoutopianism and secular belief systems, finding meaningful cosmologies even within the coldest scientific discourses. How do people prepare for the inevitability of death itself? What fantasies and imaginaries are underlying people's ways of addressing mortality? How is the afterlife changing and refracting back on present life? Temporality—as anticipation, memory, planning, prolonging, and actuary forecasts of probable futures—is a key theme in the chapters.

Abou Farman draws on his previous work on transhumanism and terminality (Farman 2017) as a temporality associated with a terminal diagnosis; when terminal, a cancer patient is uncertain of how much time they have left, but they are aware that time is limited. This liminal and uncertain state affects treatment plans and the roles of caregivers and loved ones, who must find ways of coping with the eventuality of death while the person is very clearly a living, breathing entity. For humanity in the face of climate catastrophe and doom, terminality is a collective condition. If the earth is beyond hope, what is to be done? Farman explores the relationship between doomsday in scientific, nuclear terms alongside the technocultures of transhumanism. Terminality as a kind of collective mortality starts to look like an ideology that underwrites everything from space exploration to white male privilege.

Picking up this last thread, Jenny Huberman follows the story of Silicon Valley transhumanism, showing how discourses and fantasies around start-up tycoon Peter Thiel's use of young blood to sustain his own life reveal beliefs about death in the Global North. Huberman uses journalistic coverage of Thiel's supposed vampirism to answer larger questions about mortality in the United States today and its relationship to capitalism and wealth inequality. Huberman also connects parabiosis to other ethnographic contexts where vampires or other monsters loom large. Cultural anxieties about growing wealth inequality and the power of tech elites are one reason for the outrage over Thiel's imagined quest for young blood. Immortality, like so much else under late capitalism, is a privilege of the white, wealthy Silicon Valley elites, while the rest of the population is sucked dry.

Tamara Kneese traces a longer genealogy of transhumanism, using late nineteenth- and early twentieth-century life insurance documents as a way to show how the notion of responsible death, as a manifestation of wellness ideology and self-optimization associated with some branches of transhumanism and tech culture writ large, is older than digital technologies. Individuals are supposed to prepare for their own burials by accumulating wealth and buying insurance policies. To fail to do so is to die a bad death. Responsible living and neoliberal self-care give rise to moralizing about responsible death. Crowdfunded funerals are one way of providing the dead with dignity when life insurance and other older forms of responsible death are not available. Preparing for death and coping with mortality require information management aligned with corporate logics, revealing which individuals and groups are valued above others. Algorithms sort out who is deserving of death care in the form of insurance protection, attention, and, ultimately, burial rites.

Casey Golomski focuses on new ways of doing death ethnography. Globally speaking, death is *not* the great equalizer. His work examines how HIV/AIDS changed funerary practices in southern Africa and how the high medical death rate and shortened lifespan affect expectations and relationships of care. The conditions of death redefine life. In this chapter, we encounter a group with a heightened sense of their own mortality verging on collective fatalism. In such a context, the politics of writing about subjects in such a pronounced state of vulnerability are amplified by the visibility of today's scholarship on the internet and the rapid dissemination of information (fact checked or not) via WhatsApp and Facebook. While Golomski revisits the colonial and racialized history of scholarly assessments of Africans, he points out that our ethnographies will have an afterlife among our informants that we cannot control.

Matthew Engelke examines the temporality of secular humanists in the United Kingdom, who conduct meaningful secular ceremonies for the dead in thirty-minute increments. In a way different from Golomski's interlocutors,

Engelke's humanists (agnostic or atheist) also have a pronounced sense of their own mortality, but theirs devolves not from an intimate experience of frequent death but from the conviction that there is no life after death. Thus, the new practice of "celebrations of life" emphasizes biographical narrative and richness of an earthly life over references to God and metaphysics. Engelke's chapter focuses on several different scales and tempos of time—the standardized thirty-minute ritual, a foreshortened humanist sense of mortality, and the overall acceleration of time under capitalism and high-speed modernity. While playing a central role in this chapter, temporality is a theme that cuts across many of the chapters in both sections, from the catastrophic future imagined by some transhumanists (Farman) and their effort to rewrite a personal ending (Huberman) to the time management inherent in life insurance epistemes (Kneese), the time-warp quality of embalming (Dawdy), and the intentionally slower pace of home funerals (Olson). Also concerned with care in the form of the celebrants who help manage the work of public mourning for humanists, Engelke's chapter serves as a bridge to our section on death care, where it would have been equally at home.

Interlude: Notes from the Field

These two shorter pieces by LaShaya Howie and Stephanie Schiavenato provide a glimpse into the future of death. LaShaya Howie and her interlocutors grapple with the present-day precarity of the Black funeral home in the United States. As leaders in one of the most segregated sectors of the service economy remaining today, her interlocutors assert that the experience of Black mortality justifies a unique approach to death care. Black funeral practices have generally been among the most conservative in the US context, with twentieth-century embalming and burial services still highly valued, but Howie notes that a sense of worry pervades the professional backstage as clients increasingly opt for cremation and as intergenerational continuity in small family businesses is at risk. Like Dawdy's chapter, Howie's work highlights how it may be just as important to account for why things break down as to hypothesize about the popularity of new forms.

Stephanie Schiavenato's powerful autoethnography is grounded in her first-hand experiences with reproductive loss and through her work as a doula. She focuses on the materiality of reproductive loss, including breast milk, the placenta, and funerary technologies that extend mourning time with infant corpses, specifically the CuddleCot, a refrigerated bassinet that has been designed to hold dead babies. Schiavenato asks, "What happens to people after they come out from the shadows of shame associated with miscarriage and stillbirth?" Going beyond arguments about the legal and philosophical definitions of personhood, she illustrates how new practices and technologies are remaking reproductive death to suit the maternal bodymind that lives on even after a baby has died.

Death Care

In this section, chapters zero in on the intimate dynamics that a newly dead person and their corpse create. Professionals and dedicated laypeople who specialize in embalming, burial, cremation, memorialization, and public mourning are a central focus, as is the relationship between the dead and the grieving. In different ways, contributors highlight changing dynamics within what we once called an "industry." The growing aversion to that word and its connotations of a dehumanizing assembly (or disassembly) line and for-profit motive is itself a flag of a changing way of death under late capitalism. While some emerging practices represent a return to preindustrial modes, others are highly technocratic and shaped by the global spread of neoliberal logics wherein the dead become another kind of customer. While some practices appear to have a transnational scope (such as the spread of cremation and, to a more limited extent, American-style embalming), others are inflected with highly local concerns, legal regimes, and structural realities.

Margaret Schwartz explores the haptics of grief, moving beyond visual representation of death and calling for a media studies that examines touch. As she argued in her earlier work (Schwartz 2015), mortality is indexed through visual representations of iconic corpses through the media. But care of the body is also a central part of grief. Embalming is both a visual medium (or a "memory picture" as the embalmers call it) and a physical process of intensified touch. Media studies has been undergoing a haptic turn, moving away from questions of representation and the image. Schwartz argues that spectacular death and iconic corpses are but one entry point to understanding death. Taking a new direction, here she privileges touch, materiality, and embodied labor in both digital and biological interactions. Schwartz's chapter, like Engelke's, bridges our themes while opening up the question of care.

Shannon Dawdy offers a historical context for the exceptional case of embalming in the United States. Challenging the reductionist "just about profit" critique of the Mitford era, she asks, What work does the corpse do in American life? Drawing on classic anthropological theory but also ethnographic interviews with embalmers, she argues that at the turn of the last century, death went from being a religious event to being a magical one. Embalming is fast dying out as a disposition of choice, but what remains is an approach to death that emphasizes the visual presence of the deceased (now often through video montage) and the magical role of the embalmer who manipulates time, fixing a memory to a moment before sickness, injury, and death. While "sleep" was traditionally the last memory picture enabled by the embalmed corpse, a recent trend in New Orleans toward "extreme embalming," with corpses set in lifelike poses for their final viewing, underscores the secular visual magic behind embalming that may have more to do with vaudevillian entertainment magic than it does with religious rituals of farewell.

Philip Olson's chapter introduces a set of practitioners in the home-funeral movement who are actively trying to revolutionize the paradigm of care in the United States. Although many of his interlocutors make the point that they are simply trying to return to a preindustrial and more "natural" form of death care in which families intimately participated, his ethnography demonstrates that their efforts do not simply turn back the clock. Rather, death midwives and home-funeral educators (who are in the majority women) must navigate the bureaucracies of coroner's offices, hospitals, hospices, and the conventional industry. They also need to educate a public who may be nervous about bringing the body of their loved one home for three days or washing and touching the corpse. Some practitioners are trying to establish certification and other forms of authentication and training, creating a tension between DIY idealism and the pragmatism demanded by medical and legal regimes. Counterintuitively, perhaps, what they are actually doing is creating a new form of folkloric expertise.

Lucia Liu also looks closely at conditions of labor and expertise in death care, but in this case in the far different setting of contemporary China, where a one-size-fits-all bureaucracy determines much of the training and options of the state-owned funeral industry. Nevertheless, death care in China is also undergoing rapid change as young funeral workers disregard traditional pollution taboos about death work and embrace new forms of labor subjectivity under post-reform state capitalism. What appears to be happening is that rather than the relationship between the death-care worker and the corpse being the defining feature of those who work in the field, professional personhood and pride in employment in the market economy override what exactly one does at work on a day-to-day basis. This development has some parallels to the professionalization and standardization of the funeral industry that occurred in the United States and many Western countries between 1880 and 1920, but there are, of course, also important differences, such as the labor precarity of college graduates in China who are eager for new professional pathways and the overriding fact that a powerful nation-state is the source of standardization, not a collection of professionals trying to establish legitimacy by riding the coattails of medicalization and sanitation regimes.

Ruth Toulson's chapter illustrates a quite different dynamic occurring in Chinese-dominant funeral homes in Singapore. While the US population is moving away from embalming, in Singapore this elaborate form of disposition is gaining in popularity. In addition, new funeral rituals influenced by Japanese culture are being introduced by young death-care entrepreneurs. One is struck in this case by the internationalism of current changes in death care. As in mainland China, old taboos about corpse pollution are falling away, but here under the active agency of young practitioners who may or may not have heard of Caitlin Doughty and the Order of the Good Death. They are convinced that there is a better way to grieve that involves family intimacy with the corpse (though in a professional setting) and permission to cry in public. As with Olson's example, we are reminded that changes do not just "happen" or are the result merely of market demands but can owe much to the agency of creative and passionate promoters.

Finally, the task of sketching the bigger picture assembled by this collection of diverse chapters falls to Ellen Badone in her commentary and Anya Bernstein in her generous afterword, which provide a global perspective on everything from transhumanism to embalming.

Some Parting Thoughts on the New Death

If we have succeeded in our intentions, this volume will serve as an important snapshot of what death looks like in the early twenty-first century and set an agenda for new research directions. Death never really stands still. Once upon a time, anthropologists thought that key "rites of passage"—most especially beliefs and practices surrounding death—were among the most conservative of customs across cultures, with funeral practices being passed down over dozens of generations and hundreds of years with little change. But as Peter Ucko (1969) noted in an important review of archaeological and ethnographic case material, this generalization breaks down under empirical scrutiny. People might say that they want a "traditional funeral," but what that means has always been subject to invention. That said, there is a tempo to any type of cultural change. In the last twenty years, we have witnessed an exponential acceleration of global influences, entrepreneurialism, and ritual creativity around death. Inevitably, this new death that we have documented here will someday become the old death. Nevertheless, if Philippe Ariès's (1974a) approach to death cultures in the West retains value (and we think it does), then the history of death can be characterized by periods of stasis, often of a century or more, punctuated by significant shifts in worldview and praxis that articulate with what is going on in the larger social landscape. This volume proposes that we are experiencing one of those significant shifts right now. And we wager Ariès would agree; what we are seeing in death practices, particularly in the United States, is an explosive heterodoxy (Bourdieu 1977) that does not fit comfortably with his description of the "forbidden death" of medicalization, sequestration, and psychological denial.

It would be foolhardy to offer a single theory as to why these changes are occurring when we are still in the midst of a seismic shift in how postmodern humans understand their mortality. While the continuing decline of mainstream religious influence undoubtedly plays a major role in both ideological shifts about what death means and in how the dead are handled, the proliferation of new death discourses and practices cannot simply be chalked up to a broad embrace of secular humanism. What makes it even riskier to hazard a guess as to why death is the subject of so much experimentation right now is that many of the changes we are witnessing pull in contradictory directions—from technological extensions of life by transhumanists to back-to-nature death positivity by home-funeral advocates.

Nevertheless, there are two common factors that unite almost all the new death practices documented here that suggest articulation with other existential shifts: temporal consciousness and the mediation of intimacy.

In almost every case presented in the chapters of this volume, the issue of temporality comes up explicitly or implicitly. How we experience, measure, and value time in late capitalistic societies is thoroughly enmeshed with how we think about and manage death. We see temporal sensitivities expressed in how funeral practices and the grief process are being sped up, shortened, or deliberately slowed down. Or we see them in how the narrative time of biography is being extended beyond what was once considered the natural ending of old age (and what/who counts as old, of course, is changing, too). There is nothing that accents our temporal consciousness quite so much as death. Imagining how to "make the most of the time we have," judging the kind of timing that counts as a good death or a bad death and whether there is a continuation in some form of afterlife—all these existential questions are undergoing heavy challenge and revision. In the last twenty years, Western cultural critics and scholars such as Frederic Jameson (2003) and Paul Virilio (1997) have noted that late capitalism is characterized by an overbearing sense of the present, where the past and the future are made irrelevant or at least very difficult to keep in focus. They also note that "accelerationism" and an addiction to speed (in the sense that anything that is faster must be better) have become a hegemonic reality of our daily lives. Thanks to the attention economy, a seemingly endless flow of real-time updates distracts people from recent history and prevents them from focusing on the future (whose plotting is left to wealthy transhumanists and futurists like Elon Musk). Under late capitalism, time management is a fundamental aspect of productivity and of both monetary and social value. Death management, one facet of time management, reflects changing social values. Is it better to die fast? Should you plan for your death or forecast it (or through self-optimization practices, avoid death altogether)? Is a funeral a waste of time (and a burial a waste of space)? How do we handle grief without stopping the rest of our lives? Outside forces are definitely speeding up death—thirty-minute committals, the decline of visitation and wakes, and, for many workers, little to no bereavement leave. But some actors are noticing these trends and actively resisting them, if not trying to reverse them. To be death positive is synonymous with being anti-accelerationist. Decay has its own time. Slowing life down so death can happen in a more healing fashion—whether that means declining emergency medical interventions, embracing embalming and viewing, or taking a loved one home and putting them on ice for several days—that is the essence of what we see as a broad movement to let death have the time it is due, the clock be damned.

Secondly, the nature of intimacy seems to be under scrutiny and open for experimentation—expressed through the haptics of death care, as Margaret Schwartz calls it, but also through ever-expanding mediation by technology through forms such as Zoom funerals, Facebook memorials, CuddleCots, and the Shower of Tears. How we experience intimacy and express care for the living has been radically opened up by new technologies. Now, new forms of mediated intimacy are being applied to care for the dead as well as the bereaved.

As shown by the ever-growing literature on digital death, these forms of mediation are altering our perceptions of mortality and the relationships between the living and the dead. As digital technologies become embedded in everyday life, they figure into everyday death as well. This is not a supply-demand market scenario where technology steps in to efficiently fulfill a preexisting need. Rather, as people engage with new media and technology, their desires and thinking about emotional connection may change. New avenues for caring for and living with the dead are opened up by platforms that allow the dead to linger as dynamic, interactive presences.

As the effects of the COVID-19 pandemic continue to reverberate, no doubt there will be more changes to come, but we anticipate that these two major fault lines currently cutting through the new death—reconfigurations of temporality and intimacy—will only grow more pronounced. In a crisis that has made life stand still throughout much of the world through the cessation of the calendrical rhythms of work, school, and travel, an awareness of how speed and clock time have been unnaturally naturalized is perhaps at an all-time high. And when social distancing forces ten-person funerals without hugs, or a long postponement, or a Zoom memorial service, what we value about farewell rituals and expressions of intimate care is increasingly on people's minds. Now more than ever, corporate platforms are mediating people's intimate relationships with both the living and the dead. But no matter how new technologies become entangled in people's expectations around mortality and death care, it is clear that people will continue to invent new ways of marking ritual time and for creating memorial objects. The relationship between the living and the dead is always a work in progress.

Notes

1. See the Radical Death Studies website at https://radicaldeathstudies.com/.
2. See Dead Social at http://deadsocial.org/features/about-us.

Part I

Mortality

Terminality

Technoscientific Eschatology in the Anthropocene

ABOU FARMAN

In the last few years of his life, the celebrated physicist Stephen Hawking, well-known for his theories of black holes and the beginning of the universe, publicly expounded on several scenarios regarding large-scale endings: on the one hand, endings of the current world, or planetary endings; on the other, the end of the universe, which renders the first concern into a rather parochial affair. The most academic of these was part of a paper he submitted for publication a few weeks before his individual exit from the world at the age of seventy-six. Titled, not without irony perhaps, "A Smooth Exit from Eternal Inflation," it predicted and calculated the finiteness of the universe as opposed to the infiniteness predicted by other inflation theories.[1] The finiteness of our universe also implies that this universe will end as the stars lose energy. But that would not necessarily mean the end of every possibility, because Hawking believed in the possibility of a multiverse. Even if this universe is subject to an ending, there might be other universes out there, he suggested. In order to exit or escape from this dying one, we just have to slip out of this universe and find those other ones. The space program, he suggested, could eventually help us do that, using probes to find a warp in our space-time fabric in order to access others. Space exploration would be a way to escape the tragic predicament of finitude in our universe.

Outer space also appeared as an escape hatch for his other endist vision, the end of the human world, which would result not from an inevitable feature of physics as such but from human activity. In a BBC documentary in 2016, he said nuclear war, global warming, overdue asteroid strikes, overpopulation, and genetically engineered viruses put humanity and the planet at great risk.[2] To survive and avoid an almost-certain extinction of their own making, humans need to colonize outer space in the next hundred years or so.

His views were received enthusiastically by the outer-space community. A year before the BBC documentary was released, Hawking had been given a free ticket to outer space aboard Richard Branson's VSS *Unity*, the commercial ship Branson's space company, Virgin Galactic, was planning to launch into space.[3] Hawking began training in zero gravity, his body floating and free for the first time to move around without the earth's gravitational field pulling on his limbs beset by ALS, the disease that kept him tied to his technologically advanced wheelchair. The unveiling of VSS *Unity* (the name was chosen by Hawking) took the form of a small media spectacle in the hangar of Branson's company. Hawking did not attend, but he sent a prerecorded video message pronouncing that space travel "will help bring new meaning to our place on Earth and to our responsibilities as its stewards, and it will help us to recognise our place and our future in the cosmos—which is where I believe our ultimate destiny lies."[4]

Hawking died before the Virgin spaceship was ready for its maiden voyage and so never got the chance to redeem his free ticket to space. Setting aside for now Hawking's belief in humanity's ultimate destiny, I can say with some measure of certainty that in his belief that the world is in great danger of collapsing under the destructive weight of its brainiest inhabitants, the physicist has been far from alone.

Since the unleashing of nuclear power in the middle of the twentieth century, invocations of the end of the world have intensified, spiking at specific junctures such as the turn of the millennium, triggered partly by the Y2K bug, or 2012, triggered by Western interpretations of the Maya calendar cycle. And the range of what is being called existential risk has grown tremendously, too. Recall, for instance, Hawking's own list of end-time fears. Or check the dozens of possibilities categorized as existential or global catastrophic risks by a range of institutes around the world, especially Oxford University's Future of Humanity Institute, on which more below.[5] An additional smattering of scenarios for the end of humanity, the planet, the species, or life itself would include AI takeover or the Singularity, resource depletion and civilizational collapse, asteroid collision or volcanic explosion, heat death or cold death of the universe. Contemplating, fearing, and mobilizing the end is not a new state of affairs, but have there ever been so many options as there are in the West today, a full mall of doom to choose from?

Climate change stands in as the great signifier for the plethora of ways in which scenarios for the end of the world have become socially manifest. Today, the latest international expert report on the states of nature releases waves of anxiety and anxiety-inducing journalism about extinction, loss, and possibly the

Figure 1.1. Extinction Rebellion protester enacting death in a pool of fake blood at the Trocadero steps in Paris. Courtesy of Armand, XRParisEst.

end of humanity. The report in May 2019 from the Intergovernmental Science-Policy Platform on Biodiversity and Ecosystem Services (IPBES) generated this headline in the *Guardian*: "Human Society under Urgent Threat from Loss of Earth's Natural Life: Scientists Reveal 1 Million Species at Risk of Extinction in Damning UN Report" (Watts 2019). The global protests organized under the banner of Extinction Rebellion started in 2018 and have proliferated, with the protesters staging massive public die-ins in Europe and North America, enacting the future of human extinction as a way to try and spur climate action (figure 1.1).[6] A climate striker who said things like, "We are now facing an existential crisis" turned out to be a fifteen-year-old Swede who has now become a global figure (Swenson 2019). While schoolkids striking around the world carry signs that read, "There is no Planet B," we hear of a new psychological phenomenon called "climate grief." Psychologists are studying traumas produced by climate change (Doherty and Clayton 2011), while other social scientists, Green Party members, and activists talk about mourning as a political force in the era of global warming (Stoknes 2015). "This reality is taking its toll on our mental health," writes Australian climate activist Rob Law (2019), "especially among younger people who are understandably losing hope for their futures on a hotter planet."

I call this contemporary affect and epistemology of collective endings "termi-nality," and I think of it as a secular and technoscientific eschatology. It raises several questions: What is the genealogy, psychology, and taxonomy of this full range of scientifically projected and predicted terminal conditions? Whose dis-course and whose condition are these? Who measures what for whom in these assessments of the looming end?

Terminal, as a concept, is most widely used in relation to prognosis and dis-ease. I originally used the concept of terminality in that context (Farman 2017), thinking about cancer and death in relation to secular finitude, measurement, prognosis, temporal increments, and absolute endings. As applied to diseases and then to persons, the concept began its trajectory in the nineteenth century but only gained widespread adoption after the 1960s as chronic but deadly dis-eases such as advanced cancer gained prominence, and prognosis became a way to manage and medicalize the span of time from diagnosis to the absolute end of secular death. The precondition of the experience of terminality is a particular, secular understanding of self, life, and death in which death is con-sidered final and continuity in any form is never guaranteed (cf. Engelke, this volume, on secular humanist views; Farman 2020). The term is taken from the Latin *terminus*, meaning the end point, the ultimate boundary. Terminus was also the Roman deity who presided over boundary markers for towns, temples, and properties, to whom the annual festival of Terminalia was dedicated and to whom burnt offerings were given when a boundary was marked and measured (Fustel de Coulanges 2001). That boundary is now the boundary of life, its unit of measure is time, and the figure being measured is the terminal patient sink-ing inexorably, hopelessly into the near horizon of death.

Timothy Leary, that guru of white Western counterculture, generalized the term, moving it from the medical condition to a social or planetary condition. Ailing, though ailing ecstatically, with end-stage cancer, he said, "Face it. At this point in human history we are all terminal" (Leary 1997, 115). He had a point. Aside from his own terminal cancer, he had witnessed decades of nuclear deterrence and Cold War politics that had people living under the sign of the mushroom cloud. That was not Leary's preferred sort of mushroom. His pre-ferred sort of mushroom contained not a split atom but rather the opposite, the all-unifying psychoactive substance psilocybin. To him and other West-ern users, psychedelics opened up the world beyond secular finitude. Psyche-delics became prominent in part because they created a sense of timelessness and undifferentiated wholeness with the cosmos, something that as a kind of subjectivity had been shed in secular scientific culture as it tried to break the world open into smaller and smaller fundamental units of discrete mindless matter. There was some undifferentiated wholeness in the mushroom cloud, but unlike the psilocybin experience, the mushroom cloud presented a less ecstatic version: everything flattened back to irradiated dust. It generated the image for a radical new futurelessness. As the psychologist Robert Jay Lifton remarked, it was an "image of extinguishing ourselves as a species by our own hand, with our own technology" (1987, 1, 41).

Leary's statement was not referring to some universal transcendent condition that held true for all humans in all times facing the inevitability of individual death — that would be what humanism has constructed as "tragedy" (Eagleton 2009), wherein the inevitability of final death renders vain all this effort at life and living. Leary's formulation historicizes the advent of terminality. "At this point," he writes. What does it mean to be "at this point," and how did we get here? And what is the temporality of "this point" — how long is its now, how sharp its point? And if *we* have become terminal *now*, what, at this point in human history, is that quality of being terminal that is new, that is about today? How have *we* become terminal in a way we were not before? Where are the cultural and scientific representations of the end taking hold? Who is the collective "we" who feels terminal? What racial and class anxieties inform images and imaginaries of the end? What kind of subjectivity, what kind of self, is required for, repeated in, or generated through the varieties of secular doom, through terminality?

Needless to say, I will be addressing only some of these questions here. I hope merely to make some general observations about the technoscientific aspects of terminality, using transhumanism as a key analytic site. Transhumanists believe that science and technology will transcend the current physical and mental limitations of the human in order to produce a much more efficient, beneficial, and rational future. Its proponents suggest explicitly that the current form of the species is not its final form and that a technologically enhanced form will develop through what they see as the exponentially accelerating development of technoscience, especially in the areas of nanotechnology, biotechnology, and the informatic and cognitive sciences. Yet they are also singularly preoccupied with doomsday scenarios. I am not analyzing transhumanism as a movement whose oddity we must behold. To the contrary, as I have argued in other places and both Kneese and Huberman demonstrate in this volume, transhumanism has affinities and a great deal of traffic with mainstream science and tech culture, especially around Silicon Valley, with its algorithmic selves and incessant attempts at death transcendence. In Silicon Valley, many of the most powerful figures of our digital present identify as transhumanists—Elon Musk, for example, and Ray Kurzweil, who is employed by Google (for more examples, see Huberman, this volume)—but it is also true for other scientific and technoscientific institutions from the National Science Foundation to national nanotechnology initiatives (Farman 2020). More relevant to my point here, these transhumanists, including Musk and Kurzweil, have elaborated significant and influential scenarios outlining collective endings of various sorts, as well as potential solutions, such as becoming superintelligent or colonizing outer space. Indeed, Hawking himself was part of the exchange with transhumanists on these matters, as he served alongside Musk on the scientific advisory board of the University of Cambridge's Centre for the Study of Existential Risk (CSER). CSER was cofounded in 2012 by Jaan Tallinn, a key developer of Skype, after he heard of transhumanist computational doomsday scenarios. The direct predecessor of CSER is Oxford's Future of Humanity Institute (FHI), founded in 2005 by transhumanist philosopher Nick Bostrom. FHI's research team includes a number of prominent transhumanist researchers, from philosopher Anders Sandberg to nanotechnologist Eric Drexler, considering various doomsday scenarios. It was during my work with immortalists and transhumanists in the middle of the 2000s that I first heard of the term *existential risk*; Bostrom and FHI have been crucial in popularizing the term.

The notion of terminality I describe is different from categories such as existential risk, insofar as it refers not to the material aspects, assessments, or facticity of a particular threat but rather to the overall social and technoscientific imaginaries (Castoriadis 1987; Jasanoff and Kim 2015; Marcus 1995; Taylor 2003) through which collective life is understood, researched, and experienced in relation to extensive and existential endings, as predicted by science, and denotes a particular representational and affective order through which the world is apprehended and under which actual practices are organized (see also Farman and Rottenburg 2019). The term *imaginary* does not mean that the assessments and their representations are false or merely ideal or that the threats themselves are made up, that climate change is not real, or that nuclear annihilation is only a figment of a paranoid imagination. But it does mean that the mobilization and representations of the threats, the production of risk-related knowledge, and the political relations that shape the response to the terminal imaginaries ought to be subject to critique and understood critically, as they propagate socially and elicit social and cultural responses—and indeed some have been subjected to critique already, especially in reaction to the popularization of the term *Anthropocene* (Barnes et al. 2013; Haraway 2015; Yusoff 2018).[7]

Unlike many other interpretations of technological end times (Geraci 2010; Gray 2011; McLeod 2012; O'Gieblyn 2017), I will not analyze these endist scenarios as Judeo-Christian artifacts, imbued with some underlying religiosity. I argue that terminality is a secular eschatology, insofar as these projections of the end are shaped by the authority and measures of science and the projected endings are absolute and unredemptive (without resurrection, return, or transcendent redemption), just as in the secular view of death itself. In turn, because the endings are absolute, the secular scientific measures of terminality produce a particular temporality—they start measuring time toward a final end, producing what I will call "the ticking." The Doomsday Clock run by the Bulletin of Atomic Scientists is a clear material and performative embodiment of the ticking. In an annual ritual, the bulletin, whose science and security board is comprised of thirteen Nobel laureates, takes it upon itself to measure and publicly declare our proximity to the end in temporal terms. In 2020, the hands of the Doomsday Clock were moved closer to midnight than they had ever been (100 seconds to midnight) (Mecklin 2018) since the clock's inception in 1947 to warn the world of the danger of nuclear war. The press release spoke of the "threat multiplier" of "cyber-enabled information warfare" that undercuts "society's ability to respond" to the major "existential dangers" facing humanity, namely nuclear war and climate change. Interestingly, two weeks earlier, the World Health Organization and China's health authorities had confirmed the discovery of a new entity in our midst: the novel coronavirus, later called SARS-CoV-2 for causing the disease now known as COVID-19. It had not yet become the focus of global attention, it was not part of the calculations—nuclear, environmental, and cyber—that gave the world a hundred seconds. In February, COVID-19 hit globally, and by March, the calculus of doom had accelerated and amplified. The ticking got a little faster and a lot louder.

Unlike modernity's open and progressive vision of the future, terminality's horizon is thus tense and contradictory, with a reinsertion of destiny (recall Hawking's phrase) into future thinking and a politics based on an "impossible future," where what is offered as a solution is an extreme and racialized version of what Elizabeth Povinelli (2011) calls the politics of abandonment: to leave the trouble behind by seeking, in Hawking's terms, space colonization or a porthole into an alternative universe.

Terminality as Secular Eschatology

From the Greek *eskhatos*, meaning "last," eschatology is the study and knowledge of last things or the end of things. Eschatology is generally linked to
religion and more precisely to theology, suggesting that only through divine
revelation or religious illusions can one access knowledge about the final end
of things, personal or cosmic. The assumption behind this is a teleological one
(Walls 2010), for the purpose of something created by the creator would be
known only by the creator. Eschatologies tend to predict not just that there
will come a point when something will have ended, but that such an ending,
whether in salvation or damnation, is its destiny, the resolution of its creation by
the creator. The teleological aspect of some eschatologies (especially apocalyptic
ones) is one reason why eschatology is not commonly associated with science
and the secular. These latter tend to abjure teleologies. But understood simply
as a kind of knowledge of the end of things, not necessarily linked to God and
religion, eschatology appears as a clear and strong strain in secular science,
which has its own fraught relations to teleology.

The visions of end times I call terminality mobilize a historically particular
sort of despair that is part of a discourse internal to science and the secular.
Although a terminal regime developed explicitly through the middle of the
twentieth century, especially after the nuclear bomb, the secular scientific concern with the end has been well developed since at least the nineteenth century,
with roots in very important strands of Western philosophy, social thought,
and scientific ontologies (see Farman 2020). The construction of a deep linear
geological timeline by the likes of Charles Lyell, the emergence of the concept of
extinction starting with Georges Cuvier in France, Darwinian evolution and the
transformation of species, theories of the heat death of the universe from Lord
Kelvin on, secular humanist views of the finality of individual death followed by
Schopenhauerian pessimism and Nietzschean nihilism, even Weberian views
of progress as a disenchanted timeline of obsolescence—these are foundational
and lasting aspects of terminality as a cultural setting and epistemological
haunting that beset science and scientists. A recent example of this comes from
the concerns of the celebrated physicist Freeman Dyson, who, prior to Hawking, worried much about the eschatology of a closed universe: "In this case we
have no escape from frying. No matter how deep we burrow into the earth to
shield ourselves from the ever-increasing fury of the blue-shifted background
radiation, we can only postpone by a few million years our miserable end. I shall

not discuss the closed universe in detail, since it gives me a feeling of Claus-trophobia to imagine our whole existence confined within the box." But given that he cannot live with his own claustrophobia, he proposes something else: "If it turns out that the universe is closed, we shall still have about 10^10 years to explore the possibility of a technological fix that would burst it open" (Dyson 1979, 448). Thus, "physical eschatology" is now a minor branch of cosmology, initiated by Dyson and others (Halvorson and Kragh 2019).[8]

Today, far from being a religious phenomenon, terminality is diagnosed, propagated, and addressed specifically through science, through its authority, symbolic language, techniques, reasoning, evidence, and accredited bodies. Massive collapses have been predicted by NASA climatologists, the most cele-brated being Al Gore adviser James Hansen, who in his book *Storms of My Grandchildren: The Truth about the Coming Climate Catastrophe and Our Last Chance to Save Humanity* (2009) paints a picture of a scorched earth in order to stir people to act. Over many decades, biologist Paul Ehrlich, the famed coauthor of *The Population Bomb* (Ehrlich and Ehrlich 1968), has been issuing Malthusian warnings about overpopulation and resource depletion leading to the collapse of civilization and human deaths on inconceivable scales.[9] Engi-neers and computer scientists are warning against an AI takeover and sub-sequent annihilation of the human species, while many others believe that we are in the midst of a major "biological annihilation" or a (sixth) mass extinc-tion (Kolbert 2014), events that, according to biologist Peter Raven, "pose an even greater threat to civilization than climate change — for the simple reason they are irreversible."[10]

The probabilistic calculations of the future through scientific evidence requires reading the signs, as much in historical events, such as US president Donald Trump's rhetoric, which made the Bulletin of Atomic Scientists move the Dooms-day Clock to two minutes to midnight, as in material processes, such as the rise in average temperatures due to which "the majority of terrestrial species ranges are projected to shrink dramatically," according to the scientists of the Intergovern-mental Science-Policy Platform on Biodiversity and Ecosystem Services (IPBES) (Díaz et al. 2019, 18). They predict the extinction of one million species. All this eschatology requires the massive mobilization of expertise and processes of cumulative hermeneutic confirmation by people trained in collecting and inter-preting the signs and classifying the facts with labels such as "well established" or "incomplete," "high confidence" or "medium confidence." According to IPBES (2018), its reports "have been prepared by more than 550 leading international experts from more than 100 countries over three years at a cost of more than U.S. $6 million."

Expert knowledge and scientific bodies come together to create matters of *ultimate* concern through quantized warnings about the future, using mass death, annihilation, extinction, and the specter of doom as their horizons. The abstractions of the end—too large in temporal and spatial scales to be apprehended locally and in the present—are transformed into authoritative perceptual future events through the repetition of probabilities, charts, statistics, and temporal frames made by experts and mobilized for social ends.[11] In the face of political apathy and infrastructural inertia, the urgency grows exponentially. Experts produce increasingly pressing papers, with mounting stakes. What was supposed to happen in 2050 is already happening; climate change effects are worse than expected; the Antarctic ice sheets are thinning five times faster than they were twenty-five years ago (Shepherd et al. 2019).[12] Time gets compressed and the horizon moves closer, in accelerating increments. The IPBES report states, "There will be a further acceleration in the global rate of species extinction, which is already at least tens to hundreds of times higher than it has averaged over the past 10 million years" (Díaz et al. 2019, 14). The media present the statements of experts such as Thomas Crowther, professor in the Department of Environmental Systems Science of ETH Zurich, who claim that the latest Intergovernmental Panel on Climate Change (IPCC) report omitted feedback loops, which accelerate climate change and global warming even more, bringing the tipping point closer.[13]

In short, terminality's future is an impending end subject to calculation and presented through prognostic numerology, such that measures turn into accelerating moral and temporal pressures: if we don't act now, by 2050 there will be a catastrophic two-degree Celsius rise in average temperature; or if we stabilize the human population at 9.5 billion in the next fifty years rather than letting it rise to 11 billion, we have a chance. "The hands of the Clock of Doom have moved again," declared the Bulletin of Atomic Scientists. "Only a few more swings of the pendulum, and, from Moscow to Chicago, atomic explosions will strike midnight for Western civilization" (Mecklin 2018). Terminality is determined and represented through scientifically authorized calculations of the relation of time to matter, in variations of this simplified form: if there are C amounts of X in a body (defined expansively to include planets, biospheres, populations, and so on), it has a Y probability of killing you/us off in T units of time. Thus, the world gains a due date and the ticking starts. As the last

Greenpeace report (2019) on corporate malfeasance phrases it, there is a "count-down to extinction."[14] This moral and temporal syntax, similar to the syntax of medical prognosis (Farman 2017), interpellates you in the ticking away of time and the ticking becomes part of the affective and political orientation toward the future. As in the case of terminal patients, the quantification enters the body, creates an affect, perching the person toward an end. In this case, the ticking is everywhere: in the body, the species, the economy, the atmosphere, the planet.

The prognostic syntax of the ticking—"If we don't do something by 2050, we will die"—ends with a key subclause: "But it's probably too late to do enough." For instance, some experts believe that we are already into the sixth mass extinction and there is no turning back; those who think we are only on the cusp think turning back will be difficult (Kolbert 2014). IPCC's special report on global warming (2018) states that the world would have to curb its carbon emissions by half by 2030 and then achieve carbon neutrality by 2050 in order to prevent catastrophic warming of over 1.5°C. Turning back the clock of doom, slowing down its ticking, appears as an impossible imperative. Articles in the scientific journal *Nature* propose that halting warming might be an "impossible dream."[15] Upon the release of the IPBES report in May, Robert Watson, the chair, said, "We are eroding the very foundations of economies, livelihoods, food security, health and quality of life worldwide. . . . We have lost time. We must act now" (Watts 2019). And yet in the same IPBES report, what we read is, "It is therefore likely that most of the Aichi Biodiversity Targets for 2020 will be missed" (Díaz et al. 2019, 15). Further, sustainability goals "for 2030 and beyond may only be achieved through transformative changes across economic, social, political and technological factors," where *transformative* means "a fundamental, system-wide reorganization across technological, economic and social factors, including paradigms, goals and values" (Díaz et al. 2019, 16). This points to an unimaginably exhaustive list, a daunting rearrangement of massive infrastructures of production and consumption that would require a dramatic transformation of capitalism to begin with. *Capitalism*, though, is a term not used in the report at all.

What's more, the roots and consequences of actions and decisions are no longer to be understood in their immediacy but across timescales and massive material processes that make them almost impossible to represent, map, predict, and so on—what Timothy Morton (2013) has characterized as hyperobjects. Often this has led to a sense that not only is it *too late* to roll things back (capitalism, nuclear armaments, climate, etc.) but that it's all so big that we do not even really know how to act. At the same time, the exhortations are to *do* something about it. Terminality is beset by that tension, a kind of a double bind, as Bruno Latour points out (2017): humans are to blame and so humans must do something before it's too late, but humans can't do anything and it's already too late. "With biodiversity . . . by the time you feel what is happening, it may be too late," declared Cristiana Paşca Palmer, executive secretary of the UN Convention on Biological Diversity (Watts 2018). To live in the ticking is to live in the *too-late times*. The Extinction Rebellion activists are performing this very condition when they stage mass deaths — for the too-late times means also the time of the already dead (Cazdyn 2012), for whom presenting and grieving their own death is the only political option left.

What too late implies, and for whom, are questions I will pursue in the next section. The point here is that the calculability of the end has specific effects on temporality, on the sense of an absolute horizon and what's left in between the now and the end, where both the calculations and the sense they generate rely on secularized notions about the finality of the end. Thus, like many eschatologies, terminality is more than just a theory about or a knowledge of the end of things. It is also an orientation toward the future; it is an epistemic and affective regime, a way of thinking, feeling, and being that orders collective ideas about what can or cannot be done in relation to the end of things.

Transhumanism, Civilization, and Survival

Even though they have been part and parcel of modern progress, visions of the end in the form of existential risk have spread in technoscientific communities over the last fifteen years, thanks to the tireless eschatological work of transhumanists. A long tradition in projections of chaos and destruction resulting from computational malfunction came to a head with the infamous and uneventful Y2K bug, but the subsequent years and the spread of AI technologies saw computational doomsday visions mushroom (see Geraci 2010).

Among the most effective of computational doomsday projections came from Eliezer Yudkowski, transhumanist cofounder of the Singularity Institute for Artificial Intelligence (SIAI), an organization focused on the hopes and dangers of the age of superintelligent beings (it has since changed its name to Machine Intelligence Research Institute, MIRI). "Eli" was excited by the prospect of superintelligent agents but worried that such agents might end up, willfully or accidentally, destroying what humans care about, namely human lives. SIAI was set up to find ways of preventing that. A common, crude illustration of an accidental case would be a superintelligence optimized to produce paperclips that would then take all matter in its vicinity and rearrange the atomic structure to obtain a lot of excellent paperclips. It may not despise you in particular, but since your atomic arrangement does not correspond to its aims, it would take you apart and transform you into a paperclip. Yudkowski urged research toward the development of friendly AI.

SIAI's work and Yudkowski's writings influenced a number of other prominent projects set up to curtail worrisome threats to human futures. For example, Skype cofounder Jaan Tallinn, who read Yudkowski's work online, contacted him and ended up funding the work of his institutes. Tallinn then went on to set up the Centre for the Study of Existential Risk (CSER) and the Future of Life Institute, at Cambridge and MIT, respectively. Conferences on civilizational collapse (inspired by Jared Diamond's [2005] book on the topic) were organized by Terasem, a group led by transhumanist lawyer and inventor Martine Rothblatt. And various blogs and digital message boards have had discussions on peak oil, climate threats, biological threats, and other factors that could cause a global crisis of survival.[16] As mentioned, Nick Bostrom's writings on existential risk have been influential inside and outside transhumanist circles. In most conversations, just as at most conferences, a strand seems always dedicated to the threat of total annihilation. I remember being surprised during several post-conference discussions at the sheer number of very "bad futures" (Harding and Stewart 1999) described and imagined. And whenever someone threw up an alarming new scenario, a transhumanist, shouldering the burden the rest of the world refused to acknowledge, would say, "Oh, now I'm really beginning to worry."

At the same time, transhumanism, a primarily Anglo-American secular scientific project, purports to be an optimistic technofuturistic movement convinced of the curve of technological progress and even at times the purposefulness of the universe.[17] Despite all the techno-optimism, transhumanism and its related groups are obsessed with doomsday scenarios, producing and reproducing them promiscuously.

Take the Lifeboat Foundation, a nonprofit inspired by Bostrom's texts and connected to various AI, nanotechnology, and transhumanist projects and figures. Lifeboat is entirely dedicated to researching extinction risks and developing more than a dozen "shields" against each, including BioShields,

AsteroidShields, NanoShields, AlienShields and more.[18] Based in Nevada, the founder Eric Klien has been known, on sideblogs, to denounce science and suggest that science is the biggest risk we face, while recruiting scientists to be on the board. He has also recruited right-wing anti-Islam activist Pamela Geller, which sparked minor concern among the board members.[19] In an interview, he told me that he felt the urgency to found Lifeboat after 9/11. But those were just planes, he noted; there are bigger risks, and he wants, in his own words, to avert "the triumph of evil" over "civilization."[20] Though counterterrorism is listed as one of Lifeboat's concerns, Klien emphasized that the majority of those risks will not come from terrorists. He is most concerned about something else; the biggest risks are built into the potential technologies themselves. "The same technology of health," he said, "becomes the technology of destruction."

This coil of progress and doom, in which the medium of one is equally the medium of the other, is crucial to the terminal affect, for whether in nuclear Armageddon or climate collapse or bioterror, it is the inseparability of progress and doom — their infrastructures, their tools, their measures and knowledge production — that makes the future impossible. The point is made magisterially by Julie Livingston (2020) in relation to development in Botswana and by Joseph Masco (2008, 2010, 2012, 2015) in relation to the nuclear threat and climate change. In the case of Botswana, the alleviation of hunger and health problems through large cattle ranches has also led to widespread health problems of a different order, as well as to drought and environmental devastation — what Livingston calls self-devouring growth. Masco's extensive body of work on the link between nuclear science, nuclear war, and planetary science has shown that the understanding of the planetary crisis has come through military scientific and engineering experiments linked to the bomb. Nuclear testing on trees, in deserts, and in the ocean gave scientists tools and data for an "understanding of the planet as an ecosystem" (Masco 2015, 138) The atmospheric fallout from the tests in the 1950s allowed scientists to map global wind patterns by tracking the atomic debris. This was then extended to studies of soil and water and the integration of a biospheric image connecting landmasses, waterways, and the atmosphere. So ironically, the institutions and the fields of science that came to track threats to the planet emerged as a result of military interest in the effects of nuclear detonations. My point here is to suggest that this imbrication of destruction and knowledge, advance and collapse, is one of the sources for the contemporary imaginary of the impossible future, the too-late times.

At the same time, the secular dialectic of futurity has always moved ahead with both progress and nihilism rolled into one, because, after all, in the secular, any conjuring of the future contains within it the negation of that future, its ending; like biological life itself, every future is already entombed. This is the neglected part of Weber's (1946) essay on disenchantment and progress, for it is the finality of secular deaths that haunt the ongoing achievements of human beings. Weber did not necessarily speak of extinction or the heat death of the universe, as some of his contemporaries did, but he did argue that finitude could lead to nihilism, and thus the problem of disenchantment was the problem of meaninglessness. In the absence of transcendence, he argued, progress was a disenchanted answer to finitude, the temporal bulwark erected against the meaninglessness of absolute secular endings, individual or civilizational—which is to say, you will not go on, but your being will have contributed to the development of some greater humanity in the future so that all the toil that pours out into death is redeemed by the progressive future. That secular insistence on continuity in progress continued through the twentieth century. People *must* believe in progress, Sidney Pollard asserted, because "the only possible alternative to the belief in progress would be total despair" (quoted in Lasch 1991, 41–42).

But the freedom taken and promised by modernity as part of the special constitution and prerogative of human progress has turned out to be more destructive—and more constraining, that is, less free—than imagined. This closing of the future as the domain of human freedom stands against the modern, progressive gambit that humans can shape the future as humans will it and against the secular notion that the future is not fated and so is open to human planning. As that capacity to plan and make futures is in large part what has also characterized the figure of the human, then what is at stake today is also the notion of what it is to be human. As all UN reports and news articles repeat, this all matters differently because it is a threat to all of humanity.

That universalized threat, ironically, is what is supposed to create a new motivation to act, when in fact the whole problem has been human action. Just as Dipesh Chakrabarty's (2008) Anthropocenic wake-up call to the social sciences, following on Crutzen's original concept, included a feeling of warmth toward the possibility of human mobilization and struggle beyond the parochialities of nations and the divisions of class struggle, so that same universal aspect is also mobilized in Bostrom's keystone transhumanist paper on "Existential Risk: Human Extinction Scenarios and Related Hazards" (2002). Bostrom defines existential risk as one where an adverse outcome would either annihilate Earth-originating intelligent life or permanently and drastically curtail its potential.

An existential risk is one where humankind as a whole is imperiled. Existential disasters have major adverse consequences for the course of human civilization for all time to come. (2002, 2)

Bostrom's taxonomy, however, becomes increasingly revealing of the dynamics of terminality's universalism. Genocide may be an evil, but it is not an existential risk of this sort. Neither is AIDS as we have encountered it. As he explains rationally, "These types of disasters have occurred many times.... But tragic as such events are to the people immediately affected, in the big picture of things—*from the perspective of humankind as a whole* [emphasis added]—even the worst of these catastrophes are mere ripples on the surface of the great sea of life. They haven't significantly affected the total amount of human suffering or happiness or determined the long-term fate of our species" (2002, 2). Over the course of human history, Bostrom contends, there have been very few existential risks to "our species," the closest being an asteroid impact—at least until the mid-twentieth century. The advent of nuclear weapons was the first instance where humanity became aware of an existential risk, the first time that our species had the subjective experience of contemplating and envisioning its own ultimate destruction. Since then, such possibilities have proliferated; global warming does count in the Bostrom taxonomy as one of the existential risks alongside nuclear holocaust, deliberate or accidental misuse of nanotechnology, asteroid impact, and on a lower scale, a repressive global regime or misguided world government, a flawed superintelligence, and/or a takeover by a rogue mind upload.

On closer examination, however, the question of humankind in Bostrom's text suddenly gets transformed. One version of existential risk is when the future entails a threat in which "Earth-originating intelligent life goes extinct in relatively sudden disaster" (2002, 5). But because intelligent life is not limited to humans alone, there is another scenario that would count, too, one in which "the potential of humankind to develop into posthumanity is permanently thwarted" *even if* "human life continues in some form" (5). The ultimate standard by which existential risk is assessed, then, is any threat to civilization and to the *future* establishment of a post-human cyborg technocivilization. What matters in the politics of transhumanist survivalism is not merely saving humanity but *producing* or evolving the transhumans of Western civilization who can leave behind the limitations of the human. Thus, perversely, existential risk applies to a form of being that is not yet in existence, whose existence is only anticipated.[21]

The fears, reactions, and preparations for doom and survival are structurally and materially differentiated by population, access to resources, and geography; they are racialized geopolitical discourses and formations. The name of the Lifeboat Foundation is indicative. "Lifeboat ethics" was an influential proposal forwarded by the conservative ecologist Garrett Hardin (1974) in the 1970s to defend rich nations against the supposed onslaught of poor ones, which became naturalized as the dogma known as the tragedy of the commons.[22] Hardin's theoretical argument about resources developed into the concrete political conclusion that in a situation of scarcity, there is no obligation for rich nations to provide aid to, or accept immigrants from, poor nations. They ought to be left to drown — which is precisely what is happening now in the Mediterranean. The issue here is not the survival of everyone but of some and the question of who is racially, structurally, and geopolitically overdetermined. As the post-COVID-19 world gets mobilized around various imaginaries of protection, as power gets organized under the sign of survival, the old problem of the subsumption of difference by the universal figure of humanity is reaching a new apex.

It is important to remark here that transhumanism is an overwhelmingly white movement, but also that these formations and discourses are not limited to transhumanists — much of technofuturism, and a good portion of the neoliberal ethos, is embroiled in the same rehearsal of technoprogressive myths of the future against the backdrop of futurelessness in which the survival of some comes at the cost of the survival of others. For more of this, let me return to Branson's hangar and the spectacle of the VSS *Unity*'s unveiling, where progress (the rocket) and doom (the devastated planet) were juxtaposed. For those willing to read "the American Grammar" of such events along what Hortense Spillers calls "the riffs of melanin in the skin" (2003, 211), the ritualized and mediatized hierarchies of the hangar event, within eyeshot of the American-built border wall separating the United States from Mexico, seemed inevitably distributed according to a racialized, even a noticeably Aryan, vector. The whiteness of the assembled applauding on bleachers was a chorus to three generations of Branson's decidedly Nordic family breaking a bottle of milk, instead of the customary champagne, on the nose of the spaceship, adorned with a futuristic pinup of a blond white woman with a space helmet, arched ecstatically across the side panel, breasts aimed heavenward, waving a flag embossed with the word, or brand, Virgin (figures 1.2–1.3). The iconography is so blunt it leaves little room for social interpretation, though our green friends on the Red Planet might well be asking, "Guess who's coming to Mars?"

Literal iconography or not, it might be questioned whether this sort of social hermeneutics has any place in a contemplation of the end of the world, when all of humanity is at stake, the whole world, the planet, the universe. While the highest knowledge and the most advanced technology are being marshaled to save human civilization, here I am parochially considering the racialized semiotics of our "smooth exit." Poor Hawking. Poor Branson. Poor *humanity*—its highest, most advanced exemplars trying to save it! But in fact, this has everything to do with the way that *our* terminal condition is understood and remediated, the way it makes its way into popular consciousness and politics and the reserves that are mobilized to counter the perceived threats. Who sees outer space as the smooth exit? For whom is that exit smooth? Whose world is ending? Histories of the end carry with them colonial histories and histories of empire, geopolitical interests as well as differential concerns and responses shaped by structures of power and capital. Pentagon reports recommend building fortresses around Western countries to stave off the hordes of "unwanted starving immigrants from the Caribbean Islands (an especially severe problem), Mexico and South America" when climate change hits (Schwartz and Randall 2003, 18).[23] The so-called One Percent, including bitcoin billionaires and some very prominent technoutopians, express their worries about social unrest and civilizational collapse as they go about buying $4 million apartments in refurbished nuclear bunkers, while Silicon Valley techno-optimists are gobbling up secluded chunks of land in New Zealand, Wyoming, and, it seems, as far out as outer space (Osnos 2017; Rushkoff 2018). In terminality's politics of abandonment (Povinelli 2011), sermons of techno-salvation come from people who are themselves preparing for the worst. The people who are buying up escape plans are the very same people who are the greatest purveyors of civilizational hope and progress, they are the technogarchs whose promises of designing better systems for everything from a geoengineered earth and biosphere to AI to drinking water are supposed to right the ship. Yet they are laying plans to abandon ship in order to survive elsewhere, because it may already be too late or because, as the transhumanist philosopher Julian Suvalescu warned in a 2009 talk, "minorities" are going to have access to the means of destruction (read, revenge).[24]

Radical-right survivalists and many not-so-radical conservatives subscribe to a "suicide of the West" ideology—a desperate plea for ensuring the survival of Western civilization as the most urgent task of conscientious people, since liberal guilt, according to them, is bent on a form of cultural suicide. The ideology of white suicide was first set out in a 1964 book of that title by James Burnham, the once-Trotskyite founder of the *National Review*, and revived in 2018 in a book of the same title and by another *National Review* editor, Jonah Goldberg, but focused more on saving the virtues of capitalism. *New York Times* columnist Charles Blow (2018) has called these resurgent worries over race, population, and immigration white extinction anxiety. European ecofascism is a real movement, invoking climate change hazards, lifeboat ethics, and the survival of Europe as the prime goal of humanity.[25] It is imperative for a critical approach to terminality to notice the close connections between whiteness, capitalism, and civilization as an ideal assemblage of survival forming what one might call the white anxious class. The white anxious class in Europe as in North America will have very different diagnoses, prognoses, and planning with regards to existential threats from, say, radical environmentalists, anti-capitalists, off-the-grid communalists, acclerationists, Luddites, anarchists, Afro Brazilian *candomblé* practitioners in coastal Bahia, Indigenous nations in the Amazon, residents of small islands, and so on and on.

Thus, the question of the subsumption of difference under the universal figure of humanity is actually as central now as it has been historically. The secular and scientific awareness or imaginary of the end has always been racialized. Perhaps the earliest vision of a secular terminal condition — as a collective death to be distinguished from individual mortality — is *extinction*, a notion that was not thought, or permitted into thought, until the end of the eighteenth and the beginning of the nineteenth century. In the pre-secular Euro-American cosmology, nothing could go extinct once created; that would go against the divinely ordered creation. The historian Mark Barrow (2009) traces the emergence of the concept as Thomas Jefferson and George Cuvier tried to make sense of objects in the world — or at least objects in various cabinets of curiosity. Miles Powell (2016) emphasizes that nationalist and racial imperatives drove notions of extinction and conservation. Jefferson's insistence on the survival of mammoths and mastodons was part of a battle against his pro-European French counterpart Comte de Buffon's inquiry into why American animals seemed to be so weak and badly off — what he called a "theory of American degeneracy," where he proposed that America was not a great land for men and beasts to prosper. For Jefferson, the possible existence of those massive creatures was a testament to the strength of the land, which he also linked to its "aboriginal inhabitants." That link between indigeneity, biology, animality, and conservation flourished during the early nineteenth century, with conservationists now speaking of keeping animals and Plains Indians in reserves that would protect their "race" and conserve them from the onslaught of civilization, which had led Native populations to the brink of extinction. Extinction was thought by Darwin, Huxley, Alfred Russel Wallace, and their followers to be the natural fate of the lower races of mankind (Brantlinger 2003, 14, 165–87). Not long after, the opposite view arose, an early version of white extinction anxiety, that white Americans were the endangered race and that European civilization would lead to the deterioration of the white race (190–95). None of this should be surprising. Because extinction came to bear on populations and because populations, like species, have been racialized formations, so extinction, like other endings, was always racialized and subject to civilizational hierarchies.

While many of the same assumptions and hierarchies continue today, the supposed universality of the existential threat erases existing differences in terms of power, class, and race—realities that get indexed by the reinvigoration of the gentler term *civilization*. Aside from the proliferation of that word *civilization* within doomsday discourse (note Hawking, Klien, and others cited above), a good representation of the problem is the visual work accompanying Alan Weisman's best-selling book *The World without Us* (2007). Weisman imagines what would happen to the world if all human life would stop now. In scientific detail, he describes the corrosion of all human infrastructure and the subsequent takeover of everything by plant life. The stunning and well-received images show this process: urban centers like Paris and the Eiffel Tower, New York and its skyscrapers, are seen covered with vine and weed. What the illustrations indicate is that civilization has reemerged as the defining container of humanity. Whatever is left outside the classical view of civilization is not the subject of terminality and so nor of humanity.

Conclusion: The Impossible Future, Nihilism, and the Post-tragic Posthuman

Reflecting on global nuclear devastation following his work in Japan, Robert Lifton (1987) claimed that the rise of nihilism was a response to visions and realities of nuclear annihilation, a sense of a collective destiny in destruction. Lifton argued that the nuclear devastation visited on the populations of Hiroshima and Nagasaki caused a radical breach in their sense of continuity between the past, the present, and the future. Such a breach, he wrote, "threatens a level of psychic experience that defines our humanity" (1987, 155) and leads to a "radical futurelessness," a loss of the desire to move forward. To be able to live out healthy lives and be motivated to carry out projects, Lifton argued, people need a sense of continuity. That sense comes out of a symbolic world—what he would later label "symbolic immortality"—constructed precisely in order for people to make sense of today's efforts in tomorrow's terms, to transcend the finitude of their daily lives and the finality of their deaths. The bomb annihilated the image of any such future and replaced it with a sense of futurelessness. His Japanese patients and interlocutors had a word for this: *munashi*, which he translates as "emptiness." One might think of *munashi* as the affect related to the emptying out of the future, a break in the possibility of continuity. Lifton thinks that under the shadow of the mushroom cloud, the whole planet got a case of the *munashis*. It is, he argued, just this *sense* of a break in continuity that has driven people to imagine space colonies, new religions, and returns to nature.

Lifton's characterization of despair reached beyond the devastations of the bomb, pointing to the underlying sense of an inevitable ending without redemption, that is, annihilation as a totalizing aspect of contemporary existence. The finitude that is so palpable at the end of secular lives is amplified in the larger envelope of collective finitude, in which not only do individual beings end but everything in the universe is also subject to ending. It is a condition in which the impossible future is all that remains, and so pleasure today becomes the order of the day.

The sense of inevitability I have been describing in terminality—the calculable secular eschatology—captures a similar shift in the phenomenology of the future in the West, a complex remapping of the experience of fate, freedom, agency, and power. If not a closing of the open timeline, it is certainly a closing of the future as open promise. So the humans of human civilizations who find themselves in the twenty-first century surrounded by all the goods—art and technology—that denote the supreme achievements of their humanity, discover that the very same achievements have brought them to the edge of their own eradication.

Secular humanists, with less of a techno-optimistic view of progress, might be tempted to read this as the perfect humanist tragedy; overcome by the ambition of mastery, drunk with fantasies of limitless power, the hubris of their ambitions, the protagonists are the agents of their own demise. They fell, and the clear-eyed tragedians, the apotheosis of the human spirit, can cast an eye back and say, "See, don't get too big, for all big men fall." Ruin is the end of everything, even of pharaohs. The head of every Ozymandias will in the end be leveled with sands that stretch far away.[26]

Aside from the optimism of progress, tragic meaningfulness has been one of the secular humanist trump cards. Having eliminated the afterlife and made death final, secular humanism has had no option but to make death the very condition of a meaningful life, pulling out of the hat of meaningless death—a hat sewn by its own milliners—the rabbit of meaning via tropes like the tragic or the human condition. The tragic as a trope is a tale for secular humanist adults who cannot appeal to the immaterial but do not want to slide down the nihilist rabbit hole either; so the hole becomes a magician's hat, the last refuge of the humanist where death is magically transformed into the meaning of life. This is no less of a fairy tale than the fairy tale of eternal life.

However, the trick of the tragic is inadequate to the current moment and at any rate can't be performed with terminal events such as extinction. Tragedy requires a subject looking back at an event and recognizing its tragic qualities. Extinction means there will be no such subject. Extinction is where human and Anthropos—the species and the image it has of itself—finally become isomorphic, but they do so in collapse, dissolving into absolute nothingness. The unique thing about extinction/annihilation as the transcendent ground of self-understanding is that it is an understanding beyond the human but also an understanding that undermines any possible meaning in present activity or imagined future (Brassier 2007). Terminality undermines any possibility of humanist meaningfulness; there cannot even be an appeal to the tragic.

Except for the rare European misanthrope or Eastern mystic, nihilism has been rarely engaged deeply as a critical political intervention—or possibility. It has been a bad word, because it could imply that nothing can be changed, so struggle is futile. Indeed, there is a difficult impasse here, if one is to think of nihilism politically. On the one end, there is the possibility of human self-extinction as a kind of political and ethical end. That is the position of groups such as the Voluntary Human Extinction Movement. The idea here is that humans have become an irreversibly invasive and destructive creature. But as ethical and conscious beings, humans can recognize that, and recognizing that ought to yield to other biological and non-anthropocentric futures—that is, by moving toward human extinction, they will allow unpredictable forms of life and intelligence to arise in the future.

At the other end, there is the possibility that nothing will arise, nothing of that sort. Secular finitude, where endings are already built into all futures, reaches its logical end in total extinction; humanity will disappear, and then, as Nietzsche said in the tense of the future insignificant, "nothing will have happened" (Nietzsche 1989, 246). All this desire, motivation, struggle, all this turning about, *for* nothing. Purpose and meaning are drained out. At that juncture, it is no longer about tragedy or progress. To ask the question in the present — "What *is* it all for?" — may produce some partially satisfying answer regarding the value of work and existence now ("You *want* to live!" or "For a better future!" or "To get this great project done" or "It's absurd but you just do it in good faith"). However, in the past tense, from the vantage of planetary annihilation, there can be no answer — there can't be a question either. After all, who would be left to ask, "What *was* it all for?"

Terminality contains this ultimate question but avoids it, falling back on progress, technology, and the salvation of civilization, its museums, universities, architectural landmarks, laboratories, and libraries included. But perhaps this occluded question of terminality holds a radical potential for rethinking the future by way of devaluing just these emblems of civilization — in other words, in imagining the end of a particular kind of world. It is what Aimé Césaire (2013, 39) may have had in mind when he imagined the end of the colonial world:

What can I do?
I must begin.
Begin what?
The only thing in the world that's worth beginning:
The End of the World, no less.

Acknowledgments

I owe gratitude to Shannon Dawdy and Tamara Kneese for inviting me to the SAR seminar on emergent forms of death. I thank all the co-seminarians for the richness of the exchange in general, Nafé Kramdi-Mayor for photo and research assistance, and Rich Blint for his comments and corrections.

Notes

1. Hawking's final paper (Hawking and Hertog 2018) received some attention after his death. I cite this without suggesting that I properly understand the

mathematics or physics of the paper. The importance for our purposes pertains to the social and cultural implications, because the statement is a social and cultural one, and by invoking the space program, Hawkings was clearly and explicitly making it so. Indeed, many media picked up on the paper and presented it as a public rather than a narrow expert-oriented matter. Thus terminalist popularizations of the paper regarding the end of the universe came out in various news media. See, for example, Meredith (2018). An accessible description of the paper may be found in a blog in *Discover* magazine (Scharping 2018).

2.   For the BBC interview, see Shukman (2016). Hawking has expounded on his views in other places as well.

3.   For example, see https://www.reuters.com/article/us-virgingalactic-rockets/bransons-virgin-galactic-unveils-new-passenger-spaceship-idU.S.KCN0VS2KL; or https://www.virgingalactic.com/articles/richard-branson-unveils-virgin-galactics-new-spaceship-named-vss-unity-by-professor-stephen-hawking/.

4.   For the recording, see Wall (2016).

5.   See the Future of Humanity Institute website, at https://www.fhi.ox.ac.uk/research/research-areas/.

6.   See, for example, *BBC News* (2019).

7.   Cf. Barnes et al. 2013, 541: "The cultural values and political relations that shape climate-related knowledge creation and interpretation and that form the basis of responses to continuing environmental changes."

8.   Dyson launched the idea of a respectable physical eschatology in his 1978 lectures at NYU that turned into the article on open time: "I hope with these lectures to hasten the arrival of the day when eschatology, the study of the end of the universe, will be a respectable scientific discipline and not merely a branch of theology" (Dyson 1979, 447).

9.   For a powerful refutation of Ehrlich and the population argument, see Hartman (2017).

10. Raven, a co-organizer of a Vatican conference on extinction, was quoted in the *Guardian* (Mckie 2017).

11. "What techniques, such as statistics, allow nonperceptual quasi-events to be transformed into perceptual events, even catastrophes? . . . How and why do things move from potentiality to eventfulness to availability for various social projects?" (Povinelli 2011, 14).

12. That was the conclusion generally drawn by the public from the 2018 special report on global warming of 1.5°C by the Intergovernmental Panel on Climate Change (IPCC) (Leahy 2018). For a summary of the IPCC report, see IPCC (2018).

13. See Harvey (2018). On feedback loops, see Madson (2018).

14. See also Corbett (2019).

15. See Tollefson (2015, 2018).

16. Terasem, Fourth Annual Virtual Workshop on Geoethical Nanotechnology, https://terasemcentral.org/articles/gn/GN4_2008/index.html; see also Michael

Anissimov, "Immortalist Utilitarianism," *Accelerating Future* (blog), 2004, https://lifeboat.com/ex/immortalist.utilitarianism.

17. Transhumanism is loosely composed of a range of scientifically minded groups with different areas of expertise, from life extension to robotics to neuroscience. Its history starts out with a very American, DIY, sci-fi and science-based orientation, with roots in the futurism of the 1960s and 70s, that was later hitched to a tech and biotech boom in hyperdrive, with immense economic growth and technical achievements.

18. See the Existential Risks Program secion of the Lifeboat Foundation website, at http://lifeboat.com/ex/programs.

19. See Mark Waser, "Please Quit/Boycott the Lifeboat Foundation," *WhizDumb* (blog), March 7, 2011, https://becominggaia.wordpress.com/2011/03/07/please-quitboycott-the-lifeboat-foundation/.

20. Phone interview, July 1, 2016

21. See Adams, Murphy, and Clarke (2009) on anticipation and technoscience.

22. For a short counterargument to lifeboat ethics and the tragedy of the commons, see Clark (2016) and Ricoveri (2013). Of course, anthropology's focus on reciprocity has long stood as a reproach to the utilitarian individualistic premises of these kinds of models.

23. This report was brought to my attention via Hartmann's important book (2017).

24. Julian Suvalescu, "Genetically Enhance Humanity or Face Extinction," lecture at Festival of Dangerous Ideas, Sydney, Australia, October 2009, 27:05, https://vimeo.com/7515623.

25. See Tammilehto (1985).

26. Percy Bysshe Shelley's poem "Ozymandias" ends:

    My name is Ozymandias, King of Kings;
    Look on my Works, ye Mighty, and despair!
    Nothing beside remains. Round the decay
    Of that colossal Wreck, boundless and bare
    The lone and level sands stretch far away

CHAPTER TWO

Old Men, Young Blood

Transhumanism and the Promise and Peril of Immortality

JENNY HUBERMAN

> *Capital is dead labor, which, vampire-like lives only by*
> *sucking living labor, and lives the more, the more labor it sucks.*
> — Karl Marx, *Capital*, Vol. 1

In the summer of 2016, as the presidential race between Hillary Clinton and Donald Trump was intensifying, a series of rumors began to circulate in Silicon Valley. It was reported that billionaire entrepreneur and self-professed transhumanist Peter Thiel was becoming increasingly "interested in harvesting the blood of the young" to help him achieve his goal of immortality.[1] While Thiel has long been an outspoken advocate of anti-aging and longevity research, this new interest in parabiosis (a procedure that seeks to reverse the aging process by providing the recipient with blood transfused from a young donor) generated an outpouring of condemnation and concern. In countless articles, publications, and online blogs and discussion forums, Thiel was portrayed as a modern-day vampire who was using his riches to expropriate the vitality of the young and secure for himself eternal life and power. Although the story broke in August 2016, Thiel's alleged interest in pursuing this path to radical life extension continued to be covered in the press for months after, along with an outpouring of articles castigating Thiel for his open support for and financial backing of billionaire president Donald Trump.[2]

In this chapter, I use the controversy and media coverage surrounding Thiel's interest in parabiosis to explore larger questions about the politics of life and death in the contemporary United States. Transhumanists and venture capitalists like Thiel eagerly espouse the promise of immortality initiatives and celebrate the idea of using science and technology to "solve" the problem of death while making a handsome profit in the process. Critics, however, claim there are clear perils. They warn that transhumanist immortality initiatives are just one more means through which wealthy, white, privileged men seek to reproduce their dominance at the expense and exploitation of others, and nowhere was this concern more powerfully expressed than in the stories covering Thiel's interest in parabiosis.

What justification is there for basing an analysis of the politics of life and death on an outbreak of vampire rumors? First, as the historian Luise White argues, "rumor and gossip" "reveal" a social world and "perhaps articulate and contextualize experience with greater accuracy than eyewitness accounts. They explain what was fearsome and why" (2000, 5). White demonstrates how vampire rumors in colonial Africa were used by Indigenous peoples to understand and articulate the violence and terror that colonialism engendered. She argues that rather than discounting these stories as fanciful tales or historical inaccuracies, we should treat gossip and rumors as historical sources in their own right.

Second, the vampire rumors surrounding Thiel are reminiscent of other ethnographic contexts in which concerns about illegitimate forms of accumulation are expressed through anxieties about the living dead. As anthropologists have long demonstrated, in many parts of the world, fears of zombies, vampires, ghosts, and malevolent spirits provide culturally salient means for articulating concerns about violations to the moral and cultural order.[3] For instance, Jean and John Comaroff argue that the proliferation of zombie beliefs in post-apartheid South Africa provides a culturally salient means through which disenfranchised South Africans express and experience the impacts of neoliberal capitalism and postcolonial oppression (Comaroff and Comaroff 2002, 782).[4] Similarly, Peter Dendle has explored how the figure of the zombie has given voice to shifting cultural, political, and economic anxieties within American society and culture. Dendle proposes that "the essence of the 'zombie' at the most abstract level is supplanted, stolen, or effaced consciousness. . . . [The zombie] casts allegorically the appropriation of one person's will by that of another . . . the displacement of one person's right to experience life, spirit, passion, autonomy, and creativity for another person's exploitative gain" (Dendle 2007, 47–48). In yet another context, Aihwa Ong has shown how spirit possession among female factory workers in Malaysia provided a key means through which "an emergent female industrial workforce" metabolized the dislocating effects of industrial labor. Drawing inspiration from Mary Douglas's (1966) work on the breaking of taboos and social boundaries, Ong (1988, 35) shows how these women interpreted their possession experiences as a response to the multiple forms of taboo violation that factory work entailed.

Taking this work as a departure point, this chapter shows how anxieties about the living dead played out in the case at hand. I argue that the vampiristic imagery surrounding Peter Thiel's reported interest in parabiosis evoked so much outrage and concern precisely because it tapped into larger anxieties that were rippling through American society. Concerns about increasing inequality, white male privilege, the preponderance of gerontocratic power, and the exploitative nature of a biotech industry that views immortality as the latest frontier for the expansion *and* expropriation of capital all came to be voiced in and through the coverage of Thiel's interest in this purportedly age-reversing procedure. However, I also argue that the rumors surrounding Thiel and his "vampiristic" tendencies would not have taken on the purchase they did if Thiel had not been actively backing Donald Trump in Trump's bid for the US presidency. That is, I want to suggest that what is at stake in this particular vampire story is not just a set of anxieties about growing inequality and the exploitative nature of capitalism but also a set of anxieties about the life and death of American democracy itself.[5]

Transhumanism and the Promise of Immortality

Over the last thirty years, transhumanism has emerged as an influential sociocultural movement. Transhumanism is predicated upon the idea that human beings can use science and technology to significantly enhance their capabilities and thereby overcome many of the limitations of human biology.[6] Transhumanists believe technology will imbue us with intellectual, physical, and psychological capabilities that far surpass what present-day human beings are familiar with. This, they argue, will transform the human species and human societies in very significant ways, ultimately ushering in a post-human future.

While Abou Farman's contribution to this volume rightly notes that transhumanists have become increasingly concerned with the looming threat of terminality, the desire for immortality remains at the forefront of their attempts to achieve a radically enhanced future. Indeed, through their respective ethnographies of immortalist communities in Russia and the contemporary United States, Anya Bernstein and Farman demonstrate the varied ways transhumanists conceive of mortality as a problem to be technologically conquered. They also explore the genealogies, imaginaries, and historical contingencies that have rendered Russian and American immortality initiatives distinct (Bernstein 2019, 5). Surveying their work, three key differences emerge that have relevance for the ensuing discussion.

First, whereas transhumanism in the United States is largely dominated by male libertarian elites who have achieved an "ideological hegemony" over the movement (Hughes 2019), in Russia, the transhumanist movement is comprised of men *and* women who hail from diverse political and socioeconomic backgrounds (Bernstein 2019, 23). Second, in the United States, immortalism is a predominantly secular phenomenon (Farman 2012). However, in Russia, immortalist initiatives "blur the lines between the 'religious' and the 'secular'" (Bernstein 2019, 67). This may make them less susceptible to critiques of crass instrumentalism or "immoral" human hubris, which transhumanist immortality initiatives in the United States so frequently evoke. Third, and perhaps most relevant for the analysis that follows, is the fact that among Russian transhumanists, the dream of immortality has long been conceived as a collectivist project or vision. Bernstein argues that transhumanists in Russia are united by a "long-standing historical sensibility . . . in which they feel called upon to unite *all* humans based on what they claim to be a shared biological condition, namely, human mortality" (2019, 24).

Indeed, Bernstein points out that long before Silicon Valley elites like Peter Thiel became interested in parabiosis, Aleksandr Bogdanov (1873–1928), who is claimed as an important precursor to the Russian transhumanist movement, won state funding to establish a major research institute in Moscow devoted to exploring the age-reversing potential of parabiosis. She writes:

> Perhaps most striking about Bogdanov's fascination with blood transfusions is the idea of "physiological collectivism." As expressed in his earlier science fiction, Bogdanov felt that in any truly egalitarian society, more than property and privileges would be shared; so would the very corporeal properties of persons. Thus, life extension and rejuvenation was only one goal motivating science. The creation of a kind of universal kinship through exchange of what he considered a key bodily substance—blood— was another. (2019, 67–69).

In Russia, therefore, transhumanist attempts to defeat death and utilize technologies such as parabiosis have been linked to larger efforts to create a more egalitarian and cohesive society dedicated to promoting immortality and equality for all. This stands in marked contrast to what Farman describes in his contribution to this volume. He proposes that in the United States, transhumanist efforts to escape "terminality" reflect an extreme politics of abandonment where sermons of techno-salvation and plans to leave and *abandon all* in order to survive elsewhere raise suspicions that transhumanists are first and foremost concerned with ensuring their personal survival rather than contributing to the common cause. As will be seen, such suspicions can be vividly gleaned in the public outcry over Peter Thiel's interest in parabiosis.

Silicon Valley and the Rise of the Immortality Industry

In the United States, media coverage of transhumanist immortality initiatives can be traced back to the 1990s. In 1994, Ed Regis published an article in *Wired* magazine titled "Meet the Extropians." The extropians were a group of highly educated, almost entirely white, libertarian men who were living in Southern California and riding the wave of the technology boom with a manic optimism. As Regis (1994) reported, they were passionately committed to the idea that "biology is not destiny" and that "genuine immortality" is "possible." In 1998, with the founding of the World Transhumanist Association, many of these technoutopians united with other like-minded futurists and assumed the mantle of transhumanists (Bostrom 2005, 15).

Over the last few years, transhumanist immortality initiatives have piqued the interest of some of Silicon Valley's most powerful elites.[7] In the process, transhumanist desires to live forever have gone from being peripheral stories covered mostly in science and technology journals (if not science fiction blogs) to mainstream news. In addition to being featured in publications such as *Time* magazine, *Vanity Fair*, the *New York Times*, and the *New Yorker*, transhumanist immortality initiatives are increasingly covered in business and investment journals.[8] For instance, in April of 2013, *Fortune* magazine published an article titled "5 Billionaires Who Want to Live Forever" (Alserver 2013). In September of 2015, *Business Insider* upped that number to "6 Billionaires Who Want to Live Forever" (Thompson 2015). In August of 2017, the *Financial Times* published an article titled "Silicon Valley Is Selling an Ancient Dream of Immortality." And in January of 2018, *Forbes* published an article titled "Who Wants to Live Forever? The Super-Rich, That's Who (And Most Everyone Else)" (Prince 2018).

This shift in coverage and publishing outlets is not just reflective of the American fascination with "billionaires" and the "super-rich" (of which I will have more to say about later); it is also reflective of the fact that immortality has become an industry. The "race to unlock the 'immortality gene,'" or pursue immortality through the use of new biotechnologies, artificial intelligence, and mind-cloning techniques, is attracting millions of dollars of investments from biotech start-up companies and venture capitalists in Silicon Valley who have now been dubbed "The Immortality Financiers."[9] Elon Musk, Peter Thiel, SiruisXM founder Martine Rothblatt, Amazon's CEO Jeff Bezos, former CEO of Google Bill Maris, Google cofounder Sergey Brin, and Oracle cofounder Larry Ellison have all invested heavily in the science of radical life extension and they enthusiastically proclaim that immortality is no longer an unattainable dream but rather a technical problem that can be solved or conquered. Moreover, for those involved in the immortality race, the anticipated promise of such initiatives includes not just rejuvenated bodies and eternal life but also staggering profits. It is estimated that by the year 2022, the anti-aging biotech industry in Silicon Valley stands to gross $85.6 billion dollars.[10]

Of course, there have been vocal critics of transhumanist immortality initiatives from the outset. Referred to by transhumanists as "bioconservatives" or "bioluddites," these opponents have decried on scientific, moral, religious, and ethical grounds the transhumanist desire to live forever. Moreover, as the article titles above indicate, even the most measured media reports suggest that immortality does seem to be an initiative largely reserved for the rich, thereby echoing a critique that has long plagued the transhumanist movement in general, namely its elitism. However, as the transhumanist desire for immortality has morphed into a lucrative enterprise and become scientifically more legitimate, the overall tone of media coverage has shifted from incredulity and ridicule to one of increasing respect and plausibility. For instance, in an article titled "Silicon Valley Is Trying to Make Humans Immortal—and Finding Some Success," which was published in *Newsweek*, Betsy Isaacson (2015) observes, "These titans of tech aren't being ridiculous, or even vainglorious; their quests are based on real emerging science that could fundamentally change what we know about life and death."

Despite this increase in legitimacy, in the summer of 2016 alarm bells began to sound when it was reported that billionaire entrepreneur, founder of PayPal, and self-professed transhumanist Peter Thiel had expressed an interest in learning more about the start-up company Ambrosia, which was offering trial procedures of parabiosis for $8,000 a client. The critiques and condemnations, quite interestingly, were not primarily targeted at the company itself. Nor were they primarily directed at its founder, Jesse Karmazin, a thirty-two-year-old medical researcher from Stanford University. While academics criticized the questionable science behind this potentially age-reversing technique, over-whelmingly, the popular criticism the story generated was leveled at Peter Thiel.[11] In fact, the association between Thiel and parabiosis gained so much traction that in May of 2017 the HBO television series *Silicon Valley* aired an episode that parodied the bloodthirsty quest to eliminate death by staging a scene of an older actor who plays oligarch Gavin Belson (and who looks very much like Peter Thiel) receiving a blood transfusion from a younger "blood boy."

Although Peter Thiel never actually engaged in parabiosis (whereas over one hundred Ambrosia clients have), he became the face of this life-extension tech-nique and was lambasted in countless articles, editorials, and online discussion forums and blogs, portrayed as a "blood-sucking" "vampire" who would stop at nothing to secure his power, life, and wealth. For instance, in August of 2016, the online website Romper, which advertises itself as "the digital meeting place for millennial moms," published a short piece by Laura Hankin titled "Is Peter Thiel a Vampire? Twitter Thinks So." In a spirit of playful mockery, Hankin (2016) wrote,

> Perhaps you've sensed him, as you've walked the streets of Silicon Valley at midnight.
>
> A fluttering of bat-wings pierced your awareness, a glint of fangs flashed in the dark.
>
> "I want to suck your blood," Peter Thiel, the vampire, murmured in your ear. "Also sign up for Paypal."

The online media outlet *Gawker*, which Thiel reportedly played a key role in bankrupting after it published a story outing him as gay, further amped up the hype when it reported that it had received an "unverifiable" tip that Thiel "spends $40,000 per quarter to get an infusion of blood from an 18-year old based on research conducted at Stanford."[12]

While some of the commentaries regarding Thiel's interest in parabiosis were clearly intended to be humorous, as was the case in the article cited above, they nonetheless gave voice to suspicions and concerns that were echoed many times over in more serious editorials and articles. From websites devoted to millennial moms to business and investment journals to the *New York Times* and *Vanity Fair*, this was clearly a story that activated the fears and fantasies of a significant portion of the American public. How are we to understand this? What is it about parabiosis as a life-extension technology and Peter Thiel as a potential consumer of such technology that so captured the American imagination in the late summer of 2016?[13] Why did this story elicit such condemnatory responses?

The Perils of Parabiosis

Part of the answer, I propose, has to do with the significance of blood. Within American culture and society, blood matters in many ways (Carsten 2011). It is regarded as the source of vitality and the substance of kinship (Schneider 1968). It is the gift that keeps on giving and that therefore should never be commodified. Alternatively, blood is also that which is sacrificed or spilled in defense of country and family. Furthermore, blood is of and in the body and to transfer it from one host to another is to engage in an act of boundary crossing that often provokes anxiety, if not outright fears of contamination. All this helps us understand why Peter Thiel's mere expression of interest in parabiosis triggered such a visceral and hostile response, whereas his actual (and well-known) practice of consuming growth hormones to stave off the aging process, for instance, has not.[14] The articles criticizing Thiel suggest that parabiosis is alarming because it threatens to turn vitality into vampirism and the substance of kinship into a commodity that can be bought and sold between strangers. As the *Silicon Valley* episode graphically conveyed, parabiosis also brings together bodies, young and old, poor and rich, that in everyday life would, and some might argue should, remain worlds apart.

Moreover, despite some very humorous framings, the articles and editorials criticizing Thiel almost unanimously depict parabiosis as an immoral and illegitimate act of expropriation. Indeed, if Thiel was cast as a vampire, it was not just because he was perceived as a literal bloodsucker but because he made such a good metaphorical one.[15] Thiel emerged as the ultimate embodiment of the capitalist subject or system that "vampire-*like* lives only by sucking living labor, and lives the more, the more labor it sucks." Within days of the story breaking, memes of Thiel sporting fangs began to circulate on the internet, and allusions

Figure 2.1. Peter Thiel with fangs.
Courtesy of Iain Thompson, the
Register.

to his vampirism flourished (figure 2.1). *Gawker* columnist J. K. Trotter (2016), for instance, pronounced, "The logical endpoint of Thiel's dystopian world vision could feature an economy in which the wealthy, who wish to live forever, subsist on the blood of the poor, who would die at normal age." Another article, titled "Let Them Drink Blood," claimed that Silicon Valley futurists such as Peter Thiel "plan to live forever by harvesting both the labor and the body parts of the working class" (Gittlitz 2016).

This is also to say that Thiel's interest in parabiosis did not just stir up concerns about the traditional capitalist who produces surplus value by cheapening labor power and working his laborers into an early grave. It also evoked and reflected anxieties over new forms of biocapital. As Stefan Helmreich and others have observed, "In the age of biotechnology, when the substances and promise of biological materials . . . are increasingly inserted into projects of product making and profit-seeking, we are witnessing the rise of a novel kind of capital: biocapital" (Helmreich 2008, 463–64). Thiel was thus cast as a predator who seeks to sustain his power, wealth, and life by seizing actual body parts and body substances from those with less economic means.

Criticisms of Thiel and his interest in parabiosis also reflected pervasive anxieties about increasing inequality in the United States and the gap between the ultrarich and a vast portion of the population who are struggling to maintain some semblance of middle-class life. The fact that Thiel and his Silicon Valley "pay pals" are not just millionaires but billionaires was indeed significant in how this vampire story played out. In numerous editorials and opinion pieces, it was suggested that their obscene wealth had come at the direct expense of an imperiled middle class. For instance, in an opinion piece titled "Modest Proposal: Let's Sell Our Blood to Peter Thiel and Redistribute Wealth in America," blogger Khan Duymazlar (2016) not only proposes that selling blood to Thiel and his billionaire friends at exorbitant rates such as $1 million dollars a pint might be an effective way to achieve wealth redistribution. He also wryly accuses these bloodthirsty billionaires of building their fortunes by cheating the middle class. He writes,

> On a societal level we are concerned with significant wealth floating (read: systematically pushing) to the top in this country and staying there. "Wealth redistribution"—AKA *"how does the middle class get its groove back from billionaires that rob them for sport"*—is a hot hot issue.
>   It seems like wealthy people want to live forever (fine by me), middling folk . . . well we just want to be quasi-healthy, enjoy our limited time, run a few errands and die an opiate-satiated death at some point when we get old. (Duymazlar 2016)

Last but not least, the perils of parabiosis were linked to suspicions that this procedure represents a perversion of the natural order of things, replacing the cherished belief that "children are our future," as Whitney Houston famously sang, with the idea that the young will be sacrificed to preserve and perpetuate the power of old men who stubbornly refuse to die or to let go. Many of the criticisms leveled at Thiel suggested that class warfare may in fact be a subspecies of more profound intergenerational antagonisms that are coming to the fore with the graying of American society.[16] For instance, in August of 2017, in an article titled "The Superrich Are Injecting Blood from Teenagers to Gain 'Immortality,'" Tomasz Frymorgen wrote:

> If you're a millennial, you might have felt for a while now that older generations are out to suck us dry . . . but the blood sucking appears to have become a whole lot more literal. Because the super-wealthy are now pumping themselves with the blood of young people in an attempt to prevent themselves from ageing. Over 100 people have participated in a clinical trial at a San Francisco start-up offering blood transfusions for older patients. (Frymorgen 2017)

The reactions elicited by Peter Thiel's interest in parabiosis thus both reflected and conveyed more pervasive anxieties that were circulating through American society in the summer of 2016. Concerns over increasing inequality, white male privilege, gerontocratic authority, and the extractive nature of a rapidly developing biotech industry clearly animated the outpouring of responses this news story sparked. However, what really sealed the deal and secured Peter Thiel's role as the leading vampire/villain in this social drama was Thiel's out-spoken political support of another old white male billionaire who was thirsty for power and who was regarded by many as an illegitimate heir to America's democracy: Donald Trump.

Democracy Imperiled

Long before anyone could even fathom the possibility of Donald Trump run-ning for president, Peter Thiel was openly expressing his concerns about the future of American democracy. In a 2009 essay titled "The Education of a Liber-tarian," Thiel writes, "I no longer believe that freedom and democracy are com-patible."[17] In addition to suggesting that democracy had been gravely imperiled by extending the vote to women in 1920, he goes on to explain, "For those of us who are libertarian in 2009, our education culminates with the knowledge that the broader education of the body politic has become a fool's errand. . . . In our time, the great task for libertarians is to find an escape from politics in all its forms—from the totalitarian and fundamentalist catastrophes to the unthink-ing demos that guides so-called 'social democracy.'"

Despite his own advice to "find an escape from politics in all its forms," on July 21, 2016, ten days before the first report of Thiel's interest in parabiosis appeared in article titles such as "Billionaire Trump Supporter Peter Thiel Wants the Blood of Young People," Thiel emerged as one of the featured speakers at the Republican National Convention.[18] In a televised broadcast that was aired across the nation, Thiel proclaimed his endorsement of Republican presidential nominee Donald Trump. "I build companies" Thiel began, "and I'm supporting people who are building new things, from social networks to rocket ships. I'm not a politician. But neither is Donald Trump. He is a builder, and it's time to rebuild America."[19]

Thiel's endorsement yielded immediate and intense criticism. On the day of Thiel's speaking engagement at the RNC, Ben Tarnoff, a journalist for the *Guardian*, published an article titled "Donald Trump, Peter Thiel and the Death of Democracy" (2016) in which he lamented the puzzling alliance between

Trump, "an authoritarian populist who promises to abolish free trade," and Thiel, "a self-described libertarian who worships capitalism," and reflected on its potentially devastating consequences for the American people. The blowback from Thiel's liberal and very much anti-Trump colleagues was just as intense. Cast as "the only living Trump supporter in Silicon Valley," Thiel, in supporting Trump, appeared to many to have breached a trust that might not be mendable (Naughton 2016). Indeed, Thiel has since moved from his home in Silicon Valley and has become an outspoken critic of his liberal, "elitist," "close minded" colleagues.[20]

While Thiel was being criticized by his colleagues and accused of contributing to the downfall of American democracy, by September of 2016, rumors had begun to circulate that Thiel would be handsomely rewarded by Trump if he won the presidential election. In the fall of 2016, numerous articles appeared stating that if Trump became president, he would consider appointing Thiel, who has a law degree from Stanford, to one of the most powerful positions in the land, the Supreme Court.[21] In October of 2016, Thiel stepped up his support for the Trump campaign by pledging a $1.25 million contribution, and at least according to the media coverage of the time, the bromance between Trump and Thiel was in full swing.[22] Within days of being elected, Trump, now the fortyfifth president of the United States, made good on his promise to reward Thiel for his support. Though he did not make Thiel a Supreme Court nominee, he did invite him into the inner corridors of power by appointing him as a member of his "transition team."[23] Media reports, and images of the two clasping hands in a much-discussed gesture of intimacy and common purpose, suggested that Trump and Thiel, now occupying some of the highest seats of power in the world, were firmly allied.

For many on the left, this alliance provided further evidence that Peter Thiel had been rightfully cast by the media as the country's biggest creep. Immediately after news broke of Thiel's appointment to Trump's cabinet, Brian Feldman published an article in *New York* magazine titled "Peter Thiel Is Poised to Become a National Villain" (2016). Commenting on Thiel's support of Trump, which earned Thiel the labels "crank" and "crackpot" from the liberal press, he wrote, "At the time, it seemed like a silly decision made by a Silicon Valley crackpot; now, it looks like an inauspicious sign that Peter Thiel's presence in our political and cultural life isn't going away."

Feldman also suggested that there were some striking similarities between the two men; both have been accused of misogyny, and both have led virulent attacks against media establishments that have covered them in a negative light. Feldman (2016) warned that their alliance should not be dismissed or ignored by the American people, commenting, "But of course, cranks can be billionaires—they can even be president—and with billions of dollars comes the material power that demands, if not respect, then wary attention. We now live in a post-election world in which Trump will be president, and in which Thiel's donation to Trump was a prescient investment, rather than baffling self-sabotage."

Numerous other writers and journalists voiced similar concerns, casting both Thiel and Trump as serious threats to the future of American democracy. On November 30, 2016, Jedediah Purdy published a piece in *Politico* titled "The Anti-Democratic Worldview of Steve Bannon and Peter Thiel" (2016). In it, he asked, "What does Donald Trump stand for? . . . Now that Trump is president-elect . . . the question has taken on monumental importance." He went on to propose that this question might best be answered by looking at "two of Trump's close advisers," Peter Thiel and Steve Bannon. "They are," Purdy wrote, "our first clear view of Trumpism as an illiberal theory of politics with deep doubts about democracy." Noting that there was "troubling commonality" between Bannon and Thiel that "goes far beyond any specific policy areas," Purdy concluded, "The speeches and writings of these two political outsiders suggest that beyond policy, there's something much deeper at work: an impulse to reshape the country, and the world, in a way that would change the meaning of democracy in unsettling ways—and maybe, ultimately undermine it."

Thus, if initially it was Thiel's interest in parabiosis that dominated media headlines and made him seem like such a threat to the vitality of the young, in the wake of the election it was Thiel's support for Donald Trump that made him appear as a threat to the vitality of the nation. In fact, as Purdy's article suggests, it became increasingly difficult to tell where the boundary between the two lay or who was responsible for the other's infamy. Was Trump a potentially dangerous leader and threat to democracy because he was staffing his transition team with people like Peter Thiel? Or was Thiel a menace because he was so closely aligned with the views and vitriol of Donald Trump? The question took its most graphic form in a meme that began to circulate on the internet depicting a "composite Thiel/Trump" with Peter Thiel wearing a Trump wig (figure 2.2).

Figure 2.2. Peter "Trump." Courtesy of Iain Thompson, the *Register*.

Conclusion: The Politics of Life and Death

What does this vampire story stand to teach us about the politics of life and death in the contemporary United States? I propose there are at least four lessons this case study imparts. The first is a lesson that anthropologists have been keyed into for a long time. Threats to the cultural, moral, and even political order often give rise to fears of the living dead. Whether they take the form of zombies, malevolent ghosts, or vampires, the living dead, as boundary transgressors and liminal beings, provide particularly efficacious symbols through which to articulate fears about the integrity of the social order.

But zombies, ghosts, and vampires also express and speak to such fears in different ways, and an anthropological account should be able to explain why one and not the other provides the dominant idiom in a given context. In the case at hand, the vampire emerged as the privileged symbol to articulate such anxieties because first, there is a literal correspondence between vampires and parabiosis. Vampires are bloodsuckers who maintain their eternal life by preying on the blood of others, and parabiosis is a life-extension technique that literally involves transfusing blood from younger people into older recipients. However, within Western society, vampires, like Peter Thiel himself, are also regarded as the symbolic representatives par excellence of a capitalist system that "vampire-*like* [emphasis added] lives only by sucking living labor, and lives the more, the more labor it sucks." If zombies typically represent a "supplanted, stolen, or effaced consciousness," an "appropriation of one person's will by that of another" for "exploitative gain" (Dendle 2007, 47), then vampires represent those who stand to benefit from such forms of extraction.

Indeed, this was the basic point Marx sought to make when he deployed vampiristic imagery in his critique of capitalism over 150 years ago, and it would be remiss to conclude this chapter without giving Marx his due for making this vampire story come to life in such a palpable and powerful way. As numerous scholars have observed, perhaps more than any other writer, Marx was highly skilled at invoking images and tropes of the living dead to articulate the destructive impacts of modern capitalism, and within his writings, vampires and vampirism held a privileged position (Berman 1983; Carver 1998; MacLellan 2013; Moretti 1983; Neocleous 2003; Panichas 1981; Smith 2001; Wolff 1988). Some scholars have explained the use of the vampire metaphor in Marx's writings with reference to literary style, arguing that Marx was an avid reader of gothic literature and primarily used references to the vampire as a literary tool because he "recognized how crucial it was to give an imaginative account of things" (Smith 2001, 44, 47).

Mark Neocleous, by contrast, argues that Marx's use of the vampire metaphor "was not *simply* a rhetorical device" but rather was deployed to "make a substantive point about the social world" and the nature of relations between human beings in the capitalist system of production (Neocleous 2003, 684, 674). He proposes that Marx's use of the vampire metaphor "can be properly understood only in the context of his critique of political economy and, in particular, the political economy of the dead" (684, 668). As Neocleous points out, "The role of the dead" occupies an important position in Marx's critique of political economy. In an 1867 letter written to Friedrich Engels, Marx himself proposed that "one of the best points in my book," *Capital*, is the realization that capital is itself a form of accumulated dead labor that comes to dominate and oppress the living (680). Citing various references to this in Marx's writings, Neocleous (680) writes:

> Dismissing the view that capital is distinct from labour . . . Marx argues that capital is nothing but accumulated labour. His distinction is thus between accumulated labour and labour *per se* or, as he often puts it, accumulated labour versus "living labour." . . . If the distinction is between accumulated and living labour, then it makes perfect sense to treat the former, capital, as "dead labour." Hence "the rule of the capitalist over the worker is nothing but the rule of the independent conditions of labour over the worker . . . the rule of things over man, of dead labour

over living." In capitalist production then, "living labour appears merely as a means to realize objectified, dead labour, to penetrate it with an animating soul while losing its own soul to it."

Neocleous argues that the distinction Marx drew between living and dead labor "picks up on a more general theme in his work: the desire to create a society founded on the *living* of full creative lives rather than one founded on the *rule of the dead.*" Neocleous thus concludes that Marx invoked "one of the most powerful metaphors," the vampire, to "force" on readers "a sense of the appalling nature of capital: its affinity with death" (2003, 684). Though Marx may not be read with the frequency or appreciation he once was, his writings have continued to play a major role in shaping the way capitalism is understood and critiqued as a cultural and economic system, particularly among those on the left who tend to be outspoken critics of Peter Thiel and Donald Trump. Moreover, the vampiristic imagery examined in this chapter suggests that capitalism's "affinity with death" is not just an academic concern but one that is increasingly being taken up in the sphere of popular culture.

This points to the second lesson to be gleaned from this case study: Marx's critique of the vampiristic nature of capitalism was indeed prescient.[24] With the emergence of new forms of biocapital, it is not just living labor power that is consumed by the capitalist in the pursuit of surplus value, but increasingly, as Helmreich and others have pointed out, body parts and substances themselves (Cohen 2001; Helmreich 2008; Waldby and Mitchell 2006). Indeed, one might argue that contemporary biocapitalism has literalized Marx's metaphor, and in so doing, it has raised new questions and concerns about the contemporary extraction of surplus value and its effects on the American people. Who stands to profit from immortality biotech initiatives? Whose bodily substances will be consumed in the process? Will these initiatives lead to a better life for all, or just a longer and more powerful life for some?

These questions point to the third lesson suggested by this case study. As new technologies make the dream of immortality ever more plausible and as powerful elites appropriate these technologies in their efforts to extend their vitality and staying power, we may need to supplement accounts of necropolitics with what I will call "vitapolitics." Achille Mbembe develops the concept of necropolitics to discuss the way sovereignty in the global order is, in large part, established through the "capacity to dictate who may live and who must die" (2003, 11). He demonstrates how the right to kill is used to subjugate human populations, confer "upon them the status of the *living dead* [emphasis in the original]," and create "topographies of cruelty" across the planet (40). Transhumanists such as Peter Thiel, by contrast, are not attempting to create topographies of cruelty but rather topographies of privilege where the capacity to dictate who may escape death and live ever longer and more enhanced lives appears to be increasingly central to their attempts to establish their sovereignty and power.

The last lesson this vampire story imparts is that in the contemporary United States, it is not just the case that matters of life and death are increasingly politicized. Americans are reminded of this daily when they fight for a living wage or a right to health care. What this story also suggests is that for many people living under and in the turbulent aftermath of a Donald Trump presidency, politics itself has come to be understood as a life-and-death struggle, and what lies in the balance for them is nothing less than the life and death of American democracy itself.

Acknowledgments

I would like to thank Shannon Dawdy and Tamara Kneese for inviting me to participate in the SAR seminar and for their very helpful comments on the first draft of this essay. I would also like to thank Anya Bernstein for answering my questions about parabiosis in Russia.

Notes

1. The story was first reported on August 1, 2016, by Jeff Bercovici (2016) of *Inc.* magazine in an article titled "Peter Thiel Is Very, Very Interested in Young People's Blood." This report was followed by many more reports variously published online and in the print media: Chang (2016), Chodorkoff (2016), Farell (2017), Ferguson (2016), Kosoff (2016a, 2017), McCarthy (2016), Riley (2016), and Trotter (2016).
2. See, for instance, Casey (2016), Feldman (2016), Morse (2016), Purdy (2016), and Tarnoff (2016).
3. See, for instance, Boelderl and Mayr (1995), Comaroff and Comaroff (1999, 2002), Dendle (2007), Greene and Mohammad (2010), and Ong (1988).
4. In an article titled "Witches and Zombies of the South African Lowveld: Discourse, Accusations and Subjective Reality," Isak Niehaus points to "the limitations" of the Comaroffs' argument. He notes that although "anthropological studies generally interpret discourses about witches and zombies in sub-Saharan Africa as critical commentary on the emergence of new forms of wealth," a

closer inspection reveals that zombie beliefs and accusations are "connected to powerful psychological motivations, such as emotionally overwhelming experiences of bereavement, loss, and mourning." He thus proposes that "witches and zombies derive their broad appeal from indeterminacy that defies interpretive control and constantly allows for alternative interpretations" (2005, 191).

5. For a useful discussion of the concept of biocapital and biocapitalism, see Helmreich (2008).

6. Transhumanism is far from a monolithic movement. It attracts followers from across the political and economic spectrum. In the United States, the most visible representatives of the transhumanist movement have been Silicon Valley elites who champion free enterprise and stand to profit handsomely from the development of new technologies. At the same time, transhumanism also attracts socialists, anarchists, and technoprogressives who variously seek to democratize technologies through governmental regulations, open source initiatives, and the cultivation of DIY cooperatives (Hughes 2004, 2012). There is, therefore, a range of perspectives and tensions that need to be considered when attempting to characterize and understand transhumanism. Both Klerx (2006) and Hughes (2004, 2012) provide useful overviews of the different perspectives within the transhumanist movement. Bainbridge also provides a very useful overview of the different "types of Transhumanism" (2017, 214). However, despite these variations, transhumanists are committed to a common goal. At the most basic level, transhumanism is a sociocultural movement dedicated to the pursuit of radical enhancement (Herrick 2017).

7. See, for instance, Gollner (2013).

8. See, for instance, Bercovici (2018), Grossman (2011), Horn (2018), and Friend (2017).

9. See, for instance, *Money Morning* (2020) and Rana (2020).

10. See Zhavoronkov (2018).

11. Ambrosia was referred to in some articles as "the vampiric start-up" company. See, for instance, Haynes (2017). For an article discussing "the questionable" science behind parabiosis, see Maxman (2017).

12. See both Trotter (2016) and Ingram (2016).

13. It should be noted that in numerous interviews, Thiel stated that he was interested in Ambrosia and parabiosis for his own personal health regime, not as a business venture.

14. See Harrington (2016).

15. Indeed, in 2018, the recording artist Unsanitary Napkin released a song titled "Peter Thiel (Literal Fucking Vampire)" (https://unsanitarynapkin.bandcamp.com/track/peter-thiel-literal-fucking-vampire).

16. See, for instance, Gnostic Warrior (2016), Williams (2014), and Vespa (2018).

17. He writes in this essay (2009), "Since 1920, the vast increase in welfare beneficiaries and the extension of the franchise to women—two constituencies that

are notoriously tough for libertarians—have rendered the notion of 'capitalist democracy' into an oxymoron."

18. See Morse (2016).
19. See Drabold (2016).
20. See, for instance, Byers (2018) and Morris (2018).
21. See, for instance, Kosoff (2016b) and Whittaker (2016).
22. See Morris (2016).
23. See Fiegerman (2016), Kokalitcheva (2016), and Lecher (2016).
24. For an extended discussion of the continuing relevance of Marx's critique of capitalism, see Eagleton (2011).

CHAPTER THREE

A Responsible Death

Valuing Life from Mortality Tables to Wearables

TAMARA KNEESE

Introduction

This chapter explores emergent death-care practices in the United States as part of a neoliberal emphasis on personal responsibility, wherein managing death is another facet of worker productivity. By analyzing archival materials from the Life Extension Institute (LEI), an organization founded in 1913 to improve health in the United States, alongside contemporary algorithmic life insurance models and crowdfunding practices, I argue that expectations around self-care extend from responsible living into responsible death—who is worthy of protection or investment and why? Predictive analytics determine the speculative value of human life and death. Life insurance assessments are based on gender, age, ability, race, and genetics. While mortality tables have been central to the insurance industry since at least the nineteenth century, algorithms use habitual data and lifestyle metrics to assess humans on individual and population levels. Rather than simply collecting information, life insurance companies seek to minimize risk and maximize profit by subtly shaping embodied behaviors.

I propose that historical self-optimization practices, propelled by insurance companies and organizations like the Life Extension Institute, are precursors of today's self-tracking cultures. New models of algorithmic surveillance and attention encourage people to remain productive, even in the face of death. Care of the self is imagined as making death less messy, or even less likely. Life extension is a goal for certain Silicon Valley–based subcultures in the United States, such as the Quantified Self movement. Transhumanists who plan to use technology to radically extend life or do away with death altogether are part of a much larger technoculture that includes mainstream figures and major corporations like Microsoft and Google (Farman 2020; Farman, this volume; Huberman, this volume). Individuals are responsible for maintaining their own health through virtuous habits, which marks illness and premature death as signs of classed and raced failure. Insurance start-ups, backed by venture capitalists in Silicon Valley, incentivize responsible behavior through rewards systems and use algorithms to calculate premium rates, utilizing data they collect from wearable devices and other data streams such as electronic health records. In the case of unavoidable death, individuals are expected to prepare accordingly by managing their estates and acquiring insurance policies to cover their own funeral expenses, else they will force their loved ones to crowdfund their death care after the fact. A good death is a planful one, and those who die so-called bad deaths may be deemed unworthy of both life insurance payouts and crowdfunded donations.

In the Victorian era, life insurance became a moral responsibility and spiritual practice, allowing a breadwinner's family to bury him and survive in his absence (and I am purposefully using male pronouns here, as the breadwinner ideal type was exclusively male). In the early twenty-first century, as life insurance has waned in popularity and is no longer provided by most employers—especially for employees in part-time, freelance, or gig economy positions—crowdfunding campaigns fill in for those who are unable to prepare for their own burials. Because of institutional malevolence or neglect, compassionate volunteers donate to campaigns on Kickstarter or GoFundMe to bury the unfortunate dead (Kneese 2018). Crowdfunding has itself become an after-the-fact, ad hoc form of life insurance.

In both life insurance start-ups and crowdfunded funeral campaigns, algorithms help determine the value associated with individual human lives; in the context of insurance, premiums go up or down according to metrics shared through digital platforms and devices, whereas for crowdfunding campaigns to cover funeral costs and other benefits typically included in life insurance policies, proprietary algorithms impact the visibility of campaigns. In a feedback loop of attention, the more likes and shares that a campaign receives, the more a platform will promote it.

While actuarial tables—large-scale statistical predictions about a given population's expected life span—have been central to insurance practices since at least the nineteenth century, predictive analytics provide novel ways of modeling based on individual habits and lifestyle metrics. Insurance companies use models not only to predict when and how people might die, but to shape consumer and worker behavior, encouraging them to stay productive for as long as possible and blaming individuals for their own ill health. Focusing on the positive public-health outcomes was a rhetorical strategy that companies hoped would save them from regulation and oversight. That users' personal data can influence insurance coverage is relevant to conversations around the ethics of data accumulation and the ways that algorithms can reinforce and even exacerbate structural inequalities, leading to increased surveillance of and discrimination against marginalized communities when it comes to education, housing, employment, and policing (Benjamin 2019; Eubanks 2018; Noble 2018). Like actuarial calculations of risk in the nineteenth and twentieth centuries, twenty-first-century predictive analytics in insurance have the potential to exacerbate existing inequalities. Borrowing from Nick Seaver's suggestions toward an ethnography of algorithms, my chapter relies on a mixed-methods approach, drawing on material and cultural artifacts including companies' promotional materials, interviews, screenshots, emails, pamphlets, and archival sources, or what Seaver calls "scavenging" (Seaver 2018). The precise workings of opaque corporate algorithms, which are a kind of black box, may not matter as much as their material effects. What imaginaries structure people's use of algorithms, and how do such imaginaries relate to embodied cultural practices? Algorithms are reshuffling responsible death, creating new systems for monitoring productivity and shaping behavior, including death-care practices.

As feminist digital humanities scholar Jacqueline Wernimont argues, "There are no data, tracking opportunities, algorithms, or patterns without bodies." Her book takes up the "ways the quantum media organize the Anglo-American understanding and representation of our embodied lives and deaths" (2019, 4). Technologies are always embodied, so death-care practices provide a grounded way of understanding the ways that even the driest actuarial data are composed of bodies all the way down.

This chapter examines algorithms as arbiters of death care, framing them as an extension of neoliberal self-care and biomedical responsibility. Algorithms impact how people work and how their productivity is measured, along with how their insurance premiums are calculated. They also determine which people are deserving of medical intervention and coverage or whose death is worthy of attention. I use the example of life insurance's trajectory to show how North American death-care practices are related to ideologies around wellness, productivity, and the value of human life.

In a counterintuitive turn for someone who typically studies emerging practices around digital technologies writing in a volume about "the new death," I use historical examples to trace responsible death as a concept back to the nineteenth and early twentieth centuries. In this achronological chapter, I begin with the case of crowdfunded death care to show how the algorithms and rhetorics of charity, as well as moral responsibility, work together to determine the value of life and death. I use key examples from the contemporary American life insurance industry and the twentieth-century Life Extension Institute to follow the genealogy of responsible death in the United States, showing how changing technologies and their associated cultural practices inform methods for assigning value to human life and predicting mortality.

Crowdfunding Death Care

Tech Workers Coalition (TWC), an international group advocating for equity in the tech industry, circulated this image (figure 3.1) in their February 2019 newsletter, published shortly after Waheed Etimad's fatal collision with a drunk driver. In the text accompanying a photograph of Etimad and six of his children, TWC emphasized Etimad's precarity as both an immigrant and a gig worker: "Uber will pay no workers comp death benefits for his family. There will be no life insurance pay out. In life, Waheed was a unit of profit for Uber. In death, he is nothing to them" (TWC email newsletter). Although Etimad drove full-time for Uber, the company did not consider him a real employee, so his family was left unprotected and without legal recourse.

Legally defined as an independent contractor, Etimad took on the risks associated with driving for Uber at his own peril. Apps like Uber and Caviar encourage gig workers to risk their lives in the hopes of earning more money; in another well-known case of gig worker death, Pablo Avendano, a Caviar worker, died delivering food by bicycle in a rainstorm. Gig economy apps prompt drivers and couriers to work in inclement weather, hinting that they can earn more in a storm: "When it rains the orders POUR on Caviar! . . . Go online ASAP to cash in!" Mysterious algorithms determine when and where they work, downplaying the company's role in the same way that classifying workers as contractors alleviates a company's responsibility for providing insurance coverage and other benefits. After his death, Avendano's family and friends petitioned Caviar to reimburse his funeral expenses (Ciccariello-Maher 2018). A GoFundMe campaign titled "All Out for Pablito" raised money to cover the

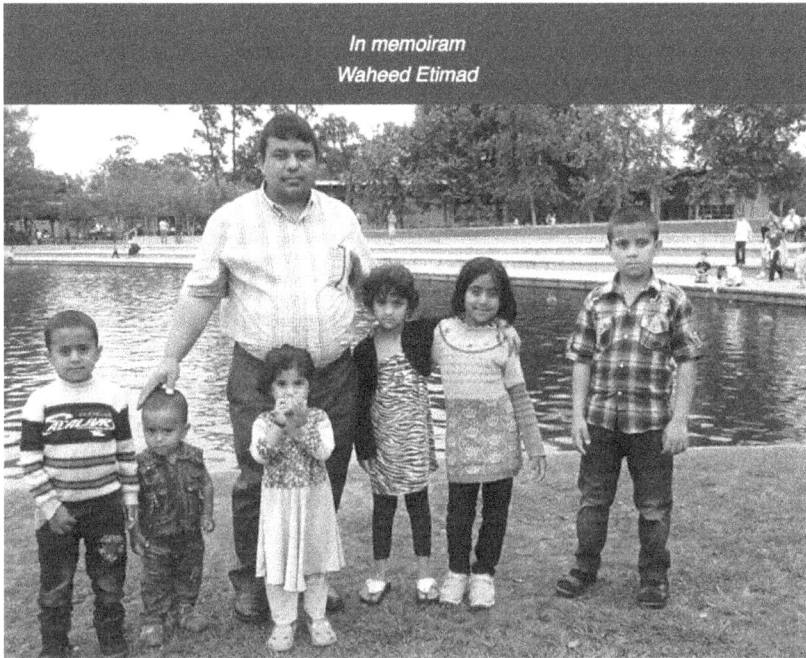

Figure 3.1. An image from a crowdfunding campaign linked to in the TWC newsletter, from an email to the author.

costs in the meantime, propelled by gig worker organizations, activist groups, and hashtags on social media.

In Etimad's case, in lieu of a life insurance payout, a combination of grassroots organizing and hashtag activism also helped raise money for Etimad's family while demanding justice in the wake of his death. Fellow ride-hail drivers arrived at Uber headquarters to hold a vigil: "They asked for #JusticeForWaheed, and whether Uber would do anything to support his family after profiting from his labor. Uber is liable for nothing. This is the lie the entire gig economy rests on: that as contractors, they are not beholden to their employers, so employers are not beholden to them. You can help support Waheed's family at this GoFundMe link" (TWC email newsletter). As a result of this on-the-ground and digital organizing, anonymous donors, Uber drivers, and acquaintances of the Etimad family could all donate funds to cover burial costs and support the family after the death of their sole breadwinner. Despite the publicity, the fundraiser never reached its

$400,000 goal. The attention economy sometimes stalls out, privileging some lives and causes over others. Depending on social status, media coverage, and the algorithmic gods of specific platforms like Twitter, Instagram, and Facebook, a hashtag or crowdfunded funeral campaign for the dead can either flourish or fade.

In the United States, many people do not have medical coverage—let alone life insurance policies—in the absence of a universal health-care system; roughly fifteen thousand people died as a result of their state's refusal to expand Medicaid benefits under the Affordable Care Act (Weinberg 2019). Crowdfunding campaigns on major platforms like Kickstarter and GoFundMe are mechanisms for raising money to pay for chemotherapy treatments and surgeries alongside pet projects and artistic innovations. Neoliberal definitions of who is deserving of care inform which campaigns are successful and which fail (Berliner and Kenworthy 2017). For those who die without life insurance, crowdfunding campaigns also cover funeral and memorial expenses, providing bereft families with financial and emotional support.

Crowdfunding has become an acceptable way to safely care for and bury the dead and is linked to larger social and racial justice movements; through its reliance on storytelling, visibility, and activism, it is a manifestation of what Casey Golomski refers to as "radical mourning" (Golomski, this volume). While crowdfunding campaigns are hosted via corporate platforms, they are intertwined with mutual-aid efforts and burial rites. In their best iterations, crowdfunding campaigns are a means of showing care. Rather than passing the collection hat at a place of worship or offering other in-person material assistance like food, flowers, or hugs as part of collective mourning, crowdfunded funeral campaigns provide another way for kin members to bury their dead with dignity. As LaShaya Howie (this volume) notes, Black death-care practices are connected to Black-owned family businesses and cultural practices that emerged out of the legacies of slavery and segregation. Black funeral homes are important spaces for Black sociality. Social movements like Black Lives Matter and the use of #SayHerName when Black trans women are murdered call attention to the precarious experiences and deaths of those in marginalized positions. For people who cannot join mass protests because of their own vulnerabilities or caretaking responsibilities, online acts of mutual aid provide a way to contribute to collective-care movements. Importantly, crowdfunding is not just organized through digital platforms but is related to direct material needs. It can be used to provide food, shelter, clothing, medical supplies, or bail funds to individuals and communities, and in some cases, it can help pay for coffins and memorial services and for childcare, rent, and therapy for mourning kin members.

Amid COVID-19, GoFundMe campaigns are omnipresent in the United States, as federal, state, and local governments have done little to support people as they lose their livelihoods and access to medical treatment. Achille Mbembe's "necropolitics" has taken on new resonances in this political moment, in which the state withholds care for its most vulnerable and conflates "essential workers" with disposability (Mbembe 2003). In the necropolitical machinations of a culture that values some lives over others, asking essential but low-paid workers to drive buses and deliver groceries, such inequities mean that crowdfunding has become a key part of sending necessary supplies to individuals and communities, as well as a means of providing material burial support to people's families after they die. The story of Valentina Blackhorse, a dynamic twenty-eight-year-old Navajo woman who died of COVID-19, appeared on *NPR* and *Democracy Now*. Despite the media coverage, the GoFundMe campaign raising money for her burial and for her grieving family members fell short of its goal. In May 2020, the Navajo Nation's rate of COVID-19 infection had surpassed that of New York. Black, Indigenous, and Latinx people, who are disproportionately dying from COVID-19 because of a long history of structural oppression and overt environmental and medical racism, are also the least likely to benefit from crowdfunding initiatives. Studies have consistently shown that crowdfunding reproduces existing inequalities, as campaigns initiated by and intended for Black people are more likely to go unfunded and donations are most likely to go to white people. Publicity doesn't necessarily work either, because people's prejudices influence which campaigns they donate to and which they pass over. The problems that exist in crowdfunded campaigns in the best of circumstances are intensified by the current collapse of support structures (Kneese 2020).

Responsible death connects to tensions within care as both a neoliberal tool and a part of radical praxis. What Hiʻilei Hobart and I call "radical care" is associated with positive affects, collective social movements, and mutual aid—or solidarity rather than charity. On the other hand, Hobart and I argue, "because radical care is inseparable from systemic inequality and power structures, it can be used to coerce subjects into new forms of surveillance and unpaid labor, to make up for institutional neglect, and even to position some groups against others, determining who is worthy of care and who is not" (2020, 2). Self-care is radical praxis when it extends outward into collective care. While self-care

is entangled with neoliberal calls for productivity and the biopolitical capture
of vitality, self-care's history is related to collective political movements, such
as feminist privileging of self-knowledge over medical expertise in the 1970s
and the Black Panthers' various social programs. Self-care is fundamental to
activism, as care of the self allows people to care for others. At the same time
self-care is increasingly related to patient compliance, wellness ideology, and
workplace productivity.

No matter the more radical possibilities afforded by crowdfunding campaigns and their ties to mutual aid practices, they are still plagued by notions of
personal responsibility and charity. Crowdfunding platforms are based on the
idea that anyone can raise money for their personal needs or desires. But the
campaigns of normatively attractive young white people attract more attention
and more money than campaigns for people who are considered less worthy,
often those from oppressed communities. Funerals are expensive, and for those
who do not have insurance or cash on hand, crowdfunding provides families
with a way to bury dead loved ones in a way they deem acceptable. Despite their
democratic appearance, however, many crowdfunding campaigns ultimately
fail. Media coverage can make or break a campaign. If a crowdfunded funeral
campaign is connected to a social movement, the campaign is more likely to
meet or exceed its goal. There are countless campaigns that don't receive funding, either because they don't inspire media attention or social media shares or
because the death is considered a "bad" one. Campaigns for victims of mass
shootings or famous cases in the news tend to be successful, whereas campaigns
for people whose deaths are complicated are less likely to compel donors. Someone who dies by suicide or overdose might be less likely to receive funding than
someone who dies in a publicized attack. In a time of mass death, as during
a global pandemic, whose deaths are counted and whose names are remem-
bered? Some affect-laden stories garner attention and money; many more are
left behind, including campaigns for the elderly, the poor, the mentally ill, and
the unhoused. The racism, classism, sexism, ableism, and ageism that exist
offline carry over into these supposedly egalitarian spaces.

Crowdfunding platforms obviously profit from campaigns that are more successful, since they take a cut of the donations, so it is in their interest to promote
campaigns that have the capacity to go viral. Platforms will sometimes include
a list of campaigns that are closing soon but not meeting their goals in the
hopes of encouraging a crowd of people to donate. Through my examination of
hundreds of crowdfunded funeral campaigns and interviews with individuals

who either donated to or initiated campaigns, I found that it is more likely that the platform will promote campaigns that are tied to news events or that are already attracting many shares, likes, and donations. In this way, the platform may exacerbate existing social inequalities by amplifying some campaigns over others. Access is also a key factor. A successful campaign depends on a verifiable creator who can craft a compelling and emotionally evocative narrative, making use of poignant photos or videos to make it clear that an individual theoretically deserves a proper burial (Kneese 2018). For instance, campaigns associated with high-profile accounts, or those reposted by influencers or people with large followings or friend numbers, are more likely to gain traction than those initiated by people without a tangible online presence.

Such deep inequalities exist in life insurance calculations as well. The United States has a long, complicated relationship with life insurance as a method for evaluating human life and death through categorization, from slavery and eugenics to neoliberal self-care and quantified self-tracking. In addition to employing a variety of technologies to surveil populations and individuals alike, the life insurance industry uses the specter of responsible death to uphold preparedness as a social virtue.

Responsible death is predicated on responsible living, which means practicing self-care and optimizing one's health to avoid sickness in the first place. The quantification of daily embodied habits is meant not only to increase productivity at work but also to enhance one's chances at extending life. Self-tracking wearables gather, analyze, and share personal habits and biometrics (Schüll 2016). A person's life is reduced to counted steps, heart rate, hydration status, weight, and oxygen levels. Self-care is thus popularly associated with self-optimization and mindfulness, or a way of preparing individuals for increased productivity in demanding workplaces (Gregg 2018). Employers may also encourage their workers to engage in corporate wellness initiatives, allowing employers to maintain new levels of control over their workers' nonworking hours (Hull and Pasquale 2018). Stress reduction and attitude modification have been taken up by the medical establishment as treatments for everything from depression to cancer (Jain 2013). In the context of terminal illness, those who fail to practice self-care may indeed be labeled as "non-compliant" and thus less deserving of institutionalized care; to earn their right to survive, individuals must perform what Beza Merid calls "responsible patienthood" (2019). Responsible death also means planning ahead or taking out insurance policies or accumulating enough wealth to leave your family well-off in your absence.

Algorithmic Risk Assessment

From the insurance industry's perspective, responsible living is inversely related to the risk of premature death. In addition to the algorithmic workings of attention and care, established insurance companies are partnering with internet start-ups to find new ways of calculating risk and attracting younger audiences; convincing millennials or zoomers to purchase life insurance policies is no easy feat. Life insurance is a dying industry, or at least it is hard to convince people to put money into something without immediate results when the majority of Americans are in debt and lack savings; *Fast Company* claims that individual sales of life insurance have dropped by 40 percent since the 1980s (Harris 2017). Some new life insurance start-ups, such as Ethos, an affiliate of Assurity Life, sell term life insurance instead of policies that persist in perpetuity in the hopes of attracting people who want to pay for a set period of time only. This might be especially appealing to those who are working in erratic industries or who are unsure of the longevity of their current employment situation. "Using population data, Ethos can offer insurance policies in roughly ten minutes based on a few bits of customer information" (Schieber 2018). On its website, Ethos pitches itself as being "for people who don't have time for fine print, unnecessary doctor's appointments or extra fees." Ethos claims, "We treat you like a person, not a risk."[1] They also emphasize that they are affordable, considering policies on a case-by-case basis. It's life insurance, personalized: "Ethos helps protect families in their most difficult moments by offering life insurance coverage that values people over profit."[2]

Speaking to the *New York Times*, an insurance industry spokesperson states that "insurers are drilling down to the precise granularity of risk" by employing algorithms (Hardy 2016). New services like Vitality calibrate life and health insurance rates according to user data from Apple Watches and Fitbits (figure 3.2), which they provide for free or at discounted rates. For insurers, algorithms imply disembodied and impartial calculation. Haven Life, a life insurance start-up founded in 2016, states that "getting life insurance should be painless."[3] Assessing risk through algorithms allows Haven Life agents to avoid collecting samples of bodily fluids like urine and blood, which is the standard procedure. Algorithms obviate the need for medical exams. However, this process still requires aggregated personal and medical data from a wide range of sources, including credit scoring, prescription data, electronic health record

Healthy living and rewards partners

Apple Watch with Vitality life insurance

To help you get active and earn rewards for doing so we're pleased to announce Vitality Active Rewards with Apple Watch Series 2.

This benefit is unique to Vitality and partners us with Apple Watch Series 2, the next generation of the world's most popular smartwatch.

Learn more

Figure 3.2. An Apple Watch with Vitality logo, from the John Hancock website.

information, and existing electronic lab data. Data become a proxy for bodily verification processes.

Data collection is easier than ever, thanks to the widespread use of mobile devices and social networking platforms. Rather than relying on medical examinations or individuals' food diaries, insurers, government agencies, or marketers can analyze data on a person's sleep cycle, sexual activity, and daily movement through the use of wearables in addition to collected data from social media platforms and mobile devices. For insurers, this means a proliferation of traits or activities that might be seen as risky or beneficial. This, of course, has direct monetary consequences for individuals, and especially for entire groups who are deemed riskier than others, such as sexual minorities (Patel 2006). Data will always have cultural implications and technological systems are not neutral or infallible. Data flows and predictive modeling may in fact exacerbate power differentials and inequalities.

Mathematical patterns and abstractions cannot help but brush up against embodied cultural practices and are continually reinforced by institutions, corporations, and organizations. In the early twentieth century, the medical establishment and life insurance industry combined mortality tables and mountains of client files with physical exams and the disciplining of individual bodies. The precision promised by today's life insurance algorithms is still shaped by human actors.

Rather than assessing the validity of algorithms in life and health insurance models, as opposed to mortality tables or other actuarial methods and tabulating machines, this chapter investigates their effects on individual behavior and cultural norms. Given the implementation of medical exams as an arm of the life insurance industry, there are resonances today not only in terms of fears surrounding data collection and surveillance but also in terms of self-optimization trends. Monitoring exercise and eating habits, smoking and drinking habits, and BMI are tied to the management of individual behaviors. Within post-Fordism, the notion of productivity itself is now bound up in participation in data accumulation, not in the creation of tangible goods or services alone. Companies' impulse to minimize risk has embodied and material ramifications. Self-investment, including all forms of self-care like diet, exercise, getting mammograms or other preventative measures, and getting enough sleep, are favored ways of mitigating risk and constitute their own form of work.

Social media data, scraped from every digital nook and cranny, are now being used to determine insurance rates. One of the largest British insurance companies, Admiral, analyzed users' Facebook posts to assess their car insurance premiums. Facebook later blocked the company from this practice, saying that it was at odds with their privacy policy and may constitute a breach of their terms. Admiral attempted to create its own algorithm to sort drivers, rating them according to their perceived personality traits such as conscientiousness or organization (Chapman 2016). Admiral assessed drivers based on their posts on social media, which were evaluated for risky behavior. Individuals who had "risky" personalities were given higher premiums. Bizarrely, risk was determined by the "excessive use of exclamation marks" or the "liberal use of words like 'always' or 'never' instead of the more measured, 'maybe'" (Chapman 2016). Through an imagined connection between online behavior and embodied risk-taking, an insurance company decided which drivers were more likely to be injured or die in accidents.

Unsurprisingly, the life insurance industry has embraced predictive analytics, which allows insurers to save labor and to reduce the influence of human decision-making: "In short, the modern paradigm of predictive modeling has made possible a broadening, as well as a deepening, of actuarial work" (Batty et al. 2010, 5). In life insurance, underwriting techniques require a great deal of time and money, usually taking an insurer over a month to complete. Underwriting is also "subject to the idiosyncrasies, inconsistencies, and psychological biases of human decision-making. Indeed, this is a major motivation for bringing predictive models to bear in this domain" (8). In many other sectors, including human resources hiring practices, algorithms are presented as a way of alleviating human bias, as if algorithms are somehow removed from the social conditions in which they are produced. Actuaries themselves can be replaced by algorithms, saving a company from spending too much money on labor.

In the twenty-first century, life insurance companies use algorithms to determine their most lucrative markets. Unlike the working-class industrial insurance policyholders of the early twentieth century, most life insurance customers today are affluent. Individuals tend to purchase insurance after they get married, buy a house, or have children. Insurance companies can assess these phenomena by examining marketing data. In fact, according to those in the industry, "a predictive model can be built to identify which characteristics are most highly correlated with the purchase of life insurance. Again, scoring a direct marketing database can help a life insurer determine where to focus limited resources for marketing and sales" (Batty et al. 2010, 16). Class, race, gender, and particular lifestyle traits, in addition to personal habits, affect whom algorithms target as likely life insurance customers.

Advocates for predictive analytics in insurance practices are increasingly incorporating prescription data records in order to target individuals for marketing, but also to assess their premium payments. "Many users are enthusiastic about its protective value, and as a result it is becoming a standard underwriting requirement for an increasing number of life insurance companies. This is another interesting source for predictive modeling" (Batty et al. 2010, 18). Insurance companies worry about including information that is at odds with the value of a company or that utilizes information that might lead to legal or public relations problems. In a stretch on the part of the industry insiders who wrote this particular white paper, life insurance is also linked to social reform, as predictive models may have the effect of increasing access to insurance and "if the final effect of predictive modeling in life underwriting is in some small way to push people toward healthier lifestyles, we would be happy to claim that as the ultimate victory" (27).

The authors note that actuaries have engaged in similar behaviors for centuries, but emphasize the new business opportunities afforded by predictive analytics:

Indeed, one of the oldest examples of statistical analysis guiding business decisions is the use of mortality tables to price annuities and life insurance policies. . . . Likewise, throughout much of the 20th century, general insurance actuaries have either implicitly or explicitly used Generalized Linear Models and Empirical Bayes (a.k.a. credibility) techniques for the pricing of short-term insurance policies. Therefore, predictive models are in a sense, "old news." Yet in recent years, the power of statistical analysis for solving business problems and improving business processes has entered popular consciousness and become a fixture in the business press. "Analytics," as the field has come to be known, now takes on a striking variety of forms in an impressive array of business and other domains. (Batty et al. 2010, 4)

Life insurance has to take into account long-term behaviors to determine policy rates, so accumulating as much data as possible supposedly minimizes the risk of signing particular policyholders. While nineteenth- and twentieth-century insurance companies attempted to alter individuals' behavior, aggregated data and predictive analytics allow for the automation of these techniques. Rather than reading a manual on how to improve their health, individuals are more subtly encouraged to conform to certain behaviors. Insurers hope to predict a commuter's routine and provide incentives to make them practice self-care, such as sending "them a Starbucks coupon to encourage them to wait out the risk" of an oncoming storm (Hardy 2016).

The large insurance firms are connecting with internet start-ups in the interest of disrupting the industry. Vitality has partnered with different insurance companies, including John Hancock, in order to lower individuals' life insurance premiums in exchange for giving the company access to their personal data (Hardy 2016). According to John Hancock's website, the Vitality program "rewards healthy behavior."[4] Customers accumulate Vitality points by going about their daily routines, including giving up smoking, going to the gym or walking regularly, and getting annual physical exams. As customers accumulate points from their lifestyle habits, they are rated as Bronze, Silver, Gold, or Platinum members, similar to frequent flyer miles. The more points individuals earn, the less they pay for insurance premiums. Fitbits are provided for "free," a token that allows the insurance company to more accurately calculate mortality risk. To sign up for plans, customers first calculate their "vitality age," which is usually higher than a person's biological age. The assessment relies on age, sex, tobacco use, weight, height, cholesterol, eating habits, and blood pressure.

Rather than using a mortality table, Vitality has users answer questions through their Life Expectancy Calculator, which assesses people's health based on a variety of factors. "Are you prepared for the possibility of outliving your retirement income, or not being able to meet your future long-term care or disability needs? Use this tool to predict the average number of years you can expect to live—and learn how life insurance can help you plan for today and the future."[5] Life insurance is a fail-safe and a step toward responsible death, especially in the face of a precarious life.

According to their calculations, Vitality gives me a baseline life expectancy of eighty-five and a projected life expectancy of ninety-five. As an aside, they note that "adult men and women who follow a healthy lifestyle can add more than 10 years to their life expectancy."[6] A disclaimer provides more context for their speculation about my expiration date; they base their assessment on a 2008 mortality table calculated from life insurance sources and social security data.

Naturally, this rather primitive calculator is not the true stand-in for the mortality table. Instead, my aggregated personal data would give insurers a much clearer idea of when I might die. My habits, in combination with information about my social networks and demographics, would make me seem like a person worth investing in—or not.

Those who subscribe to Vitality are promised a more secure financial future in addition to a healthier life. Individuals are rewarded for healthy choices and receive gift cards and discounts at Amazon and Whole Foods for acquiring fitness gear and nutritious food. Institutional support is also provided to customers, as the Friedman School of Nutrition Science and Policy at Tufts University gives subscribers access to information about nutrition, diet, and health. In addition to saving money on premiums, individuals who maintain their bodies are more productive in later years: they can continue working later into life while also enjoying their golden years. Stock images on the Vitality site show thin, athletic, silver-haired couples on golf courses. This allows them to remain financially secure in addition to active and healthy. "The new program also upends the traditional approach to life insurance underwriting, which typically bases its pricing on a detailed but static snapshot of a person's medical status. Now, John Hancock's term and universal policies will be priced continuously, at least for consumers who choose the Vitality program" (Bernard 2015).

Vitality is a program intended to benefit people who have enough leisure time and physical energy to enjoy a gym membership. To entice users by promising Whole Foods discounts limits the program to people in cosmopolitan urban centers or wealthier suburban communities. Vitality also limits itself to those who are young and well enough to engage in physical activities, while implying that following their regimen can help to slow the aging process or even extend life itself.

I cannot help but see connections between Vitality's promises and the goals of the Life Extension Institute (LEI). Founded in 1913, the LEI helped produce a perceived connection between information and wellness. Irving Fisher, a Yale economist and social reformer, and Harold Ley, a wealthy New York City–based contractor, cofounded the LEI to enhance American health and male-worker productivity. The LEI was composed of "men with large means at their command, and the new health promoting agency is heavily backed with capital" (*New York Times* 1913). Prominent men from medicine, business, and philanthropic organizations, including former president William H. Taft, the founder of the Mayo Clinic, and Alexander Graham Bell, served on the LEI's board. Even if these powerful board members were not instrumental to the LEI's day-to-day operations, they lent the organization symbolic weight. From the start, the LEI was intertwined with the insurance industry. The Metropolitan Life Insurance Company was one of its biggest and most powerful clients; the LEI conducted annual physical exams of MetLife policyholders to calibrate premium rates that benefited MetLife and employers. The LEI thus prefigures contemporary concerns about surveillance and discrimination, highlighting disparities between ordinary workers and corporations.

Through its many health pamphlets, the institute advocated for healthy living, including moderate exercise, careful hygiene, and abstention from alcohol, tobacco, and drugs. By encouraging self-optimization, LEI proponents believed that old age could be curtailed and death overcome. Adherents also connected physical self-improvement to practical and moral issues; individual restraint could supposedly alleviate social problems like venereal disease, prostitution, and excess alcohol consumption, as well as illnesses like typhoid and tuberculosis.

Some members of society seemed better suited to these disciplinary practices than others, and health data collection and analysis emphasized differences between men and women and the young and the old, as well as between different racial and ethnic groups. A productive economy excluded women, immigrants, and people of color, instead privileging white middle-class male breadwinners. Life insurance is a way of managing death, but it is also a means of categorizing individuals and populations as potentially valuable or inherently risky. Employers' surveillance of workers' health theoretically ensured increased productivity. The LEI performed data collection on factory workers for Ford and General Motors, conducting physical exams over time, while comparing the health of white-collar bankers to the health of industrial workers. Workers were evaluated according to ethnicity and race, as LEI cofounder Irving Fisher and several other board members were staunch eugenicists. They considered disease a depreciation of investments, placing moral responsibility on workers to remain healthy (Zelizer 1979).

The LEI used physical exams and mortality tables to surveil and categorize the working classes, whereas for elites and for wealthy white men in particular, self-tracking was a way of extending the life span and potentially beating death. Thus, the history of life insurance is related to movements like eugenics and transhumanism. Their actuarial calculations were not meant to merely capture information as it was but to change habits and effect social reforms through the monitoring of populations. Today, actuarial work has expanded, and real-time fluctuations can be tracked through digital means, including wearable devices, GPS data, and social media metrics. In the context of life insurance, proprietary algorithms, not actuaries and mortality tables alone, determine the value of human life and death. Algorithms' capacity for surveillance and attention is much greater in part because of their invisibility and opacity. The LEI conducted medical exams on factory workers and used graveyards as data, but today's corporations can simply gather data from their employee's devices while managing them through algorithms.

While the Life Extension Institute conducted mass surveillance of workers through observation and medical exams, today's data collection is tied to ordinary wearables and familiar social networking platforms. This may appear to be a softer form of control, based on data management and a reward system. Algorithms are a kind of prodding mechanism, allowing users to modify and track their own behavior while providing data to insurers and corporations.

Drawing the connections between the LEI and algorithmic life insurance practices shows how self-optimization is tied to notions of productivity and the valuation of life and death. Numerous scholars have noted how notions of well-being and health are continually remade through technological biomedical enhancement. Michel Foucault's concept of "technologies of the self" positions self-care as the basis of morality, stemming from the Greco-Roman tradition. Technologies of the self include "operations on their own bodies and souls, thoughts, conduct, and way of being" to transform "themselves in order to attain a certain state of happiness, purity, wisdom, perfection, or immortality" (Foucault 1988, 16). While there are liberatory aspects of self-care, it can be taken up by the neoliberal state to place responsibility on individuals while subjecting certain populations to control through biopower. Nikolas Rose (2007) describes how this epistemological shift emerged from new "technologies of optimization," which seek to control the body's vital forces through the blending of biology and genetics with informatics and computational methods. Technologies of optimization do not just try to cure diseases or enhance individual health, but they also "change what it is to be a biological organism" (Rose 2007, 17).

Rose imagines optimization as central to molecular biology and genetics, but he also discusses the ways in which new products like Viagra have shaped definitions of sexual health for older men. Biopolitics is thus closely tied to bioeconomics. The logics behind optimization are extendable to other contexts beyond DNA. At the heart of optimization is the desire to transform, through an act of transubstantiation, one material, body, object, or product into another entity. Optimization as an epistemology also infuses movements like the Quantified Self and certain genres of transhumanism, where tracking applications measure calorie intake, sleep patterns, or sexual activity. The founders and elite proponents of the Life Extension Institute delighted in self-optimization, much like technologists do today. But data are harvested from others' bodies as well and used to make predictions about entire populations. The blood-sucking imagery Jenny Huberman recounts with respect to transhumanist capitalists like Peter Thiel is connected to longer histories of self-optimization through the exploitation of others (Huberman, this volume).

On the other side of a movement based on extending life is one just as concerned with predicting and managing death. As Wernimont puts it, "The generative functions of life tracking, including the making of English and American nation-states and citizens, depends on death tracking. Our quantum media count death in order to open up the space to count life in particular ways and in order to protect particular people" (2019, 2). Quantum media within the context of lived reality eventually translate into quantified death.

Wernimont compares histories of mortality tables and insurance for enslaved people, the census and its counting of different people according to different values, and current digital death registers. In the United States, the Centers for Disease Control and Prevention use the Modern Mortality Register to count the dead through health and medical trends. The register focuses on specific diseases, not all, and the interface is designed to be used and read by medical professionals, not the general population (Wernimont 2019, 76–80). Aggregated data at the population level disconnect data from the embodied experiences of the individuals they quantify (150).

The mortality table is still present in algorithmic assessments of human value and speculations about when people will die. But with the rise of big data and predictive analytics, insurers can dispense with physical exams and more obvious forms of surveillance. They can assess risk, or so they believe, through the data themselves. And data in this context are almost always relational. Individuals are labeled risky based on their social context: demographic information, social networks and "friends" on social media, and location data.

Life Insurance as Speculative Death

Life insurance attempts to address mortality through information management, using predictions about risk and calculations of value to determine how people might die and when, and what their lives and deaths are worth. It is future oriented, in that the precise time and cause of death is a still-unknown factor. The value of individuals as workers and policyholders is dependent on speculation. Abou Farman (this volume) describes "terminality" as a future-oriented individual and collective state where death is in the air, whether because of a terminal cancer diagnosis or, on a more collective scale, the climate catastrophe that threatens all life on earth, noting that radical life extension in Silicon Valley transhumanist circles is one method of mitigating this mode of existence. Life insurance, too, steps in as a way of managing such uncertainty in the face of impending doom.

While life insurance has been in operation in the United States in some capacity since the mid-eighteenth century and gained in popularity in the 1840s, it did not become a fixture until after the conclusion of the Civil War. In 1889, the Actuarial Society of America held its first meeting. In 1890, members of the ASA encountered the punched-card tabulator, an instrument first used by census takers and later taken up by the insurance industry. Tabulators were a physical means of managing large datasets, in many ways a precursor to the computer (Yates 2005, 35). The mortality table is itself an algorithm, albeit one calculated by hand. While US mortality tables were developed to determine risk and potential margins for profit in the late eighteenth century, the insurance industry settled on the American Experience model in 1868 (Hustead 1988). Sheppard Homans created the American Experience table, drawing on the findings of the Mutual Life Insurance Company. It was the most commonly used actuarial table in the insurance industry from the late 1860s until 1948, when it was replaced by the 1941 CSO (Commissioners Standard Ordinary) mortality table (Hustead 1988). The actuarial table served as the life insurance industry's lifeblood as it became entrenched in the American experience. A mundane instrument for a macabre task.

Massive social changes, new technologies, and institutional needs facilitated the spread of life insurance. The growth of life insurance coincided with the changing class structure of antebellum American society, with the emergence of urbanization and industrialization and the rise of the middle class (Murphy 2010). Crucially, rather than just predicting health outcomes as they did in the nineteenth century, twentieth-century reformers worked in tandem with corporations, bureaucrats, and medical professionals to actively change health-related behaviors to manage risk. A focus on public health and life extension acted as a public relations buffer, allowing insurance companies and employers to avoid regulation and reform (Bouk 2015, xiii).

Anthropologist Michael Ralph (2012) highlights the relationship between slave insurance and life insurance policies for workers when it comes to the valuation of human life. Enslavers who sought financial compensation for enslaved people who were injured, lost, or had died took out insurance policies. Plantation owners and traders also took out policies on enslaved people working in particularly dangerous roles or for the passage itself. Likewise, plantation owners developed statistical methods for tracking the productivity and output of enslaved people in relation to hours worked. Enslaved people with defined skills, like carpentry or blacksmithing, were valued at higher rates than unskilled laborers (Ralph 2012). Work and productivity became intrinsically tied to the monetary value of human beings, who were categorized according to age, gender, race, health status, and occupation.

After the Civil War, industrial insurance flourished as a practice. Business owners insured workers according to the risks of their workday routines. Initially, industrial insurance companies experienced higher mortality rates than ordinary insurers, in part because of the hazardous work conditions experienced by employees in factories and mines. Ralph argues that the rise of industrial insurance, where corporations would take out policies betting against the longevity of the poor, indicates the cultural affinity between slave insurance and emerging life insurance practices. Job-related injuries could diminish a worker's productivity, thus decreasing their value to the employer and costing money to the insurance company. Work output was thus directly associated with individuals' value. Insurers applied actuarial assessments to large populations, ranking them according to gender, age, ethnicity, race, ability, and even religion. For example, insurance firms charged African Americans much higher premium rates than whites (Ralph 2012). From its inception, life insurance was predicated on a system that valued some lives and deaths over others and that made its profits by betting against those in marginalized positions to enrich both insurance companies and employers. Daina Ramey Berry's groundbreaking work (2017) shows how every aspect of the life cycles of enslaved people was monetized, including their "ghost values" after their deaths.

Rather than just using mortality tables and statistics to predict the life spans and health futures of their employees, business owners and insurance companies actively sought to change workers' physical conditions to maximize their profits. Kate Crawford, Jessica Lingel, and Tero Karppi (2015) write about the predigital technologies of self-tracking, including weight scales and pedometers, versus the data-driven varieties used in the contemporary moment. They draw a distinction between self-improvement through knowing the self, or the ways by which patients learned to monitor their own weight and movement before reporting that data to medical professionals, versus tracking today, which more directly provides data to corporate platforms and third parties, from insurers and advertisers to government agencies. They argue that the new self-tracking methods are more directly tied into embodied surveillance.

As historian Dan Bouk's work shows, however, there is a longer history of surveillance directly related to self-improvement and associated data collection. During the early twentieth century, insurance companies began to conduct large-scale health studies on industrial workers (Bouk 2015). For business owners, healthier workers could be more productive for longer. Analysts attempted to find the optimal number of work hours and the right conditions to enhance worker productivity and reduce the risk of injury on the job. Insurance companies also directly benefited from workers' health, because good health allowed them to avoid paying out money to policyholders. Along with the notion that breadwinners had a moral obligation to acquire life insurance to support their loved ones, the twentieth century saw the spread of health as a marker of individual responsibility. Workers, whether working-class individuals or middle-class managers, were expected to improve their productivity through self-care practices. Personal self-tracking became a moral imperative and a contribution to the social good (Hustead 1988). Individual workers were expected to take care of their bodies and spirits to improve productivity, while employers were advised to regularly check in on the health status of their employees to ensure quality output. For employers and insurers, convincing workers to practice self-care helped them live longer, healthier—and thus more productive—lives. For an industry based on speculative death, encouraging responsible living helped companies maintain their profit margins and it also made them seem like morally responsible institutions—using risk rating to justify their own classist, racist practices. There was little evidence that life extension and risk assessment methods were effective, but a focus on self-care as moral imperative placed responsibility on individual workers rather than on employers or insurers.

Insurance as Salvation

Importantly, insurance and associated responsible-living techniques were associated not just with better life expectancies and maximum productivity but with spiritual practices as well; responsible death is a moral calling. Sociologist Viviana Zelizer (1979) argues that life insurance helped bridge sacred social ritual with monetary exchange. While death is supposedly a metaphysical phenomenon and outside of the fluctuations of the market, life insurance commodifies death and puts a speculative, monetary value on human life (Zelizer 1979). While mutual aid and community support provided financial assistance to widows and children prior to the nineteenth century, in the nineteenth century, "the financial protection of American families became purchasable commodity" (Zelizer 1978, 593). Life insurance coincided with the growth of urban centers and manufacturing, with the largest companies in cities like New York and Boston. Zelizer claims that "life insurance was part of a general movement to rationalize and formalize the management of death that began in the early part of the 19th century" (593). Speculation went from being morally suspect to acceptable, even mandatory, as a means of providing for kin members after death.

Life insurance promotional materials reveal the logics and imaginaries behind companies' business models. How did major insurance companies portray responsible death as an extension of family life and workplace productivity? In an industrial life insurance pamphlet published by the Prudential Insurance Company of America in 1918, Protestant self-reliance takes center stage. Life insurance "has been termed 'The greatest thing in the world'" because it prevents "privation and want" (Five Minutes Talk with The

Prudential on Industrial Life Insurance 1918, 1). Through industrial life insurance policies, policyholders pay small deposits every week, theoretically helping poor individuals to "save steadily, a little at a time, week by week" (2). This money-saving aspect resonates with Ethos and other life insurance start-ups today that similarly target middle-class markets and precarious workers. The pamphlet claims that this method of payment is advantageous because premiums are "completed within the ordinarily vigorous and productive years of life and relief thus be secured from what might thereafter become a burden" (3). This implies that able-bodied, young male workers can ensure their families' comfort by paying weekly amounts, avoiding payments in old age. The pamphlet's position echoes Michael Ralph's analysis of life insurance policies for enslaved people and others working in dangerous conditions, situations in which disability and the loss of productivity are equivalent to death in the eyes of the insurer. The Prudential pamphlet emphasizes that its policies have provided for the poor, including the burials of children, a common need given early twentieth-century child mortality rates and the 1918 influenza pandemic, as well as the substantial policies of prominent businessmen. However, the working class is clearly the pamphlet's intended audience. In one image (figure 3.3), a widow happily sits reading to the toddler on her lap while another daughter looks on and her son sits reading at a table. The family is shown in comfortable surroundings even after the breadwinner's death, with art on the walls and a Tiffany-style lamp on the table. A caption states, "This home was Prudentially protected." In an image on the adjacent page, the same woman is shown in an empty dwelling, as men in overalls carry away her furniture while a well-dressed man who appears to be managing the repossession of her belongings takes inventory. Her baby is now depicted in tears, and the other children are missing from the portrait altogether. The caption to the second image says, "This one was not [Prudentially protected]." In the second scenario, the breadwinner failed to preemptively manage his own death and is personally responsible for the destitution of his family.

Inside the pamphlet, a white middle-class family teeters on the edge of ruin. With insurance, they can continue on as before, but without it, they fall into penury. It is the male breadwinner's duty to prepare for the future. The pamphlet reinforces the moral dimensions of life insurance and hints at the loss of a worker's productivity. At the end, it claims that "if the insured should lose permanently the sight of both eyes or suffer the loss, by severance, of both feet or hands or of one hand and one food, one-half the amount of insurance would

Figure 3.3. A 1918 Prudential Insurance Company pamphlet found at a flea market in Portland, Oregon, from the author's personal collection. Photos by the author.

be paid in cash and the policy endorsed as fully paid up for the remaining one-half" (Prudential Life Insurance 1918, 7). Severe injury is equated with the total loss of productivity and is therefore likened to death itself. According to the pamphlet, domestic bliss is entirely dependent on the male worker's sustained productivity and his careful planning for a responsible death.

Like the Prudential pamphlet, materials from the Life Extension Institute provide a glimpse of the moralistic gender-, race-, and class-based logics behind the rise of life insurance. The LEI also lends a rich, embodied element to actuarial mortality charts. While the calculations of risk and assessments of different groups appear to be removed from daily life and individual experience, medical practitioners in fact conducted medical exams on individual bodies. These statistical analyses, in turn, had real material effects, informing public policy, education, and popular culture.

As Dan Bouk recounts, a statistician for the Prudential Insurance Company in the early twentieth century, Frederick Hoffman, traveled to graveyards to record the birth and death dates of white southerners to predict their future mortality and to figure out which regions were more worthy of Prudential's investment (2015, 116–17). Hoffman also visited hospitals and sanitariums to observe care practices and living conditions. Prudential captured data from the dead as well as from the living, making assumptions and predictions about entire populations. In the Jim Crow South, gathering data about the life spans of wealthy southerners from hospitals and gravestones to decide whom to insure would only add to existing oppression. Deciding not to insure poor Black southerners or people living in areas with high illness or mortality rates would also leave them without protection. Responsible death practices were intrinsically

tied to existing social and racial hierarchies. The spectral promise of life extension and good health was an excuse for discriminatory practices.

How to Live Forever

Calculating mortality risk and value based on race and class led to prescriptions
for responsible living as well as responsible death. Insurance was a major backer
of and reason for the existence of the Life Extension Institute, but public health,
including an emphasis on responsible living and self-care as solutions for social
ills, was an essential part of the LEI's work. A May 1913 conference at Reed College
in Portland, Oregon, helps to contextualize the priorities of the LEI in relation to
hygiene, sexuality, and social reform. The conference was held just seven months
before the LEI's announcement in the *New York Times* and a year before the LEI's
doors officially opened. On the first day of the Reed conference, Eugene Lyman
Fisk, who would soon be named the LEI's medical director, gave a talk on "Life
Insurance Companies and the Health of Policy Holders." At the time, Fisk worked
for the Postal Life Insurance Company, conducting medical exams on policyholders. Fisk's presentation at the conference was later published as a pamphlet, which
included an image of the Postal Life Insurance Company exhibit at the Conference on Conservation of Human Life. The caption below the photograph states,
"One of the many ways in which a Life Insurance Company can cooperate in the
movement for Physical Welfare." The display's many charts and graphs abstractly
present a disinfected version of the deeply embodied, sometimes morbid work
of life insurance underwriters, who scoured graveyards and hospital wards. Here,
we see respectable middle-class women gathered around Fisk's table at the Reed
conference, seeing how life insurance data are related to better health outcomes
and life expectancies (figure 3.4).

The three-day gathering at Reed was widely attended (according to newspaper reports, there were three thousand conference goers) and publicized.
It was open to the public and included exhibits, lectures, outdoor games, and
meetings of academics, social reformers, and state agencies. The conference
program reveals the ways that reform movements were connected not just to
the insurance industry but to practices surrounding social hygiene, or eugenics,
and reproductive health. The first day of the conference started with a section
on public health. Along with Fisk's presentation was a report on public-health
education among women. Other panels included a segment on "Conditions
of Labor," which examined hours and wages, along with industrial accidents

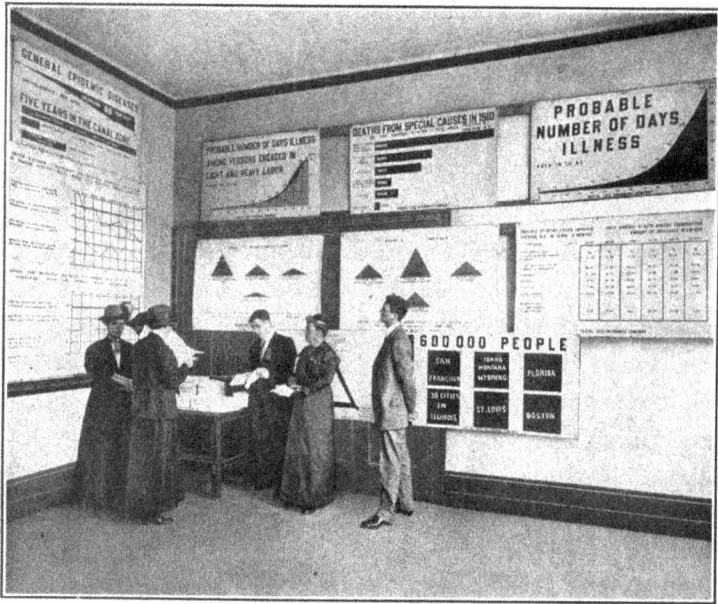

Exhibit of the Postal Life Insurance Company at the Reed College Conference on Conservation of Human Life, Portland, Oregon, May 9, 1913.   One of the many ways in which a Life Insurance Company can coöperate in the movement for Physical Welfare.

Figure 3.4. An exhibit of the Postal Life Insurance Company at the Reed College Conference on Conservation of Human Life in Portland, Oregon, May 8, 1913. High-resolution image courtesy of the New York Academy of Medicine.

and compensation law. A panel on "Defectives" included talks about "mental deficiency," "The Care of Our Delinquent Girls," and "Psychological Tests for Juvenile Offenders." Disability is directly related to crime and other social ills. Calculations of risk were also deeply rooted in eugenics, relying on ableist, sexist, and racist notions of productivity and value. In addition to advocating for diet changes, temperance, and more exercise in public parks, conference attendees called for the classification of schoolchildren according to their physical and mental status, separating "normals" from "defectives." Conference presenters spoke about topics like "Medical Aspects of Sexual Hygiene," "The Pedagogy of Sex Education," and "Moral and Religious Aspects of Sex Education," linking public health to social reform and religion.

Conference goers hoped to extend human life and to prevent "needless deaths" due to disease, injury, and war. Within Reed College's Special Collections and Archives, archival boxes from the Conference on the Conservation of Human Life contain an untitled and undated newspaper clipping of unknown origin that lists the conference's goals. After recognizing the usefulness of extended human life for the social good and the nation as a whole, reformers sought to extend the life span, attempting to "stretch it out tenfold. . . . Not only the prolongation of the action of the actual lifetime of human beings, but increased health, happiness, and intensified citizenship, are the objects contained in the lessons being taught through pictures and story and instruction, by the exhibits and noted speakers included in the diversified program of the undertaking." Crucially, the article claims that it is incumbent on individuals to engage in "clean, careful living" in order to stave off suffering and death. Rather than medicine, doctors advocated for parks, playgrounds, and wholesome foods over "incantations and doses." Lifestyle changes, which require personal willpower and healthy habits, are ways of extending the individual life span and bettering the overall health of the nation. In this moment, reformers believed that premature death was a sign of societal decay caused by individual moral failings. Healthy choices automatically translate into a longer life.

Two years later, in 1915, Eugene Fisk and Irving Fisher published a successful book, *How to Live*, which provided instructions on how much and what to eat, ideal forms of exercise, and tips for effective sleeping. In the same way that Ray Kurzweil and many other transhumanists and futurists of his ilk recommend taking nutritional supplements and perfecting the body in preparation for radical life extension technologies to cheat death, LEI proponents believed changes in diet and lifestyle could help people live longer, if not forever. They equated old age with disease itself. *How to Live* also included a section on sexual health and eugenics, asking readers to protect their racial "germ plasm." *How to Live* was very popular and went through many different editions. Until the 1950s, the book was used as a textbook in high schools to instruct students on personal hygiene (Hirschbein 1999, 93).

In addition to instructional pamphlets, the LEI worked with insurance companies to advocate for mass surveillance to assess Americans' living habits. The Postal Life Insurance Company started conducting regular exams of its policyholders after 1909. The Metropolitan Life Insurance Company followed suit. In 1911, the Equitable Life Assurance Society started its own Conservation Department in order to keep tabs on policyholders. While they relied in part on statistics from hospital records, private medical practice records, or population statistics, Eugene Fisk describes this as limited. To Fisk, even scientific experiments in laboratories are suspect: "To accurately measure such influences, large masses of lives must be kept under observation for long periods of years. Only in the offices of life insurance companies can such material and such opportunities be found. These records cover the family and personal history, the physical type, and to some extent the manner of living of millions of individuals" (Fisk 1913, 2). The LEI's holistic interpretation of individual health relied on both the close monitoring of everyday habits and on the collection of contextual data. Fisk sees life insurance companies as the arbiters of health data, and the institutions that can best assess individual and collective risk as well as potential value.

In a published pamphlet based on his presentation at the Reed College Conference on Conservation of Human Life, Fisk (1913) claims that the public will be more willing to take the advice of life insurance companies specifically because they are businesses, not just social reformers. Life insurance companies also have money and can thus influence public-health legislation: "Entirely apart from any moral obligation to employ life-insurance knowledge of life-influences in the service of humanity, it is becoming apparent that there is a business waste and a business neglect in permitting risks to shift for themselves after once being admitted to a company instead of aiding them in prolonging their lives and thus increase their value as business assets" (Fisk 1913, 2). Rather than abstractly determining risk through actuarial tables or statistics, life insurance conducted physical exams on individuals and also tried to manage their behavior. Policyholders would benefit from longevity and a higher quality of life, "while the cost of the net cost of insurance will be reduced by the mortality-gains returned to the policyholder in the form of dividends" (Fisk 1913, 3). Fisk uses the American Experience Table and Medico-Actuarial Table to determine the amount of money potentially lost to insurance companies by groups exposed to risk. Saving or prolonging lives is directly related to saving money. He then goes on to argue that the "death rate is not a fixed quantity," as lifestyle changes, including living more "hygienically," influence mortality rates (Fisk 2013, 6). British moderate drinkers were found to have a higher mortality rate than abstainers, which leads Fisk to argue in favor of the temperance movement.

Predictive models are not just used to measure death rates, but to make changes to individual health. Reformers sought to influence personal behavior through public-health campaigns and institutional action. Individual bodies were in fact tied to a much larger apparatus, which looked to profit from the shaping of their habits.

In an LEI pamphlet on fatigue, Eugene Fisk (1922) offers possible solutions to the problem of young workers aging faster than they should. He writes that shorter working hours and a lighter workload might improve workers' health, especially in combination with improving social and working conditions. But he argues that maximizing productivity relies on individual workers' own habits, so it is ultimately their responsibility: "The individual must be better taught how to live and build up a strong body, free from defects, competent to do a full day's work, and holding something in reserve for emergencies" (1922, 274). Insurers and employers attempted to find the optimal work hours and conditions to maximize productivity, but they also pressed individual workers to maintain their bodies as they would machinery.

Within the context of the Life Extension Institute, cooperation between the life insurance industry and the medical establishment bridged actuarial projection and embodied action. Through mathematical patterns and calculations of risk, certain groups were determined to be more valuable than others. These assessments led to mobilization, as corporations, state and federal government agencies, health advocates, and religious organizations applied these findings to actual human lives. Rather than just calculating risk, those in power actively attempted to alter their findings by encouraging individuals to change their habits.

Algorithms supposedly replace the need for experts, for physical exams, and even for the scientific method. In this way, they contain a spiritual essence, even as they are mobilized to influence material concerns. Algorithms target particular markets or audiences and can frame populations and behaviors, but algorithms themselves are also marketed. In many new insurance start-ups, as for companies like Uber and Amazon, the algorithm is itself the product. What are algorithms imagined as doing, and whom do they benefit? Beliefs about their capacity and nature can shape human life and death.

As with actuarial tables and tabulators in the past, current algorithmic insurance programs assume some groups, from smokers or drinkers to sexual and racial minorities, are riskier than others. With the ascension of far-right ideologies in places like the United States, Brazil, Australia, the Philippines, and Europe, how might proprietary algorithms be deployed to normalize and justify oppression? Today, as in the Life Extension Institute's heyday, algorithms are used by government agencies, major corporations, advertisers, and the medical establishment. Facilitated by the incessant production of personal data, algorithmic insurance practices are a realization of the Life Extension Institute's information management fantasies.

Conclusion: The Future of Responsible Death

This chapter provides a framework for understanding the ways that algorithms are imagined to participate in responsible death, building on a longer genealogy of coerced self-care and surveillance technologies in life insurance. While this chapter and our broader seminar were not about the process of dying per se, projections about life and death are part of the same system of abstraction and valorization. If death is a problem to be solved, how do various factions propose that work be done?

Care of the corpse and the materiality of mourning are related to other social conditions. In the United States, the link between self-care and productivity is part of a neoliberal wellness ideology, but it is also connected to an older system of assessing the value of human life and death. Life insurance is a kind of death management, whether it relies on information organized through tabulators and mortality charts or from algorithmic calculations based on data from social media and wearables. Today, life insurance start-ups attempt to disrupt the industry, which is imagined as catering to older generations. In some ways, however, the practices of responsible death promised by the new wave of venture-backed start-ups mirror those found in industrial insurance pamphlets, which also targeted those without security or accumulated wealth.

Acknowledgments

This chapter began as a paper at a 2016 UC Berkeley Algorithms in Culture workshop and conference. Thanks to workshop participants there and to those at UC Davis, where this paper was further workshopped at a Food for Thought symposium. I want to especially thank Alexandra Lippman, Dan Bouk, Hannah Zeavin, Theodora Dryer, Robyn Caplan, and Ksenia Tatarchenko, along with my fellow SAR Advanced Seminar participants, for their feedback on various incarnations of this work. As a digital media scholar, I welcomed the opportunity to hang out in archives and look for longer histories of self-optimization and life extension, including at the New York Academy of Medicine, American

Philosophical Society, the Chemical Heritage Foundation, and Reed College Special Collections.

Notes

1. See the Ethos website, https://www.ethoslife.com/.
2. Ibid.
3. See the Haven Life website, https://havenlife.com/.
4. John Hancock Vitality Program is at https://www.johnhancockinsurance.com/vitality-program.html.
5. Ibid.
6. Ibid.

CHAPTER FOUR

Deathnography

Writing, Reading, and Radical Mourning

CASEY GOLOMSKI

What happens when people read
writing about death
in our communities, a place we call home

Wondering this faces a mirror
we look in together.

In a list of gemstone tips for writing, Ruth Behar ([2015] 2020, 50) says we should "understand the mutuality of gazes." Mutuality is participation in another's being. It is about being sociable, being interactive and cooperative with one another. These are enlivening encounters common to interactions of caregiving and receiving, learning from and collaborating with one another in field research, and generally working and living together. Being together in these ways also does not mean we will fully know each other or that our relationships will be reciprocal or equitable—or if they ever have or ever will be—but we should want them to be as part of our ethnographic praxis.

A gaze is perspective on embodied aspects of relationships between observer and observed, like ethnographers and readers about whom we write. In it, we are imbricated in aspects of each other's being. Dialogical ethnography can show this imbrication in representing our interactions and collaborations. A gaze and the relationships it builds up and embodies have existential aspects, in that establishing mutuality with others in our method also exposes our mortality, says Behar: "Our genre will always be quirky because it comes about through the magic of a unique intersection in time and space between a set of people and a person who wants to tell their story. This moment of shared mortality is improvised and fleeting, won't ever be repeated. . . . We try to honor, with accuracy and poetry, a fragment of what was revealed to us" ([2015] 2020, 49–50).

Mortality, then, is always some part of a mutual gaze in our writing. This chapter examines this shared dimension in deathnography specifically (a shortcut to say writing about death, and a term we thank Henry Lee Heinonen for coining on social media) and how mortality affects both its writers and people about whom they write. It uses the case of describing new death-care cultures that arose in the wake of mass AIDS-related mortality in eSwatini, the southeast African kingdom formerly known as Swaziland. As the country with the world's highest HIV prevalence for more than a decade, eSwatini has been the site of major changes to forms of dying and death. This chapter foregrounds dialogues with ordinary Swazi people on a book I wrote about it (Golomski 2018) and what these discussions can show us about writing death as it is shifting on a global scale.

Death today is multifarious. Its diverse forms and processes are flourishing under biomedical, technoscientific, political, and cultural regimes, insofar as thoughts about death and engagements with it differently affect life as intentionally lived around the world. Dawdy and Kneese (this volume) write that this leads "different forms of imagined death [to] arc back and shape different kinds of life. It is this arc that we call 'mortality.'" Mortality then bridges phenomenal and material dimensions of death and life and our modulated engagements toward them in practices of "anticipation, memory, planning, prolonging, and actuary forecasts of probable futures." To these theoretical insights I add ethnographic representation. Through time and our respective life courses, our own arcing back or reorientations to mortality affect how we collect, author, and curate stories from the fragments of deaths retold to us in the field.

Deathnography should honor those fragments, to use Behar's terms, by also make them meaningful and relevant to those they represent. Next, in a poetic-reflexive mode, I offer a few dialogical examples of critical engagements with the book that span North America to southern Africa. These engagements show how deathnography globally circulates today and how its mutual gaze emerges among writers and communities whose deaths we write about. They also show how the gaze incites consciousness of necropolitics, for which deathnography can become a form of what I call radical mourning. In our writing, we can bring this mourning into being by foregrounding recognition of our shared mortality—or what activist-scholar Cindy Milstein (2017, 8–9) calls our inter-vulnerability—by building trust in commemorative storytelling and writing against racialized orders that differently condition our deaths and knowledge about them.

Naming Death, or, Can I Trust You to Tell This Story?

A word that can define how to write better about death and dying is *trust*. In several southern African languages, the word for *trust* is *themba*, which is also used as a first name. Themba is one of those general names you might adopt on the first day of a beginner's Zulu language class, which for me was at Boston University's African Studies Center. That name Themba has followed me since. People call me by this in eSwatini, as my first name, Casey, is stranger to say, and my surname more so; the first four letters of Golomski begin to spell a sexually vulgar offensive in siSwati. Addressing someone by their surname there is a standard formal greeting and primary act of showing respect. In extenso surnames recall one's clan history through their praise names. They recall one's ancestral dead. I think some people hid confused repulsion behind laughter when I introduced myself and my research to them by saying my surname, a mixing of sex and death. I have a feeling these are reasons why it was misspelled in a headline about my book that was published in one of the kingdom's two newspapers (figure 4.1).

I trust that whatever happened in the editorial process, it was not done carelessly. Conventionally, anonymity and confidentiality build trust in ethnographic writing about illness, suffering, and death. It tends to mean assigning pseudonyms, which I gave to every individual and most places written about in the book. One reason was to try to follow anthropology's professional code of

Figure 4.1. Digital image via WhatsApp of newspaper article. "Book Review: Casey Glomoski on Being a Writer." *Times of Swaziland*, February 17, 2019.

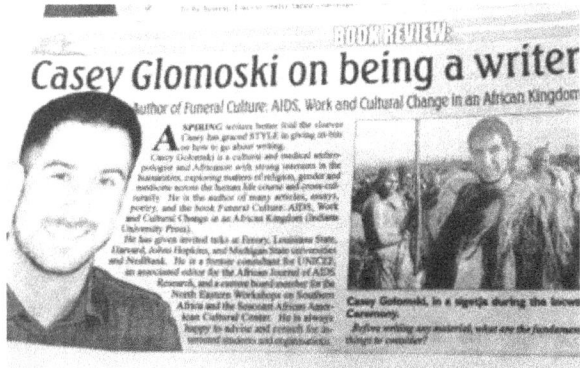

ethics. eSwatini borders South Africa and Mozambique and is home to 250 to 300 clans who claim varying degrees of geographic belonging to the land and larger polities, not limited to the reigning royal Dlamini clan, who consolidated the Swazi ethnonationality that defines the country today. With a population of only 1.3 million, people know other families' names and histories. From the start, I suspected that full anonymity and confidentiality in a small-scale society like this was going to be impossible, if not an anthropological myth.

One citizen I spoke with, Pius, confirmed this. In 2019, he was a twenty-six-year-old graduate student in international development at a university in the northeastern United States. As a teaching assistant, he led discussions of the book for his mostly white American undergraduate students. Discussing anonymization of research subjects, he told me about a conversation he had with his adviser, an anthropologist and professor of global public health: "One comment I had for the professor was that considering how tiny Swaziland is, if I wanted to find out who this person was in the book, it would probably take me one day! It is a very small country. Like that person you mention who is a school principal in Mbabane. There are not that many schools there, like seven, so it's not hard to find out who."[1]

I laughed, being embarrassed. I quickly told him that I also sometimes changed place-names in addition to peoples' names ethnographically. I had not actually changed the place-name of the administrative capital Mbabane in that instance. In that moment, telling this to Pius was my pivot to save methodological face and to skirt potentially identifying the otherwise anonymized principal. In part, it was a gut-reaction aversion to settling into the gaze, an aversion to some kind of failure in writing.

Another reason I used pseudonyms was because, in another sense, dying and death from untreated HIV or its complications was unnamable. For all people I met in eSwatini, AIDS was a bad death. Today, in the supposed "post-AIDS" era, dying of AIDS signals a horrible breakdown of mutuality in a lack of caregiving or inabilities to access health care and its allied infrastructures. It signals biosocial expulsion. AIDS deaths often involved forced or mutual silences, denials, or inactions to care that were often due to circumstances beyond one's control. Bearing witness to all this was painfully difficult — *kulukhuni*, in people's own words.

When someone told me about a relative or neighbor dying of what was likely an AIDS-related illness — even sometimes up to ten years *after* ARVs were rolled out nationally by the government and nongovernmental global health organizations—inherent in their telling was also some statement about their own role—active or not—in that other person's dying. A lie that there was no extra seat in the car to drive someone to the clinic. An unanswered phone call.

Would could they *not* tell me?

What had they *not* done?

What have I done?

That unknowability marked a limit of trust in how I recounted stories of others' deaths. Naming someone as peripheral to the field of care that constellates around a death was perhaps like too brightly shining an interrogation lamp upon them. The light would not reveal a singular truth about a death but rather blind the field, whitening out irreconcilable visions about what had happened. I feared I would lose sight or maybe fail to fully name the ethical decision-making surrounding a death. I explained it this way in the book:

> I met many people in Swaziland who told me deeply personal stories of slow AIDS deaths. . . . Stories of neighbors who locked increasingly sick family members in bedrooms or out of latrines or took away their eating utensils out of fear of contagion or anger. . . . Stories of orphaned children's movement into homes of distant relatives who were reluctant to accept them—perhaps out of spite or because the children were uncomfortable reminders of the dying process. Stories of finding neighbors in their homes who had died alone, or whole families who died over time, their empty, overgrown homesteads, unplowed fields, and tombstones remaining silent material testaments to lives lost. Stories that cannot be retold here fully—a decision I made along with those who first told them to me, for to do so would force an account of death in ways that would be too painfully direct or reductive. Telling such stories could never fully convey what had been sacrificed. (2018, 42)

In trying to name this unnamable process, I retold the story of one young man whom I called Nik and his near-death experience from the disease. Based on my time living with him and interviews with him and others years later, I at first interpreted his near-death illness to have resulted from a social breakdown among kin. Nik had moved from a small city to the rural homestead of his mother's brother "Vuyo" and Vuyo's wife "Nokwenza." In the six months I lived there with them, Nokwenza became my gatekeeper to their extended families, community members, and the chief. I recounted Nik's physical decline as AIDS related and compounded by verbal and physical fights with Nokwenza over his lack of helping out at home and alleged theft of domestic items like eggs and soap. He ultimately survived the disease, a process I first framed based on his own account of overcoming it through medication and a will to move back to the city with the help of his maternal aunt, the Mbabane-based principal whom Pius read about and pointed out.

While I was writing the book, I also saw this story line as a breach of trust with Nokwenza. I worried it mischaracterized her—someone I still talk to weekly and love for her kindness and willingness to allow me to live in her home—as a villain mistreating someone dying of AIDS. I had settled instead in a gaze with the dying person, Nik, focusing on his narrative of survival, which also converged with my inabilities to push further on that narrative and whom it occluded. Six months after the book came out, I gave Nokwenza a copy and asked her to read the chapter describing the events of Nik's near death. A week later, she initiated this exchange on WhatsApp using the pseudonyms I had given them in the book rather than their real names:[2]

> Nokwenza: . . . Themba, the stories are funny like the egg and soap story. I think Nik had needed to adjust as he had tasted living in his rented room and was doing things his way. Nokwenza is the one who took Nik to the hospital when he was about to lose his mind [from AIDS-related delirium], and she is the one who asked for Nik's transfer from the clinic he was using and got him a sick leave form [from his job] from the specialist doctor in the hospital. At that time of the first visit, he was weak and small weight so he was given food from World Food Organization. It was cooking fat and yellow maize meal. The doctor added that he has to eat green vegetables for [a] balanced meal every [day]. Then when he was able to do things for himself, he was taken by *make lomncane* (his maternal aunt, the principal).
>
> Themba: Wow this is so wonderful. *Nangikhuluma naye* (When I spoke with him) he didn't explain that you helped him like that.
>
> Nokwenza: But his mother *wabonga* (she was thankful) for [what I did for] Nik *wabonga* (she was thankful).
>
> Themba: You have really helped me a lot. So you took Nik to hospital and helped him get better and [Nik's mother] was very grateful. Do you think Nik was also grateful?
>
> Nokwenza: Yes. Yahh he was so grateful because he was in stage 3 and his

hair was like relaxed and he looked pale with a 4 CD 4 count . . . he took
the medication wrongly because they advised him to take them at night
because the doctor [said] he will see like scary animals after taking them
so with his night shift I [helped him and he] applied for a sick leave
[from his job] so that he can have enough time to rest.
Themba: Incredible. You really saved him.

Trust is the initial opening key of a gate turned by a keeper like Nokwenza.
It makes or marks the opening of a gaze, and a passage from death back into
enlivening conditions, like aiding Nik amid food and job insecurity and a fragmented health-care system. Then, trust is the sound of that gate's swinging, suggesting things that continuously pass through. It may be someone or something
like the wind, or *moya*, which in siSwati also means "breath" or "a spirit." Or it
may be like what Dawdy and Kneese again see as mortality itself, an arc along
which our perceptions of life and death modulate or reorient through time.
Deathnography isn't made from a single passage through the gate. It comes out
from consistent, sometimes jammed or interrupted, traffic that not everyone
observes or moves in simultaneously.

There are still risks both socioeconomic and physical in being identified as
a person living with HIV/AIDS. There is also a social risk in being mischaracterized as an uncaring person by an ethnographer. Naming and non-naming
practices are both meant to protect people from these risks, even as a deathnography in which they are situated can easily be opened up by an investiga-
tive local reader. Still, by entrusting their spaces, interactions, and stories to
me, Nik, Nokwenza, and others perhaps also indirectly name the conditions of
death and dying they face in a vernacular register. And this may never be a full
disclosure. Pius said:

It doesn't really matter so much as to who these people are. It's just a personal feeling [I have]. We have touched on this [issue of anonymity] in
several of my [public-health] classes. I do not see as it as a bigger problem.
It helps to destigmatize the HIV epidemic when you put a face on it. This
is the issue when it comes to anonymity or secrecy. But it's not my place to
talk about [what people disclose]. The people in the book reserve the right
to disclose that or not.

Maybe Nokwenza was not more critical in describing my representation of the situation because she loves me, insofar as the siSwati word for "to love" is the same as "to like," *kutsandza*. Maybe she hesitates because I also regularly chip in for their daughters'—now my goddaughters'—school fees.

Maybe she does not need or want to undertake critiques of deathnography, or perhaps WhatsApp is an imperfect venue for doing so. Maybe it is all of these things. Or none of them. To the question, "Do you feel it was unfair the way I wrote things? Or do you think anything was wrong?" she replied, "No, because you wrote what you saw and were told."

Maybe she just came to trust me.

Reflections: Mirrors for Society

When I walked into the kitchen under the light strung from a moldering rafter, her daughters squealed "Themba!"—their faces obscured in the partial darkness. I tended to show up late in the evening when visiting. The few flights to eSwatini route from Johannesburg, South Africa, and land in the newly opened airport in a remoter part of the country named after the reigning absolute monarch King Mswati III. A project meant to drive development in this underdeveloped district, its construction involved the forced mass exhumation of 186 bodies from family and community cemeteries. After landing, driving across the undulating landscape to rural hamlets like Nokwenza's can lead you to arrive after sunset, around the time nightly soap operas play on television if there is electricity to light the otherwise snowy screen.

September 2018 was such a trip. A conference at the University of eSwatini on fifty years of the country's independence I planned to attend was canceled at the last minute due to institutional lack of funding. With three free days, I made my way to their home with three copies of the book, one for Nokwenza, one for her husband's older sister—who was my former language instructor and the one who first invited me to stay at her family's homestead—and an extra copy I eventually left unsigned. That was Nokwenza's suggestion—a blank copy for whomever they might wish to gift one to themselves.

Still, darkness
or a blank page,
a mirror draped for mourning,
can't obfuscate a gaze.

I did not look directly into Nokwenza's or other interlocutor-readers' eyes when I gave them these copies. At the time, I felt that I couldn't. Here was a book that was ostensibly about "you," people who helped me come to an understanding about their lives and lifeworld that was also about one of life's most shattering aspects. The word *funeral* is capitalized on the cover. There is a color photographic image of a grave festooned with a rainbow of artificial flowers (it was not the cover image I chose).[3] They knew I was writing such a book, but there was still an uncomfortable immediacy in beholding it together, reminding us of our shared time together at their neighbors' and relatives' funerals and our own respective losses and prospective deaths. This is the mortal dimension of the gaze.

"It is starting a dialogue by putting a mirror in front of us." Dr. Betty S. Dlamini, a Black Swazi scholar of gender, drama, and literature shared these words at an author-meets-critic roundtable at the African Studies Association meeting in Atlanta in November 2018, one of four panelists reflecting on the book. They included Dr. Joy Chadya, a Black Zimbabwean social historian of gender, and two white cultural medical anthropologists of HIV/AIDS in sub-Saharan Africa, Drs. Ruth J. Prince and Fred Klaits. What I found key in the forum were Drs. Dlamini's and Chadya's critical perspectives on funerals, based both on their women-centered research as well as their lived experiences as women cultural insiders witnessing these dynamics for themselves in their home communities. Notwithstanding criticisms of his interpretive speculation (Bernard 1949) (interestingly a mode now in anthropological vogue), Clyde Kluckhohn's (1949) original poetic phrasing of anthropology being "a mirror" resounds in Dr. Dlamini's words to characterize deathnography's necessary mutualism, or more expansively representing the people being written about.

Drs. Dlamini and Chadya both began by noting the methodological importance of using ordinary peoples' stories and oral histories, especially those of women, in research on topics like death. Dr. Dlamini recommended that studies should involve retranslating vernacular terms from different age-gender vantage points. I used vernacular as a means to theorize, homing on the siSwati term *umsebenti*, or "work," which as a noun means both general wage and nonwage labor, as well as life cycle rites like funerals, to understand how changing deathways incite historical consciousness about the postcolonial value of culture (Golomski 2018). The meaning and applicability of such concepts, Dr. Dlamini noted, vary subtly among older and younger and married and unmarried people and men and women. Although most of my main interlocutors were women like Nokwenza, my understanding of aspects of their respective "work" was also limited by local sex and gender norms. I gender identify and express as a man and thus cannot access some women's spaces, and I am more sexually anomalous as a gay man.

One aspect of death here that obfuscates the gaze is the space of women as widows. They are still often rigidly sequestered at their marital homesteads for ritual mourning for a period of one to three winters. This is a result of local perceptions of their *sinyama*, a supposedly "black," contagious death pollution. Widows' main, if not only, visitors during this time are kinswomen and some neighbor women. To understand their gendered vantage point on *umsebenti*, Dr. Dlamini said, it would be important to hear stories from "those women who are sitting in mourning," as their lived experience of bereavement and seclusion could offer insights into cultural ascriptions and negotiations of bodily, emotional, and social affliction.

Like Nokwenza, another main informant in the book is an educator I named LaGija. I knew her to be wary and critical of traditionalist funerary prescriptions for women. At the funeral of her estranged husband's sister, for example, LaGija and her sisters complained to me about having to visit these secluded mourning women, namely LaGija's antagonistic mothers-in-law (mothers- and daughters-in-law are stereotypically averse toward each other in eSwatini), and how they would have to deferentially serve them tea and scones, among other domestic duties.

Reading LaGija's experience as a disjuncture between traditionalist Swazi cultural norms and lived experience, Dr. Dlamini questioned why and how the mothers-in-law were rude to LaGija despite her best efforts and her husband's caustic behavior. "We must learn more about those women who produced LaGija's husband," she laughingly commented, asking why the bereaved women would, in Dr. Dlamini's eyes, be antagonistic toward other women in the space of death and reproduce what she and other Swazi women scholars deem as a patriarchal dimension of HIV/AIDS there (Nyawo 2018; Thwala 1999). Perhaps it is the social and emotional conflict surrounding death that people fear as contagious or polluting. Liu and Toulson show in this volume among their Chinese and Singaporean informants that fears of death pollution and its taboos are waning or of less concern for younger professional, educated, cosmopolitan individuals like LaGija. Perhaps people see bigger risks in disrupting their social relationships, even as death reveals some of them to be oppressively gendered and culturally overdetermined.

In her comments, Dr. Chadya shored up the importance of feminist and historical analyses by reflecting on her own past experiences. "I am a daughter-in-law" like LaGija, she said, "and we became scone eating people" with respect to the aforementioned funerary foodstuffs she had to serve. The custom of eating scones and drinking tea during night vigils is today common across the southern African region, originating in colonially induced urbanization and the rise of material-culture–related consumerist class distinctions (Lee and Vaughan 2008). Differences in rural and urban funerals coincide with class differences, Dr. Chadya explained, and these became the basis for what people now perceive to be cultural newness. Today in Zimbabwe, one can find what are called "English" versus "Shona" funerals, she noted. In the former, some upper-class women bring their maids to do funerary labor on their behalf (substituting someone for their ascribed duties like LaGija's). The latter funerals are sometimes called "poor" or "woeful," *nhamo* in Shona, and with respect to widows' expression of grief in unkempt appearances at the rite, "the dirtier you are, the more you are showing you're mourning," a conflation of class and social deprecation in an invention of tradition.

In their eyes, looking into deathnography's mirror—itself an artifact of our discipline's racist history of removed viewing of the lives and suffering of nonwhite peoples around the world—offers a critical, sustaining view into one's own gendered and historical experiences. As the conversation turned broadly to the past, Dr. Dlamini recalled the insights of former Swazi national leaders Queen Gwamile and King Sobhuza II, both of whom steered Swazi communities through British colonial rule into independence in 1968: "Sobhuza told us that we can discard some of what whites and Europeans gave us, but he also said that you maybe can also give up something that you relearned about yourself" in such contact. "Here is a moment to ask where we are as a country fifty years later on things and big questions like gender equity and how oral history and storytelling can tell us things about culture."

Dr. Dlamini's words point to the usefulness of deathnography as historic text. It is writing that focuses on a past that is still with us, on people who are gone physically but remain ancestrally and in memory, and on the decisions people made to prepare for those deaths and prevent others. As it endures as a text across generations, deathnography can be an important educational or informational resource for interrogating and newly inventing tradition. Colonial-era ethnographies describing deathways in formerly non-scribal African communities have long been used in the postcolonial era as documentary evidence in legal, medical, and policy disputes about custom, with the biases of course being that these dispute arenas were also the product of colonial and culturally scribal conditions of power. Texts were also authored by white outsiders often working with local male elites (Kalusa and Vaughan 2013).

Today, youthful readers are reassessing the value and use of deathnography with this history in mind. Pius the graduate student in the Diaspora noted how age, rather than gender in Drs. Dlamini's and Chadya's cases, came to the fore as shaping his capacity for self-reflection in the book. As he explained in our interview:

> For me, it was learning about many aspects of funerals and other things I did not know much about because of who I am. Young people do not generally attend funerals, and I left and spent most of my formative adult years in this part of the world [United States]. I do go home every single year, but I have only been to four funerals in my entire life, two in my family and two in the community outside of my family. So some of the details of what goes on during funerals I knew from general knowledge or my relatives reporting on it when coming back. So there were new things to me sometimes in the scenes that were portrayed. It was helpful because it situates you in the scenario and then you are able to take a bird's-eye view if I can say that.

For Pius, deathnography offered a chance for familial conversation and corroborations of custom that could possibly (re)define his relatives' past and future funerals, a point I return to later. Because mortuary ritual knowledge has typically been the prerogative of elders and passed verbally and transgenerationally, written accounts can offer additional and alternative access to this information, albeit changing with time. Many of the stories shared with me during field research were also corroborated in local newspaper media, the National Archives, and by local scholars in local journals. The gaze then emerges from collectively curated local knowledge.

Although the conference on fifty years of independence was canceled, I still stopped to share copies of my book with colleagues who hosted me in the Department of Theology and Religious Studies. It was important to show their writing in the bibliography and as an iteration of Christen Smith's ongoing

#citeblackwomen movement (embarrassingly, not citing local scholarship is still a problem in anthropology). The book would also be a useful metric of research impact. Like other faculties worldwide, scholars there are expected to show how their work is cited. Lacking licenses to databases like Web of Science or reaching a search limit in Google Books that would show this, a copy of the book's bibliography would be easier to use.

The other main constituents of the university, the students, offered me another perspective akin to Pius's, that their generation, born in an era of mass AIDS mortality, might take this record as an opportunity for reflection and future-making. My colleagues received their copies with the hook that I would guest lecture for them the next day. On a hot Wednesday afternoon, I was then standing in a hall in front of over two hundred second- and third-year undergraduate students from courses in social work and theology and religious studies. The first thing I thought was "You all look so young," and then "What do *I* have to tell you about death in your community?" I had the chalkboard and my general command of siSwati that I hoped would legitimate or endear me to them somehow.

I began by talking again about the siSwati vernacular for *work*, asking them to reflect on the term's associations with death and its situational use. In small-group conversation, students noted that they saw value in thinking with terms from their own language and that death and funerals were indeed hard things to deal with. In a few silent rounds of a show of hands, many volunteered that they spent their weekends on some activity related to a funeral, whether in food preparation, traveling to a bereaved family's or neighbor's home, or beholding their parents talk about money-related death matters. We didn't do a show of hands about personal losses. Many were likely representative of youth whom policymakers described in the literature of the past three decades as infamously "orphaned and vulnerable children," or OVCs, of their society. They were the ones who had survived the disease, were now living as young adults, and here, hard at work as university students. Regionally, some youth as OVCs have already learned how to do their own ethnographies of HIV/AIDS (Hunleth 2017). They already know too well about death and dying through their generationally particular experiences of facing it in their own communities.

A year later, in September 2019, I found myself doing the same exercise across the border in South Africa, facing a similar classroom of students at the University of Johannesburg. Though some of the material was ethnolinguistically familiar to them (siSwati being one of South Africa's eleven official languages and intelligible to many Nguni and Sotho-Tswana language speakers there), discussions about the kingship, clan-specific rites, and the overall solemn tenor of their geopolitical neighbors' funerals surprised the students. They mentioned their own country's history of funerals as major sites of anti-apartheid protests in the 1980s and that their funerals strongly contrasted to eSwatini, only four hours away by car. In South Africa, some laughed and some lamented, today's funerals are succeeded by parties called "aftertears" where younger attendees indulge in heavy drinking, house music, mobile phone selfies, sex, and "gangsterly" fun (Lukhele 2016).

My colleague and copresenter that day, Black Swazi medical anthropologist Dr. Thandeka Dlamini-Simelane, forced that contrast on the students so that they might reconsider how their own raucous postmortem parties could be seen as both familiar and strange when compared to their neighbors' rites, to use another phrase common to us in anthropology like the mirror. In small-group conversation, the South African students came to conclusions that death-care cultures are central to collective identity and that they change via economic and political forces. Their own suggestions to us that big-name mortuary-service providers in their country might try to innovate their products for their Black majority consumers (see also Howie, this volume)—commercials for which they see nightly between segments of those same soap operas watched by Nokwenza's daughters—was a case in point that day.

Maybe Black southern African youth, like many Black youth globally, do not need to read a conventional deathnography about their communities to know any of this. They see it in real time on social media and television and in the neighborhood.

Maybe by partying for the dead, or by studying theology, social work, and public health, they are fabricating a new mirror of their own, and on their own terms.

> They're aware
> what we write has obsolescence
> and writing death's a resurrection
> and an insurrection

Radical Mourning: Reading and Writing against Necropolitics

Racialization has been a primal mechanism for dehumanization. Worldwide, Black, Indigenous, and nonwhite peoples' lives and deaths have been made to matter less as historically extinguishable (non)beings of modern states' settler expansionism and as specimens coterminous with nonhuman nature subject to modern anthropological observation and writing. These are aspects of what Achille Mbembe (2003) elaborates as necropolitics, a now-prevailing order of many sovereign nation-states globally marked by authoritarian consolidations of power and powerful dynamics of othering (of nonwhite, as well as women, nonheteronormative, poor, nonelite, and nonhuman peoples). Ultimately these lead to tacit or explicit exterminations of life. It is an aspect of power that Mbembe coins as "nocturnal."

This shadowy necropolitical configuration also takes form in the funereal. Again, people across cultures experience afflictions of transcendent phenomena surrounding death that anthropologists call "pollution" (see also Liu and Toulson, this volume). In southern Africa, again, this is known as *sinyama* or *umnyama*, which variably translate as "blackness" or "darkness" and differently coalesces as a malodorous quality among bodies and spaces marked by death, violence, and precarity. In eSwatini, the absolute monarch King Mswati III and royal Dlaminis are extremely susceptible to *sinyama*, insofar as they actually relieve themselves of all preparations of and being near dead bodies for funerals of both majority citizens and their own relatives.

Royals conscript ritual specialists known as *bantfu bentsaba* (people of the mountain) from specific clans to handle their deceased relatives and other procedural affairs at their funerals. Royal funerals also tend to be more austere or "traditional(ist)" in using grass mats for wrapping bodies rather than enclosing in caskets and using herbal purgative medications for mourners. Later, the ritual specialists are involved in bodies' entombment at the Mdzimba Mountains near the royal capital Lobamba. The area is also militarily guarded. Ordinary citizens who work for royals as guards, chauffeurs, or other personal attachés are often prohibited from attending funerals for their own relatives under workplace policies outlining the potential risks of later contaminating their employers by attending.

This is all public, albeit discreet, knowledge in eSwatini, but there is certainly a lack of moral consensus around traditionalist funeral practices of the authoritarian monarchy, even for some royals who also die by these same practices. The recent tragic tales of two queens darkly show this. In 1999, royalists removed eighteen-year-old citizen Senteni Masango from her high school and betrothed her to King Mswati III. She became his eighth wife, known as LaMasango. Her entry into public life was rocky, as a writer for one of the nation's newspapers labeled her a "high school dropout." (He was arrested, fined by the state for defamation, and fired from the newspaper.) She and the king had two daughters. On April 6, 2018, LaMasango was found dead at her palace, apparently from a medication overdose for treatment of rheumatism and depression. Reports leading up to her death cited an increasing if not total social isolation from her family and others, an effective imprisonment by her royal kin. This included a prohibition against attending the funeral of her own sister, Nombuso, the week prior to her own death. LaMasango was buried by the "secret rites" at the nation's royal capital (Waweru 2018).

Eleven months after LaMasango's death, another of King Mswati's wives, LaDube, also died and was "buried by royal Swazi rites at the designated royal mountain" (Zwane 2019). Born in 1987, Nothando Dube was married at the age of sixteen to King Mswati III in 2005 as his twelfth wife. He first met her at a birthday party for one of his other children and later when she danced for him with her age regiment at the annual Reed Dance, Umhlanga. In 2009, Dube was put under house arrest for having an extramarital affair with the former minister of justice. In 2010, she was fully expelled from the royal household, her three children being kept from her by her royal in-laws per patrilineal, patrilocal prerogatives of state-authenticated "Swazi culture." According to media reports, LaDube lived in South Africa and was hospitalized frequently for depression, passing away on March 8, 2019, from an illness related to skin cancer. She was thirty-one.

Perhaps like other authoritarian elites, Dlamini royals in eSwatini are caught in a necropolitical paradox embodied in rituals of mortality. Royal funerals are effectively ethnonationalist by supposedly embodying forms of stereotypically patriarchal Swazi culture, but they are also anti-spectacular, in that they're not public for ordinary citizens to see, be near, or participate in, contra the norm of other postcolonial African state funerary spectacles (Mbembe [2001] 2015). They are also precisely nonmodern affairs in contrast to other elite funerals worldwide, which nation-states often stage as vehicles to modernize populations (Engelke 2019). To remain legitimate as a deep well of cultural authenticity, Dlamini royals reify their mortality as somehow fundamentally traditional in form, a God-Father's immutable law that is somehow mysterious, out of sight, and untouched by the public.

Yet as a result of long-term effects of HIV/AIDS (converging, of course, over time with tuberculosis, COVID-19, and in other syndemics and pandemics), royals' funerals end up undermining themselves or perhaps becoming less meaningful, because they turn out to be so unlike ordinary people's funerals and commemorative practices. In contrast, mass public funeral culture in eSwatini today is strongly defined by an imperative for "dignity" and produced in typically Christianized ceremonies with the foodstuffs, accoutrements, and antagonisms also described by Drs. Dlamini and Chadya. Unlike their royal counterparts, "anyone can go to a funeral," people often told me.

And they did. Ordinary citizens' funerals are often large affairs, their size and diverse attendees described with a sense of ambivalence and awe in public discourse. Funerals were also chances for some neighbors of the deceased to get a meal from a funeral feast amid widespread food insecurity. A demonopolized and widely expanded life insurance market and efflorescence of private commercial mortuaries (as described by the South African students) offer new products and services that have combined uneasily with how longer-standing local burial cooperatives and families mobilize resources. eSwatini also opened its first crematorium in 2007, the first public reiteration of this postmortem rite since the 1850s, when this clan-specific practice was phased out under consolidating royal Dlamini cultural hegemony. Tellingly, it was the former practice of the graduate student Pius's clan, a fact he had not previously known but confirmed after reading the book and asking an older relative about it for clarification.

Today, ordinary citizens' commercialized burials and commemoration in overcrowded public cemeteries are what's come to redefine the physical and sociocultural landscape of the country and the broader region of the continent. These new deathways make up what I called a kind of "radical mourning" (Golomski 2018) or what anarchist activist-scholar Cindy Milstein called a "counterhegemonic culture" (2017, 5) of mourning to prevailing orders that would dispossess, disavow, or make caricatures of the value and memories of ordinary people's deaths. These are on-the-ground actions of death care that both emerge from bio- or necropolitical dynamics of sovereign nation-states and critically counter them as well.

Documenting and writing about these everyday mourning processes are also radical textual actions that solidify historic evidence of necropolitics, racialization, and other violent abuses of power, wherever and however it manifests. Reading this evidence, importantly in dialogue with people about whom it is written, stimulates the emergence of a critical consciousness necessary for sociopolitical change. Deathnography, then, is educational and potentially antinecropolitical. It becomes a form of radical mourning, in that it beholds and respects losses as articulated in peoples' own terms. Deathnography assesses the origins of violence and structural pathways that condition death and knowledge about it in the communities with whom we work as well as our own. This is not always easy to do, even if it is necessary.

Conclusion

In our March 2019 interview, Pius told me more about his classroom experience with the book and what students found interesting:

> Many were really fascinated by the idea of the royal family. I had to struggle to be as fair as I could be. I am not really a big fan of the royal family in Swaziland. I had to give them the facts as they stand and not try to inject my political beliefs in terms of what was going on. Students were taking the class at the same time of the elections and placement of the new cabinet and ministry. It allowed us to explore America's descent into what I characterize as . . ."

He devolved into laughter and recounted a classroom discussion of how one of King Mswati III's daughters, Princess Sikhanyiso, was installed as eSwatini's minister of ICT in 2018. This led his students to questioningly comment how it was dissimilar to Ivanka Trump's moving into a White House advisory capacity for her father, the US president. I confessed to him that I was practically uncertain about doing an overt political critique of the Swazi kingship in the book. I thought I might not be able to return to the country if I had and that some of my informants would be endangered. Through the police and military forces, the state imprisons and censors political oppositionists or critics both physically and in writing. During elections, young women and people living with albinism, somehow symbolic of fecundity, are subject to "ritual murders" (see also Huberman, this volume). Political parties are illegal, and public protests are met with brutal police violence. The affinities among what's experienced in postcolonial African countries like eSwatini and other sites worldwide deemed sliding toward authoritarianism should be increasingly clear to a (necro)politically conscious reader.

"What were you going to say about the descent or characterization of America?" I had asked Pius, returning to that moment where he broke down in laughter. "I was trying to look for the right term, what would be maybe quasi-dictatorship, let's put it in those terms," he said, again laughingly:

The point I was trying to make is that many of the things we have grown to associate with liberal democracy [in the United States] are not enshrined into law, many are just based on expectations that if you are a president you don't get to do that. One thing I did was show a clip from the *Daily Show* with Trevor Noah at the height of the primaries where he was saying that Donald Trump is the typical African dictator, it is a fascinating clip juxtaposing what Trump was doing with Robert Mugabe or Jacob Zuma who was president at the time. There are some things that happen that are part of the political discourse, and as a Swazi you are very quick to recognize it as a dictator. The students here [in the United States], they have no point of reference. They say that is just the president is being crazy. No, no I know exactly what is happening here; people here don't take it as seriously as they should. The things that typically happen in a monarchy are very recognizable to me.

Maybe because I have been working in Pius's home country for some time, I, too, see much of what has happened in the United States since the 2016 presidential election (and before it) as a momentous, unsettling political shift. Inquiries into foreign governments' compromising information and national elections were obstructed by the president and his appointees (including his family members). The velocity of the state's informational errors or outright lies was high, a way to shield itself from scrutiny in confusion. State rhetoric, policy, and populist fervor aired and inflamed centuries of the country's structural racism. Citizens across gender, sexual, religious, and racial spectra have faced open acts of violence in hate crimes and in their protests against this necropolitical order. Life and livelihood for many feel at risk.

As for Pius's students as readers of one book about a small, foreign place in southern Africa, this all becomes more familiar, and precisely so through stories about the deaths of nonwhite others. This, again, is also part of anthropology's colonial, racist legacy. There is no escaping it. Instead, we have to acknowledge it, to write things differently with, for, and among the individuals we feature in our texts. Focusing on dialogical engagements before, during, and after our writing about death helps activate and sustain the gaze noted by Behar. The gaze collects and makes mutual long-standing, immediate, and future concerns of life and death among researchers and people about whom they write. And it emerges most palpably in those microlevel, often awkward moments and relationships of fieldwork that career directly into our shared mortality.

Maybe the awkwardness or discomfort among ethnographic topic, method, and text is metonymic for the multifarious but collective work we must put together in the face of global necropolitical urgencies.

And maybe deathnography's usefulness for all this is that it beholds the immanence of our mortality. It is an ultimate mirror through which we can collectively and radically mourn ourselves and world, and in doing so, reimagine death.

Acknowledgments

Thanks go to my original informants-as-readers, as well as Cal Biruk, Brooke Bocast, Joy Chadya, Betty S. Dlamini, Nhlanhla C. Dlamini, Thandeka Dlamini-Simelane, Ellen Foley, Fred Klaits, Victoria Massie, Ramah McKay, Abigail Neely, Sonene Nyawo, Stacy Leigh Pigg, Ruth J. Prince, Gcobani Qambela, Agostino Zamberia, University of eSwatini students in theology and religious studies and social work, University of Johannesburg students in anthropology, and Shannon Lee Dawdy and Tamara Kneese for their comments and invitation to contribute.

Notes

1. Throughout the chapter, I have preserved the speakers' chosen use of the country name or its original dated context of use amid the official geopolitical name change.

2. Discussing HIV/AIDS in northern Nigeria, Rhine (2016) identifies a similar furtive shift in pronouns during interviews as exercising a self-referential identification that discloses sensitive information about the speaker without compromising respectability and co-implicates listeners in the high stakes of the topic and context. In the following quotes, Themba, again, is the author (Casey Golomski); text in parentheses contains my translations of the original siSwati, and brackets clarify content and context.

3. I provided this image among several others to the press. The first mock-up showed an ornate beaded tapestry in eSwatini's National Museum made by a local artist Sabina Elizabeth featuring grandmothers, children, and a white Jesus among graves in a farmstead scene. Several white American students told me they liked the press's chosen cover because it looked like a home and garden magazine and not something necessarily about Africa, so unsuspecting (American) readers might be more likely to pick it up.

CHAPTER FIVE

"For the One Life We Have"

Temporalities of the Humanist Funeral in Britain

MATTHEW ENGELKE

Since the early work of Robert Hertz (1960), anthropological understandings of funerary rites have emphasized the role they play in the symbolic triumph over death. If any given funeral concerns the rent caused by the death of an individual, the ritual process offers repair and reinvigoration. "The last word must remain with life: the deceased will rise from the grip of death and will return, in one form or another, to the peace of human association" (Hertz 1960, 78). In their elaborations on Hertz's key theme, Maurice Bloch and Jonathan Parry have cast this in more general terms as "the conquest of time" (1982, 13).

In this chapter, I explore time and the matter of its conquest through a consideration of funerals conducted by celebrants in the British Humanist Association (BHA). What interests me about these funerals is the extent to which they are framed and performed according to a set of distinctive understandings about life, death, and time. The most important of these is that there is no life after life. Humanists consider death the end, at least of the self. This is reflected in part through one of the BHA's precepts, captured in a widely used humanist motto: "For the one life we have." Humanism, and the humanist death, is thus very much about time. In championing a certain kind of time, humanists seek to offer an alternative to religious worldviews, especially those in which the human life is but one rendering of the life of a subject, some identifiable person, soul, or being with agency. Furthermore, many members of the BHA find fault with worldviews in which a belief in heaven, reincarnation, or other afterlife/alter-life shape a person's approach to mortality; the humanists see it as dereliction of duty to the ethical and social demands of the here and now. For these and other reasons, the BHA's funerals are often referred to not only as "humanist" but also as "non-religious." Exactly what this means can differ, but it has ramifications for how we understand the temporalities of the funeral.

Before turning to such matters of time, though, it will be helpful to provide some background on the association.

The BHA

The British Humanist Association's roots stretch to 1896, with the union of ethical societies that had grown up in the Victorian era.[1] Broadly speaking, such "Victorian infidels" (Royle 1974) promoted secularism not only as a political arrangement, but as a more general outlook and disposition. During the course of my research, which began in 2011, the BHA promoted itself on its website as "the national charity working on behalf of non-religious people who seek to live ethical and fulfilling lives on the basis of reason and humanity" (www.humanism.org.uk). At that time, it had roughly thirty thousand members and supporters; today, the figure is closer to forty thousand. The BHA is part of a larger dynamic in Britain, the United States, and well beyond of people self-consciously identifying as non-religious; such organizations, and the larger zeitgeist, are gaining an increasing level of attention by anthropologists and sociologists (see, for example, Blankholm 2014; Lee 2015; Quack 2012).

Since the early 2000s, the BHA has gone about its work and served its membership via three main avenues. The first is to promote values of secularism and liberalism through public campaigns. The BHA opposes state funding of faith-based schools, for example, and seeks reform in the House of Lords over the right of station for twenty-six Anglican bishops. In a similar vein, the BHA advocates for the right to assisted dying and the legalization of humanist weddings. The second main line of action is the cultivation and support of local humanist groups (see Engelke 2014, 2015b). There are several dozen of these groups throughout England and Wales, ranging in size from five to seventy-five people. Most groups meet one evening per month, usually in a pub or community center, to discuss politics, social policy, and ethical issues, often with a guest speaker. Some local groups are more elaborately organized, hosting subsidiary events (pub lunches, book groups, country walks) and sponsoring opportunities for community service (staffing homeless shelters, volunteering in prisons, visiting the housebound elderly). The third main area of work is the provision of humanist ceremonies (see Engelke 2015a, 2015c) and, more recently, chaplaincy-style services in hospitals and prisons. Funerals are by far the most popular of the ceremonies on offer, but the BHA also runs weddings and naming ceremonies. These ceremonies are performed by celebrants accredited by and affiliated with the BHA. The celebrants perform about nine thousand funerals per year. The vast majority of these funerals are not conducted for card-carrying members of the association but, rather, members of the general public seeking an explicitly non-religious ritual. What I often heard from celebrants and families alike was the phrase "not the vicar," when it came to the deceased's wishes.

The BHA maintains a London-based staff of about a dozen personnel, the majority of whom work in one of the three main areas of activity. The head of ceremonies, for example, acts as a coordinator, liaison, and source of support for the network of celebrants. There are about three hundred celebrants in the BHA, the majority of whom have undergone association-based training to conduct the ceremonies. These celebrants are not employed by the association, but they remit a small percentage of their ceremonial fees (usually in the range of £120–£180) to the BHA to help meet the costs of the network's infrastructure. In a survey of 195 celebrants that I conducted, a set of demographic figures emerged that matched up with my fieldwork findings, through which I got to know about a dozen celebrants well (having met several dozen more, too, at meetings and an annual conference). About two-thirds of celebrants are female (this is the inverse of the wider BHA membership), and just over three-quarters have a background in music, drama, or other performing arts. In terms of household income, only 33 percent of celebrants described the celebrant work as a necessary source of income. In any case, I never met a celebrant who spoke anything less than passionately about the meaning and sense of purpose they derived from their work. As one celebrant put it to me, "It is incredibly gratifying to play a small part in easing people through such a difficult time in their lives." Celebrants are also ethically committed to the importance of choice; one of their deepest concerns is with what they (and their clients) identified as an "authentic" rite of passage. Any given funeral should reflect "the person" and not simply default to the presumed, Church-of-England norm. As another celebrant put it, these funerals should be seen as "a public service" and help "spread the word about Humanism."

While Charles Taylor does not ever locate or contextualize his arguments in relation to a particular community, there are many ways in which members of the BHA could be said to embrace Taylor's rendering of "the immanent frame"—a frame, that is, which "constitutes a 'natural' order, to be contrasted to a 'supernatural' one, an 'immanent' world, over against a possible 'transcendent' one" (2007, 542). Members of the BHA are "those who see immanence as admitting of no beyond" (550).

Time and the Rites of Death

How is the death of a person temporalized in the ritual action of such an immanent frame? This question can be addressed in several ways.

In a straightforward sense, what is often notable in the ethnographic record is just how long funerary rites can take. In many parts of the world, it is not unusual for the proceedings of a funeral to last several days and to have multiple parts or stages, sometimes separated by a year or more. For the Bara, of Madagascar, three ceremonies are held for the dead, the first of which, involving the burial, lasts three days. This is followed by a large gathering, much grander than the burial rites and marked by conspicuous consumption, held after the next harvest season. Finally, the smallest yet most significant ceremony is the reburial. This is conducted much later, up to several years after the death, and marks completion of the process. Such secondary burials are very common throughout the world and are commonly long in coming (Metcalf and Huntington 1991, 116–22). They often symbolize the final passage of the soul or spirit to the afterworld or afterlife; the importance of the exhumation is to make sure the passage is a smooth one, which is determined by the "dryness" (i.e., purity) of the bones. Reburial also marks the vital potential of the death—its enfolding into the regeneration of life. In his study of death rituals in rural Greece, Loring Danforth (1982, 14–17) tells us how one Orthodox peasant family waited nearly five years before undertaking the obligatory exhumation and secondary burial of a lost daughter. We know from work on the interment and placement of ashes that British customs can also involve multipart staging: a family scattering the ashes at sea, for example, or along a favorite hiking trail on the anniversary of the loved one's death (Prendergast, Hockey, and Kellaher 2006). But whichever way you cut them—and even if we include the longer arc of time in the overall process of mourning and commemoration—death rites in contemporary Britain are on the short side.

Another aspect of the interest in ritual time is with its more experiential and ideological components. Rituals take a certain amount of time, but they also have, or help to induce, a distinct temporality. It is often said that ritual takes us "out of time"; ritual marks a break with ordinary life and daily routines. The regularity of many ritual forms and performances has the effect of desensitizing participants to the contingencies and quirks of their own lives. Times change, but ritual does not—or so we are supposed to think. The Catholic Mass is the Catholic Mass is the Catholic Mass. Through repetition and predictability, rituals offer an order that transcends the everyday (Bloch 1989). In some cases, such a break with mundane life is meant to restore vitality or energy to that life and its routines, be it through spiritual uplift, some form of ethical reflection, or contemplation of the larger social order. In other cases, including rites of passage, stepping out of time is necessary for the socially recognized transformation to take place. "We are presented, in such rites, with a 'moment in and out of time,' and in and out of secular social structure," as Victor Turner puts it (1969, 96). Rites of passage provide a "stage of reflection" (Turner 1967, 105), a temporary wayside from which to take a view in the forward march of life. Johnny, who was one of the BHA celebrants I got to know best—a blues guitar player and long-time resident in southeast London—understood this well. In the funerals he conducted, he always prefaced his remarks on mortality by saying, "And what better place, as we sit here somewhat stunned in [this crematorium], torn away from our busy lives and routines, for me to offer you some thoughts on life and death."

The Ticking Clock

The chapel in a London crematorium is a stage, and as such, to direct and push forward the matter at hand, it contains things hidden. These include important spaces behind the scenes, such as the chapel attendant's room and antechamber to the crematorium itself, in which staff are busy at work, even if for most of the time that means watching a closed-circuit TV, simply waiting for their cue to play the Frank Sinatra track, to slide the coffin off the catafalque, and so on. In some London chapels, there is also an organ off to one side or in a balcony overhead, just in case Sinatra is too modern for the family in question. At the City of London chapel, the organ also serves as a convenient cover for the range of sacred signs that might be needed, from the Om to a cross to the Star of David, any of which can be taken out and placed up front to set the appropriate scene. On the lectern, where the officiant stands, is the button that closes the curtains around the catafalque. BHA celebrants, I came to learn, treat this button with great respect and due care; I knew several who made a point of always knowing how long it takes for the curtains to finishing closing. The goal is to have the curtains close and your words of committal finish at the same time.

Timing, as I came to learn, is everything in a funeral. And no one involved in delivering a funeral should ever treat this fact lightly. Crematorium managers do what they can to make sure of this, above all by providing the most

Figure 5.1. The time limit at Eltham Crematorium, discretely placed on the lectern. Photo by the author.

important stage direction, which is often taped or glued to the top of the lectern; a small notice that reads (as at Eltham, a cemetery and crematorium in Southeast London), "Please ensure your SERVICE does not exceed 30 MINUTES. Thank you" (figure 5.1). In some crematoria, it's only twenty-eight minutes; sometimes just twenty-five. Not very long at all.

The pressing importance of the clock may not be the first temporality one associates with a funeral. A funeral, after all, is about grander timescales than all of that. Yet there is something about the exigency of the London funeral—the funeral that takes place under modern, industrial conditions and is shaped not only in relation to the mourners but, more generally, by "the inward apprehension of time of working people" (Thompson 1967, 57)—that deserves our attention. E. P. Thompson's classic study of time and industrial capitalism is especially valuable here. A funeral is a ritual, but it is also a jobsite, or, rather, an overlapping set of jobsites, conditioned by the infrastructures of contemporary urban life, which we increasingly recognize as pressed for time. This fact is reflected in several of the other chapters collected in this volume, from LaShaya Howie's account of African American funeral homes to Huwy-min Lucia Liu's of the market economy in China.

All the same, I never heard people who attended a thirty-minute BHA funeral characterize it as being short; mourners don't have to stare at that emphatic reminder of the strict limit. And there are no clocks in crematorium chapels—none visible to the mourners, at least. So the time is what the time is. True, celebrants would often remark on the difficulty of encapsulating a life in such a short period, but then again, they always managed to do it; the only serious challenge they felt, as far as I could tell, was making sure that any tributes by family and friends stuck to an agreed schedule. A good celebrant makes sure that all tribute givers provide the text of what they're going to say in advance. If necessary, sensitive and diplomatic arm-twisting can be applied to make sure that Uncle Nick keeps his remarks to five hundred words. When it comes to music, careful instructions will be given as to when a song should be faded out.

The "moment" of reflection in a humanist ceremony is an important point of transition within the ritual action; it comes near the end of the ceremony and is usually marked by playing one of the deceased's favorite pieces of music. While longer than a moment, the pace of the funerals means these reflections can rarely last for the full length of even a Rolling Stones tune, to say nothing of a symphony movement or a cello concerto. "Fade at 2:12." "Fade at 2:35." These are common directions to the chapel attendant manning the sound system. Managing the time isn't that difficult, as long as you're careful. If anything, celebrants worried about the longer funerals, those that get booked as double slots and so take fifty or even fifty-five minutes. A double slot (which of course costs more to the family) is often necessary if there will be a lot of guests. Getting 50 or 60 people in and out of a crematorium chapel in 25 minutes is not a problem; if you're talking about 150 or 200 people, however, the simple logistics of entry and exit can eat up too much time. When this was a practical necessity, however, I often found that celebrants worried about having too much time to fill. The pace and tempo of ceremonies that were longer than forty minutes could be difficult to control. How many tributes should there be? How many musical interludes of Cindy Lauper?

Sometimes, then, less is more. In any case, celebrants seemed well attuned to what Sarah Sharma (2014) refers to as the limits of "speed theory," a key aspect of which emphasizes the shortness of time a late-modern subject is assumed to face as a result of technological developments, the enlargement of social scales, and, not least, the premium placed on productivity and efficiency. Ritual is one avenue through which "the complexity of lived time" (6) can be crafted, felt, and enacted.

Where the thirty-minute scheduling becomes troublesome is when funerals get delayed. Gene, a police officer I got to know during his training for the BHA, had a horrible experience in this regard. The celebrant conducting his mother's funeral was forty minutes late, forcing Gene to step into the breach; he ended up conducting the funeral himself. Gene turned his frustration and upset into something positive and productive; this experience is what prompted him to train with the BHA. He thought he could do a better job.

Sometimes, then, the force of clock time comes bearing down. It doesn't happen a lot, but I did have one experience of this myself, at the ceremony of Addison Albridge, one cold, wet late winter afternoon in 2011.

Addison Albridge

Addison's ceremony was held at the St. Marylebone Crematorium in North London, not far from Crouch End, the neighborhood in which he had lived for over thirty years. The funeral was conducted by Frances, a woman in her fifties and sometime actor who had been a celebrant at that point for a decade. Because I always arrived early, at first it didn't seem odd that there was a vicar standing in the crematorium chapel's foyer, still wearing a drenched mackintosh. He was there with an elderly widow and about a dozen other mourners to perform a committal; the full funeral service had been held at his church. Frances wasn't sure what the holdup was—maybe the coffin hadn't arrived? But then, wouldn't the man's widow have been with it? People were starting to arrive for Addison's ceremony, and the foyer was getting crowded. Frances kept very calm; she was always calm, and the vicar did not appear fazed, either. After a few minutes, however, as more fifty-something Crouch Enders sporting Hawaiian shirts and ponytails started arriving, Frances and the vicar swung into action, liaising in whispers with the chapel attendant. Presently, the elderly widow and her guests were ushered into the chapel, as the rest of us stood by, trying to keep quiet out of respect. Frances still wasn't fazed, or at least didn't look it. Whatever it was that was holding up the committal before us—we never did learn—clearly hadn't been resolved, though, and within a few minutes, the crematorium staff had the poor elderly widow and her handful of friends and family file back out of the chapel. We were going to go first. With fifty or sixty mourners now gathered for Addison's ceremony, Frances and the funeral director had us file in, against the background of "Across the Universe," by the Beatles. Addison's flower-strewn coffin was then processed in and placed carefully on the catafalque.

It quickly became evident that Frances had no intention of cutting corners. In fact, the funeral that unfolded was the most leisurely I attended, in terms both of its pace and the extent to which the tempo crafted the character of Addison.

Addison, aged fifty-three, suffered a brain hemorrhage. He collapsed at home and spent ten days in a coma before dying. On the front of the ceremony program was a picture of him, somewhere near the sea, maybe Lyme Regis or Norfolk, two of his favorite places. His shirt is open, his straw hat held in place by his left hand, a ring on his pinky finger (but not a pinky ring) just visible, proper sideburns, a mustache, and a mop of still blonde hair falling out the back of his hat. He is looking into the distance with a slight open-mouthed smile.

Everything about Addison came across as laid back. He dropped out of a polytechnic, where he was studying biology, but never lost an interest in nature and the stars. Far from being all dry science, though, Addison was well-rounded and also something of an autodidact. He loved P. G. Wodehouse, Elvis Presley, Dr. Who, Arsenal, Guinness, and cooking (saffron buns, spaghetti carbonara, hamburgers, apple pie). Addison was a musician and a playwright, too; in Crouch End he helped form a pantomime group that played each year at a local pub. He wrote all the pantos himself, and he and his musician mates donated the ticket proceeds to charity. That's how he met Jane; she was working for an infants' charity that the panto group was supporting, back in 1995. Jane wrote him a letter for the funeral, which was read out by a family friend; she couldn't bear to read it herself. "A love letter from Jane," it began,

Dear Addison,
Three weeks ago, it was like time had slowed down and stood still, but simultaneously events moved far too quickly. Was this the Space, Time, Parallel Universe stuff you had tried to explain to me? I'm afraid I never really grasped it then, but perhaps I'm beginning to now . . .

   Last Christmas I bought you a copy of Keith Richards's autobiography. You read it in one sitting and I'm looking forward to reading it too. You always had a lot of time for the Rolling Stones and in particular Keith Richards when he played the Blues . . .

   My world changed when I met you and fell in love. It can never be the same now you're gone.

Addison and Jane's daughter, Billie, who was no more than eleven or twelve, also wrote a tribute. She called him Addison, rather than Dad, because that's what Jane's son, from a previous relationship, called him. Addison liked that. The letter was read out by the same family friend:

> You took me to school and collected me every day, holding my hand and listening as I chatted and letting me walk along the walls and jump off at the end. You kept your cool on the playgroup trip to Paradise Park when I didn't want to get on the coach and then I didn't want to get off. . . . You knew exactly how to make a glowing log fire in our fireplace. . . . I miss you Addison, I miss you Dad. I will never forget you.

The rain had let up by the time Addison's ceremony was over, so people were able to gather in the garden out behind the chapel. Jane came out last, having asked to stay back for a final moment with the coffin; there wasn't a committal. She lit up a cigarette and rested her head on a friend's shoulder, her eyes puffy from crying. I found myself standing with three women, one of whom, in a gray dress, said to the others, "I've never been to a humanist funeral before. That was brilliant. I'm definitely going to have one." "You know she's an actress," said one of the other ladies, who was very old and hunchbacked. "She took her time," said the woman in the gray dress. "She really concentrated on the person. It wasn't rushed."

It wasn't rushed, despite the bottleneck produced by the delayed committal. (As I was later to learn, coming before or after a simple Christian committal has its advantages, because in nearly every case, the funeral itself has already taken place, so the vicar or priest needs no more than ten minutes of the time slot.) What had started out with some dramatic tension resolved itself well. Once the rules are broken—once the schedule is thrown awry—it is almost as if the officiant has free rein. Everyone becomes aware of the time, but that makes time less important. Objectively, Addison's funeral was not longer than it was supposed to be, even if the twenty-eight minutes it took were not the twenty-eight minutes allotted to it; subjectively, however, the combination of the cock-up and the laid-back demeanor of who Addison had been—the kind of reader who sinks into a chair to devour an entire book in one go; the kind of father who lets his daughter walk along the walls on the way home from school—stamped the event.

The time-space zone of the crematorium chapel is nested within others.

Figure 5.2. The speed limit at City of London Cemetery and Crematorium. Photo by the author.

If what happens in the chapel is brief and yet not rushed, even its unhurried aspects appear fleeting with respect to the larger setting. Crematorium chapels are always located within cemeteries, in which all those gravestones are supposed to signal permanence, if not also eternity. The special character of a cemetery is also marked by the regulation of movement within it. The speed limit in Britain's cemeteries is set at five miles per hour; anything more than this is understood to be disrespectful and out of place (figure 5.2).

Time is slowed down. At the funeral of Dave Simons, Johnny's eyes nearly popped out of their sockets as the hearse, pushing 20 mph, pulled up to the chapel. "Whoa!" he exclaimed. (Traffic on the roads had been heavy; they were running late.) This slowing down of time is mirrored behind the scenes of the chapel, in the crematorium itself. Here, the laws of matter, physics, and chemistry take over. It takes about ninety minutes to cremate the body of the average-sized adult. At a busy chapel, by the end of the day, there might be a queue of two or three coffins waiting to go into the ovens. It is not unusual for a body to be kept overnight before being burned—a fact that is not hidden, but not exactly advertised either, since for many families, the idea of a loved one's remains waiting in a queue to be turned to ash is not a happy thought.

Secular Times

Another aspect of interest in ritual time has to do with how the ritual itself sets out what we might call a cosmological frame. This gets us to the conquering of time. In some cases, this involves a focus on how the unpredictability of an individual death—the snap of time's arrow—gets folded into a cyclical view of time in which any given death is necessary for the furtherance of life. In other cases, the individuality is minimized in the effort to assert society's (eternal) power. In both types of cases, "death is consequently transformed into a process which is essential for the continuation of life" (Bloch and Parry 1982, 10).

Here it might be helpful to point out the ways in which humanist approaches to death and time mirror those found elsewhere in the ethnographic record. Yet we need to pay close attention to one key aspect of how the continuation of life is recognized in ritual—namely, whether it is eternal. This is where the immanent frame can make a difference, where a secular distinction gets forged. "Almost everywhere religious thought consistently denies the irreversible and terminal nature of death by proclaiming it a new beginning" (Bloch and Parry 1982, 9). Can this claim be extended to traditions of thought which disavow "the religious"?

By far, the overriding concern of a BHA funeral is to underscore the strapline "For the one life we have." This is it. If nothing else, celebrants want to suggest that death is the end—at least of personhood. For most members of the BHA, the promise of an afterlife is one of the most baffling and detrimental aspects of a religious worldview. It is baffling because there is no reasonable standard of evidence with which to support such a belief. In many cases, what I found was not an outright rejection of the possibility, for how could we know for sure? It had more to do with the elaborate detail of what that afterlife contained, with much mocking of pearly gates and much derision of awaiting virgins (as picked up from mass-media renderings of why Islamic extremists seek martyrdom). And the baffling feeds into the detrimental, for above all, what humanists conclude is that belief in an afterlife shifts the focus of social and ethical projects away from this world to another world. To organize what you do around the promise of eternal life is, for humanists, an abrogation of our responsibility to the here and now. They view the very idea of an afterlife as a challenge to the truth of time.

Another way of putting this is to say that humanists only recognize what we might call, after Taylor, "secular time" (2007, 54–59). By this I mean the standard of time by which we measure the age of the earth (4.5 billion years), how long it takes to soft boil an egg (three minutes), the number of weeks in a year (fifty-two)—or, for that matter, the length of a funeral at Eltham Crematorium (thirty minutes). This rendering of time is similar to what Walter Benjamin referred to as "homogenous, empty time" and Benedict Anderson, after Benjamin, elaborated as the time of "clock and calendar" (1991, 24). It is homogenous and empty because it is the same everywhere and cannot be shaped by anything other than itself, such as an invisible hand or supernatural agent. This type of time stands in contrast to what Benjamin called "messianic time," which he used to describe how, in Jewish and Christian framings, an invisible hand is understood to direct the course of history (and its eventual end). The idea of messianic time is one of several ways in which religious traditions have allowed for alternative readings of secular time. To draw further on some of Anderson's interests, one example would be the Christian interpretation of Abraham's sacrifice in the Old Testament as prefiguring Christ's sacrifice on the Cross at Calvary. In such a framing, events have meaning and links to one another along—and beyond—the pathways of clock and calendar. For Taylor, messianic time is one example of what he refers to in a more general way as the overlay of "higher times" upon secular time (2007, 54–55). In summing up the difference between secular time and higher times, Taylor says that "one is concerned with things in ordinary time, the other with the affairs of eternity" (55). For the humanists, there are no affairs of eternity. There is only secular time.

During the training courses to conduct funerals run by the BHA, one of the things the trainers emphasize is that funeral scripts should be approached as vehicles for social history. Capturing the person should always involve capturing something of the events—local, national, and international—that shaped her life. Developments in technology, job markets and the economy, and popular culture were also highlighted as helpful for setting the scene of a life, as well as adding depth and color to the imagery in the celebrant's tribute. Johnny regularly appealed to nostalgia, here in the life story of Roy Watson Jr. (1947–2011):

> Dad Roy worked on the footplates of locomotives for the Great Western Railway and he would take young Roy-boy down to get his wages, which he would collect in a little tin cup, as was the way then. And Dad would read The Eagle comic to young Roy in bed, embellishing the stories. He'd also devour the 2-D comics Dad would buy him, enjoying going to Wembley for the speedway and cheering on the Wembley Lions and masters of

the shale like Bill Kitchen and Tommy Price. Making plastic aeroplane kits
and in time discovering the allure of the Electric Cinema, Portobello Road,
often followed by a slap-up meal of pie and mash.

For older generations, this emplacement and appeal to remembrance of
things past was even more important. For those of a certain age, one's experience of the Second World War was requisite. In one case, Sophie, a young celebrant with a background in acting, was even able to relay this experience in the
person's own words. For the funeral of Mildred Spark, Sophie, a celebrant in her
thirties—who, like Frances, also worked as an actor—drew liberally (and with
the family's warm welcome) on an autobiographical essay that Mildred had
written for her grandsons. Sophie was also able to be very direct about the value
of a link between Mildred and the time. Sophie said, "Demonstrating her flair
for contextualizing personal history in the wider historical backdrop, Mildred
starts her chapter on the war":

> My father had been in the City of London's National Guard during the
> First World War, machine-gun instructor aged eighteen! In 1937 he joined
> Bromley Air Raid Precautions Service at its inception. I was soon involved,
> delivering leaflets door-to-door, and later I manned the telephone in his
> "District Head-quarters" in our brick air raid shelter during air raids. At 14
> I took the Warden's exam, and so at the grand age of seventeen and a half
> was put on the strength, to become Bromley's youngest Air Raid Warden.
> On that dreadful day, Third September, the world came to an end; shud-
> dered, and somehow started again looking, at first as though nothing was
> any different. But nothing was really the same ever again.

Humanist funerals make great use of nostalgia; invocations of the past, in
small and seemingly trivial detail, help produce the structure of feeling desired
by celebrants—and, nearly always, the mourners. It was not at all unusual for
the kinds of cues employed by celebrants to stick with the family and friends—a
favorite old song, talk of the days when wages were collected in tin cups, first-
hand accounts of world-historical events. If you go to the humanist funeral of
an octogenarian, afterward you may well overhear a cousin or old friend express
their surprise and delight at being reminded of something long gone: "I haven't
thought of Rita Hayworth in forty years!" or "Boy, now those were the days—
they don't make Fords like they used to!" As a funeral feeling, nostalgia contains

a perfect mix of sadness and happiness, longing and fulfillment. It is also worth noting the ingredients of nostalgia. As Svetlana Boym argues, nostalgia cannot spring only from individual memories. Its force is dependent on the connection between self and society: "Nostalgia is about the link between individual biography and the biography of groups or nations, between personal and collective memory" (Boym 2001, xvi). In this other way, then, to say that BHA funerals are about "the person" actually obscures the importance of society and of history in the humanist regime of values.

To sum up so far, part of what we see here is something more than a homogenous, empty time, à la Benjamin. While this sets the foundation of the ritual temporality, the recollections of a life and historical periods fill the emptiness — not with some metaphysical bedrock, but a meaningful biographical time nonetheless. Invocations of time are saturated with emotion and affect.

Nostalgia in humanist funerals also foregrounds the primacy of historical/secular time. Because the afterlife is denied, and because a humanist funeral is about the celebration of how one person made his or her mark in the world, the temporal horizon of now and then tends to dominate. This is not to say there is no concern for the future in the humanist worldview, or, still less, for the course of mourning and grief. Like all funerals, those performed by celebrants in the BHA contain elements of social and psychological comfort through assertions of life conquering death. You will never hear a celebrant say that everyone in the family will one day be reunited with mother in heaven. But celebrants nearly always emphasize two means through which the pain of grief can be alleviated by recognizing the ways in which a life continues.

The first, and most prominent, is memory. Every BHA celebrant enjoins mourners to keep memory of the dead alive. The ceremony itself is a foundation and catalyst for being able to do so. "We must leave Dave's body here in the safe hands of the chapel attendants, but he will live on forever in our hearts, minds, thoughts, and dreams," as Johnny said with respect to Dave Simons. "With love we shall always keep his memory and, in gratitude, we recall the human image he has left us and he will remain forever in each and every one of you." "Hold on to Jean in your thoughts and in your hearts; there is no need to part from her too quickly," is what Sarah, a celebrant in West Midlands, told the family and friends of Jean Baker. "Talk about her often," she urged. "Remember the things she said and enjoy your memories of her, just as we have done today. When we return to our homes, our schools, and our work, let us be inspired to live our own lives more fully, enriched by memories of Jean and the part she played in our lives." What Sarah's enjoinment also does is reinforce the distinctiveness of ritual time. She makes full use of liminality to emphasize how the ceremony can affect a transformation, here in terms of mourners' efforts at ethical self-cultivation.

The second way in which humanist celebrants emphasize continuity and continuation is from a scientific point of view. Most frequently what you hear concerns genetics. Pointing to the deceased's children and/or grandchildren sitting in the front row of the chapel, a celebrant will describe how that person "lives on" in the younger generations. It is often so plain. "Eileen will continue to live," Laura, one of the BHA course trainers and a long-standing celebrant, said at the graveside of Eileen Parks, "directly through her children, her grandchildren and the generations that follow, and in the memories you all have of her." With respect to Mildred, Sophie told those gathered that "her genetic inheritance will move into the future through her grandchildren." On occasion, this emphasis on genetics is complemented by a recognition of what cosmology tells us about matter and, concomitantly, our own atomic makeup. "Essentially every atom in your body was once inside a star that exploded," explains the theoretical physicist Lawrence Krauss. (A prominent humanist, Krauss delivered the BHA's Darwin Day lecture in 2017 to an audience of over one thousand people in central London.) "We are all, literally, star children, and our bodies made of stardust" (Krauss 2012, 17). At a funeral, there is neither the time nor the bandwidth to go into details on thermodynamics—less familiar, perhaps, than genetics—but humanist celebrants do sometimes relate the dead to the stars and the organic makeup of the world. "Luke lives on in the earth around us" is how Janet, a celebrant in her fifties and a registered nurse, once put this. Ironically, then, the old Anglican image of "ashes to ashes, dust to dust," drawn from the Book of Common Prayer, comes in handy. So does the famous passage from the Book of Ecclesiastes—"To everything there is a season"—which is occasionally used by the celebrants (albeit with the reference to what is "under heaven" being replaced with "under the sun").

In these several respects, what we find in humanist ceremonies corroborates the conclusions of ritual theory, in which funerals signal the "triumph over death" (Hertz 1960, 86). What humanists prompt us to consider, however, is that the form of triumph can make a big difference, certainly in terms of the work a funeral does and the temporal horizon it sets. To frame triumph over death in terms of memories and DNA is not the same as doing so in terms of salvation by Jesus Christ. Taken together, celebrant appeals to individual biography, memory, and genetics underscore the BHA's emphasis on "the one life we have." These appeals are an assertion that what we have in that life—all that we have in life writ large—is history, not heaven.

The D-word, *death*, is a red line for the humanists and helps underscore this point. Facing up to the facts of mortality—and helping others do so—is a central aspect of the celebrant's work. In the raw and vulnerable moment of a funeral, however, some celebrants use terms of temporal reckoning that work around the insistence that death means death. In short, celebrants say things in ceremonies that they don't mean literally. The most common example of this is something along the lines of what Johnny said with respect to Dave, mentioned above: "He will live on forever in our hearts, minds, thoughts, and dreams." In the context of an everyday conversation, Johnny would readily acknowledge that there is no "forever." The people remembering Dave will die, too. So what the celebrant really means is "So-and-so will live on in your thoughts until you're all dead, as well." But saying this would be ridiculous. Above, I also referred the funeral of Luke Bolton, conducted by Janet; she said near the start of the funeral that Luke "lives on in the earth around us." In the committal, this stardust-style point was linked to Janet's emphasis on a humanistic understanding of mortality, grief, nature, and time. It is worth quoting this "final goodbye" in full:

> We are now going to say our final goodbyes to the physical existence that was Luke, with love, with honor, and with respect.
>
> Luke has made the same passage from life to death as he did from death to life. All living things are subject to death; it is the basis of our growth; it is in the order of things; it belongs to the life of the world. All of us who accept the unity and completeness of the natural order and believe that to die means the end of conscious personality, look death in the face with honesty, with dignity and with calm.
>
> And so death has come to our friend and loved one. It is in sorrow but without fear and knowing that he is eternally at peace, that we say our final goodbye to Luke.

Some of the phrasings here are adapted from Jane Wynne Willson's guidebook, *Funerals without God* (1990). This is a must-have on the shelf of every

BHA celebrant. "In sorrow but without fear" is something you will hear at many BHA ceremonies. Again, note the ways in which Janet builds up an imagery of the natural order, of the passage of time and of "the life of the world" (another popular BHA phrase) as part of a cyclical process. One of the things that struck me, however, was Janet's invocation of the eternal. Because eternity is a very un-humanist reckoning with the concept of time.

Eternity is not time. Certainly within the Christian traditions most proximate here, eternity cannot be contained by such a term; eternity is more than time, other than time, beyond time. It is unhelpfully metaphysical. I had a chance to discuss this with Janet after the funeral. She asked me what I thought about her ceremony and I mentioned that I was struck by her appeal to eternity, since it sits at odds with a humanist view of what I referred to above as the cosmological frame in which we live. She took the point, but like many celebrants, she wasn't terribly bothered by it. She also didn't think she was offering false promises; people knew what she meant. This is even more the case with talk of "forever"; there is no need to be 100 percent literal in a humanist ceremony. The language needs to be poetic, to be felt in the gut. But it doesn't need to kick you in the gut—at least not more than the D-word does. All the same, a few days later, Janet and I had an exchange of text messages, in which she further parsed her phrasings. Celebrants, I found, often thought very carefully about the words they used and the potential indices they contained (figure 5.3).

The semantic looseness of terms like *eternity* and *forever* is partly ensured by the otherwise regular insistence on secular time and natural order. By celebrating a life that has been lived rather than an afterlife that is to come, humanist ceremonies reinforce the pivot around events, dates, and other specificities of personal biography and cultural history. The argument is that this should be enough, that it is a lot in itself. Secure in our knowledge of the earth sciences and cosmology and comforted by the potentials of memory and genetics—whose time horizons are distant enough—it is indeed in sorrow but without fear that we must approach mortality.

Here we might reflect on the different path that humanists take from their close kin, the transhumanists. As Jenny Huberman and Abou Farman relate in their chapters for this volume and as Anya Bernstein discusses in her afterword, for transhumanists, "the new death" is no death at all. I was certainly struck, after the fact—in conversations with these colleagues—how similar and yet different humanists are from the likes of a Peter Thiel or Nikolai Fedorov. In all my time with the BHA, I never heard discussion of transhumanism; humanists

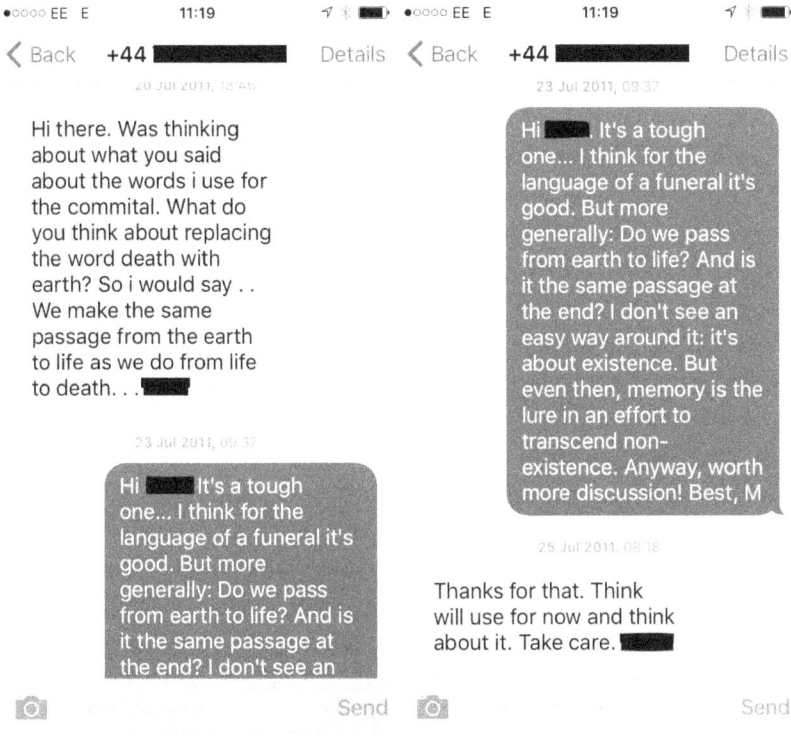

Figure 5.3. An exchange of texts between the anthropologist and a celebrant.

share commitments to science and technoprogressivism yet clearly not the felt need, either emotionally or rationally, to conquer death literally.

Speaking of close kin, alongside the transhumanists, the BHA's rendering of humanism relates to Protestantism. Elsewhere I have discussed the ways in which the BHA is marked by Anglican forms and history (Engelke 2014). How could it be otherwise? It is certainly true that BHA ceremonies are not always so different from Anglican funerals held in crematorium chapels. For one thing, as we might now note, both are given the same amount of time; unless you pay more, you get thirty minutes at Eltham no matter what the service: humanist, Anglican, Catholic, Hindu, "not stated," or anything else. Then there is the emphasis on the person. Some Anglican services have no more than a fill-in-the-blank rendering of liturgy, but many contain love letters, tributes from friends and family, and ski boots set atop the coffin—just like humanist funerals. The sociologist Tony Walter (1994), one of the leading figures in death studies in Britain, has been documenting this trend among Christians (and others) since the early 1990s. This, at least, is not brand new.

Where you do get a consistent difference is in the layering of temporalities. Even when there is a lot of secular time in an Anglican service—Nigel's trip to the Austrian Alps in 1998, Bessie's experiences as a great-house maid in 1940s Berkshire—it is always framed in relation to a higher time, one set above even the stars. Of Roy, a ninety-year-old man whose Church of England funeral I observed at Mortlake, the priest said he had gone "to that new country, where Christ is King." Of Ruth, about whom the mourners heard nothing (though she must have liked Bob Dylan, since "Hey Mr. Tambourine Man" followed the commendation), the priest said, "Ruth, though she's gone from our sight, is now with Him." These particular invocations of higher times—and higher places— were buttressed by the liturgical staple, which is an invocation of Jesus's words in John 14:6: "I am the way, and the truth, and the life."

The kinds of moves embraced by the BHA have the effect of bringing eternity and other higher times lower and lower. Within anthropology, this dynamic has been remarked on at some length by Roy Rappaport. In his (1999) view, the more history and the time of clock and calendar come to dominate within a society, the harder it is to hold on to any sense of eternity, even within ritual:

> It follows that the numbering of days and hours and, finally, minutes and seconds, joins the numbering of years in undoing eternity. If durations great and small are all numbered, we can no longer escape time's undoing by entering ritual's eternity even for a little while, for when we return we can hardly avoid knowing that our sojourn lasted, let us say, from 3:00 until 5:00 p.m. on a certain day of a certain month of a certain year. Endless time not only is not eternity but overwhelms eternity, reducing it to insignificance or superstition. . . . Number gives eternity, which once informed life and was infused by it, into the hands of death. (235)

So, what, then, of the conquest of time that marks so many funerary rites around the globe? Where does the insistence on secular time in humanist funerals—and its prominence in the wider context in which such funerals take place ("ensure your SERVICE does not exceed 30 MINUTES"; 20 mph, "Whoa!")— sit? *Death* is a hard word to swallow, but swallowed it must be, and it would be a mistake to cast the authority of science and "the order of things" (as Janet put it) as cold comfort. For it is only when we acknowledge time's inevitable conquest that we can shake off the fear of it. This acknowledgment in itself is, for the humanists, a fulfillment of humanity's potential. Within the context of their funeral ceremonies, the argument is that we conquer time by recognizing that we cannot conquer time.

Acknowledgments

Funding for the research in this chapter was provided by the United Kingdom's Economic and Social Research Council (RES-000-22-4157). My sincere thanks go to all the members of the British Humanist Association who helped with the research and proved such generous hosts and interlocutors. I would also like to thank the family members and friends of the people whose funerals I attended, many of whom gave generously of their time. An earlier version of this chapter was presented at "Death Cultures in the Twenty-First Century" at the School of Advanced Research, in September 2018. I would like to thank the participants there—Anya Bernstein, Shannon Lee Dawdy, Abou Farman, Jennifer Huberman, Rebekah Lee, Tamara Kneese, Phil Olson, and Margaret Schwartz—for their helpful feedback, as well as much conviviality.

Note

1.   In 2017, the BHA underwent a public rebranding to Humanists UK. Because the officially registered name of the organization remains the British Humanist Association, and because my fieldwork (2011–2014) took place when the organization was publicly known as such, I keep this moniker.

Interlude

Notes from the Field

CHAPTER SIX

Loss in/of the Business of Black Funerals

LASHAYA HOWIE

When we are in a group, Cynthia frequently asks her peers what they see in the future of the funeral business. I have been around her long enough to know that she isn't just asking for my benefit or because I am conducting fieldwork with her funeral home. She is far from pretentious and too blunt for that. She is asking sincerely, because she is preoccupied with the question and has yet to come up with an assuring answer. It is certain, however, that "funeral service," as it is called among its initiates, is changing. And that worries Cynthia and her colleagues.

On this particular occasion, we are having a late lunch following a long morning of presentations at the 2019 National Funeral Directors and Morticians Association Convention in Mobile, Alabama, the largest professional gathering for Black mortuary practitioners worldwide. Cynthia has gathered a small intergenerational group of her friends. A couple of the women are faculty members at a mortuary college in Chicago where we live, and the others own and manage their own funeral homes in Mississippi and New Jersey. Their positions inform their concerns about the future of their field, which range from the challenges new mortuary school graduates face in finding employment to the funeral directors' struggles to remain relevant in their local communities. Hearing the near exasperation in their voices as they recount anecdote after anecdote to illustrate the insecurity they feel, I detect an anticipation of loss as the subtext to this conversation.

Loss is an expected subject of conversation among funeral professionals and a graduate student researching contemporary Black funeral practices in the United States. But this discussion, not about grief or mourning because of the loss of life but about the uncertain status of Black death care, surfaces frequently in my dissertation fieldwork. While extensive changes are impacting the American funeral establishment at large, my research with Black funeral professionals shows that the fear of losing both profit and their place in the fabric of Black social life looms over funeral homes and their proprietors. Their anxieties are fueled by shifts in consumer preferences, gentrifying neighborhoods, and competing generational expectations and fragile familial dynamics within family-run businesses. All these changes are perceived as threats, and the effects are cumulative.

Relevance and vitality are always pertinent concerns for businesses, and with industries like media and retail undergoing radical transformations, funeral homes worry that the onslaught of changes is a harbinger for the end of their own livelihood. What I am suggesting, however, is that the angst within Black funerary circles is not solely the result of overall market shifts, nor are the effects of such changes solely commercial. Anthropology has long held death practices among the most important social practices for a group of people and that by studying them, collective understandings of life, death, the body, and kinship might be revealed (Hertz 1960). The commercialization and professionalization of modern death care in the United States hardly attenuates its social function; in fact, they augment the questions that can be asked (Ariès 1974b; Suzuki 2000). For instance, despite the near uniformity in commercial death practices, how has racial segregation remained a hallmark of the American funeral industry?

Beginning around the mid-nineteenth century, death care emerged as a formal enterprise, and the funeral home eventually became the location for preparing the corpse and often for holding services. Today, with few exceptions and despite some changes, Americans still overwhelmingly rely on funeral directors, embalmers, and morticians when a death occurs to prepare the corpse for services and/or dispose of it, to handle bureaucratic processes by filing death certificates and liaising with insurance companies and government agencies, and to plan and conduct memorial services when requested (Laderman 2005).[1] Despite the common practices of commercial death care, funeral service remains one of the most racially segregated sectors of the American economy. While the technical practices are arguably one and the same, historically, the Black and white funeral professions developed along parallel but separate paths, and competition for clientele rarely crossed the racial divide. Although histories of the "American" funeral industry tend to focus on white Protestant funeral businesses in the northern United States,[2] Holloway (2002) and Smith (2010) document the particular history of the Black funeral industry in the twentieth century[3] by charting key developments in professional organizations and the celebrated status of funeral directors within Black communities because of their economic and political power.[4] Consequently, Black funeral professionals over-whelmingly, and nearly exclusively, provided death care to Black people, and today they continue to do so.[5] Thus, changes in Black funeral service might be understood as an unraveling of intimate and often insular cultural practices and the undoing of the funeral directors' social role. At stake is what Black death care provides: the funeral as a site of Black sociality, the deceased's body as part of that sociality for a final time, the funeral home as a Black neighborhood insti-tution, and the funeral director's specialized cultural work.

Scholars in Black studies and related disciplines agree that racism and anti-Blackness have fatal effects for Black people in the United States and across the globe (see Gilmore 2002 on environmental exposure; Roberts 1997 on Black maternal mortality; Costa Vargas and Alves 2010 on police violence and geog-raphies of death). As a result, theorists argue that Black people have a unique relationship with and to death (Hartman 2007; Holloway 2002; Sharpe 2016). While these arguments provide important structure-level analyses, fieldwork has allowed me to more closely interrogate how such structures come to bear on lay and professional understandings of death management. My collabora-tors seldom articulate such a directly causal connection between race and an individual's death. Instead, the funeral directors and people who seek their ser-vices more commonly suggest that Black people's experiences with death elicit unique emotional, spiritual, and social reactions. How each respondent defines what is distinctive may vary, but the sentiment is consistent. As such, accord-ing to many practitioners and their clients, Black funeral professionals are best poised to address the particularities from within a shared social world.

But funeral directors, and funeral-home owners in particular, feel the secu-rity of that position abating. Of course, their investment in maintaining a tight grip on Black clientele and favoring more expensive funerals benefits the funeral homes' bottom line, but to dismiss their objections as purely profit motivated or as mere attachment to convention would overlook other lessons to be learned at this current juncture of Black funeral service and, by extension, the status of American death care in the twenty-first century. Do the changes in the Ameri-can funeral business portend the end of Black death practices? Do these shifts in consumer preferences and new market realities foreshadow a loss of a crucial aspect of culture?

Change as Loss

Funeral professionals are justified in feeling like the ground is shifting beneath them. For much of its history, the modern American funeral business was seemingly uniform and effectively unchanged, and its contours were mostly dictated by the professionals rather than their clients. Now, considerable transitions are happening that affect the entire industry: once completely dominated by small family-owned-and-operated businesses, funeral corporations are now encroaching ever so slightly on the market; consumer preferences have shifted in favor of cremation, which is more economical, over embalming and burial; while funeral directors used to manage all aspects of a relatively standardized process, people preplanning services for themselves or making arrangements for loved ones now want a greater say and a more personalized experience (Dawdy 2013).[6] Lastly, the majority of funeral directors were once men, and the profession was effectively passed down from generation to generation, but today, mortuary college graduates are predominately women, and the numbers of first-generation professionals greatly outweigh those from "funeral families" (Shaffrey 2018; Siner 2019).

Since race significantly influences this industry's organization, how the changes listed above impact Black funeral homes in particular and what other considerations may be specific to them is of great interest among Black funeral professionals and to my research. The neighborhood-altering effects of rapid gentrification in Washington, DC, forced the historic Hall Brothers Funeral Home to close after almost eighty years (Schwartzman 2019; Stanley 2016). Funeral homes are often embedded in physical communities, which are commonly bound by race and class. If those neighborhoods change, the standing of local funeral homes is threatened. In the areas where I work, on Chicago's South Side, gentrification is less imminent, but closures still occur, though for other reasons. When we discuss funeral homes going out of business, my collaborators don't celebrate less competition in an already difficult market, they are saddened by it, implying that the sense of loss is not solely financial. In a closely intertwined professional community wherein funeral directors may have grown up together, or attended the same church or school, or belong to the same social organizations, their personal connections exceed the business. Also, they fear that the fate that befell those funeral homes might await their own. According to the National Funeral Directors and Morticians Association, there has been an overall decrease in the number of Black funeral homes across the country.[7]

If closing is the most definitive end to a funeral home, selling out to a funeral corporation—and I use that phrase deliberately—might allow a semblance of continuity, but it is deemed more a threat and a taboo than a viable possibility. I have heard mumblings about local owners possibly having sold their funeral homes to one of these corporations. Per the agreement, the conglomerate rearranges the inner workings but maintains the face and name of the funeral home in order to capitalize on its established status and to continue the appearance of Black ownership. Directors speculate that these corporations court Black funeral homes intentionally and exactingly, because unlike white people who are overwhelmingly choosing cremation and thus spending less money on memorials, "we still pay good money for a funeral."[8] Because a takeover invariably means a loss of Black ownership and dissolution of family ownership, it is seen as a failure among Black funeral directors.

From an anthropological perspective, a shift away from tradition has no moral bearing; it is neither inherently good nor inherently bad. In fact, changes in funeral norms provide opportunities to analyze emergent death practices alongside commercial developments and what they may suggest about evolving notions about mortality (Dawdy 2013; Huberman 2012). Likewise, changes like the greater number of women and first-generation funeral professionals signal a break from a once exclusionary line of work and usher in a greater diversity of people who can bring fresh perspectives to a field already undergoing change. However, rather than rushing to project the long-term consequences of these changes, my work currently necessitates pondering some of the immediate effects for death-care professionals, namely anxiety and uncertainty. Doing ethnography with funeral professionals amid these transformations in death care requires being attentive to their worries, how and when their worries surface, and what we might learn from them.

The growth of cremation and the threat of discontinuity of family ownership are two of the most commonly discussed sources of angst. While funeral customers imposed cremation's popularity on a reluctant funeral profession as a whole, the familial and intergenerational dynamics of family owned funeral homes feel like personal attacks from within.

The proliferation of cremation is probably the most significant shift in American death care in recent history. In 2015, cremation superseded burial as the most common choice for final disposition for the first time in the United States, and its popularity will continue to rise. The National Funeral Directors Association (NFDA) projects that by 2035, 78.8 percent of Americans will choose to be cremated (NFDA 2015). Where I am conducting fieldwork, funeral directors have noticed a marked increase in cremation requests. Funeral directors frequently cite cremation as *the* symbol of a death-care system that is drastically different from its past. Because the cost of cremation can be a fraction of the cost of embalming and burial, its monetary impact is readily recognized, but the rise of cremation and decline of embalming and restoration has implications for both the profits and the practice of Black death care.

Embalming, the process of replacing bodily fluids with a chemical cocktail to preserve the body for viewing and burial, is a distinctively American practice performed few other places in the world and was once the uniquely American cornerstone of a funeral director's professional identity (Dawdy, this volume). In the early days of the profession, morticians sought social status as professionals in large part by insisting that embalming was a scientific practice that required skills and training, sometimes going as far as likening it to surgery (Farrell 1980, 151). In my fieldwork, embalming and the related skill of restoration, which combines a myriad of artistic techniques including cosmetology and building prosthetics when needed to create the most visually pleasing presentation of the body for viewing, remain a quintessential part of how many funeral directors see their work and how they describe their personal style.[9] It provides an opening for creativity and for practitioners to develop a signature approach. Rodney, who is a funeral director and embalmer at another field site, apprenticed with a funeral director in Florida who saw himself as an artist and attracted clients with his distinct style. "This guy liked to make people up like dolls, so he didn't worry too much with the color or texture that came with embalming. . . . But I took from my dad, we prefer a more natural look: less with the cosmetics, and more with calibrating the embalming liquids." According to Holloway (2002), restoration is more than aesthetic; African American embalmers had to develop extensive skills in the "restorative arts" because Black people are disproportionately victims of violent death that might have caused physical trauma. In Chicago, where I primarily conduct fieldwork, the prevalence of gun violence unfortunately still demands these special skills.

Notwithstanding the increase in cremations and funeral directors' anxiousness around it, the uptake of cremation has been substantially slower among Black Americans. Therefore, the continued prominence of the intact, embalmed body most commonly presented in a sleeplike state partially differentiates Black funeral practices in the United States—if only for now.[10] Funeral directors anticipate the cremation rate to continue to rise among Black funeral customers, and as it does, a defining feature of Black funeral service slips away. Additionally, Black funeral homes most commonly have to outsource cremations to white-owned crematoria, which means a reduction in profits. Besides their professional affinity for embalming, funeral directors also insist on the therapeutic benefits of traditional viewing, and they worry about psychic ramifications for loved ones if the practice is abandoned. Examined this way, preparing and presenting the body brings people together and includes the deceased in a recognizable form. It is a cultural and spiritual practice that maintains social bonds through the funeral service.

Unlike the changes forced on funeral professionals from outside, owners worry that dynamics within their own families challenge the sustainability of family ownership. Competing notions of professional and personal boundaries, obligation, and the role of work in one's life complicate the already fragile inner workings of family-owned funeral homes along generational and gendered lines. Kinship hierarchies are often reproduced, causing tension in the workplace between spouses, parents, children, and siblings on the one hand, and between family and nonfamily staff, on the other, with the first usually receiving the owner's preferential treatment. Uneven levels of involvement in the family business can be a source of tension between siblings, especially when gendered expectations allow brothers more leeway, and sisters feel more inhibited. When I asked Cynthia how funeral service will change, now that most graduates of mortuary colleges are women, she eschewed the optimism most people express: "The business is still male dominated, and it will take much longer for that to change. I had a tough time [even though] I had the family backing."

Given that the funeral business has historically been male dominated and fathers pass the businesses down to their sons, Cynthia emphasizes that her parents handed their business over to *her*. She is also careful to mention that both her parents started the funeral home. Her mother performed administrative duties, while her father took care of the duties that required a funeral director's license. Today, her brother also has a funeral director's license but chose a career in local politics; her father is semiretired and she manages a very small staff. Rodney's parents run the funeral home where he works. He and his sister, Erica, assist their parents in managing a slightly larger staff. Both funeral homes have two generations working together, and despite the different configurations, both are led by baby boomers.

The concept of generation is so ingrained in the business that it is part of funeral directors' professional identity and how they describe their funeral homes. For instance, owners regularly introduce themselves according to whether they are second- or in some cases third- or fourth-generation funeral directors, followed by the origin story of their family's business. Employees in leadership positions in larger funeral homes who are not part of the family are not shy in describing how they earned their place in an industry where nepotism rules. Owners who establish their own funeral home without "growing up in the business" proudly say so.

While the generational structure is taken for granted among funeral directors, the concept of a generation as it relates to societal cohorts and kinship structure may also be useful for tracing owners' anxieties about legacy and longevity against the experiences and desires of their employees, who are often part of the same family. Because owners establish funeral homes with the intent of continuity, second-generation funeral directors may feel that they had little choice in joining the family business. And for millennial funeral professionals like Rodney and Erica working under their baby-boomer parents, competing perspectives on family duty, sacrifice, and work-life balance are never far from the surface. Less enthusiastic funeral directors may resent the time-consuming and emotionally taxing nature of being surrounded by death and grief on a daily basis or begrudge maintaining a respectable comportment in public, because they feel pressure to always represent the family and its funeral home. Erica once told me, "Sometimes I'd rather be doing anything else. Anything."

And for many funeral families, the younger adults *are* doing anything else, which worries their parents and grandparents, who planned to pass the business down to their descendants. Cynthia knew that none of her children or stepchildren would enter funeral service. Having grown up with her own father as a funeral director, she knew she could not mount a convincing argument in favor of her chosen career. With the long hours, erratic schedules, little pay in smaller funeral homes, and no realistic chance of career advancement within a small organization, she understood their opposition and chose not to pressure them. But now, as she fantasizes about her own retirement, she also laments not having the guaranteed succession plan her father had when he stepped aside.

With waning investment in the business with each generation of a family, some baby-boomer owners blame a loss of cohesion within the family. Their children, however, celebrate being less tethered to a lifestyle they don't want. In contrast to the dwindling interest from "funeral kids" who grow up in families who own funeral homes, more than ever, graduates from mortuary colleges are first-generation funeral directors (Siner 2019).[11] This trend will bring in new leadership for an already changing funeral industry, but it also gives credence to current owners' nervousness as they anticipate the loss of their own legacies. Millennial presence in funeral service is increasing and will inevitably take over leadership, whether these funeral directors are related to the funeral homes' founders or not. Their perspectives as funeral professionals and as people who are planning funerals will shape the future death care in the United States in terms of workplace culture and consumer preferences.

Conclusion

In part because they want to make a greater impact on their community and in part because they are strategically looking for ways to maintain relevance despite the changing landscape of death care, the funeral homes where I work engage in philanthropic outreach or host community events that have nothing to do with funeral service. Cynthia, for example, has implemented advice from business leadership courses she has taken and now rarely uses the phrase *funeral home* in branded materials. Instead, her business cards and event flyers bear her family's name only. When she renovated the chapels a few years ago to make them rentable event spaces, the chosen design could just as easily accommodate a book club meeting (and yes, there is a book club that meets there) as a funeral. While some strategies push owners further outside of death care, others reimagine possibilities within its changing terrain. Rodney hopes his family will go beyond their traditional offerings to respond to newer, consumer-initiated funerary preferences. "No matter how people decide to do it—whatever trends may come—we must adjust." He adds, "[Funeral homes] must ask ourselves, 'What are we in the business of?'" Using the iPhone's popularity as an allegory, he asserts that companies in the cell phone business became obsolete, but by contrast, Apple thrived, because it saw itself as a leader in the business of *communication* and focused on consumer desire instead of the product as such. In his opinion, funeral homes do not yet fit that model, but they can, and they should.

Unfortunately, Black funeral homes are less like Apple and more like other Black institutions and industries, including the Black press, Black banks, and Black health care services that occupied crucial commercial and social roles in Black life in the late nineteenth and early twentieth centuries but suffered eventual declines when integration opened Black consumer markets to white businesses and, with similar results, when larger companies increasingly made survival difficult for small businesses.[12]

Will Black funeral service undergo a similar fate in the twenty-first century? Broader consumer trends have certainly crept into the funeral business. Personalized touches are being added to services to make funerals less formulaic, and Americans, now accustomed to comparing products online before making purchases, can rely less on funeral professionals by shopping around for deals on obituary printing, flowers, and even caskets, with retailers like Amazon and Walmart selling them directly.

Yet death is unlike any other occasion, making funeral decisions more than just purchases. Does the social purpose of a funeral offer somewhat of a safeguard for the business? Does the funeral directors' unenvied proximity to the dead and those in mourning secure their role, regardless of the extant particulars of the enterprise? More specific for my research, race has not only helped shape American funeral service as an organizing societal structure in the United States, but, I anticipate, will be present in twenty-first-century American death care, whether its influence is palpable or obscure. How it manifests remains to be analyzed. Even as funeral directors worry about their standing, what does the still persistent preference of Black people for Black funeral homes suggest about how Americans understand death, the dead body, and transgressing racial boundaries? More than anything, the anxiety and fear of loss in the internal discourses among Black funeral professionals signal not necessarily an inevitable demise, but rather an uncomfortable uncertainty. They are unsure about the final outcomes and can only speculate about what it all means. But they fear that something important is being upended.

Notes

1. Muslim, Jewish, and Hindu mortuary practices that occur within the United States are faith-based and differ from what are conventionally and historically considered "American" death practices. Still, legislation necessitates a licensed funeral professional's involvement for some purposes such as filing the death certificate. Also see Hagerty (2014) on the small but growing home-funeral movement, wherein loved ones of the deceased adopt a do-it-yourself model, taking on the responsibility of preparing the body and holding a service, often at home; and Olson (this volume) on home-funeral practitioners who are developing their own notions of expertise as alternatives to industrial death care.
2. See, for example, historians Farrell (1980) and Laderman (1996, 2005) and Mitford's famous exposé *The American Way of Death* ([1963] 2000). Although the discipline has since moved on from these assumptions, foundational studies

in the anthropology of death (e.g., Metcalf and Huntington 1991) similarly overlook Americans' differing relationships to death and attendant death practices.

3. Smith and Holloway both forecast significant changes in the funeral business by the twenty-first century. The contrasts become more apparent when ethnographies of current death care are situated within a longer history of death and funeral practices in the United States.

4. In contrast to the esteemed position Black funeral directors enjoy within Black social life, Thompson (1991) argues that white death-care workers' labor is stigmatized by nonprofessionals.

5. I use "Black" and "white" funeral industries to reflect the predominant racial division within the death-care industry, for example, in terms of customer base and professional organizations. While they might flatten the diversity within those groups and seemingly do not account for other groups, these descriptors accurately describe how separate *industries* developed in a way that mirrors the binary racial structure that is fundamental to American society and is first predicated on Indigenous erasure. Religion, ethnicity, and class are often collapsed into the business's race-based organization. It has proven difficult for me to find statistics on the racial makeup of funeral homes and their clients, but historians of American death care have treated them discretely, either intentionally like Farrell, Holloway, and Smith or by presuming uniformity in death practices while only studying white Americans. In my own field research, I work in African American–owned funeral homes that have an overwhelming Black clientele that vary by class and ethnicity.

6. For more on consumer preferences, see the website of the National Funeral Directors Association, https://nfda.org.

7. These two articles feature the same Washington, DC, funeral home. While the Hall Brothers' story exemplifies the staggering gentrification in the LeDroit Park area of Washington, DC, it is not anomalous. Like funeral homes, historic Black cemeteries in numerous cities have been uprooted or threatened because of urban development aboveground. Considered together, the presence of Black funeral homes and Black cemeteries exemplifies how American segregation historically permeated death and burial practices, creating the need and opportunity for their establishment. Today's political economy renders these same spaces of Black death precarious (a topic I explored in an opinion piece I wrote for my hometown newspaper following a discovery of African American graves during construction of a golf complex; see Howie 2017). Archaeologists have been at the forefront of research on Black burial grounds. In addition to the watershed discovery of the New York City African Burial Ground in the 1990s and scholarship following the discovery published by Michael Blakey, Cheryl LaRoche, and Warren Perry, see also Brittany L. Brown's (2013) work on Black cemeteries in Jacksonville, Florida, and Delande Justinvil's efforts with the Bethesda African Cemetery Coalition profiled in Waddell (2019).

8. A local funeral director offered this comment during a seminar at the 2018 NFDMA convention in Kissimmee, Florida. Similarly, Isiah Owens, a Harlem funeral director featured in the documentary film *Homegoing* (Turner 2013), discusses his refusal to sell his business to corporations despite their offers.

9. Embalming and restoration work is, expectedly, set apart from the other happenings within the funeral home. It happens physically and metaphorically "in the back" of each funeral home where I conduct fieldwork. The status of embalming and restoration among practitioners varies. For some like Rodney, it is the part of the job that they enjoy most, because it is a challenging, embodied practice. For others, it has less social status compared to funeral directing (actually conducting funeral services and handling the administrative work), because it is more technical and hidden from public view.

10. Dawdy (this volume) argues that the emergence of "extreme embalming," in which the body is arranged in a wakeful tableau instead of in a coffin in a state of "deep sleep," signals an effort to combat the expansion of cremation as well as a literal demonstration of the American desire to interact with the dead in American funerary preferences.

11. In 2017, 83 percent of mortuary college graduates were the first in their families to join the funeral profession, according to the American Board of Funeral Service Education.

12. For even closer examples, we can look at the antecedent decline of Black casket manufacturers and Black-owned cemeteries in the United States.

CHAPTER SEVEN

Cuddling Death
Exploring the Materiality of Reproductive Loss

STEPHANIE SCHIAVENATO

Leaky Grief

Two weeks after prematurely delivering twin girls who died shortly after being born, my partner and I decided to adopt a dog.[1] It was a bitterly cold day, and as I buttoned up my winter coat, I was stung by the now-roomy fit that had only recently been stretched to capacity by a growing abdomen. We walked against the icy wind gusts, and warm blood trickled out of me, a reminder of the large wound left inside my uterus, where two placentas had implanted.

At the shelter, an employee asked us what size dog we were interested in. As a New Yorker, I understood the practicality of owning a smaller dog, but I have always been drawn to the vexed pit bull. "Let's start with the big ones first," I said. As we were led toward the back of the building, the employee told us that they had just received a female pit bull that was used for breeding and had recently delivered puppies that were taken away from her. "She is still lactating," he said almost apologetically.

I went into labor at six months, too soon for my babies to survive outside of me but late enough that my body did not understand there were no babies to feed. My breasts began to fill with milk as soon as I came home from the hospital. I was prepared for this, because I am a birth doula and understood at the time that at around four months of pregnancy, the body begins the process of providing nourishment for a potential life.[2] What I was not prepared for was the suggestion that I could attach a mechanical pump and extract that milk to donate it. My midwife offered me two options: actively suppress a process that would inevitably happen or encourage it by pumping regularly and taking herbal supplements known as galactagogues that would increase my supply.[3]

Standing in front of the pit bull's cage, I crouched down and said, "Hello, little lady." She stood up and gently wagged her tail. I noticed her swollen breasts. I reached my hand in to pet her and as we locked eyes, my breasts began to leak.

When a pregnancy ends, each gestational stage activates bodily matter, ranging from tissue, corpses, lochia, breast milk, emptied abdomens, and stretch marks permanently etched onto skin.[4] Reproductive loss is an experience saturated in materiality, but one that has often been diluted in the realm of the immaterial. Arguments over what existed (and later, what was lost) have largely focused on the legal and cultural definitions of the embryo, fetus, or baby (Conklin and Morgan 1996; Dubow 2011; Morgan 2009). In the United States, the material experience of the pregnant person—including how to interact with what remains—is seldom addressed.[5]

In these notes from the field, I begin to explore what the materiality of reproductive remains engenders. After my delivery (figure 7.1), I continued to work as a doula for over a decade, attending hundreds of births and supporting clients as they coped through various losses: infertility, miscarriage, stillbirth, and hysterectomies.[6] Many of these visceral experiences, including my own loss, provide an ongoing scaffold for understanding the growing importance given to the artifacts of reproduction. My research focuses on three areas in which the relationship between reproductive potential and loss is uniquely animated in the mother's bodymind: breast milk, the placenta, and funerary technologies that facilitate increased time with fetal corpses.[7] In this chapter, I focus on the material practices of mourning reproductive death, practices that I suggest are moving beyond existing debates on fetal personhood. My fieldwork is ongoing, so my observations here are exploratory and preliminary. I provide ethnographic descriptions of a stillbirth to introduce some of the possibilities and anxieties activated by the corpses of dead babies. Then I explore how innovations in understanding parent-child bonding have influenced bereavement protocols in hospitals. I introduce a device called the CuddleCot, a refrigerated bassinet designed for dead babies and manufactured by a funerary company based in Gloucester, England. The bassinet is just one of several technological interventions and innovations within reproductive demise that my research tracks, but its dynamism is significant. Finally, I conclude with a suggestion to reconsider the significance of the maternal bodymind that the reproductive loss occurs within or beside.

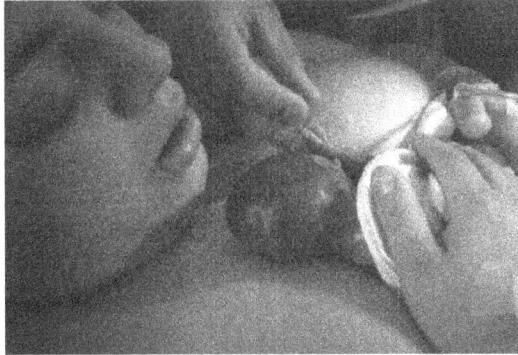

Figure 7.1. Author holding
one of her twin daughters.
Courtesy of the author.

Beyond Personhood

How does one mourn the end of a life that never came to be? In recent decades, the work of feminist anthropologists and science and technology scholars has rigorously addressed the liminality of pregnancy (Layne 2003; Thompson 2005), the contingent personhood of fetuses (Morgan 2009; Morgan and Michaels 1999), and the blurred categories of nature and culture in assisted-reproductive technologies (Becker 2000; Franklin 2013; Ragone 1994; Strathern 1992; Teman 2010). Anthropological knowledge has documented the dissimilar treatment of dead babies across cultures (Conklin and Morgan 1996). Funerary rites extended to fully incorporated members of society are frequently denied to miscarried, stillborn, or newborn bodies. In New York City hospitals, for example, if a fetus is born dead and the family does not make arrangements to take the remains home (itself only a recent option), the body will be discarded in the incinerator. American laws governing the treatment of corpses do not apply to certain liminal bodies whose histories are rooted in who counts as a person, and by extension who can be mourned (Casper and Moore 2009).

But emerging postmortem practices in the United States dealing with pregnancy and infant loss point to a significant shift in the cultural scripts that surround an untimely demise. Since the early 2000s, a move away from the tendency to silence reproductive loss is making room for concerted efforts that immerse families in the temporality, materiality, and sense-making of the death. My ongoing fieldwork in New York City and Gloucester in the United Kingdom has revealed that parents are increasingly encouraged by mental health professionals, medical staff, and funerary operators to recognize all pregnancy loss as equally significant to the end of any other life. More specifically, parents are being persuaded to break the silence around miscarriage and stillbirth through intimate interactions with reproductive remains. What happens to people after they come out from the shadows of shame associated with reproductive loss?

In 2016, an article in the *Atlantic* reported on a newly passed law that requires women in Indiana who experience an abortion, miscarriage, or stillbirth to arrange for a state-regulated burial or cremation. The previous statute treated most fetal remains as medical waste, but women would soon have to arrange for funeral homes to complete their reproductive procedures (Green 2016). The author, Emma Green, traces this monumental shift to an effort, originating over a decade ago, by parents who wanted access to the corpses of their stillborn babies against existing hospital regulations. In the article, a law professor suggests that pro-life activists joined this movement and pushed for it to apply to all recognized pregnancies.[8] The suggestion is that a law was created following two distinct but related emotions: the anger of the pro-life activists and the sadness of would-be parents.

Predictably, this law was challenged by pro-choice activists around the country, as other conservative states followed Indiana's lead, and the legal debate eventually reached the federal courts. In May 2019, the Supreme Court upheld the statute. Justice Clarence Thomas wrote that neither the Constitution nor other court rulings "[prevent] a state from requiring abortion facilities to provide for the respectful treatment of human remains" (Williams 2019). Following the ruling, Vice President Mike Pence, who as governor of Indiana signed the law into effect, tweeted, "A victory for life!"

The regulations require a burial or cremation, but no birth or death certificates are administered. The remains do not have to be named or registered as having lived in any other capacity, as, for example, in potential child deductions on income taxes. Nonetheless, it is not difficult to see how these legislative moves, while initiated by grieving parents of stillborn babies, are also a backdoor entry into legitimizing and institutionalizing personhood at the moment of conception. We tend to bury human matter that previously lived.

As evidenced above, when addressing the experience of pregnant bodies and pregnancy loss in the United States, it is impossible to ignore the abortion debate. But that debate is not my focus here. What is interesting to me about the tensions playing out around abortion is not the conflict between religious, juridical, and scientific justifications of when life begins but rather how the politics of personhood are used to address the materiality of death. The language that imbues how we talk about reproductive potential and loss is already overdetermined by those existing debates and the limited linguistic, philosophical, and ontological options within them (Conklin and Morgan 1996). Regrettably, this toxic, embattled political landscape often eclipses the embodied experiences of pregnant people.

By focusing on the postpartum and postmortem matter that lingers, my fieldwork broadens the scope of how we think with and about reproductive potential and loss by going beyond the philosophical and legal arguments regarding personhood. I appreciate that debates on when life begins and what counts as life are critically important to issues of access and justice, but my hope is that my research will honor the myriad and varied experiences of the flesh.

A Kidney Stone Birth

A year after my own loss, a pregnant client called to let me know that her baby had suddenly died. Nadia was only three weeks away from her due date, but after not feeling the baby move for several hours, she went to the hospital and after a tense and quiet sonogram, she was told there was no longer a heartbeat.[9] She was in shock and devastated. In an instant, Nadia was transformed from expectant mother to a woman with a corpse in her womb, a corpse that had to be delivered before decomposition caused a life-threatening infection within her. I spent the following two days helping her give birth.

At the hospital, we were placed in a regular room on the labor floor, amid the moans of contraction pain and the raw cries of newborns. Our door had a teardrop taped on the outside, a coded image the purpose of which is to alert any medical staff that past this particular threshold, there would be no reassuring fetal heartbeats coming from the monitors. The hospital staff wanted to know if after the delivery, she and her husband would like to hold the baby, name it, and arrange for a funeral home to pick up his body for a private burial. I asked them to give us a moment to discuss the plan. In our eerily silent room, Nadia was clear that she did not want to see or touch anything. Her husband, Sam, awkwardly likened the dead baby to a kidney stone — "They wouldn't bury that, right?" When I relayed this back to the nurses, they were aghast. Since we had many hours to go, they hoped that I would be able to convince them that holding the baby would be the "best way to grieve."

Doulas provide nonjudgmental and unconditional support. We do not try to convince our clients to make decisions that we think are the better ones; rather, we provide a platform to help them make the best choices for themselves. So despite the challenge of staying neutral, given my own history, I promised I would keep Nadia from seeing anything that came out of her body. Nadia and Sam are Jewish, and as we passed the hours making conversation, they acknowledged that part of what influenced their unyielding decision was an awareness that Jewish law does not recognize the loss of a stillborn baby as one equal to any other life. One is not compelled to mourn. Increasingly, it is possible to find compassionate rabbis who will bend the rules and even allow the body to be buried in a Jewish cemetery, but it was an effort that this couple did not want to initiate (Tessler 2014). They did not budge for close to forty-eight hours.

As we got closer to pushing, Nadia told me that she felt like something was coming out of her. I carefully lifted the sheet that was covering her legs and saw that the top of the baby's head was sitting outside of her vagina. I put the sheet back down and told her it was time. I reminded the doctor and nurse that they did not want to see the baby, and through a carefully orchestrated choreography involving many white hospital sheets recruited to act as barriers and shields, Nadia pushed out a dead baby boy that was hidden from their view, put into a bassinet, and immediately wheeled out of the room by a nurse.

About an hour later, I went outside to get Nadia some water, and one of the nurses called me over with tears in her eyes. She brought me into a small auxiliary room near the nurses' desk where the baby had been wiped down and carefully swaddled in a hospital blanket. They had also put a hat on him. Apart from his pale color and uncanny stillness, he looked like a normal sleeping baby. The nurse was particularly upset that he would be sent to the incinerator, along with biohazard waste. I was deeply moved by this swaddled corpse and the nurse's tender care of it and used this moment to take some pictures on my cell phone. When I went back in the delivery room, I let Nadia and Sam know I had taken some pictures. I told them I would hold on to these images and if they ever wanted to view them, all they had to do was ask.

Two weeks later, Nadia called and asked me to come over so she could look at the pictures. She looked at only one image, very briefly, and never looked again.

Bonding with Death

Twenty years before Nadia and Sam gave birth, Dr. Irving Leon, an obstetrician based in Michigan, warned of a troubling turnaround. In a 1992 article, he wrote, "About 20 years ago, medical caregivers typically tried to prevent parents from mourning a stillborn or neonatal death by prohibiting any contact with the dead child, disposing of the body unceremoniously and anonymously, prescribing tranquilizers for the parents to dull any expression of shock or grief, advising them to forget the experience, and often suggesting another pregnancy soon. Today, a completely opposite approach is recommended" (Leon 1992, 366).

Dr. Leon highlighted three trends that he felt required immediate reassessment: "institutionalization of bereavement, idealization of contact with the dead baby, and a homogenization of grief" (1992, 366). Caregivers had shifted the site of pathology around reproductive grief from recognition to disregard. Whereas before, it would be frowned upon to want to hold your dead baby, now it was concerning when a parent chose not to. The transformation in bereavement protocol can be theorized in divergent ways, but for the purposes of this chapter, I want to highlight a particular trend in perinatal literature that Dr. Leon cites as influential to the about-face: theories on parent-infant bonding.

During the 1960s and 1970s, pediatricians John H. Kennell and Marshall H. Klaus revolutionized hospital procedures following labor and delivery. In *Mother-Infant Bonding* (1976), they theorized that the first hours after birth were crucial for the lifelong connection between a parent and a child.[10] The environment in which the doctors worked routinely separated mothers and babies and did not encourage partners at the bedside or allow siblings to visit (Vitello 2013). Klaus and Kennell focused on the influence of certain hormones, like oxytocin, also called the "love hormone," and the behavior that supposedly flowed from it as a crucial mechanism to healthy attachment. If this time was not protected, they argued, babies would suffer lifelong consequences. Their work dramatically changed hospital protocols (still in effect today) and contributed to shifts already occurring around attachment parenting during the 1960s and 1970s. But they also came under heavy criticism for their implicit sexism, small sample size, and the simplification and routinization of an extremely dynamic process (Brody 1983). For Dr. Leon, the influence of Klaus and Kennell's work on bonding when applied to the management of perinatal loss risked flattening out an equally complex process like mourning. He writes, "The assumption that pregnancy loss inevitably and solely involves mourning the death of one's baby is open to question" (1992, 370). This sentence is so bare that it has the potential to be overlooked. But what Dr. Leon is challenging is quite nuanced; it is not abundantly clear what is being grieved.

Despite the indeterminacy of what was lost, this kind of institutionalized hospital bereavement protocol suggests that one could bond with a corpse. What role does oxytocin play in a postmortem setting? Is the aim to become appropriately attached to this loss? Dr. Leon does not address issues of personhood; he is not debating whether what was lost actually lived and therefore deserves mourning. Rather, he urges caregivers to make room for a multitude of responses to the death of a baby. Against his concerns, bereavement protocol has not changed much since the publication of his article. In fact, it has only intensified, as the stillbirth described earlier highlights. Nadia and Sam were ultimately respected in their choice to not interact with the corpse, but everyone who came in contact with them argued that it would be best if they did.

Cuddling Death

A few months after being with Nadia and Sam, another client of mine experienced a stillbirth. Supporting her birth was entirely different, as she and her husband wanted to hold the baby after the delivery. Jenna and Tom stayed with their baby for several hours after he was born. He was held by both parents, three grandparents, a family friend, and me. Elan had died about four days before he was born, and the longer he was in the room, the more the effects of decomposition appeared.[11] The nurses at the hospital provided a memory box where a lock of hair, footprints, pictures, and the blanket that he was swaddled in could be taken home by the parents. Following the birth of this death, I became interested in exploring these kinds of reproductive postmortem practices, and soon after starting graduate coursework, I learned about the CuddleCot.

FlexMort produces mobile mortuary units that aim to "cool the deceased with dignity." The company was founded by former policemen who were influenced by the coordinated terrorist attacks that occurred in London on July 7, 2005, where fifty-two people died and over seven hundred were injured. The prevalence of mass casualties along with the challenges of storing very large corpses led Simon Rothwell and Steve Huggins to create flexible mortuary solutions like the Mass Fatality Mortuary Dome that is designed to store over two hundred bodies in situ or the Hospital Covercool bariatric mortuary cooling system for corpses with elevated BMIs that do not fit into the standard hospital morgues. The CuddleCot is just one of many products designed at FlexMort, but it has put the company on the global map of mortuary innovations.

Flexmort sits on a quiet industrial street in Gloucester, a city of 150,000 in southwest England. Steve, the commercial director, described the extant problem of managing stillbirths in hospitals as a "rugby pass"—the dead baby quickly passes from mother to dad, onto the midwife, and finally to the morgue.[12] This urgency with the handling of the corpse is necessitated by the reality of decomposition. An adult human begins this process immediately after death, and for a baby that is born dead, the decay often begins in utero. This means that when the body comes out of the pregnant person, it is already more fragile and in a more advanced state of breakdown. Stillborn babies usually have extensive discoloration, oozing fluid from the nose and mouth, and skin that peels off easily. It is part of the reason why nurses immediately swaddle dead babies in hospital blankets: it covers up their disintegration. Understandably, this is a deeply upsetting experience for parents. Steve told me that the idea for the cot came from a mother who had experienced a reproductive loss and felt that the company could develop a unique product to help grieving families. Promotional materials for the CuddleCot suggest that their product buys parents time to get to know the baby to say goodbye, phrasing that is common across emerging reproductive postmortem practices. The cot, mainly consisting of a refrigerated cooling pad tucked inside of an innocuous-looking bassinet, aims to slow down the inevitable chain of physiological events (figure 7.2). Flexmort is a very small company (four employees), but the CuddleCot has been propelled to international recognition. Cots are made to order in the factory and shipped globally. Their website reports the cot's appearance in Australia, New Zealand, Canada, southern Ireland, the United States, and in over 95 percent of hospitals in England.[13]

The CuddleCot costs around US$3,000 and is often purchased by a family who has personally experienced a stillbirth and afterward decides to donate one to the hospital where they delivered. Families are motivated by a desire to offer an opportunity they did not have to help future grieving families. Before finalizing engineering on the cot, the company conducted research with families, who explained that babies were disturbingly "ice cold." Steve told me that most morgues, where stillborn babies are kept, cool corpses to around 40°F (5°C). The cot keeps the bodies of the babies at around 46°F (8–9°C), where they are "cool enough to present." When I interviewed Steve, we sat on a small couch in the lobby that was cozy and generic. The only clue that suggested we were talking about corpses was a series of framed news clippings about the CuddleCot hanging on a wall above Steve's head. The one that caught my eye was about a couple who used the cot for sixteen days, taking their dead baby on walks in a

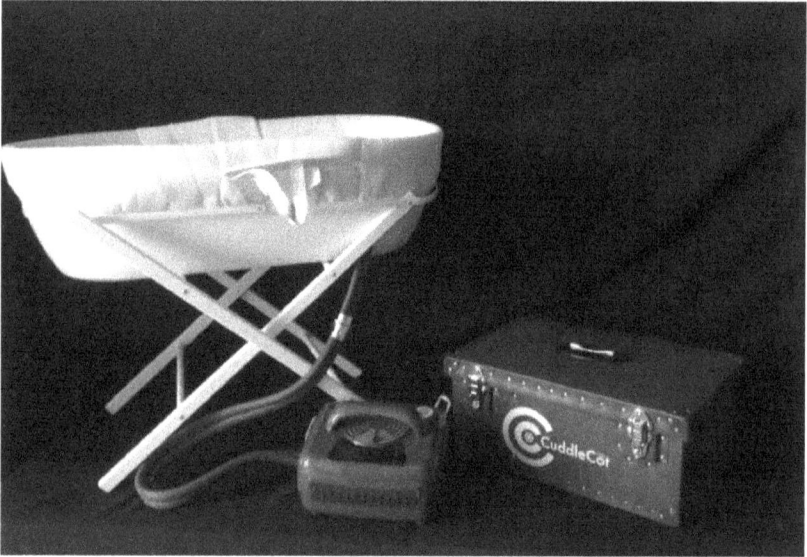

Figure 7.2. CuddleCot, from the Flexmort website.

pram and to the local playground (Roberts 2017). Acknowledging the apparent macabre nature of these kinds of reproductive loss stories, Steve told me that the company made a conscious decision not to post any pictures of dead babies inside the cots. Steve said they did not want "to inflict that on everyone." On their Facebook page and on their website, they only promote images of donations of the cot to hospitals.

Still Leaking

The CuddleCot is venturing into terrain that most Euro-American societies have historically moved away from: sitting with a corpse for an extended period of time. Families can spend numerous days taking pictures, changing the baby's clothes, "introducing" the baby to other family members, or just holding the baby for hours while the cot softly buzzes with cool air. Steve turned one on for me. The sound was familiar, like a humidifier in a dry urban apartment; it is quiet and strangely comforting. The cot has made it into the *New York Times*, NBC's dramatic television series set in an NYC hospital, *New Amsterdam*, and the now-infamous controversy around Charlie Gard, a terminally ill UK infant who died in 2017 (Bever 2017).[14] The language on Flexmort's website and in most journalistic articles written about it emphasizes that parents need time — time to get to know a baby they are meeting for the first time, albeit postmortem; time to make memories; time to say goodbye. But what does time mean in the face of decomposition?

Time in this context is inextricably linked to a manipulation of temperature, or to borrow Joanna Radin and Emma Kowal's development of the term, *cryopolitics*, to describe "what happens when temperature is used to reorient life" (2017, 12) or how "in the realm of the cryopolitical, life and death both exist to be remade" (7). The CuddleCot may be remaking reproductive death, but it also inadvertently ignores what occurs in the just recently pregnant person's body. The emerging mourning practices following reproductive death, like the CuddleCot or a memory box that collects individual pieces of the baby, foreground the corpse, while making no mention of the body that until only recently housed it.

Artist and anthropologist Abou Farman's work on cryogenics foregrounds the body in discussions on the secular. Farman focuses on bodies who have been declared officially dead by the medical establishment but are subsequently suspended in a postmortem limbo, aided by submersion in liquid nitrogen vats. Farman argues that the body in general, and liminal bodies like corpses specifically, represent the secular tensions that exist between materialist foundations and rationalist claims to autonomy (2013). The site of contention is not only what materiality might index in terms of personhood, but perhaps an even more recalcitrant metaphysical dilemma: What is left after death? It is here where I locate the tension between the material and immaterial that is activated in the similarly liminal postpartum/postmortem body.

A few days after giving birth to a corpse, the maternal body begins to come alive again with breasts that begin to leak milk to sustain life. Further, bleeding from the lingering wound where the life-giving placenta implanted in the uterus can occur for up to six weeks, a reminder of the vulnerability and risk required to reproduce life. Fetal microchimerism occurs, a process by which fetal DNA from every single pregnancy remains in the mother's body, almost indefinitely, lodging itself into the pregnant person's brain and other vital organs (Zimmer 2015). Reproductive loss is unique within discussions of death care (Dawdy and Kneese, this volume), in part because the death occurs inside of another body or adjacent to other acute biological processes. The postpartum body is a palimpsest of beginnings and endings. Recalling Dr. Leon's concern about an assumption that pregnancy loss directly equals mourning for the baby, what else is being mourned here? What else has died?

Notes

1. In her magnificent study on pregnancy loss in America, anthropologist Linda Layne writes, "Nearly all of the other infertile couples using my adoption agency had gotten a dog as an interim child" (2003, 252).
2. Anthropologist and doula Megan Davidson (2019, 15) defines a doula as a "professional birth support person who provides physical, emotional, and informational support throughout pregnancy, labor, birth, and the postpartum period."
3. I pumped for about three weeks and donated my milk to a friend who had a four-month-old baby and needed to augment her own supply.
4. The normal discharge from the uterus after childbirth.
5. Linda Layne has written extensively about this, both in *Motherhood Lost: A Feminist Account of Pregnancy Loss in America* (2003) and in numerous articles.
6. A hysterectomy is a surgical procedure that removes the uterus, making the possibility of a future pregnancy impossible. Hysterectomies are rarely done during labor and delivery, but at times they are necessary in order to save the life of the pregnant person.
7. I use the term *bodymind* following feminist disability studies scholars Margaret Price's (2015) and Sami Schalk's (2018) important contributions. In *Bodyminds Reimagined: (Dis)ability, Race, and Gender in Black Women's Speculative Fiction* (2018), Schalk writes, "Bodymind is a materialist feminist disability studies concept from Margaret Price that refers to the enmeshment of the mind and body, which are typically understood as interacting and connected, yet distinct entities due to the Cartesian dualism of Western philosophy. The term bodymind insists on the inextricability of mind and body and highlights how processes within our being impact one another in such a way that the notion of a physical versus mental process is difficult, if not impossible to discern in most cases" (5). In this chapter, I want to emphasize how the physiological processes of being pregnant and giving birth inextricably influence the experience of reproductive death.
8. I follow Faye Ginsburg's approach when it comes to terminology within such a polarized context. In her groundbreaking ethnography, *Contested Lives: The Abortion Debate in an American Community*, she writes, "I have made every effort to respect the integrity of both positions in the abortion debate, as I understand them. So for example, I refer to each group, as would any anthropologist, by the appellation its members prefer" (1998, xxxv).
9. Names have been changed.
10. In 1982, after receiving considerable pushback for their work and as a nod to

the feminist critique in particular, the book's title was changed to *Parent-Infant Bonding.*

11.   Jenna and Tom decided to name their baby.

12.   Most births in the United Kingdom are attended by nurse-midwives, in contrast to the obstetrician-dominated environment of the United States.

13.   See http://flexmort.com/cuddle-cots/. There are about ten stillborn babies born every day in England.

14.   The well-known personal health columnist for the *New York Times*, Jane Brody, reported on the CuddleCot, writing, "The device gives parents a chance to bond with their babies—to love and hold them, take pictures, even take them home and take them for walks, creating memories to last a lifetime" (2019). Interestingly, thirty-six years earlier, Brody wrote an article that reported on the criticism that Klaus and Kennell had received on their theories of bonding, writing, "The critics say that if early contact affects how well a mother cares for her baby, the effect is small and limited to some mothers under some circumstances" (1983).

In the *New Amsterdam* scene, which lasts about two minutes, the main character of the show, Dr. Max Goodwin, wheels the CuddleCot into a hospital room where a crying woman is curled up in bed. He says gently, "Gabby . . . Sophie is here. This is called a CuddleCot; it's a special bassinet that keeps stillborn babies cool so that they can stay with their parents a little longer . . . even after they are gone." The mother responds, "How can you . . . it's so . . . ." "Morbid?" The doctor offers, "These devices can give you something that nothing else can . . . time."

When it was time to push out my daughters, I remember that the obstetrician said to me, "You won't have to push for long since they are so small." However accurate this statement was at the time, it was eclipsed by its inane insensitivity. I did, in fact, feel incredible physical pain from the small but very hard heads making their way through my pelvis, but more importantly, I wished that I could have pushed indefinitely. Had they not emerged from my insides, they would not have died. Had they not died, who would I be now? After their breathing efforts subsided and they started to become increasingly cold, I was ready to say goodbye. Because they were born alive and warm, having just come out of my equally alive body, their subsequently cold bodies were a clear signal that they had gone somewhere else. Perhaps in the milk that I would eventually pump out of my body or maybe pieces of them microscopically nestled within my frontal lobe. The maternal bodymind does not cease to exist the moment a baby dies. In fact, in many ways it comes alive with unexplored power and potential.

Part II

Death Care

CHAPTER EIGHT

The Haptics of Grief
A Taxonomy of Touch in Death Care

MARGARET SCHWARTZ

Hail to the thumb, the useful thumb,
The grasper, the holder, the doer of deeds,
Where fingers are futile and tools succumb,
Stolid, ungainly, the thumb succeeds.

And hail to the men who are like the thumb;
Men who are never sung by a bard,
Men who are laboring, modestly dumb,
Faithfully doing the work that is hard
— From "The Thumb" by Amos Russel Wells

Clasping ours through life and death,
Lovingly to latest breath,
Sweetest thing that comforteth, —
A woman's hand.
— From "A Woman's Hand," by Amos Russel Wells

This chapter explores haptics of death in a technological age, how the hand is a mediating device organizing relations between the living and the dead. Specifically, I am interested in the different kinds of touches—instrumental and caring—that are involved in preparing a body for rituals of memorialization. I work from the premise that technological mediation is as inextricable as death from the human condition. In death care, the hand is an instrument of mediation, organizing a number of contingent relationships including, but not restricted to, those between loved ones and strangers, men and women, individuals and families, family units and institutions, public and private, contamination and purity, and authentic and inauthentic care or feeling.

Something akin to what Foucault (1978) called the repressive hypothesis is at work in mainstream understandings of Americans' relationship to death. The story goes that death was once incorporated into every aspect of daily life—literally incorporated; without any official training or authorization, people—usually women—held, washed, moved, watched over, and disposed of dead and dying bodies. Death was part of the family and the home, and mourning was a practiced art. As vaccination, antibiotics, and risk management made sudden and untimely death less frequent and less expected, this practice of mourning waned. With the rise of modern medicine and hygiene, as well as new disposal practices—principally embalming—death moved out of the home into hospitals, and disposal moved to funeral homes where trained professionals—usually men—were licensed and paid to manage the social experience of death. By the mid-1960s, this set of practices was so ingrained, and their alternatives so distant from living memory, that Jessica Mitford could call her critique of commercialization and disenchantment *The American Way of Death* ([1963] 2000), as if there no longer existed any other way.

There is a kind of nostalgia for an imagined past that takes hold when "death positives" and other advocates of home death practices decry the coldness of corpses prepared by (male) strangers in a laboratory and advocate for (female) death doulas to help the bereaved prepare the body at home. While this critique certainly carries an emotional truth for those who wield it, this taxonomy of the haptics of death care is designed to illustrate the rhetorical nature of such claims. After all, the embalmer is in close physical proximity to the body and must handle it with care. And the death doula is herself a paid professional, whose services are rendered in the context of a struggle for equal recognition and certification from the state regulatory bodies that at the moment privilege the embalmer and the funeral parlor. Attending to touch reorients the analysis, allowing a fuller recognition of diverse forms of death care.

As I have argued elsewhere, contemporary death culture as exemplified by embalming and photography has a strong visual bias; fidelity in the texture of the flesh, for example, or its internal composition, is willingly sacrificed to fidelity in the appearance of death as peaceful sleep (Schwartz 2015). The corpse must look like the person it was in life, even if it does not feel or smell like that person. But what laying on of hands occurs in embalming? What does the instrumentalized mediation of the hand do to construct the relationship between the embalmer and the body? More particularly, how is the touch involved in embalming managed so as to make something clinical and scientific that, under different circumstances, is read as intimate and caring? As we will see in an example below, the specter of necrophilia always haunts the embalmer's laboratory.

Exploring the rhetorical differences in death care, then, I turn to movements that see themselves resisting dominant practices of death care. These movements, as read from their promotional literature, cast their brand of touch as antithetical to what happens with embalming and corporate funeral homes. How does the construction of touch as care in these movements work to reorganize the relationship to the body and to perceived dominant death culture?

To engage touch and the human hand in practices of death is to unpack cultural investments in "true" intimacy, "proper" mourning, and "real" connection. In her work on grief and social value, Judith Butler points toward the stakes in denaturalizing such investments. To this I would add that not only does there exist a hierarchy of lives worth mourning, but also a hierarchy of how to do the work of death care. Those who are considered not worth grieving are also not granted proper access to what are understood as proper or authentic modes of death care. The privilege of demanding a mode of death care that feels personally authentic and meaningful is unequally distributed. According to reports of those present at the scene, the body of Michael Brown, for example, lay on the street for hours, even as his mother fought with authorities to be allowed access to the body (Hunn and Bell 2014). As I have argued elsewhere, the right to mourn privately is often denied the victims of police shootings, who must witness footage of their loved one's death streamed and broadcast endlessly throughout the news cycle (Schwartz 2016). Putting these examples next to the people who hire a death doula to help them achieve a more authentic relationship to death and care for the dead body illustrates the enormous inequalities inscribed via the hand on the bodies of the dead.

Although touch is complex and not at all a synonym for care, it is my hope that this conscious pivot from the eye to the hand may offer different knowledges, intimacies, and values. My book *Dead Matter* (2015) argues that contemporary death cultures, particularly those involving public figures, are biased toward the visual. *Dead Matter* traces the emergence of embalming out of the practice of funeral photography and illustrates how significant and sometimes violent alterations to the substance of the flesh were tolerated so long as they served to create the appearance of death as peaceful sleep. Likeness thus took precedence over substance, and while those terms carry a particular moral weight, any such emphasis on them here is merely a reflection of the way these practices have come under criticism from people who claim that the dominant American way of death is crass, lacking in substance, and materialistic. The haptics of death, then, are a conscious pivot away from the dominant approach to death cultures, and a careful attending to *all* modes of touch involved in death care, including those that some might consider cold, medical, or opportunistic. Moreover, the hand as device denaturalizes the distinction between the technological and the natural, a binary often deployed in contemporary death cultures to hierarchize modes of death care.

Contemporary death cultures are plural, but each one stages a particular relationship between death, media, and technology. Media are not only extensions of the human body (McLuhan 1964) or manipulations of space and time (Krämer 2006). They are also, as Amanda Lagerkvist (2016) writes, existential— they bring up essential questions about what it means to be human, thrown into a particular place and time and with a particular set of tools. Just as embalming was a technological advance that supplemented and eventually supplanted postmortem photography (Schwartz 2015), so digital archival technologies capable of storing and circulating indexical traces of the deceased have shifted the experience of mourning and remembrance. These kinds of shifts can invoke nostalgia for an imagined premodern relationship to technology; this nostalgia, in turn, is constructed around practices that variously reject or reinscribe media practices of remembrance. Dana Luciano (2007) describes how the nineteenth-century middle class shifted its mourning practices in response to the changes wrought by modernity, industrialization, and the rise of electronic media. The media of our present moment lean heavily on the image to express and manage ideas about the human, about memory and loss. These practices have in turn given rise to counternarratives that raise questions about the limits of the image to do all that existential work.

Technology's role in practices of mourning and disposal is sometimes construed as antithetical to so-called healthy mourning, defined by Freud as a kind of acceptance or reintegration of the fact of death into the grieving psyche. For example, Ernest Becker's *The Denial of Death* (2007) associated modernity with a distancing from the physical reality of the body's limitations by posing the question of technology in relation to human finitude. While this is also what is happening in Heidegger's "Question Concerning Technology" (1981) (and in his phenomenology overall, where death forms the "horizon" that makes meaning possible), it was Becker who psychologized the argument, asserting that technology use itself is a social practice for denying death. Becker makes media into techniques of oblivion, refusal, and repression. Peruse the cultural iconography of any gone-too-soon screen icon—Marilyn Monroe and James Dean spring to mind—and it is easy to see why this was a tempting analysis. Archival media make possible an unconscious belief that the iconic do not die but pass fully fleshed into a technological eternity. But do they work the same way on all bodies? Do archival videos or sound recordings of the ordinary dead allow us to believe that they have not left us? I am inclined to think not, for unlike public people who were only ever present in mediated form, these departed bodies mark the lived present with their absence, an absence if anything made more palpable by their resuscitated images.

But if technology does not defy death or soothe mourning, that does not make its use irrelevant or even harmful in everyday, private practices of grief. If to be human is to be technological, as Marcel O'Gorman and other posthumanist philosophers have argued, then use of technology in and around death and mourning is a direct encounter with that finitude. O'Gorman (2015) actually seeks to reintegrate Becker into media philosophy by prescribing a kind of therapeutic use of technology, one that engages with the materiality of the technological object and by extension with the finitude of all bodies. While I prefer a language of engagement and praxis to the therapeutic deployment of technology, I do follow O'Gorman in his considered refusal to separate the technological from the human, whether epistemologically or existentially.

Hence the turn to the hand both as a moment of human contact and as a mediating apparatus or device. Analyzing touch in death care is a way to open up to a larger, more interdisciplinary notion of mediation. This chapter turns to the encounter between the living and the dead in terms of its material and symbolic actions. How does materiality function in the deeply symbolic process of preparing a body for disposal? Such practices of care for the dead body are also sites where the material and the symbolic intertwine. Touch is both tactile and meaningful, its registers modulated by cultural understandings of appropriate boundaries, contamination, and purity. Working in touch, itself both tactile and symbolic, on that most meaningful of material objects, the corpse, offers an apprehension of fundamental interdetermination of the textual and the material (Coole and Frost 2010, 3).

Touch has also become a vexed site under the conditions of contagion in the

COVID-19 pandemic. Deaths that might otherwise occur surrounded by loved ones instead happen in the isolation of a quarantined ward. Families who might otherwise have opted for a more hands-on approach to preparing the corpse for burial may have seen those plans thwarted by new protocols to contain contagion. The sheer number of deaths meant that careful care for the corpse was a luxury that death-care and health-care workers could not afford. Corpses awaited preparation in refrigerated trucks because of storage overflow (Hicks 2020), people died at home alone and were buried before their bodies could be claimed (Giuffrida 2020), and families gathered to mourn via Zoom (Ohlheiser 2020). These disruptions are happening in the context of changing practices around death. The home death movement has moved the conversation around care of the corpse away from the hygiene-focused, scientific/rational model where that work was done by professionals—board certified, and usually male. The return of traditional models of family preparation offers a feminist/female-centered practice of care for the dead body that elides historical women's work with less-excavated articulations between women's bodies, loving care, and social reproduction. The COVID-19 pandemic has brought a high death rate (especially in certain demographics) along with an insistence on a medicalized, sterile, and often remote set of practices around care for the dead (Parveen 2020).

The stakes, therefore, of these changing narratives about care for the dead take on new urgency—who should do it, what counts as care and what is only medical processing, and how the hand as a mediation literally articulates those values.

In what follows, I will explore embalming and the home death movement from this perspective. I think of it as a kind of taxonomy: the different interventions of the hand, of touch of the hand, in care for the dead body. I start with some descriptions of the care of the corpse of Eva Perón to set the scene for how the hand articulates values about appropriate care for the body. I then move on to embalming more generally and end with the home death movement.

Dressing the Corpse's Hair

In the early 1970s, when the deposed dictator Juan Perón saw an opportunity to return to Argentina, he knew he could not do it without his wife, Evita. In Peronism's complex iconography, Evita was the "bridge of love" connecting Perón to his working-class base. However vulgar this bridge—born of Evita's radio celebrity in an emergent mass media—it was also material. I do not only mean the grain of her voice, the traces of embodiment engraved on an analog medium (Barthes 2009). I mean also that her body was a literal emblem of the Peronist redemption of the working class. Evita's body bore the mark of illegitimacy; a nameless child, her parents never married. Perón gave her his name and by extension legitimized all those she represented. For six brilliant years, Argentina lived a national passion play as Evita's ardent Peronism became a national exemplar. She then became its first martyr, as she succumbed to uterine cancer with all the pageantry of a secular saint.

A return to power, then, was unthinkable without his most powerful symbol of its popular roots. But every Argentine who had lived through the spectacle of her death knew that she had also been specially embalmed for a public monument whose construction had been halted by Perón's overthrow and exile. A generation of young militants, who had been children during his first presidency and had grown up with Evita's hagiography, opened the way for Perón's return. The return of her corpse, which had been missing for nearly twenty years, was an explicit part of their demands.

The corpse was exhumed and brought to Perón's home in Spain. There, with the help of a Rasputin-like figure named José López Rega, Perón and his third wife, Isabel, conducted a séance. López Rega instructed Isabel to lie on the coffin so she could receive Evita's spirit, transforming her into the second coming of the Bridge of Love.

My favorite part of this scene is a detail I found in only one source. Evita's signature feature was her long hair, dyed blonde and worn in a tight chignon. The years underground had left her corpse's hair damp and disarrayed, rusted hairpins staining the blonde coils. Maryssa Navarro writes that before the séance, Isabel herself dressed the corpse's hair (Navarro and Fraser 1996). I imagine her shaking fingers gently, gingerly combing and twisting and smoothing. When the corpse was eventually brought back to Argentina for burial, it was restored by professional embalmers. In photographs taken of the restoration process, it is clearly evident that they have replaced her natural hair; spread out on the embalmer's table, it glows a garish yellow with a plasticky smooth texture, like a doll's hair. I like to imagine that Isabel was combing the original hair, terrified lest it pull away from the head.

This possibly apocryphal detail strikes me as far more intimate than the business of lying on the coffin. It is intimate not only with the body but with its postmortem vulnerabilities—rust stains and soil and decay. She would have had to work delicately, slowly, gently. Yet Isabel and Evita were not intimates. The relation between Isabel and the corpse was one crafted from the social position of wife, the metaphorical connection that the séance was designed to cement.[1] Yet it was the hand, in this case, that mediated between their strangeness and their intimacy.

When leaders are embalmed for public display, usually a secular hagiography is at stake. Like Lenin, Eva Perón, too, was embalmed in a society with deep Christian roots that had, at least during the era in question, put them aside in favor of a secular cult of personality. Isabel—a tragic figure in Argentine history, both laughable and cruel—may have relied on the medium López Rega, but her hands also mediated the transfer of power. She was neither embalmer nor bereaved; she had never met Evita, nor does history give any record of how she may have felt about her predecessor. I cannot help but imagine that the feelings were complicated. What does the horror and fascination of this scene stem from? Is it the juxtaposition, in death, of physical intimacy and temporal/relational distance? And yet there are all manner of proximities and distances—in short, mediations in flux—involved in the haptics of death care.

On the other end of the spectrum of mediations we have Pedro Ara, the Galician scientist and master embalmer who prepared Eva Perón's body for public display. His relationship to the corpse surely involved all manner of technical intimacies in the sense that he had to touch the body in multiple ways over the span of the two-year period he had to complete his work. Yet his role, unlike Isabel's, was professional, not familial, gendered masculine, not feminine. His hands are the gloved hands of the scientist, his touch the impartial, steady pressure of procedural ease.

These two figures, Isabel and Ara, anchor this partial taxonomy of the haptics of death care. As we will see, Isabel, with her (imagined) reverence and delicacy, occupies the space where the home death movement hopes to intervene in a space dominated by figures akin to Pedro Ara: men of science whose hands mediate between the body and the state without involving the bereaved at all. At stake, I argue, is the question of whose hands are a proper device for the transformation that occurs when a corpse becomes a memory, a legacy, or a bereavement. What is the proper means by which this should occur, and who has the right to decide it? When Michael Brown's body lay in the street, his mother was not allowed to handle it, because it now belonged to the state, to law enforcement, to the courts and evidence. It was the autopsy and the forensics that would decide how to remember him, as martyr or victim or thug. That this distancing had to be achieved through violent means—reports have the police holding her back (Hunn and Bell 2014)—indicates the incredible pressure placed on death care, both emotionally and culturally.

Defining Touch

To what, exactly, does touch refer in this taxonomy of the haptics of death? Classification is by necessity violent in the sense of a strategic cut, an organizing principle. The *Oxford English Dictionary* lists at least seven definitions of *touch* as a verb, only some of which involve intentional contact between human hands or bodies. Touch may also involve ingestion, proximity, reach, or influence, all of which are metaphorically linked to the notion of intentional bodily contact but not identical to it. Nonhuman surfaces, territories, or substances may touch.

I have suggested that the hand works in death care as a device mediating between corpses, gendered bodies, and social/textual/symbolic meaning. Therefore, my taxonomy will be restricted to one species of touch: intentional contact with the human hand. Importantly, there is no requirement that this touch signify as caring or loving. Rather, I am interested in the moments where hands work on corpses in the process of preparation for disposal and how that work also constructs a relationship between the corpse, the memory of the deceased, and the larger social framework in which that memory will live on. As the other chapters in this volume show, these processes are as varied as contemporary American death cultures.

Intentional touch also highlights the instrumentality of the hand in media cultures. Human interaction with information technology is almost always manual, even if other senses, such as vision or hearing, are crucial to the interaction as well. Moreover, the analysis of "screen cultures" seldom emphasizes the tactile relationship between human body and device, network, or infrastructure. Deployment of electric devices at the touch of a button has indexed fantasies of human control over the elements since the nineteenth century (Plotnick 2015). How, then, do these manual commands, now so deeply ingrained in everyday American life, appear in the context of an existential crisis like death? How do they inform ongoing practices of memorialization and grief? Perhaps the death-positive critiques are in some ways a critique of death at the touch of a button, whether that be the crematorium or the phone. If these positions tend toward the Luddite, they are often not incompatible with certain forms of push-button interaction, specifically online spaces. Looking at the hand as an instrument of tactile interaction with other bodies allows for a demystification of the oft-romanticized laying on of hands. The hand is neither a guarantee of physical immediacy nor a barrier to it. It is simply an embodied mediating unit—the source, indeed, of the digital (Peters 2016)—in a social world that is always and already mediated.

Where is the hand, and what are its practices, both in modern embalming and in one of its alternative cultures, the home death movement? For the discussion of embalming, I will return to the example of Eva Perón. We have a detailed account of the process from her embalmer, Pedro Ara, which replicates the kinds of naturalized assumptions about the role of the embalmer that the home death movement explicitly critiques.

Embalming

Embalming and the corpse preparation undertaken in a funeral home surely involve hands intentionally touching the corpse. Embalmers must by law wear latex gloves, so this is not a skin-to-skin handling of the corpse. Some of the touch is recognizable as care that one might take with an ailing body, washing and cleaning the body, applying makeup, dressing the hair and body, trimming nails, and so on. Other kinds of touch are invasive; embalmers make an incision in the body, usually near the groin, so as to introduce embalming fluid into the circulatory system. Here, touch is mediated by a simple machine (a pump) and by the infrastructure of the body itself. The effect of this touch is dramatic at a cellular level and at the level of touch and feel. As Angus Whyte (2013, 35) describes, the tissues change in a way akin to how an egg white goes from clear, liquid, and slippery to white, solid, and firm when it is boiled. This kind of dramatic change is not available to the eye, but it is to the hand or even the microscope; the dramatic change in tissues supports the creation of death as an image of the deceased in the medium of the corpse's flesh, even if (as I have written about my own experience in the preface to *Dead Matter*) the results may appear uncanny or ghastly to the bereaved.

There is no requirement in this scenario, however, for emotional attachment or non-instrumental intimacy. As Aulino (2016) writes of long-term care in Thailand, even those with an intimate family relationship to the person for whom they are caring may routinize, instrumentalize, and otherwise make impersonal and automatic the care that they give. It is worth noting, however, that morticians may be community members of long standing whose families have served in that capacity for generations. John Troyer, who now heads the Center for Death and Society at the University of Bath, comes from a family of morticians, as does Philip Olson in this volume. Family funeral parlors would then have prepared the bodies of people who were their friends and neighbors. There is a long history of segregation in the business of death, so that Black morticians often served only their communities, thus reducing (if not eliminating) the chance that the deceased would be a total stranger to the embalmer (see Howie, this volume). Religion would also make a similarly narrowed field of customers. This business model is changing, however. Large corporations like Service Corp. International or Carriage Services have been buying family owned funeral homes since the 1980s, making them into chain organizations that, in the words of one mortician, aim to make their establishments feel "like a Starbucks" (see Dawdy, this volume; McIntyre 2011). Thus the preparation for disposal here, while still involving the same kinds of contact between gloved hands and dead body, would reflect a different social relationship between the deceased, the bereaved, and the person doing the preparation.

The case of Evita Perón offers an entire volume of information about the relationship between the embalmer and the corpse. The Spanish (Galician) master embalmer Pedro Ara spent two years preparing the corpse for public display and recorded his process, experiences, and the details of the corpse's eventual seizure by the Argentine military. The resulting book is called *Eva Perón: La verdadera historia contada por el médico que preservó su cuerpo* (Eva Perón: The true story as told by the doctor who preserved her body) (Ara 1996). Ara writes, "My story will be as objective and direct as humanly possible, with no other limits than those imposed by respect for the persons and feelings involved, and those imposed by prudence" (35; all translations are my own). Ara's entire account is written in this almost comically solemn register, where references to destiny and Nietzsche mix with vehement accusations of slander and lamentations for the sufferings of Evita. Evidently because of his self-imposed limits of respect and prudence, descriptions of the actual physical process of embalming are written with clinical distance, in the passive voice, with little account of the actual manipulations of the body. In fact, he spends more time countering false accounts of his involvement; for example, he cites a *Time* magazine article from 1955 that alleged that Ara was at Eva's deathbed to make sure she was given no drugs that would affect the embalming, saying that this "false and grotesque" account was given by "some reptile seeking to either trick or extort the journalist" (67). What descriptions there are take place in the context of expositional dialogue, so the reader is never left alone, as it were, with Ara and the body. For example: General Perón asks about a particular ingredient or procedure, and Ara answers with a layperson's explanation. But these exchanges are very few, and most are limited to the hours immediately following Evita's death. Arrangements of the hair and nails are also undertaken at that time by Eva's maid, not the doctor/scientist. The embalmer's art, he writes, is not aesthetic but documentary. Once the maid finishes, General Perón tells Ara that he wants no spectacle of the embalming, that neither he himself nor any other member of the family will disturb his work until it is completed in time for the body to be viewed by the public. In the chronicle, the reader is herself escorted from the room and allowed to visit Ara only in his study as he reflects upon the process of the work and the events taking place politically outside his laboratory. Thus the black box of embalming is left intact, and the work of the doctors' hands is shrouded in the veils of respect and prudence.

Although somewhat exaggerated by the high drama of the situation, Ara's attitude is in some ways exemplary of embalmers as a profession. Embalmers are supposed to be discreet, scientifically detached clinicians. They operate in laboratories, with instruments; they use mechanical pumps to introduce chemical solutions that only they are licensed to possess and deploy. The assumption is, even in the "Starbucks" model, that the bereaved do not want to see into the black box, that what is happening there is unthinkable. And yet from a practical, material perspective, it is incredibly intimate in the sense that bodies are unclothed, they are open in the vulnerability of death to surgical penetration. And because the hands to which they are vulnerable are not those of the bereaved, their distance must be maintained.

I have mentioned that Pedro Ara anxiously answers his critics in his chronicle of Evita's embalming. This is because in the folklore of her death, Ara is often depicted as violating these professional distances; he is covetous, obsessed, enamored. In Rodolfo Walsh's 1966 short story about the theft of the corpse, "Esa mujer," the nameless colonel rages against Ara, explaining why he had to take the body away: "That disgusting Galician . . . he was pawing her tits!" Fears about the contagion of death here meld with the uncertain gendering of both the powerful Eva ("I buried her standing, because she had balls!" howls the colonel in "Esa mujer") and the fussy doctor, the caretaker of the body. In the handling of corpses, bodies must have firm boundaries; touch must be caring but not covetous, intimate but not sensual.

As the rumors of Ara's necrophilia show, these boundaries must be continuously maintained against the danger of too much intimacy. However, the home death movement takes the opposite tactic, rhetorically positioning itself as an appropriately intimate form of death care in which touch is always equivalent to emotional connection.

The Home Death Movement and End-of-Life Doulas

The home death movement, discussed at more length in chapter 10 of this volume, positions itself as a critique of contemporary funeral industry practices. Proponents, who sometimes refer to themselves as death doulas or midwives, are employed to help educate families on what might be possible for them to undertake on their own, separate from state or corporate involvement, with regard to the preparation and disposal of a loved one. As state and local laws vary with regard to these practices, one of the death doula's biggest jobs is to help families navigate these different options. The documentary film *A Family Undertaking* (Westrate 2003) is a snapshot of the range of practices that the bereaved may employ; some simply prepare and dress the body themselves before transporting it to a crematorium or other disposal method, while other families built the coffin themselves and buried the body on their own land. The rhetoric of this growing movement is to wrestle away from a disenchanted world the sacred duty of caring for the dead.

End-of-life doulas see themselves as providing ethical, holistic, nonmedical care and comfort to the family and to the dying person. Because they are not medical providers or providers of hospice/palliative care, their area of expertise is precisely emotional support and guidance. This is not the only thing end-of-life doulas do, however. According to the National End-of-Life Doula Alliance (NEDA), they also provide information. The NEDA mission statement stresses that this information should be provided neutrally, that is, without judgment or preference. Much as birth doulas often describe their services as offering agency within the medicalization of childbirth, end-of-life doulas offer the bereaved information to facilitate an empowered encounter with the funeral establishment. And as with birth doulas, there is a tension between their implied critique of the industry and regulations and the recognition and equal status that they seek from it. The NEDA webpage explicitly states that it seeks equal status for its members alongside medical end-of-life care providers. At the same time, the notion that there is a need for the end-of-life doula's services implies that the traditional providers are lacking, specifically in the kind of compassionate care that, in NEDA's (2019) words, empowers families to demand from an uncaring industry a meaningful and individually tailored funeral experience.

As the name suggests, end-of-life doulas are often female, and the home-funeral and death-positive movement levies a warranted critique of the funeral industry that its providers are overwhelmingly male, a shift from centuries of death work done by women. The rhetoric of this kind of death-care service, therefore, might be characterized as essentialist-feminist, a return to the traditional women's role of caretaker. The poem "A Woman's Hand" quoted at the opening of this chapter illustrates how "women's work" is articulated via the hand to the care of the dying. A closer look at the specific touch provided by an end-of-life doula illustrates how the discursive elements—the rhetoric—of this kind of care shift the meaning of the touch without making radical changes in kind. The end-of-life doula may do washing and arranging of the body much as an embalmer would do, or she may help the family do this work. For the doula, handling the corpse would be structured by the regulations of her industry, which may require the use of latex gloves and would prohibit the kind of invasive techniques used by embalmers. Nevertheless, her *rhetorical* positioning is that her hands, even if they are sheathed in latex and are paid to be there, are the hands of a loving caregiver, an ally, or even a friend.

Family members' touch would be structured by a different set of regulations, such as religious observance. In Orthodox and Hasidic Jewish communities, for example, a society called the Chevra Kadisha (literally, "sacred society") does work that one might associate with a death doula—watching over the body of the deceased before internment, cleaning the body and dressing it in the prescribed funeral garments, and even providing assistance in preventing secular practices that are forbidden in this community, like autopsy and cremation. Family members do not perform these duties, as they are considered too painful for the mourners. As these communities are strictly observant of the Jewish law that no material gain may be taken from the dead, there is a sense that preparation and internment are community responsibilities and should not be done for hire (Vaad Harabonim of Queens 2020). According to a handbook for Chevra Kadisha, women may prepare men's bodies if there is no suitable (i.e., Jewish) man available, but it makes no mention of men preparing women's bodies (Kavod v'Nichum and Gamliel Institute 2020a). Presumably, there is always a Jewish woman on hand willing to undertake the work of death care.

The tradition of Chevra Kadisha is just an example of how highly observant religious communities' funerary practices may well mimic what the death doula is trying to do in a secular context (for more on secular funerals, see chapter 5 in this volume). Religious observance may share with the death doula, then, a certain disdain for modern disposal methods, particularly their invasiveness, their association with monetary gain, and their medicalization. The difference is thus not so much what the hand does but how the hand mediates between the corpse and the bereaved and the social memory for which it is being prepared. The actual touching would not be much different from what a mortician would do, again exempting the actual embalming. Hands would gently move limbs; force might need to be exerted when limbs have stiffened. Hands would lift and move bodies and smooth facial features, wash and dress bodies. And indeed, while the Chevra Kadisha is a volunteer society, the information I found about existing societies included a list of for-profit Jewish funeral homes with which they worked. Similarly, the death doula charges for her services. But their touch is rhetorically constructed as a metonym for community, as a kind of unpaid social reproduction or a service of the heart. The hand, here, becomes the mediating device for these rhetorical constructions: a hand that is properly Jewish, a hand that is gendered female, a hand washing with water, not with funerary detergents.

The difference, then, comes not from the actual touch, but from the discursive and cultural context in which it occurs. Cleaning the body, for example, might be done by a mortician on a metal table, with hoses and detergents not available in the average home, where cleaning the body would likely be done with hand soap and water, a washcloth, and perhaps a plastic sheet to keep the bed or floor from getting too wet. As I mentioned at the beginning of this chapter, touch could refer to the contact between the body and these cleaning agents or between the body and the object upon which it lies. In this chapter, however, I am talking about the intentional touch of hands. And in this case, the actual actions of the hands are not materially different except in the case of the practice (embalming) that is restricted legally to those who are licensed to perform it.

Therefore, an attention to touch in this instance highlights the rhetoric that gives it meaning. End-of-life doulas frame their touches as "ethical, compassionate and holistic" in implied contrast to the touches given by morticians and others in the funeral and medical establishment. They imply that something is missing in the touch of these others, something that their presence alone can adequately supply. Nevertheless, the end-of-life doula is not in most cases a family member, nor, in contrast to the Chevra Kadisha, is she someone who offers her services for free. Her compassion is purchased. While monetary exchange in emotional relations is deeply engrained in the American economy, there is still a long-standing cultural association between money and emotional coldness, impersonality, and greed (Zelizer 2009). End-of-life doulas walk the same fine line that other care workers must walk between a paid service and an implied critique of the industry that demands that service be paid for. Their professional rhetoric demands equity with others in the industry because, they claim, ethical and compassionate care is a service not currently offered by that industry but desperately needed. Their hands thus move in a discursive situation wherein care is equated with compassion and emotional intimacy, with gentleness and love.

Conclusion

In this preliminary taxonomic examination of the different kinds of touch present in contemporary death care, I have argued that touch structures relations of kinship, community, privacy, and gender. In this sense, the hand is the mediating device articulating the corpse to its proper gender, its proper memory, its religious community, its family, and its place with regard to public and private concerns like hygiene and contagion. I identified two broad categories of touch, instrumental and caring, and showed how the values articulated to each worked to organize ideas about proper death care within different communities.

The poems I used as an epigraph illustrate neatly how the hand articulates gender to the social via different kinds of work. "The Thumb" celebrates the instrumental work of the male hand and the unsung but vital touch of dutiful labor. "A Woman's Hand," by contrast, is what holds us through life and death, "lovingly to the last breath." My work in this chapter has been to denaturalize these articulations by showing them at work in contemporary death cultures.

The COVID-19 crisis and the racial uprising in its wake put touch in death care into high relief. Bodies killed by police or in a crime are not the property of the bereaved until they have been released after investigation. When the killer is also the state apparatus charged with investigating the death, there is a cognitive dissonance that cries out for the body to be returned to kinder hands, to the hands, for example, of a mother who would care for the body as the state seems so evidently not to.

In the pandemic, the high death rate combined with quarantine protocols and a shortage of health-care and professional death-care workers meant that hands-on care of the dead, particularly for nonprofessionals, was nearly impossible. In a crisis where care work has become visible in its breakdown, death care of all kinds also becomes visible through its loss.

A larger, more theoretical aim has been to shift discussions of death care away from the visual and toward a material, haptic interaction between the corpse and those who are caring for it. In so doing, I hoped to break down some of the normative ideas around gender and care that are so neatly illustrated in Wells's poems. Hence, a taxonomy of the hand, understood as a mediating device between the ritual object of the corpse and the society from which it is being separated, would foreground the role of touch and care in these vital processes.

Note

1. Politically, this connection was made explicit when Perón successfully regained the presidency and named Isabel his vice president. Twenty years earlier, Evita's bid for the vice presidency had been thwarted by her cancer. Isabel would fill the role of which death had robbed her predecessor. Isabel—or Isabelita as she was styled to echo the diminutive Evita—would find herself president after Perón died, only months after his return to Argentina. A young woman whose only previous job experience was as a cabaret dancer, she was no match for the military junta that ousted her, inaugurating a decade of state terror.

CHAPTER NINE

The Embalmer's Magic

SHANNON LEE DAWDY

Uncanny Introductions

I first met Wilson (not his real name) at the National Funeral Directors Association meeting in Indianapolis in 2015.[1] Although in his early thirties, he was already well regarded by his colleagues as a senior spokesperson for the industry. He was thinking ahead but not rocking the boat. As my collaborator and I set up to talk to him in front of a one-hundred-year-old hearse that had been installed in the convention center lobby as an exhibit piece (and which, in its white and gold cheerfulness, looked more like a fancy ice cream truck), many of the people streaming by stopped to greet him and exchange chitchat.

Upon meeting Wilson, I was immediately struck by his appearance—he is handsome, with curvy cheekbones and a conventionally well-proportioned body and face. Almost too handsome. Like an actor who could play Dorian Gray. He was dressed impeccably in a blue-gray suit, obviously tailored for him (Italian, if I had to guess), complete with cufflinks, an expensive-looking watch, and well-polished classic men's dress shoes (again, my guess was Italian). His skin was very pale (I accidentally typed "blue" at first), and he had dimples. His eyes were large and intense, and they matched his tie, also blue. But most unsettling to me, for some reason, was his hair, which was slicked back with a heavy pomade. He looked to be a person of uncertain vintage in both body and dress. He could have been a friend of the Great Gatsby. Or he could have just stepped out of *GQ* magazine into the reality of a death convention. I was mesmerized by his appearance but also a bit repulsed for reasons that weren't immediately clear to me. This is totally unfair to him, but I share my reaction here as an ethnographic confession. Later, I realized that my reaction to his personal presentation went to the heart of what I want to tackle here. I need to unpack my feelings, as well as an institutional history that led to that moment.

Wilson is a fourth-generation funeral director from the southern United States. He talks about current changes that "the industry," as he calls it, is experiencing. Despite his conservative style, he generally embraces these, which include the relaxation of formality and a growing demand for personalization and attention to the uniqueness of the individual who has died. He talks a lot about ritual. But he also says that because Americans are becoming less ritualistic in their daily lives, we are at risk of losing something, particularly when it comes to rituals around death. He doesn't mind if the rituals change or become more humanist (i.e., not religious), but he does not want them to go away. He then credits Abraham Lincoln with the line, "You can measure the moral fabric of a society by how they treat their dead" (interview transcript, et passim). Later on, I tried to verify this quote and couldn't find it. It seems to be a mashup of sentiments Lincoln expressed in his Gettysburg Address and a line from Sir William Ewart Gladstone, an English prime minister born the same year as Lincoln. It is not fake history exactly. It is truth-like in that it expresses well enough the earnest message that Wilson wanted to get across, as well as my own anthropological proposition—that how Americans are now treating the dead is an index of larger cultural tides.

After we talked for a while about how the business is changing, about how it needs to become more like Starbucks, or luxury hotels, I asked Wilson what has become a standard question in my interviews with death professionals and people on the street: Had he given any thought to his own arrangements? Wilson lit up with a smile. He was happy that I'd asked: "I *have* thought about what kind of service I want to have and what my funeral looks like—I would like to be embalmed and viewed." At that point, I realized that what was making me so uneasy about his appearance was that he looked like someone who had just emerged from the embalming room. And I don't mean the embalmer.

So many writers both before and after Freud ([1899] 2003) have characterized the human corpse as an uncanny object that this status is often assumed to be a cultural universal. That assumption should be debated. But what I puzzle over here is why Americans, despite the religious and ethnic diversity of an immigrant nation, so thoroughly (with the notable exceptions of Orthodox Jews, Muslims, and some Asian immigrants) embraced the embalmed corpse in the twentieth century. Internationally, it stands out as another kind of American exceptionalism. Or, if you find the embalmed body uncanny, a kind of

American peculiarism. By 1960, an estimated 95 percent of the American dead were embalmed. In the United Kingdom, Europe, and Latin America, embalming was by and large reserved for public figures lying in state, a small number of elites who could afford to emulate kings, for medical dissection, and occasionally on those bodies that needed to be transported over long distances. Embalming came only very recently to Africa and Asia, although in the last two decades, it has started to pick up speed for quite different cultural reasons (Lee 2011; Peck and Bryant 2009, 404; Walsh 2017; Liu, this volume).

Foreign observers have been commenting on the strangeness of American death for some time. From Evelyn Waugh in *The Loved One* (1948) to Jessica Mitford's ([1963] 2000) well-known critique *The American Way of Death*, to Philippe Ariès's more scholarly reflections on the American way of death (1974), writers have paused on the peculiarity of the US case. While Mitford and Ariès read the ritual as an extreme modernist taboo that denies death and bans mourning, Waugh recognized that the American funerary complex revolved around the embalmed body in a way that could also be understood as quite attentive, if not obsessed (see also Gorer 1955a; Jackson 1977).

It has become a kind of orthodoxy in the death industry, and in many scholarly publications, to point to the catastrophic losses of the American Civil War and the spectacle of President Lincoln's embalmed body as a turning point in American death (Farrell 1980; Faust 2009; Laderman 1996; Laqueur 2015). Yet across the Atlantic, embalming never became the solution to large numbers of war dead lost abroad, much less spread like wildfire to the civilian population as it did in the United States after 1880. The US pattern is extraordinary for the twentieth century, and it persisted well beyond the conditions that might have birthed it. I am convinced that rather than just being a contingency of the Civil War or a con job of unethical salesmen, embalming must *mean* something. It must *do* something. I will argue that the embalmed body in the United States was the result of mystery-making by a class of neo-Egyptian magicians who met a historically rooted American need to visualize and commune with the dead. That sounds pretty out there. But if I am successful, at the end of this chapter the reader will understand how I got there.

The popularity of viewing and embalming in the United States is now rapidly declining among white Americans, giving way to cremation with or without a public ceremony (for reasons that are not yet clear, the "traditional" American funeral remains more popular in Latinx and Black communities; see Howie, this volume). Although this shift is often couched as an economic or pseudo-environmental concern with bodies taking up "too much space," the fact is that the embalmer's magic is no longer working for many Americans. The embalmed corpse has become uncanny rather than comforting (Dawdy 2019; forthcoming). But before we can understand why it is changing and how funeral professionals are responding, we need to understand how widespread embalming came to be embraced in the first place. This chapter is about that history, reinterpreted through the anthropologist's eye for ritual meaning.

The Historical Object

Sources on American death practices cohere around several important points. The first is an agreement about what the traditional American funeral entails. The mortuary staff pick up the body from the place of death (these days usually a hospital or nursing home) and transport it to their facility where it is washed, embalmed, "restored" with fillers and cosmetics, dressed, and placed in a hinged-lid casket made of metal or wood and lined with satin or other soft material. The lid is usually split so that the top half can be opened by itself for viewing of the face and torso. This assemblage of objects is the centerpiece of a ritual of viewing before, during, and/or after a service, which can take place in either the funeral home or a place of worship. After the ceremony, the body and casket are transported to a cemetery where they are deposited in a cement-lined vault. A newer practice follows this sequence up through the end of the ceremony, upon which the embalmed body and sometimes the viewing casket are incinerated in a crematory retort (alternatively, viewing caskets can now be rented).

Historians agree that this practice in the United States developed between the Civil War (1861–1865) and the end of World War I, by which time it had become so commercialized and standardized that it became the target of criticism (Farrell 1980; Laderman 1996). Nevertheless, from 1920 to 1980, embalming and conformity to this "traditional" American ritual were near total. After Mitford's influential exposé ([1963] 2000), cremation rates started to climb. Still, nearly 40 percent of Americans today opt for embalming, far above international rates (NFDA 2018). As I will relate toward the end of this chapter, rather than watch their art die away, innovative funeral directors are changing the face of embalming to respond to shifting attitudes toward the afterlife and what the living want from memorial events. What remain the same in these practices are a desire to interact with the dead, the centrality of the body, and the magical role of the embalmer.

Although the recipe has changed over time, modern arterial embalming goes back to late eighteenth- and early nineteenth-century European experiments to preserve specimens for medical dissection. Body fluids are replaced with chemical preservatives via a pump that circulates through the arterial system (Chiapelli 2008; Peck and Bryant 2009, 404–6). A widespread misconception exists in the United States that embalming is practiced as a form of postmortem sanitation. Corpses smell bad, but so long as they are not leaking into drinking water, they usually pose few health risks to the living. In fact, opening up the corpse and draining its fluids presents more of a hazard from contagious disease than natural putrefaction, a point brought tragically home by urgent calls for PPE (personal protective equipment) for funeral directors and guidelines issued by the National Funeral Directors Association (NFDA) to help embalmers prevent exhalation of COVID-19 spray from dead lungs (NFDA, n.d.). The NFDA went against the World Health Organization's recommendation that the practice be avoided during the pandemic. The United States, as ever, decided to go its own way. That said, the preservative effects of embalming did serve a practical purpose during peak outbreaks when funeral homes were overwhelmed, allowing mortuary workers to store dozens of embalmed bodies for a few days at a time in chapels cooled by air conditioning, reserving their limited refrigerated space for the un-embalmed (Montgomery and Jones 2020). The ritual of visitation that embalming supports, however, was so foreshortened and limited in audience by social distancing rules that its efficacy may be further eroded after the pandemic. Families who before may have been torn between cremation and embalming probably chose the first out of expediency and the fact that few people would be able to see the corpse anyway. Media coverage of the pandemic has underscored how the inability to say goodbye, either in the hospital or in the funeral home, has compounded the grief of families. The loss of parting rituals has been mourned in its own right.

Gary Laderman (1996) notes that the popularization of embalming in the US case enabled the continuation of an antebellum habit of viewing the corpse before burial. Sometimes this took place during a two- to three-day wake in the family parlor. But even when the body was buried quickly (due to weather, disease, or travel), the coffin lid was left open for viewing at a graveside ceremony just before burial (cf. Farrell 1980, 147). Laderman quotes several English travelers who thought the practice odd, if not repugnant. The exceptionalism of this practice is reinforced in an 1878 article by a British embalmer and inventor, who connects it to the growing popularity of embalming in the United States:

> Embalming at the present day is, in England, an exceptional process, and when we are called upon to perform it here, it is, in ninety-nine out of the hundred, for some one foreign to country [so that they can be transported home]. . . . In the United States of America the embalming process is carried out to a great extent, and I believe the number of persons embalmed in that country increases every year. . . . The embalming has been sought after that the relatives may retain the dead body as long as they can with the face exposed to view. For such purpose coffins of a special kind have to be made, in the lids of which a pane of glass is placed. In England these receptacles for the dead are not often constructed; but in America they are specially constructed. (Richardson 1878, 915–16)

In 1848, American inventor Almond Dunbar Fisk patented a cast-iron coffin in the form-fitting shape of an Egyptian sarcophagus. Nicknamed the "Fisk Mummy," his design included a glass window over the face for viewing. However, this was only a luxury version of wooden coffins with glass windows that had become popular by the 1820s. It is sometimes claimed that these windows were a safety feature to verify death—that breath clouding the glass would distinguish an actual sleeper from an eternal sleeper. More likely, it allowed for viewing the person from wake to interment while simultaneously sealing off the smells and signs of putrefaction. A priority on preventing decay is evident in the language of Fisk's patent: "From a coffin of this description the air may be exhausted so completely as entirely to prevent the decay of the contained body on principles well understood; or, if preferred, the coffin may be filled with any gas or fluid having the property of preventing putrefaction" (quoted in Meier 2013; Wescott et al. 2010). Fisk was also one of the early inventors of the rectangular metal *casket* with a hinged lid for easy viewing (*coffins* are typically six sided with a fixed lid and remain popular in the United Kingdom, Australia, and parts of Latin America).

Clearly, an interest in viewing the corpse and delaying decay predated the spread of industrial embalming, and these preconditions had already marked off the United States as peculiar. Contemporary embalmers claim the purpose of their practice is to provide a "memory picture" for the living. The term may have a long history. It has been argued that embalming is primarily a visual medium that mimics the effects of postmortem photography (Schwartz 2015). Capturing images of the dead was one of the first uses to which Daguerre's invention was put, preceding widespread embalming by nearly forty years (Ruby 1995). Mark Schantz's cultural history of antebellum death provides a clue as to why Americans valued images of the dead: "No idea about heaven was more important in the early nineteenth century than the notion of what was called 'heavenly recognition': Individuals who had known each other on earth would be able to identify each other in heaven" (2008, 62). In order to recognize a friend or loved one for this joyful reunification, it may have been important to burn an image of their appearance into memory.

Charles Jackson also recognizes the visual importance of embalming: "The Civil War presented the problem of returning home large numbers of corpses. Yet the aesthetic motive in the quest for means of body presentation is clear and becomes more so with the gradual growth in popularity after the war of arterial embalming" (1977, 304). Jackson's central argument is more worldly than Schantz's: Americans developed several methods of "keeping communion with the dead." In his words, "In every way possible the dead would not be allowed truly to die. Those alive would draw the dead world into the living world as never before" (1977, 301). One reason for this desire to keep a channel open between the living and the dead might have been the astounding mortality rate that antebellum Americans experienced at levels that were "almost medieval" (Schantz 2008, 10). Jackson's focus on communion with the dead implicitly connects the popularity of Spiritualist séances in the nineteenth-century United States to a fascination with viewing, beautifying, preserving, touching, and talking to the corpse (and haptics are still quite important—see Schwartz, this volume). It is therefore not so much of a leap to say that embalmers were—and are—imbricated in an occult practice.

Egyptomania and Sleep Magic

These histories of affect and material spiritualism in the United States provide an important context for the rise of embalming, but why did the practice spread between 1880 and 1980, even as the social conditions that created it subsided? Here I trace a different but parallel genealogy that takes seriously references to Egyptology in the early days of professional embalming and attends to the specific visual vocabulary that developed in the mature form of the American funeral suite—death as sleep. Together, they suggest that embalmers developed a quasi-magical power over a public who wanted to believe in the healing power of the corpse. Like many magical forces, this is a power they attempt to master, but is not always under their control.

Egyptomania arrived belatedly in America, a couple of decades after this strain of Orientalism had taken hold in Europe following Napoleon's expeditions. In the United States, the fad hit in the mid-nineteenth century, epitomized by the erection of the Washington Obelisk in 1846. Scott Trafton (2004) argues that Egyptomania in America was particularly powerful because it became a means for expressing racial anxieties and aspirations in a nation split by a double consciousness, first in the abolitionist era and then under the rise of scientific racism in the late Victorian period. But also that it was a displacement for a deeply conflicted Christianity.

"Mummy Fever" was part of this story (Brier 1980; Pringle 2001; Taylor 2014; Wolfe 2009). In the 1840s and 1850s, mummies were ceremoniously unwrapped in scientific and public spectacles in many American cities. These events were featured in the literature of the nation's leading writers such as Alcott, Poe, and Hawthorne. Egyptian mummies captured the American imagination in a way that endured in American popular culture. Simon During (2002) argues that mummy fever and Egyptomania were entangled with the rising popularity of stage magic in the nineteenth century (a co-occurrence to which I will return) while Laderman (2003, 10) notes that their popularity lasted well into the early twentieth century, when they became a favorite subject of early cinema. To be sure, the horror genre suggests that mummies represented the uncanny—but an uncanny that was fixated upon, not avoided, in popular American culture. Enter the embalmer.

This cultural backdrop of mummy fever is why we should not dismiss the frequent claims of early American embalmers to be practicing the "Egyptian art." Farrell acknowledges the influence of Egyptian ideas, but more as a colorful anecdote than a possible clue to the self-understanding of embalmers. He quotes one Victorian writer commenting that New Yorkers were, in their treatment of death, "'becoming rapidly Egyptianized.' . . . Eventually Americans almost universally adopted embalming, which they traced to Egyptian origins" (1980, 170). One of the earliest training institutions was F. A. Sullivan's "Oriental School of Embalming which used a chemical solution that Sullivan marketed through the 'Egyptian Chemical Company'" (163). Embalming "made the people marvel at the 'mysterious' and 'incomprehensible' processes of preservation, and made them respect the practitioner" (153). In fact, embalmers worked hard to produce this mystery, and they quickly became quite secretive about their techniques. The first meeting of the NFDA in 1882 hailed "the varied improvements in your art [that] enable you to conceal much that is forbidding in your calling" (cited in Farrell 1980, 146–47). Industry language suggests that funeral directors deliberately produced an aura of mystery around this new ritual element in American life (143).

Laderman also briefly acknowledges this influence in the history of the American funeral business: "The funeral industry was not alone in its fascination with ancient Egyptian culture at this time, of course. This exotic civilization appealed to many Americans thanks to the colonial expeditions pilfering, and then displaying, cultural artifacts—often dead bodies, from this time forward popularly identified as 'mummies,' snatched from their eternal resting places" (2003, 10). He goes on to cite a 1934 professional publication dedicated to "the Ethical Funeral Directors of America . . . that examines the relation between ancient Egyptian practices and the modern 'science' of embalming. . . . A critical element of these narratives is precisely this advantage: royal treatment available to all citizens. Or, in other words, the democratization of what was once an exclusive, highly valued, ritual for important personages" (11–12).

Early critics of embalming also recognized the Egyptian influence and objected to its "pagan" character. As one said, "We were incensed at the funeral customs which cause every John Doe to view death with the eyes of an ancient Egyptian pharaoh" (quoted in Laderman 2003, 61; see also 60). If one critique of the modern American funeral was that it had become too commercial, another was that it had become too magical: "Preparation rooms, where washing, embalming, and cosmetic work were carried out, transformed the corpse into a suitable ritual object of devotion. Indeed, the increasingly common criticism from the first half of the century [was] that, with the advent of embalming, the American funeral had turned into a form of pagan body worship" (22).

In my interviews, I have found that the Egyptian narrative continues to be a key origin story for American embalmers. This self-presentation can be traced back to their training and possibly to fraternal organizations.[2] A contemporary textbook on embalming has seventy-eight entries for Egypt in its index—and not all these are in the history chapter (Mayer 2011). References to dynastic Egypt are used to justify regulations, to explain the preference for desiccation over putrefaction, and to laud the ancient bond of respect between doctors, priests, and embalmers.

I am not suggesting that Americans believed, like the ancient Egyptians,

that they could "take it with them." What I am saying is that embalmers—
through secretive techniques—have deliberately created an illusion that there is
no death, only a deep sleep. Hagerty rightly notes that this was by design: "The
intended effect of embalming is the production of a corpse that appears lifelike
and sleeping. . . . A life-like corpse is the only acceptable corpse in the traditional American funeral. . . . The embalmer ensures that the body will not be a
'horror' by erasing any signs of death. . . . The embalmer produces the corpse as
something that is not quite dead—all traces of death are banished" (2014, 431).
Margaret Schwartz (2015) and others have noted that the image of a sleeping
body was the desired effect of most postmortem photography as well. The eyes
were forced closed as necessary and the body was often positioned on a bed,
couch, or a mother's lap to stage sleep (cf. Laderman 1996, 77).

A reporter covering embalming at Civil War field hospitals in 1862 informed
his public that "the bodies look as lifelike as if they were asleep" (quoted in
Laderman 1996, 28). This effect is precisely what embalmers promised in
their earliest advertisements from the same period: "Bodies Embalmed by Us
NEVER TURN BLACK! But retain their natural color and appearance . . . so as
to admit of contemplation of the person Embalmed, with the countenance of
a one asleep" (115).

Some versions of Christianity posit that the baptized dead are asleep until
Judgment Day, when there will be a mass awakening. However, this doctrine
has been vigorously debated within American Protestantism and only the
minority millenarian sects of Seventh Day Adventism and Jehovah's Witnesses
uphold a strong version of it. This eschatology contradicts the more common
doctrine that upon death the individual spirit is immediately transported to
heaven or hell. Over time, antebellum faith in a literal heaven that could be
vividly depicted in lithographs (Schantz 2008) gave way to a nondenomina-
tional vagueness grading toward secularism. In the twentieth century, Americans became less certain about what might lie beyond, but the illusion of sleep
still dominated the funeral rite. The safest answer to "What next?" was not denial
but deferral—to sleep on it. Depicting the loved one as sleeping rather than
dead means that embalmers are in the business of creating a kind of undead.
During a traditional funeral, Americans worship the undead. The allegation of
pagan magic is not so preposterous.

The same embalming textbook cited above reinforces the association of sleep
and death, as well as the magical effect of this illusion upon the beholder: "One
of the world's oldest and best known examples of modern-day embalming is a

2-year-old child by the name of Rosalia Lombardo. Little Rosalia died in December of 1920 in Palermo, Italy. Her father full of grief over the loss of his child, called upon a local embalmer. . . . Today, Rosalia is known as 'Sleeping Beauty' as she appears to just be sleeping" (Mayer 2011, 2086). Her body, encased in a glass coffin, is still on view today and is referred to as a mummy. The Disney film *Sleeping Beauty* may have been inspired by Rosalia; in the United States, it remains the most-viewed Disney film of all time. I don't mean to be cute; I think this fact is significant. This *is* the American dream—that dreamers can sometimes wake.

The bedchamber design of coffins and caskets became quite elaborate by the late nineteenth century. Soft, fine cloths like silk, satin, and linen were used to line the interior of the casket and make it resemble a bed to such an extent that pillows became a standard feature. On monuments, in cemetery names, and in eulogies, references to heaven and hell were gradually replaced with references to sleep and rest. But to be sustained, the illusion of sleep must not be disturbed by the idea that even unseen, after all the visitation and corpse worship is done and the deceased lies in their bed six feet underground, the body could become something undead in a different way—a seething, organic mass of small worms and microorganisms. Thus, the concrete vault and sealed caskets should be understood as part of the embalming complex; their aim is to forestall decay for as long as possible, to extend the magic for at least as long as the mourners care to imagine what might be happening out of sight. The website for a contemporary American funeral home makes the consumer's choice clear: "Most metal caskets . . . have a thick rubber gasket surrounding the entire lid which creates a sealed enclosure making it more difficult for outside elements to penetrate the interior of the casket. . . . Because of the porous nature of wood, it is virtually impossible to completely seal a wood casket. If protection is a priority, a burial vault, which is a container that encloses and protects the casket, may be utilized" (DeBord-Snyder Funeral Home 2015). There can be no sleeping beauty without beauty. There can be no rest when outside elements intrude. The (un)dead need to be protected.

The magic of the embalmer involves creating an undead creature—a nonbreathing but sleeping human. The embalmer mysteriously manipulates earthly materials to have a supernatural effect, an effect that intervenes with nature as we know it. This is the classic ethnographer's definition of magic. Embalmers advise one another to conceal their techniques and, to be sure, how many people know where the incisions are made, how many gallons of chemicals are used, how long the process takes, or where the extruded blood goes—except the embalmer and her apprentice, or the curious anthropologist exploring backstage?

Embalmers are adept at manipulating not just materials but the immateriality of time. They do this in a way that is beyond the capacity of most humans, including the professionals to whom they like to be compared—doctors and ministers. Not only can they create and extend a liminal period between life and death, they can reverse time. The appearance of a body that is merely sleeping sets the clock back to a time before suffering, before a traumatic injury or lingering illness. Embalmers assert that this is one of the reasons that corpse viewing is healing. So important is this type of medicine that the embalmer's art quickly expanded from as-is preservation to restoration. The use of injections, wax prostheses, and cosmetics is designed to turn back the clock to a healthier, happier time for both the dead and their survivors. While rituals by definition involve a manipulation of time and the creation of a liminal state, as seen in Matthew Engelke's quite different secular humanist context (this volume), there is a kind of specialist power claimed by embalmers. They are a kind of time lord.

The Magical Object

Back at the NFDA convention, I tried to get at the international comparative question with Eliza, who is a professional "celebrant" (officiator of humanist rituals) from Australia. She thinks Americans are strange, particularly when it comes to the open casket. When I asked her if back home she had fielded any particularly unusual requests, she mentioned one case in which a woman in her forties who had died after a long illness had requested that the coffin at her funeral include a fake bloody arm sticking out of it, the kind you can purchase at a dollar store for a Halloween tableau. The woman was beloved by a wide circle of friends, in no small part for her humor, but it was a rare case in which Eliza advised against the deceased's last wishes.

The story of the would-be prank, though, uncannily anticipated an interview later that day with Beverly, a traditional American funeral director. We spoke to Beverly on the floor of the exhibit hall, which was a noisy, busy place full of wares and services that were a bit dizzying in their range and variety, from luxury hearses and biodegradable urns to cemetery reconnaissance drones. Beverly was dressed in a dark, manly suit, her snow-steel hair cropped short. She was warm and direct, but not motherly. She runs a family business, inherited from her father. She was businesslike and reminded me of a high school gym teacher or a nun. She deals with a lot of bodies but tries not to get too close. She sees the changes the funeral industry needs to make as "going back to basics." It is the interpersonal skills that are critical: "Our body language, our tone of voice, our words and phrases. You know, historically in our profession we've used the word 'removal' or 'transfer,' but we need to change that, you know, we are going to come and bring your mother into our care." After telling me about her father, who was apparently an odd child who created his own personal pet cemetery complete with little handmade caskets and who drew pictures of his friends in caskets, she added something that I heard other funeral directors say in one fashion or another: "I believe a lot of us are called to this. We look at it as a ministry. You know, it is an honor."

She then talked about how she believed the movement toward cremation can be accounted for by a more mobile society. People no longer live near their family or hometown cemeteries. But this worried her: "It seems like there's a little transition here of families not having the body present. But it is *so* critical. That is part of the grieving process." She was firm on this score: "I think it is important to have an open casket if you can because there is the reality of what we do — that this has happened and you need to see the loved one. In mortuary school, they train us to create a pleasant memory picture." She made it clear that embalming and restoration should be applied as much as possible, even in cases of physical trauma. "It is important for a funeral director — an embalmer — to give her or his talents to create that person back." I was intrigued by her choice of words, which she herself had said are so important. It is an act of creation, a way to bring them back from the trauma of death.

One technical thing I learned from Beverly about restoration was that in the case of a disfiguring trauma, particularly to the face, they use waxwork to re-create the missing parts. Maybe this is why the wax figures in Madame Tussaud's are so eerie. They look like corpses. Or maybe it is the other way around. "A person, say, that is real emaciated, that's lost a lot of weight — what a talented embalmer can do is use tissue builder and kind of bring that person back where it almost erases that hard time they went through with that loved one and they're almost transported back when the mom was up and going. We get her hair done, her makeup."

But in some cases, the trauma is too great. In some cases, the bodies are shattered, parts separated from one another. As challenging, both emotionally and physically, as such a violent wrench from life can be, Beverly does not give up on the healing properties of the dead body. When I asked her if there were any experiences that were particularly memorable as a funeral director, she told me the story of a man, his wife, and their daughter who were flying into the local airport in his small private plane on Christmas Day. The plane crashed, and both parents died. The daughter in the back seat survived unscathed; she has an adult brother who missed the trip because of work. The mother was disfigured, and the dad, Beverly said in a peculiar choice of phrase, "You couldn't see at all." The son struggled to understand what happened—how his parents were gone but his sister looked like she hadn't been on the same plane. He viewed his mom and accepted her disfigurement:

> Nothing would do him but to see his dad, so we took the family out, and what we did is [she pauses, searching for words]. You know, the body was so mangled from the wreckage—his left foot was pretty well intact. And we took it out of the body bag, cleaned it, and we put a nice little velvet throw over it. And I can still see him today sitting on that end of that daybed, just rubbing his dad's foot. Now for some people that would be gruesome, or "How could you do that?" But I knew that he probably wouldn't be able to go on if he didn't. He could see his sister. He could see his mom. But he had to see something of his dad—that this really happened to me.

Of course, the young man probably *would* have gone on without his father's foot, but Beverly was saying that he would have gone on differently. There is a strange time management that occurred in Beverly's reckoning. She says on the one hand that funeral directors are there to help the families slow time down, to get them not to rush decisions (such as cremation) that are irreversible. This is important, because a funeral only happens once. But facilitating visual and physical contact between the dead body (or at least parts of it) and the living also speeds up the grief process so you can get to the healing part faster. Funeral directors claim that their art is exactly the opposite of death denial. However the healing mechanism works (through communion with the dead or confronting the trauma), it is clear that viewing—or what we might call corpse therapy—is effective for some people. Beverly will try to honor any request that is "dignified." The foot stroking qualified.

I suggest that viewing the dead worked for one set of reasons in the mid-nineteenth century and another set of reasons in the twentieth and twenty-first. The embalmed body—or body part—in the traditional American funeral went from being a snapshot so that the dead could recognize one another in a Christian heaven to something like a medieval saint's relic with the power to heal the living. Even the Vatican has become uncomfortable with the thin line between magic and religion that relics represent and has generally disavowed their veneration. But most American embalmers are not so constrained. They are more likely to understand what they are doing within the medicalized frame of "therapy," but they are hard-pressed to explain how their own cure works.

Another insight into the function of embalming in American life may be gleaned from looking at its most extreme practices. What Beverly did with the foot was not extreme, but what two funeral homes operating in New Orleans, Louisiana, have been doing since 2012 has raised eyebrows even within the death-care industry. One funeral director I spoke to about the practice calls it "extreme embalming." What he is referring to is a practice of embalming individuals in naturalistic, *wakeful* postures set up for viewing with a tableau of artifacts from their everyday lives. The first cases that rose to media attention originated in Puerto Rico in 2008. The uptake of this practice in New Orleans appears to be an example of the globalized influences cross-fertilizing and transforming the new death today. It is a case of emulation and adaptation by local funeral directors rather than a direct importation (neither the families nor the embalmers involved seem to have any personal connection to the island).

The first local case was Uncle Lionel Baptiste, a beloved jazz musician. The newspaper account of his arrangements suggests both similarities and differences with the traditional American funeral:

[H]is body was propped against a faux street lamp, standing, decked out in his signature man-about-town finery. He wore a cream sport coat, beige slacks, tasseled loafers, ornate necktie and matching pocket square, bowler hat and sunglasses. His bass drum and his Treme Brass Band uniform were positioned nearby. His head was cocked slightly to the left. He appeared ready to step from behind the velvet rope and saunter off to Frenchmen Street, where he reveled in dancing and drinking beer. "He looks better today than when I saw him the Thursday before he died," said Storyville Stompers tuba player Woody Penouilh. (Spera 2012)

Baptiste's son said that since his father was original, his funeral needed to be; he promised his father he would send him out in style. Humor was definitely at play, but also a sense of what was natural and a good fit for the deceased's personality. One attendee reported, "I was looking for him to move. . . . That's something I've never seen before. It's perfect. It's a wonderful, strange thing." The embalmer adapted his magic to the light mood of the day, but secrecy remained a part of the art.

> During his 50 years in the funeral business, Louis Charbonnet had never before embalmed a body in such a life-like pose. . . . "You have to think outside the box," Charbonnet said. "And so he's outside the box. We didn't want him to be confined to his casket." Charbonnet declined to share the "trade secrets" of how the effect was achieved. "Five or six of my competitors have been through today, asking how we did it," he said. "It was a challenge." (Spera 2012)

The second case was Mickey Easterling, a larger-than-life socialite and philanthropist who for her last rite was seated on a garden bench wearing a hot pink feather boa and holding a champagne glass in one hand and a cigarette holder in the other (Vanacore 2014). She went out as she lived, the life of the party.

The third case is perhaps the most poignant in that the deceased was, before her death, not a public figure. "Ms. Mae" lived in a modest house in a rough neighborhood and was on and off public assistance for most of her fifty-three years. She died from complications after a stroke. Her niece, whom she had raised as a daughter and who directed her final arrangements, told me she was beloved by many people in the neighborhood. In our extended interview, Zymora told me that she needed a little more time with her aunt. She needed to talk to her and tell her that she loved her. Maybe if she was asleep or in a coma (as Ms. Mae was for several months), it would be less likely the message would be heard. As another attendee at Uncle Lionel's funeral noted, you rarely see people sleep. But you do see them doing other, normal things—like sitting at the kitchen table in their Saints football jersey, smoking a cigarette, working on a crossword puzzle, and drinking a Busch beer. That's how Ms. Mae was last seen. Guests were invited to sit at the table and truly visit (figures 9.1 and 9.2).

> She's my everything. She's the family everything. She was just different. She had a big heart. She can be the funniest. She can be the meanest—but in a good way! Her personality is really indescribable. And I know what she wants. She loves her family. She loves to party. I organized a whole party. I

Figure 9.1. Ms. Mae at her funeral. Courtesy of the author.

Figure 9.2. Zymora and family with Ms. Mae postmortem. Courtesy of the author.

had tables set up with beer, shot glasses. They took shots of alcohol at the funeral. It was a party but she was just deceased and not physically there. I was just looking for peace. I wanted happiness and it was happy. Mae was loving. She was a teenager. And I missed that. I know she's not going to forget this.

In our conversation, Zymora shifted back and forth from present to past tense when talking about Mae. Given that she was both very present, and not, for her final event, this makes sense. A blurring of the present and past tense is exactly what extreme embalming does—it creates a gerund, a leave-taking, through a protracted in-between state. This is a deliberate liminality rather than a finality. And the deliberateness is important. Rather than being uncanny, which is how the corpse is usually interpreted, this type of in-between person is comforting. I noted that Zymora said her aunt was not "physically" present, but she also describes how her sister did Mae's nails and a close friend did her hair. It wasn't "the body's" nails and hair, it was Mae's nails and hair. The confusion between past/present also muddles absence/presence. What was *un*present? Perhaps Mae's ability to respond to the love that was being shown. In all three of these cases, the absence of a talking, agentive person seems to somehow elevate, through the creation of a tableau reflective of their lives and personality, an intensified if distilled *presence* of their personhood—the spirit of the individual is accentuated and made present. They cannot speak, but they might be listening. The embalmer's magic is about manipulating time, creating a possibility for communion with the dead, and even an occasion for entertainment. It is not about reassuring us about the afterlife. It defers the question and instead creates a pleasant ambiguity, whether the embalmed corpse is set in a sleeping or a wakeful posture. As Zymora and the majority of Americans I have talked to say, death is a mystery: "The truth is, once you gone, you don't know *where* those people are at."

Several months later, in a very different part of the country, my collaborator Daniel and I arrived at the apartment of Michael and his husband, Lawrence, in a quiet neighborhood in San Francisco. Michael is an embalmer. Michael's quiet demeanor and passion for his work came across in his interview as he sat in an antique chair upholstered with images of angels. He sees embalming as a way for families to have more time with the deceased. It slows down the goodbye. He came to this work through a combination of skills in makeup and health care: "My craft is an unusual craft. I knew right from the beginning that I could be useful. It opened a whole different doorway to work for me. It was much more than work. It was an opportunity to be with an individual and this is their last [pauses]—what people are going to see. It's you and the individual."

I am not sure that Michael protected any craft secrets with me. He was forthcoming when I asked technical questions. But he did say that "the body is a temple" and "death is a mystery." He also accounted for the history of embalming through the Egyptians, but back then, this option was "only for the rich." In America, everyone is royal. Certainly, one gets the feeling that Michael sincerely treats his individuals with a reverent care. But now what sticks with me most

Figure 9.3. Michael's home altar. Courtesy of the author.

from our interview is not anything he said. It is the altar that we encountered in the entryway of their home as we took our recording gear up the stairs (figure 9.3). I do not know what all the objects were, or what they meant, but I did recognize an ankh, a statue of the cat god Bastet, a scarab beetle, and two urns with the heads of Anubis (god of mummification) and Horus. I wish I had been a little nosier.

Conclusion: "A Willing Suspension of Disbelief"

As Matthew Engelke (2019, 32) observes, one of the most pervasive narratives in studies of death and dying in the modern West, and particularly of the United States, is a story of "sanitation and disenchantment." But in this closer look at the interior logics of embalming, I wonder if we are not seeing a case of "sanitation and *re*-enchantment." Almost all the conventional funeral home directors and embalmers I have interviewed (including Wilson, Beverly, and Michael) answered the question about why American funeral practices are changing by pointing to the decline of organized religion in the United States. I don't dispute that the decline in religious influence is leading to a proliferation of funeral practices, but I am not convinced that this means they are becoming any more secular or any less supernatural. Unless we are talking about what Simon During (2002) calls "secular magic."

Anthropology and comparative studies of religion were for a long time bogged down in arguments over the taxonomic lines between science, magic, and religion (Frazer 1890; Levack 1992; Malinowski 1948), despite Marcel Mauss's ([1950] 1972) best efforts to argue for a spectrum. According to the classic (and now outdated) taxonomy, magic is similar to science in that it is "based on man's confidence that he can dominate nature directly, if only he knows the laws which govern it magically" (Malinowski 1948, 3), whereas religion admits to human impotence, especially in the face of death (Hertz 1960; Malinowski 1948, 29–35). While I follow Mauss in believing that there is no perfect classificatory system, it is helpful to expand the spectrum even wider to include entertainment magic. During (2002) presents a cultural history of secular magic, from mesmerism to card tricks, demonstrating that it isn't really all that secular, except in extreme forms, and that a continuum exists in magical practice from the supernatural to the trivial. When we include entertainment magic in the suite, the parallels to embalming and the ritual of corpse viewing become even more striking. To reinforce the argument I have been building—that embalming can be understood as a form of magic—I highlight here four traits of the practice that justify including American embalming in what During (2002) calls the "magical assemblage": secrecy, transformation, mediation of the dead, and illusion.

> *Secrecy.* "Science is born of experience, magic made by tradition. . . . [It] is occult, taught through mysterious initiations, handed on in a hereditary or at least in a very exclusive filiation" (Malinowski 1948, 3). Among the many traits that embalmers share with magicians is the secrecy of their techniques and the family lines through which the profession passes. The NFDA reports that 89 percent of American funeral homes are family businesses; the number of these that are in their third generation and beyond is probably the highest of any other small-business sector in the country. During (2002) observes that trade secrecy is also one of the many threads that connect occult magicians to stage musicians.
>
> *Transformation.* Magical practice involves a transformation, a change from one state to another, usually a physical one: "The actions vary according to the initial state of the individual, the circumstances determining the significance of the change, and the special ends assigned to them. Nevertheless,

they share one feature in that their immediate and essential effect is to modify a given state. The magician . . . is always conscious that magic is the art of changing" (Mauss 1972, 76). The magician often needs assistance in effecting the desired transformation.

Mediation of the Dead. In many overtly magical practices around the world and throughout history, among the most important helpers and interlocutors of the magician are the dead. If priests are the intermediaries for living souls, magicians are the intermediaries for dead souls. Ghost-raising of various forms is a special domain of magicians at either end of the occult-secular spectrum. In the nineteenth century, the line between spiritualists leading séances and stage magicians was quite thin, and the same individuals could perform in both genres (During 2002). Like the medium in a séance, embalmers provide the possibility of a ghost-raising for those who might have questions or who might find comfort in being able to talk to the dead. In this way, the "extreme embalming" cases may offer, for those who are not too distracted by their uncanny qualities, an even greater degree of short-term comfort. Someone who appears to be awake is not only more familiar but also provides the illusion of listening attentively.

Illusion. During's most intriguing argument is that stage magic involves a kind of willful double consciousness that is a peculiarly modern orientation toward "illusions as illusions" (2002, 56) that can stimulate wonder, fear, delight, and comfort—a type of winking gap between experience and wish fulfillment that ultimately led to the development of cinema. This devotion to illusion and the rise of American show business from Barnum to vaudeville coincided with the rise of embalming. Entertainment magic (conjuring, escapology, legerdemain) has a long history around the world but enjoyed significant growth and professionalization in the United States during the same period as embalming, from the mid-nineteenth through mid-twentieth centuries. It also was heavily entangled with Egyptomania and mummy fever.

While most embalmers would prefer to be thought of as healers, their work is operationally much closer to that of magicians, falling somewhere in the middle of the occult and secular types. Their magic "may offer the possibility of communications between the natural world and a veiled, supernatural order separated from everyday life by a barrier which is also a threshold" (During 2002, 546). This veiled threshold is materialized literally in the separation between the "back stage" of the embalming room and the "front stage" of the viewing room, often bedecked in curtains. The funeral director's main task is to whisk the corpse away from the place of death as quickly as possible, affect a transformation in secrecy, and then unveil his or her handiwork to a special audience in a very limited engagement (this magical effect may have international appeal; cf. Liu, this volume). After the female assistant is sawn in half, she is miraculously made whole again. This is not to trivialize what embalmers do or to minimize the solemnity with which they perform. To make the deceased whole again, appearing to be healthy and sleeping or the life of their last party, is the illusion they knowingly perform. The aim is sometimes to entertain but always to comfort. The illusion of the undead is easier than the truth of death and decay. This is the double consciousness that embalming enables.

In the opening to his erudite psychological history of magic, Ioan Couliano states, "Magic is primarily directed at the human imagination, in which it attempts to create lasting impressions" (1987, xviii). While Couliano credits the magician with significant powers as a master manipulator, During astutely observes that for magic to work, the audience has do their part to sustain the illusion. Magic is a type of real-time material fiction that requires a "willing suspension of disbelief" (During 2002, 641). This includes a suspension in disbelief in natural laws and linear time. In an act of magic, "abstract categories like time, space, and causality (which are taken for granted in everyday life or rational thought) modulate, bend or fragment. To enter the magic domain may be to access a cosmic simultaneity, in which events can be foretold and the past is never erased" (During 2002, 554). Recognizing that the illusion of death's reversal is at the root of embalming helps us understand that there is a continuity between the traditional embalming of the sleeping beauty type and the extreme embalming of the living, upright type. In both cases, as a form of magic it "fictionalizes by simulating reality rather than truth" (880).

An additional element that underscores embalming as a magical practice is found in the ubiquitous claims by funeral directors that viewing the (restored) corpse is therapeutic. As During (2002, 1198) notes, the line between therapy and magic has also been historically thin. Embalming aims to heal by means of magical illusion. Or at least that is the intent. Lately, however, a gap has been growing between the good intention of embalmers and its reception by grievers. In interviews with dozens of nonprofessionals in the course of my fieldwork, less than 5 percent of them would choose embalming for themselves or their loved ones. Most share the opinion of Jed, who, dressed as a zombie on Halloween night in New Orleans in 2015, said, "I think the ritual of burial and viewing the dead body is the most morbid thing that anybody ever came up with." The embalmed corpse can be *too* uncanny. The creation of automatons, dolls, mannequins, puppets, and dummies played a central role in the development of modern stage magic. Fascination with uncanny, almost-human figures helped popularize magicians who were master inventors of new technologies and manipulators of the visual (cf. Couliano 1987, 91). But the danger of the uncanny is that fascination can easily tilt toward terror and repulsion. It appears that more and more Americans view the embalmed corpse in this way. And this, too, is the danger of a practice that requires a "willing suspension of disbelief" on the part of the audience. Like the premise of a Disney film, if they stop believing, the magic stops.

Acknowledgments

This project would have been impossible without my collaborator Daniel Zox and the generosity of our interlocutors. Students enrolled in the "Death and Being" graduate seminar at University of Chicago helped launch me into the writing phase of this project, while research assistant Charlotte Soehner helped me with the historical background. Interlocutors at the SAR seminar "21st-Century Death Cultures" (who were also a lot of fun) emboldened me to think in magical terms. William Mazzarella helped focus that path with some suggested reading. Any risks, quirks, errors remain my own.

Notes

1. The ethnographic research extracted here was conducted under University of Chicago IRB protocol IRB15–1236 (exempt). The larger project involves both filmed interviews recorded with my collaborator Daniel Zox and informal solo interviews, focused on changing American death practices around disposition of the body. I have changed the names of all my interviewees to protect their anonymity; I have eliminated ellipses, false starts, *ums*, and so on, from the transcription for flow. Daniel Zox's cinematography provides images for the figures, reproduced with his permission.

2. The organizations may include Freemasonry, which draws heavily on Egyptian symbolism and is known for a special focus on customized funeral rites and special cemeteries for its members.

CHAPTER TEN

To Bear a Corpse

Home Funerals and Epistemic Cultures in US Death Care

PHILIP R. OLSON

When the infant son of Karen Santorum and her husband, former US senator Rick Santorum, died in 1996, the Santorums did not call a funeral home; they drove their son home, where they cared for his body themselves and held a private wake. The Santorums' DIY funeral was met with fascination, confusion, sympathy, and even scorn in popular media. Described as "bizarre," "sad," "sick," and "crazy," but also as an "understandable" and "important" "way to grieve," the twenty-week-old Gabriel Santorum's "home funeral" (as it would now be called) provoked questions about the legal, cultural, psychological, and public-health interests involved in the handling of dead human bodies. Who is entitled to take custody of human corpses? Where do dead bodies belong or not belong? Are dead bodies a danger to the public health? Are there better and worse ways to grieve and memorialize the dead? What kinds of public interests are at stake in the private disposal of human remains? These are among the many questions that arise when customary death-care practices are disrupted or overtly challenged.

The Santorums were not alone in wanting to hold a home funeral for the body of a loved one. One year earlier, Silver Spring, Maryland's, Elizabeth Knox chose to keep the body of her seven-year-old daughter, Alison, at her home for three days after Alison's death in an automobile accident. And in 1994, in Sonoma County, California, Jerrigrace Lyons followed the instructions of her friend and Reiki instructor, Caroline Whiting, who asked that her friends not turn her body over to funeral professionals but instead lay out her body themselves and deliver it to a crematorium. Unaware of one another's home death-care actions, Lyons, Knox, and the Santorums were among the first of growing numbers of Americans who have begun to question the prevailing custom of calling a funeral director immediately upon the death of a loved one.

Participants in the early twenty-first-century US home-funeral movement argue that private citizens may reap financial, social, emotional, and political benefits from caring for their own dead without the mediation of licensed funeral professionals (whom I will call "funeral industrialists") and with minimal technological intervention into the care and management of dead bodies.[1] Through websites, blogs, online and in-person trainings, public talks and community discussions, written guides, storytelling, videos, and media coverage, as well as through numerous local and national organizations like Knox's Crossings: Caring for Our Own at Death, Lyons's Final Passages Institute of Conscious Dying, Home Funeral & Green Burial Education, and the nonprofessional, nonprofit National Home Funeral Alliance (NHFA)—a social movement organization that identifies itself (without apparent contestation) as "the leading body of home, after-death care support and education in the U.S." (NHFA 2019c)—home-funeral advocates seek to educate the public about the ins and outs of do-it-yourself death care.

Broadly, the aim of the home-funeral movement is to empower people to care for their dead themselves and to empower home-funeral advocates to aid those who would like to arrange and conduct home funerals. In stark contrast to transhumanists and "immortalists" (Farman, this volume; Huberman, this volume) who seek to overcome death through technoscientific means, home-funeral advocates join the ranks of the "death positive" (Order of the Good Death 2020a), who embrace human mortality and seek to facilitate frank conversation about and planning for the inevitable "terminality" (Farman, this volume) of human bodies and human lives.[2] The home-funeral movement is a complex social movement that embraces the interests of various groups whose death-care knowledge and skill have been marginalized by the dominance of industrial death care. The movement is predominantly led by well-educated, progressive, white women, many of whom have experience with home birth or at-home hospice care and for whom home-funeral advocacy is historically and politically connected to home-birth advocates' challenges to the gendered medicalization of birth (Olson 2016a). These women have found allies in conservators of traditional Muslim and Jewish funeral traditions, including the Janazah Project, a Brooklyn, New York–based nonprofit that helps Muslims care for their own dead, and Kavod v'Nichum, a nonprofit based in Columbia, Maryland, that helps Chevra Kadishas—Jewish burial societies—"to fully participate in funerals and burials in their communities, in accordance with their own Jewish orientation."[3] Far from being guided by the sensibilities and practices that shape secular ceremonies like those discussed by Engelke (this volume), the home-funeral movement aims to facilitate the private performance of creative rituals that express the participants' values and beliefs, whatever they may be.

Home-funeral practices can vary considerably, but they differ from the industrial funeral practices that have dominated US death-care culture ever since modern, arterial embalming thoroughly transformed US death care into a technically skilled profession (Faust 2008; Laderman 2003), while turning dead bodies into industrial commodities. Home-funeral practitioners typically wash, dress, and adorn the bodies of their dead at home or at a funeral home and shroud or casket bodies themselves, often making bodies and burial containers into sacred, intimate, and elaborate craft objects. Rejecting invasive and toxic embalming technologies, home-funeral practitioners preserve bodies by keeping them cool—using dry ice, ice packs, air conditioning, body coolers, or, weather permitting, outdoor temperatures—for home vigils and funeral rituals that can last for hours or even several days. Home-funeral practices may involve the personal transportation of the body from the place of death to the home-funeral location or from the home-funeral site to the site of final disposition (for example, a crematory or cemetery). Beyond caring for the physical remains of the dead, home-funeral practices may involve a variety of other projects, including organizing and performing funeral rituals, writing obituaries, filing death certificates and other legal documents, and managing digital legacies.

Although it is legal to take custody of and care for one's own dead in every US state—with only ten states requiring that a licensed funeral professional be involved at some point in the process of death care—home-funeral practitioners and advocates have shared numerous stories about the resistance they experience when seeking to take custody of their dead from health-care institutions or when attempting to deliver their own dead to the site of final disposition.[4] Adding to home-funeral practitioners' and advocates' frustration, this reluctance persists even when health-care professionals and disposition service providers are made aware of next of kin's legal right to claim custody of their own dead. While the policies of health-care institutions and disposition service providers are not always congruous with applicable funeral laws, those policies both presume and produce a continuum of action across the seemingly distinct social contexts of health care and death care.

Drawing on five years of ethnographic research I have conducted as a participant observer in the US home-funeral movement and on narratives and training materials that home-funeral practitioners and advocates themselves have authored, I show in this chapter how the US home-funeral movement challenges a shared "epistemic culture" (Knorr Cetina 1999) that spans health-care and death-care institutions by drawing critical attention to bureaucratically managed "sequences of action" or "chains of action" that shape the movement of bodies from health-care institutions to death-care institutions. Knorr Cetina's idea of epistemic *culture* helps to reveal what lies behind (or within) individual, occurrent acts by drawing attention to the background conditions that support and are supported by the habitual articulation of "chains of action." As Star (1995), Wajcman (1991), Cockburn (1985), and others have shown, these background conditions can harbor persistent biases that unevenly grant and restrict social authority and power.

As a complex social movement, the home-funeral movement challenges multiple biases animated by the epistemic culture spanning health-care and death-care institutions (Olson 2016a). In this chapter, I will focus primarily on the movement's efforts to challenge a bureaucratic and strongly expert-driven approach to managing and understanding the human body. Home-funeral practitioners' and advocates' efforts to take custody and care of dead bodies force an interruption in the habitual "chains of action" that bind medical and mortuary expertise, thereby drawing attention to the contingencies of the medico-mortuary epistemic culture *as an epistemic culture* (see Knorr Cetina 1999, 10). Leaders of the home-funeral movement seek to cultivate an alternative epistemic culture—especially with respect to the care of the human corpse. Yet as I will explain toward the end of this chapter, home-funeral movement leaders disagree about whether the movement should position home-funeral knowledge as an alternative form of expert knowledge and skill, or whether the movement should promote a more radical opposition to death-care expertise in general. At stake in these internal debates are the social role and identity of the home-funeral movement as a whole.

The collaborative work of writing this volume began long before the start of the COVID-19 pandemic, which will undoubtedly persist beyond the volume's publication. As I write these words, the global number of reported new cases is growing faster than it has at any time in the still-early history of the pandemic.[5] Around the world, health-care and death-care workers and institutions have struggled to keep up with the timely and dignified handling of the bodies of people killed by COVID-19. This disruption to business as usual has drawn increased public attention to the social, professional, and institutional mechanisms that sustain various taken-for-granted death-care norms and practices.

Uncertainties around these norms and practices have generated a variety of "funeral insecurities" among different groups of death-care stakeholders. I will conclude this chapter with some preliminary, exploratory thoughts about the pandemic's impact on "funeral security" and on ongoing contestations about death-care authority and expertise.

Two Continuums of Care

As death-care scholar Glenys Howarth points out, "Modern funeral directors acquire control over funeral service via their custody of the corpse" (1996, 15). Likewise, home-funeral practices depend on home-funeral practitioners' and advocates' capacity to take custody of dead bodies. Yet as a response to the dominant regime, the home-funeral movement must contend with a death-care culture in which, over the course of more than a century, the authority of funeral industrialists' knowledge and skill has become harbored in law, infrastructural arrangements, corporate expansion, broad public acceptance, and routine habit. The home-funeral movement seeks to denaturalize industrial death care by revealing its historical, cultural, and political contingency. As home-funeral advocates and practitioners frequently point out, "A home funeral is what used to be called [simply] 'a funeral'" throughout most of American history, "since all funerals took place in the family home" (Order of the Good Death 2020b) before the thoroughgoing professionalization and industrialization of US death care.

CHAINS OF CUSTODY

In the late nineteenth and early twentieth centuries, as Americans increasingly turned to physicians to care for their living, ill, and dying bodies, Americans also progressively abdicated the care of their dead bodies to morticians. Indeed, the same social, political, economic, and industrial processes that account for the "medicalization" of the live body also explain the "funeralization" of the dead body. The inconspicuousness of the parallel trajectories of American health care and death care in the late nineteenth and early twentieth centuries is due largely to morticians' and physicians' successful efforts to define and control separate social and professional spaces for themselves (Olson 2016a, 2016b).

Many historians and social scientists (notably Armstrong 1987; Howarth 1996; Laderman 2003; Lofland 1978; and Rundblad 1995) have pointed out that the formation of these distinct spaces involved complementary shifts in the epistemes of body care, as physicians and morticians alike grounded their social and legal authority over the body in the formal, technoscientific trainings they received in medical or mortuary science schools and in a decidedly public-health-minded approach to understanding and managing human bodies. Indeed, US funeral industrialists have long relied on embalming's perceived public-health benefits (namely, as a means by which to sanitize unclean and dangerous corpses) to justify embalming's routine adoption—though Dawdy (this volume) points out that embalming's broad, public embracing in the United States may be explained by Americans' early twentieth-century fascination with Egyptian culture.

According to Armstrong, in the mid-nineteenth century, "great medical, legislative and public interest in the proper management of the corpse" was driven by the intensifying medicalization of the body, which included the "extension of public surveillance over the dead" (1987, 652). According to Gilligan and Stueve, authors of *Mortuary Law*, "Public health and safety concerns, as well as public morality, necessitate the disposition of the dead by regulated methods" and justify the enforcement of those methods through "the police powers of the government" (2011, 6).

Following Blauner, Lofland draws attention to the bureaucratization of death: "There is nothing at all peculiar about the fact that modern societies should handle death and dying bureaucratically since "'bureaucratization [is] our characteristic form of social structure. Max Weber has described how bureaucratization in the West proceeded by removing social functions from the family and the household and implanting them in specialized institutions autonomous of kinship considerations'" (Lofland [1978] 2019, 20–21, citing Blauner 1966, 384). Professional funeral directors have been happy to fashion a professional identity in fulfillment of the bureaucratization of death care and in coordination with actors in similarly bureaucratized institutions, including health-care professionals and government agencies.

The functional coherence of health-care and death-care institutions is not automatic. Death-care industrialists and health-care industrialists must *work* to create and maintain coherence within and between their respective regimes. Medical and funeral institutions have established norms and practices for identifying (and reidentifying), tagging, tracking, and documenting the locations and movements of the human bodies within their jurisdictions, as well as the transfer of bodies out of or between medical and funereal jurisdictions. Indeed, the toe tag used to identify and track dead bodies is among the most iconic features of the image of medico-mortuary corpses.

Discussing the professionalization of death care in France in the 1980s, Trompette and Lemonnier theorize that the "structuring work and inter-professional coordination" of health-care and death-care professionals has created "socio-technical networks" that have "reconnect[ed] two physically adjacent but socially and organizationally divided worlds (the medical world and the funeral world)" (2009, 10).

> The work involved in formatting and channeling the circulation of the deceased includes the entire chain of people treating the dead. This chain is based on cooperation and affiliation between health professionals and death professionals. Socio-technical networks connect spaces and create a continuum of action between the health-care establishment (hospital, old people's home, etc.) and the funeral parlor. . . . The management of the interface between life and death relies on powerful material and practical links that organize the standardized circulation of the deceased. (2009, 22)

These networks act as sites where bureaucratic norms (e.g., tracking, documentation, repetition, confirmation) can be performed through the circulation of bodies through and between bureaucratic regimes. These norms may be performed in a number of ways, ranging from highly conscious, ritualistic performances to unconsciously rote, mechanical performances.

Health-care professionals work to facilitate the smooth transition of bodies from the medical regime to the funerary regime. In a set of guidelines for funeral directors, the Department of Health (DOH) in the Commonwealth of Virginia stresses, "It is extremely important that we maintain the chain of custody for bodies in our care. This is especially critical when we receive a body after regular business hours. Please remind your staff that the necessary information must be entered into the morgue record completely and legibly."[6] These guidelines aim to manage risk and facilitate the smooth transfer of bodies between health-care and death-care regimes. The DOH prefaces its guidelines for funeral directors by stating, "We value our relationship with funeral service providers," who "often are called upon to act as a liaison between the Office of the Chief Medical Examiner and the families of deceased residents."[7] The Virginia DOH provides no similar guidelines for releasing a body directly to the decedent's next of kin.

Funeral directors, too, work to facilitate the smooth transition of bodies between medical and funerary regimes. In a February 2019 webinar produced by funeral industry publisher Kates-Boylston, Dan Funchess, a nurse and director of funeral operations at a cemetery real estate company, stresses the importance of establishing relationships with hospice organizations as a means by which to maintain the official status of the funeral industrial episteme. According to Funchess, "Funeral Homes have always had working relationships with the Medical Community . . . (e.g., MDs; Long-term care facilities; Hospitals, etc.)" (2019, 15, 55), but "we [funeral directors] have become complacent . . . and think that we're probably the drivers of everything death-related" (14, 35). Funchess insists that funeral directors must *work* to build and maintain their professional identity as "the death care expert[s] in [their] communit[ies]" by cultivating relationships with health-care professionals and institutions (16, 30).

BONDS OF INTIMACY

Reflecting on her daughter's death, Beth Knox writes:

> When the life support at the hospital was about to be removed, I was told that the hospital could only release her to a funeral home.
> I had given birth to her. She had lived with me every day of her life. I had carefully chosen what she was exposed to, what she ate, where she went to school. I was required by law to care well for her. But now that her heart had stopped beating, I was being told that her care was no longer my concern. (Knox n.d.)

From Knox's point of view, the relevant continuum of action regarding the care of her daughter did not extend from the hospital to the funeral home; rather, it centered on her continued care for her child. Keeping her daughter's body at home for three days, Knox says she "was able to continue to love my daughter by caring for her and by doing that I could begin to accept what had happened and begin to heal" (Harris 2007, 106). Knox experienced the care for her living and dead child as a natural continuum of action based in bonds of intimacy between a mother and her child.

Knox's experience is familiar to others who see themselves as conservators of long-standing, sacred traditions. For nearly fifteen years, Brother Noor—as he has asked that I call him—has led the Janazah Project, helping Muslim families prepare the bodies of their dead for burial, washing them, shrouding them, and reciting the Janazah prayer.[8] I met Brother Noor at the NHFA's biennial conference in Reisterstown, Maryland, in the fall of 2017, where he participated in a panel devoted to discussing various religious communities' perspectives on home funerals. Joining Brother Noor were David Zinner, executive director of Kavod v'Nichum, and Lucinda Herring, owner of Thresholds Consulting and Ministry, Limina, and a self-described "student of both Western and Eastern spiritual traditions," who offered thoughts on a Buddhist perspective on home funerals.

One month after the conference, I interviewed Brother Noor over the phone to follow up with him about a story he shared during the panel discussion about a Muslim father's frustration at not being able to take custody of his dead baby's body. The hospital at which the baby died would not allow him to take his child's body home, even though, Brother Noor states, "legally speaking [New York] state law does not require to have a licensed funeral director remove the body or . . . sign the body out."[9] According to Brother Noor, the baby's body remained in the hospital for nearly a week before the family relented to the hospital's insistence that a funeral director take custody of the corpse. Funeral laws in New York State are among the most restrictive in the United States with respect to home death care, requiring the presence or signature of a licensed and registered funeral director at multiple stages between death and final disposition.

Brother Noor relates another story about an Easterville, Pennsylvania, cemetery's refusal to accept a body that Brother Noor and a Philadelphia family brought to them for interment. Having called ahead to inform the cemetery that he was about to deliver a body for which he possessed a burial permit, Brother Noor was surprised, on his arrival at the cemetery, by the cemetery owner's insistence that a funeral director be present to transfer the body to the care of the cemetery and to oversee the body's interment. Brother Noor correctly pointed out that Pennsylvania law does not require the presence of a funeral director, but to no avail. Understandably anxious to bury the body of their loved one, the family relented and paid a local funeral director to attend the interment. After this event, Brother Noor sought help from the NHFA, David Zinner, the nonprofit Funeral Consumers Alliance, and from Pittsburgh-based rabbi Daniel Wasserman, each of whom reported having similar experiences with cemeteries' refusals to accept bodies from persons other than licensed funeral directors. According to Brother Noor, the Easterville cemetery remained reluctant to change its practices even after he and his allies presented the cemetery owner with information about relevant Pennsylvania funeral laws. "I lose this fight all the time," says Brother Noor, "but hopefully [I'm] not going to lose the war."[10]

The home-funeral movement articulates an alternate ontology of the corpse, one that is grounded in a conception of the corpse not as an aberrant public-health concern warranting the intervention of state-regulated experts but rather as a natural, normal body that calls for continued care from intimates (friends, family, close-knit community members). And instead of viewing home-funeral practitioners' or advocates' efforts to take custody of their dead as an interruption of standard practice, the home-funeral movement considers industrial death care an extended interruption of a much longer tradition of home death care.

In a chapter titled "Then and Now" of the home-funeral training guide, *Undertaken with Love* (2007), home-funeral movement leaders Donna Belk, Margaret Eden, Wendy Lyons, and Holly Stevens frame the home-funeral movement within a narrative about the recollection or reinvigoration of a form of knowledge and skill—frequently identified as feminine—that has been denigrated, forgotten, or lost: "Historically in America, after-death care was considered the exclusive duty of women [who] . . . possessed specialized knowledge in the laying out of the dead." Yet, the authors point out, the US Civil War marked the beginning of a time when "little by little, caring for our dead went from being an act of love freely carried out by families and communities to a trade that allows for little—if any—hands-on family involvement." Today, the narrative continues, "modern-day pioneers in family-led home funerals . . . have contributed to our understanding of the practical skills involved in caring for our dead," helping people "reconnect" with the "sacred tradition" of home death care, and to "welcome the funeral back into the intimacy of the home." Through the home-funeral movement, the authors emphasize, we are "reclaiming our past" (Belk et al. 2007, 3).

The home-funeral movement has developed, in part, out of a broad critique of male-dominated body-care practices in both health-care and death-care contexts. In particular, home-funeral advocates' attitudes toward and understandings of the dead body resonate with home-birth advocates' conception of pregnant and birthing bodies. Just as the home (or natural) childbirth movement has resisted the medicalization of childbirth, insisting that pregnant and birthing bodies are natural, normal, and generally not in need of medical intervention, so too the home-funeral movement resists the funeralization of the dead body, contending that dead bodies are natural, normal, and generally not in need of oversight or technical intervention from professional funeral directors or embalmers. In fact, many of the same women who championed natural childbirth when they and their friends were having children in the 1960s and 1970s have now reached a point in their lives when the death of friends and family members is becoming a more central part of their life experiences (Olson 2016a). As Lisa Carlson, author of *Caring for Your Own Dead* (1987), stated in a 2005 *Washington Post* interview, "It's the other end of the spectrum from natural childbirth. . . . The baby-boom generation took control of critical life events, wrote their own wedding vows, had home births. . . . They're fueling the interest in taking control [of death care]" (Cox 2005).

Meeting Administrative Concerns

Bureaucratic arrangements and epistemic cultures can have a life of their own beyond the dictates of the law, which does not *determine* routine death-care practices. We gain some insight into why various institutions (including hospitals, nursing homes, cemeteries, and crematoria) resist families' efforts to exercise their legal right to take custody of their own dead by talking to institutional administrators about their refusals to work directly with intimates of the dead. Moreover, we gain insight into understanding home-funeral movement leaders' strategies for overcoming these resistances.

Decedent Affairs

During the same NHFA conference at which I met Brother Noor, I also met Ruth (as I will call her), a former decedent-affairs program manager and now manager of pathology (a position that encompasses her former position) at a large health-care system that operates multiple hospitals in the Eastern United States. Knowing she would be addressing an audience generally unsympathetic to her hospital's policy and practices of only releasing bodies to licensed funeral directors, Ruth bravely participated in a panel discussion titled "Building Bridges: Advocating to Hospices and Hospitals." Her fellow panelists were then president of the NHFA, Lee Webster, and Fabio Lomelina, a clinical counselor and former bereavement support and outreach coordinator for Gilchrist Hospice Care in Baltimore, Maryland. The last panelist to introduce herself, Ruth stated with humorous self-deprecation, "Today, in this room, I am 'The Man.'"[11]

In November 2017, I followed up with Ruth to learn more about her role in managing the release of human remains. Ruth works in a liminal space in the hospital, managing the transition of dead bodies out of the hospital, and she sees herself as part of a team providing continuous care for the body across the boundary between life and death. When giving tours of the pathology department to hospital nursing staff, Ruth tells the nurses, "Just because your patient dies doesn't mean that we stop caring for them at the hospital."[12] Although she works for a hospital system, Ruth says she is "thankful" to be "part of the death care community," referring to herself as a "death-care professional." Ruth is sympathetic to the home-funeral movement, having helped organize a home funeral for her own grandfather. For Ruth, her family's choice to have a home funeral "was a personal choice that we made, but I wasn't necessarily seeing it as [part of] a movement." Nevertheless, when it comes to performing her job, Ruth says, "I'm in a position where I'm not always able to exercise personal beliefs."

Ruth recognizes that families have a legal right to claim custody of their dead, but, she explained during the NHFA panel discussion, hospital policies are "more restrictive than the law." In our subsequent phone interview, Ruth elaborated: "In terms of risk it's not always about how the law is written. It is very much—especially with something as sensitive as death is, [and] as disconnected as we are to it—we have a huge emotional connection, and when we see something we don't like, you know, it raises [pause] it's a high emotion item." Ruth defends the hospital's policy, saying it secures the safe and dignified treatment of the dead, while also ensuring the proper bureaucratic rituals are performed. Funeral directors have "the right equipment to transport the [deceased] person," Ruth says, "and they reliably file paperwork." Ruth expresses concern that the removal of bodies by people other than licensed funeral directors exposes both the decedent and the hospital to unnecessary risks: "Unfortunately, the things that can go wrong in these situations, you know, you can read about it anytime you want with a Google search. The terrible things that can happen. . . . You don't know what's going to happen to that person [the decedent]." When I ask her to provide specific examples, she speaks not from personal experience, but instead relates stories she has heard, or evokes potential scenarios involving "someone being dropped," "body fluid exposure," families' failures to "fill out paperwork" (notably death certificates), or home-funeral families "not having the right equipment to transport the person" and therefore "having to [carry] the person out, you known, like a fireman carry or something" or letting the body fall out of a person's van and "[end] up on the road."

For Ruth, managing public perception is key to establishing the public trust she feels she possesses through her job: "People trust you, and that's a *huge* gift." In turn, Ruth trusts funeral professionals, whom she calls "a special kind of people" with "integrity" who work in "a noble profession," stating that she feels "honored" to work with them. She knows how funeral professionals operate. She trusts their training and the knowledge and skills that they possess. But home-funeral advocates and home-funeral practitioners have yet to earn the same degree of trust with her, and it is this lack of trust that underlies the hospital's policy of not granting custody of the corpse to persons other than licensed funeral directors.

Managing Home Funeral Knowledge and Skill

There are now dozens of home-funeral trainers and teachers offering a variety of educational programs designed to teach people how to care for their own dead or to train those who would, as "home-funeral guides" (HFGs), assist families with the care of their own dead.[13] Different programs teach different sets of skills and use different pedagogical techniques. Some relay information primarily through print and online media, while others rely on in-person, hands-on trainings ranging from half-day workshops to weekend-long intensives. Increasingly, training programs have begun offering business advice for those interested in hanging out a shingle in the nascent alternative death-care market. On the one hand, this variety of training is a strength of the home-funeral movement's folk episteme, allowing for flexibility with respect to local contexts. On the other hand, the indeterminacy and unpredictability that variety entails can engender apprehension among persons and institutions who value reliable consistency of practice.

Many home-funeral advocates and movement leaders have resisted the professionalization of home-funeral work. As the NHFA states on its website, "Requiring licensure or certification would force guides into becoming industry professionals, which is in direct opposition to what home funeral guides stand for, specifically keeping the care of the deceased in the hands of the family and not in the realm of industry professionals" (NHFA 2019b). Other home-funeral advocates maintain that professionalization could elevate the social standing of the home-funeral movement in a bureaucratized death-care culture that values professional expertise. Merilynne Rush, a former NHFA board member and author of the training guide *Home Funeral Guides: Illuminating the Path* (2015), considers herself a death-care professional, albeit not a funeral service provider. In a 2014 interview, Rush told me:

> I'm not a funeral director. I'm not in the industry. I'm a natural death care educator who is outside of the profession. . . . Licensed funeral directors shouldn't have a monopoly on the term "funeral professional," but public perception gives them this. So I can't *now* call myself [a funeral professional], but one day I might be able to do that. Yes. I am [a funeral professional], but I don't call myself one.[14]

Rush suggests that being able to claim the status of "funeral professional" would indicate public recognition of the value of her knowledge and skill, validating her work in the eyes of families seeking help with home funerals and in the eyes of members of the techno-social networks (like Ruth), whose countenance home-funeral guides are likely to need.

While the NHFA neither offers certification in home-funeral practice nor endorses any independent certification program, the organization "acknowledges the value of certificates of completion awarded by home-funeral education providers for the purpose of ensuring that home-funeral guides and the public receive appropriate and consistent information to aid them in carrying out a home funeral or teaching others how to do so" (NHFA 2019b). But certificates of completion can fulfill that purpose only if there *is* consistency across the training that home-funeral guides receive.

In October 2018, the NHFA (2019a) posted on its website a set of "core competencies" that all HFGs ought to possess. Former NHFA president Lee Webster describes herself as the "point person" for the development of HFG core competencies, stating that the topic of standards is "near and dear to my heart. . . . I love systems! And I want them to work. What do we do to make them work?"[15] Webster believes that defining core competencies and offering a "badge" to those who demonstrate proficiency in those competencies proffers a compromise between centralized control over certification standards, on the one hand, and curricular over-opulence on the other. Webster refers to this compromise approach as a form of "microcredentialing," which, she says is "in keeping with cutting-edge credentialing around the country in different areas."

Webster hopes that core competencies will provide HFGs with the "professional" validation that they have always wanted—a validation that could help the home-funeral movement achieve its goal of capacitating home funerals: "It's being viewed as a professional. . . . We want to be accepted in this community, just like everybody else who provides services to the dying [or intimates of the dead], that we do have the knowledge, we can now demonstrate that we have the knowledge, you know, once we get this whole proficiency thing up, and we need to be treated as though we have this knowledge." Movement leaders like Webster continuously "[get] calls from individuals with individual problems. They are crises. They need to be dealt with immediately and it sucks up all your time," says Webster, who further explains, "We'll have people calling all the time saying, you know, 'I can't get my brother out of the hospital. They won't let us take him home.' . . . And we'll have to then get on the phone with various authorities, including hospital bureaucracies and work our way through all that, explain the law case by case." According to Webster, microcredentialing could lead to acceptance in (or at least by) professional death-care networks and may help address some of the bureaucratic obstacles that home-funeral advocates and practitioners regularly face.

Yet many leading home-funeral advocates believe that professionalization and certification are anathema to the goals and identity of the home-funeral movement. Elizabeth Knox insists, "Advocates of professionalization are missing the point!"[16] She wants to preserve what she sees as the folk character of home funeral practices:

> It's an oral tradition, honestly. We're at the day and age where everybody wants to professionalize and certify, and . . . [b]ut that's not what home-funeral care is about. . . . This is essentially an oral tradition. You know, we're renewing the way this was done throughout millennia. You take the humanity out of it as soon as you start to certify and professionalize, and the whole point of home-funeral care is that it brings the humanity back into death care.

Knox sees the home-funeral movement as offering not only an alternative to industrial death care but also a check on contemporary society's overvaluation of knowledge credentialing and professional status. Her appeal to a millennia-old tradition of home-funeral care represents an effort to disrupt bureaucratic conventions that "[take] the humanity out of [death care]." Knox would seem to agree with Engelke's (2019) suggestion that Max Weber's thoughts on bureaucratic disenchantment may shed light on the home-funeral movement's critique of the medicalization and funeralization of the human body. As Engelke notes, the home-funeral movement is part of a broader trend—one that includes death midwifery and natural burials—that seeks to "establish values of intimacy" and which, borrowing a phrase from Weber, "marks commitments to 'the blood-and-the-sap of true life' (however defined)" (Weber 1946, 141, quoted in Engelke 2019) that bureaucratic efficiency has drained from death and death care (Engelke 2019, 32).

Knox is not alone in resisting the professionalization and bureaucratization of home-funeral work and the certification of HFGs. In an October 2019 phone interview, current NHFA president Dani Lavoire told me she "struggles with [fully embracing] the proficiency badge" and that she is unwilling to promote the professionalization of home-funeral guides.[17] While she recognizes that the movement "takes all kinds" (including those who support and those who oppose the professionalization of home death care), Lavoire insists, "I don't think the NHFA should be supporting home-funeral businesses." For Lavoire, the overarching aim of the home-funeral movement is to empower people to care for their own dead outside of the professional setting of industrial death care and with minimal bureaucratic administration. "The last thing you want to do while grieving," Lavoire writes in the May 2019 NHFA newsletter, "is to make a trip to the county building."[18] Moreover, she is unconvinced that proficiency badges will enhance the credibility of home-funeral practitioners and advocates in the eyes of health-care professionals, death-care professionals, or the general public. Lavoire is a licensed and certified midwife who has been practicing for twenty years, but, she notes, these credentials have not enhanced her credibility among the doctors and nurses: "When I'm in the hospital, I'm treated exactly the same as Aunt Mary."

In keeping with cultural-historical narratives that cast the home-funeral movement as a reclamation of old knowledge and forgotten tradition, Lavoire maintains that both birth knowledge and death-care knowledge are grounded in "primitive" knowledges or skills that are "in [human beings'] DNA to do." According to Lavoire, this kind of embodied knowledge is not appropriately credentialed by social movement organizations or by adherence to professional standards. Instead, Lavoire appeals to experts in evolutionary biology, neuroscience, and clinical psychology—specifically Stephen Porges's (n.d.) polyvagal theory of neurophysiological stress response and Peter Levine's trademarked "Somatic Experiencing" approach to trauma treatment (Somatic Experiencing

Trauma Institute n.d.)—to underwrite home-funeral knowledge with scientific credentials, thereby proffering a biological foundation for home-funeral proponents' belief in the grief-therapeutic benefits of home death care. "Part of why we're doing this [promoting home-funeral practices]," says Lavoire, "is because it affects our grief processes in a way that's beneficial to our stress responses."

The particular ideas articulated by Rush, Webster, Knox, and Lavoire may not represent most practitioners' or advocates' views about home death care, but they draw attention to an important aspect of the movement's challenge to industrial death care. The home-funeral movement is not—and cannot be—a simple revival of preindustrial death-care practices. Indeed, to view the movement as a mere recovery of past practices would be to strip its leaders and practitioners of their creative, social, and political power. The home-funeral movement is seeking to construct a *new* epistemic culture that is built around a conception of the dead human body as a natural, normal body that generally does not require the technological interventions of state-sanctioned experts, but that calls for continued care from intimates. Home-funeral proponents naturalize this understanding of the dead human body through cultural-historical narratives (and even scientific narratives) about labor, the human body, and humanity. By exposing the contingency and constructedness of industrial death care's epistemic culture, home-funeral proponents also reveal the contingency and constructedness of the alternatives they themselves are fashioning. Indeed, the home-funeral movement does not offer a more "authentic" appreciation of death and dead bodies than does the dominant industrial death-care regime. As Armstrong (1987) points out, the bureaucratization of death has not entailed a "denial" of death but rather a transformation of the discourses, materials, and rituals involved in the "progression of the newly dead from the world of the living to the world of nature" (652). Moreover, there is no a priori reason to think that bureaucratized death care cannot be richly affect laden or that it can offer none of "the blood-and-the-sap" of a full-bodied relationship with death, as Engelke (this volume) demonstrates.

Home-funeral movement leaders disagree about how best to represent and promote the character of the movement as a whole. Rush and Webster tend toward embracing professionalization and curricular standardization for HFGs, believing that microcredentialing could raise the credibility of home-funeral practitioners within the bureaucratic chain of custody that ushers the dead from the world of the living to the world of nature. But Knox and Lavoire believe the movement should instead resist professionalization and bureaucratization in an effort to put death care literally in the hands of intimates, whose knowledge and authority are grounded in continuing personal, caring relationships with the decedent. Movement leaders disagree about "the machineries of knowing in which [home-funeral] agents [wish to] play a part" (Knorr Cetina 1999, 9), and thus continue to grapple with the kind of epistemic culture the movement wishes to cultivate.

Funeral Insecurity during the Pandemic

On March 12, 2020, the day after Italian actor Luca Franzese's sister, Theresa, died of COVID-19, he posted an emotional plea for help on Facebook: "I have my sister here in bed, dead. I don't know what to do. I can't honor her as she deserves because institutions abandoned me. . . . I contacted everyone, but nobody was able to give me an answer" (Steinbuch 2020). Franzese's selfie video, featuring his sister's dead body lying in bed at her home in Naples, Italy, quickly spread through international media, contributing to growing, global awareness of sudden disruptions to standard corpse management. In the ensuing months, "funeral insecurity" has become a well-traveled concern among public-health experts and funeral directors, pundits and politicians, intimates of the dead and dying, cemetery and crematory operators, pathologists and coroners, health-care institutions and professionals, and, of course, home-funeral proponents. All these groups share a common concern for, at minimum, the management of large numbers of dead bodies and the timely and dignified disposition of human remains; but each group has a different set of things to feel insecure about and different ideas about how they might help to restore funeral security. Franzese's plea for help raises questions to which there are no obvious answers. Which "institutions" left Franzese feeling "abandoned"? Who has the authority to care for the bodies of the dead? Who has a responsibility to care for the dead? Why didn't Franzese "know what to do"? Who *does* know what to do? What is at stake in seeing funerals as a security issue? And who has the authority to answer these questions?

International relations scholar Jessica Auchter writes, "Dead bodies are considered a problem *for* governance in that they require some kind of management, yet rarely considered a problem *of* governance in that they rarely cause us to reflect on structures of authority and power" (2016, 44). The home-funeral movement's primary aim is to make visible and to challenge the structures of authority and power that shape the management of dead bodies, but COVID-19 has generated greater awareness of the politics of dead bodies than the home-funeral movement could. And as Auchter notes, this increasing awareness "is intimately linked to . . . how an issue becomes conceived of as a 'security issue' and thus a policy imperative" (48).

The pandemic has elicited novel articulations of the differing death-care expertises already discussed in this chapter. Frustrated that the dangers of their "forgotten" work are being overlooked by public officials who remain focused on "hospital[s] or first responder[s]" (Kopp 2020), funeral directors like Ellen McBrayer and Stephen Kemp refer to themselves as "last responders"—others have called themselves "last of the first responders" (Sanburn 2020)—whose job is, as Kemp puts it, "to complete the chain of protecting the general public" (Root 2020). Positioning themselves in a chain of action that extends across the boundary of health-care and death-care institutions, funeral industrialists have sought not only to emphasize their public health expertise but also to increase awareness of the public-health dangers that they themselves face, in hopes that this awareness will amplify their requests for increased access to personal protective equipment. Home-funeral movement leaders, too, have sought to promote their knowledge and skill as especially important during the pandemic, emphasizing their role in fostering intimates' care of their dead. "Our job as [home-funeral] educators has suddenly expanded," says Lee Webster in a webinar video posted to the NHFA website (Adams et al. 2020) and further promulgated by *Newsweek* in late March (Rahman 2020). In addition to providing HFGs with guidance about home body care during the pandemic, the video encourage HFGs to broaden and deepen their presence in US death-care culture by "contact[ing] as many leaders, organizations, and agencies [as] you can to let them know that you have a skill and knowledge that can help families with learning how to care for their own [dead] at home" (Adams et al. 2020).

Yet funeral insecurity during the pandemic has also drawn attention to other "problems *of* governance," notably problems of social inequity that span health care and death care. In a July 5, 2020, article, the *New York Times* reported that "Black and Latin[x] people have been disproportionately affected by the coronavirus in a widespread manner that spans the country, throughout hundreds of counties in urban, suburban and rural areas, and across all age groups" (Oppel et al. 2020). The death care industry remains a highly segregated industry (Fletcher 2020; Laderman 2003; Plater 1996), with Black-owned and -operated funeral homes tending to serve primarily Black clientele and white-owned and

-operated funeral homes tending to serve white clientele. Given this segregation and the disproportionate impact of COVID-19 on African Americans, we should not be surprised when Black-owned funeral homes become overburdened during the pandemic, as did Brooklyn, New York's, Andrew T. Cleckley Funeral Services, which resorted to storing decomposing bodies in unrefrigerated rental trucks in late April (Feuer, Southall, and Gold 2020). But we ought to be wary of judgments—like those issued by New York City mayor Bill de Blasio (Feuer and Kim 2020)—that lay blame directly on disproportionately affected Black funeral homes for circumstances like these. And as the Movement for Black Lives coalition raises greater awareness of police violence (in the wake of the police killing of George Floyd), untenable mass incarceration, and draconian sentencing practices, we should be especially sensitive to the severity of private and public legal sanctions levied against Black funeral homes that have difficulty managing mass death during the pandemic.

Like Auchter, I hope the management of dead bodies will receive more attention within the field of security studies, which may provide a framework in and through which a variety of actors—including scholars, activists, policy makers, nongovernmental organizations, laypersons, religious leaders, professional societies, and industry leaders—may collectively bring diverse knowledges, skills, and intersectional perspectives to bear in order to identify and respond to issues of funeral security. If, as science, technology, and society and securities studies scholar Saul Halfon says, "Security truly is what the experts make of it, where expertise is that which can be sold as expertise to powerful communities of practice" (2015, 147), efforts to diversify and make audible a wider variety of voices in the marketplace of expertise may be a good place to begin to make processes of securitization more epistemically just.

Notes

1. I choose the term *funeral industrialists* for two reasons. First, home-funeral advocates frequently self-identify as funeral "professionals" of a sort, though they actively resist identification as members of the funeral industry. Second, most licensed funeral directors readily self-identify as professionals and as members of the funeral industry.
2. In the present context of the COVID-19 pandemic and ongoing protests against deadly police violence, it is especially important to think critically about what it means to think positively about death in general and about the meanings of different kinds of death.

3. Janazah Project (2020); Kavod v'Nichum and Gamliel Institute (2020b).
4. Aside from the Federal Trade Commission's "Funeral Rule" (16 CFR 453), funeral laws and regulations are almost entirely authored at the state level. I use the term *advocate* to refer, broadly, to anyone who works to educate the public about home death care or who advocates for other peoples' right to care for their own dead. I use the term *practitioner* to refer to people who have performed or participated in (or who have attempted to perform or participate in) home-funeral practices. Home-funeral advocates and practitioners may or may not self-identify as members of or participants in the US home-funeral movement.
5. *New York Times* (2020).
6. Virginia Department of Health, "Information for Funeral Directors," https://www.vdh.virginia.gov/medical-examiner/information-for-funeral-directors/.
7. Ibid.
8. In both traditional Muslim and traditional Jewish death-care practices, the body of the deceased is generally washed by persons of the same sex as the decedent; men wash the bodies of dead men, while women wash the bodies of dead women. Thus, in Islamic and Jewish death-care practices, postmortem body care has not been dominated by one sex or another, as has been the case in US death-care culture.
9. Phone interview conducted on October 31, 2017.
10. Ibid.
11. NHFA Conference (Reisterstown, MD, September 22, 2017).
12. Phone interview conducted on November 6, 2017. (All quotations and references made in this section will be to this interview unless otherwise indicated.)
13. Many (but not all) of these programs are listed on the NHFA website, https://www.homefuneralalliance.org/directories.html#!directory.
14. Phone interview conducted on April 26, 2014.
15. All subsequent references in this section will be to my October 16, 2018, interview with Webster.
16. Phone interview conducted on July 6, 2015. All subsequent reference in this section are to this interview, unless otherwise noted.
17. Phone interview conducted on October 28, 2019. All subsequent quotations from Lavoire are drawn from this interview, unless otherwise noted.
18. National Home Funeral Alliance member newsletter, "Notes from the Field," May 2019, distributed via email (on file with the author).

CHAPTER ELEVEN

Making a Living from Death
Chinese State Funeral Workers under the Market Economy

HUWY-MIN LUCIA LIU

In March 2009, every major national newspaper in the People's Republic of China (PRC) and several international papers reported on a job fair at the Shanghai Talent Market. This job fair was a special recruitment event—twenty-three funeral-related institutions in Shanghai (including state funeral parlors, state and private cemeteries, and other funeral-related companies) were offering 395 positions to college graduates or those holding higher-degrees). Many headlines used titles such as "5,000 College Graduates Fighting for Positions in the Funeral Industry" to sensationalize the event. Almost all reports emphasized how well the funeral industry paid and how stable its positions were to explain why college graduates would compete so fiercely to work in a profession that had for so long been considered both low-status and taboo. To unpack the uniqueness of this event, we need to understand the special mix of tradition and commonality that characterizes the funeral profession in Sinophone cultures (Chinese-speaking societies) in general and in the PRC in particular.

This chapter illustrates changes that have occurred in the Shanghai funeral industry by situating death workers in the context of the socialist transition as the PRC changed from a planned to a socialist market economy (although this was not in any way a teleological transformation). I do so by delineating and analyzing the life history of a Shanghai funeral worker, Lin Wu, one of the best body restoration artists in China. My analysis of Lin Wu emphasizes two aspects: ambiguity and existential crisis. This reorientation allows me to consider funeral professionals as individuals who, similar to other Chinese people, must navigate their lives under a socialist market economy and choose between different ethical ideas of being proper persons.

Death in China

The Chinese Communist Party nationalized the Shanghai funeral industry soon after it officially defeated the Chinese Nationalist Party in 1949. By the mid-1950s, all funeral homes, cemeteries, and other funeral-related institutions were nationalized in Shanghai. Such nationalization of funeral institutions provided the infrastructure that allowed the Chinese state to modernize and secularize preexisting mortuary practices. In Sinophone cultures, traditional funerals were based on concepts of spirits, afterlife, the unclean and polluted nature of the corpse, and a Confucian social hierarchy. Properly performed death rituals transformed dead bodies into ancestors—the classic kind of regenerative process described by Hertz ([1900] 1960). However, the Chinese Communist Party saw these assumptions about death as feudalist superstitions, a cause of China's perceived weakness in the face of Western imperialism. As such, the Chinese Communist Party promoted cremation to replace body burial and secular civil rituals to replace religious rituals. The idea behind this state conception of proper death is actually quite similar to those of secular humanists in the United Kingdom who believe that there is no life after death (Engelke, this volume).

After the Chinese Communist Party nationalized the Shanghai funeral industry, state funeral workers became quasi-governmental officials. As such, their main task was to promote state-sanctioned ways of handling and disposing of dead bodies. Although Shanghai state funeral workers did not usually rely on force in their policy implementation, enforcement did happen (Liu 2020b). The Cultural Revolution, lasting roughly between 1968 and 1978, was one of the most important political events that shaped death in Shanghai. Almost overnight, all cemeteries in the city were closed, and universal cremation was implemented via the two crematoria that were allowed to remain open. At the national level, Chinese funeral parlors took on a distinctive function (Chinese funeral parlors are synonymous with crematoria), becoming key sites for state-enforced mandatory cremation in urban areas. This long process of state-initiated modernization and secularization of death is known in China as Funeral and Interment Reform (*binzang gaige*). While the specific policies governing death and the intensity of implementing those policies have changed over time, Funeral and Interment Reform, with its goal to "modernize" death, has been an ongoing governmental effort that continues to this day.

Following the death of Mao Zedong in 1978, which marked the end of the

Cultural Revolution, the Chinese Communist Party began experimenting with market-economy principles. This change has affected every aspect of social life, from the loss of guaranteed lifelong employment, to increased private and personal space, to a moderate revival of religious practices, to just name a few. For funerary matters in Shanghai, introducing market-economy principles has created several new trends. In terms of death ritual, while Shanghai funeral parlors hoped to generate profits by promoting personalized funerals that commemorate the deceased as individuals to replace socialist civil funerals that memorialized the dead as model socialist citizens (a type of ritual that was popularized during the Cultural Revolution), what actually happened was the reincorporation of religious practices within the secular socialist civil funeral (Liu 2019 and 2020a). At the national level, the Qingming Festival (also known as Tomb Sweeping Festival), which was once discouraged because of its association with religious ideas and practices of managing death, became a national holiday in 2008. In other words, if the first half of the Chinese Communist Party's modernization of death was about secularization, the second half is about religionization. In terms of death work, Shanghai state funeral parlors were changed from being a part of the bureaucratic apparatus to being units that were financially independent, if not profit-making. To facilitate such a transition, the Chinese state worked to transform death workers from being solely policy-enforcement officials to being both officials *and* entrepreneurs motivated to maximize their productivity (Liu 2015). In other words, this transition from planned to market economy required not only a new kind of death institution that generated profit but also a new kind of death worker who was capable of doing so.

This change in political economy brought about two specific trajectories for death work in China: professionalization and commodification. In contrast to what happened in Europe and America, where death care moved from the family at home to professionals in funeral homes (Ariès 1981), in Sinophone cultures, there has been a long history of paid funeral professionals. In imperial China, while parts of funerals depended on family members, a wide variety of death rituals required paid professional services that were provided by nonfamily members. The main concern over funeral professionals emerged from the concept of the pollution of the corpse—both as a perception and as a very real issue of sanitation and hygiene—inherent in the management of dead bodies. This association of death and dead bodies—and the people who deal with them—with uncleanness, as being polluted, which has long marginalized funeral professionals in Sinophone societies, was precisely why a job fair inviting college graduates to compete for positions in the funeral profession was so newsworthy (Douglas 1966; and see Toulson, this volume, for a discussion of death pollution in the Singapore context).

James Watson's (1988a) work on funeral specialists in rural Hong Kong is one of the few anthropological accounts exploring funeral professionals in Sinophone studies. Watson argues that funeral specialists' physical proximity to decaying bodies and the skill, training, and literacy needed in these jobs created a social hierarchy. Within the funeral profession, fengshui masters ranked highest, followed by priests. Additionally, there were "pipers, musicians, nuns, and general helpers," who played a part in handling death but who did not have direct contact with the dead bodies. At the bottom of the hierarchy were corpse handlers who had direct contact with the dead. While Watson's fieldwork was based in British Hong Kong in the 1960s, his portrait of the social hierarchy of funeral specialists was considered to be consistent with life in imperial China (before 1911). On the other side of the social hierarchy in imperial life were scholar-officials, or scholars who enjoyed the highest social status based on Confucian ideology. While college graduates were not exactly the contemporary version of scholar-officials, the contrast between them and funeral professionals was based on this old divide.

This centuries-old concept of death pollution continues to be a powerful force in Sinophone societies today. When Ruth Toulson (2013) conducted her fieldwork among ethnic Chinese morticians in Singapore—an economically and technologically well-developed city-state—in the early 2000s, she saw restaurant staff purposely shattering rice bowls outside the restaurant because those bowls had just been used by her mortician interlocutors. During my fieldwork in Shanghai in 2011, it was standard practice for state funeral workers to not visit relatives during the Lunar New Year holiday, even though everyone else was expected to visit during this time. This urge to avoid death has to do with people's desire to stay away from the malicious spirits and bad luck brought by pollution. In Euro-America, however, scholars have argued that the denial of death, motivated by people's desire to pursue happiness and scientific modernity, has driven people to avoid public recognition of death (Ariès 1981; Becker 1973; Gorer 1955b). Of course, to what degree death avoidance still exists in Euro-American societies today is another question. As Dawdy and Kneese suggest in the introduction to this volume, the popularity of death in the media and the emergence of death salons, among other social phenomena, seem to indicate that Americans have moved away from their denial of death.

Nevertheless, this persistent view of death pollution in Sinophone societies contrasts with what had happened in Japan. In her pioneering book addressing funeral professionals in Japan, Hikaru Suzuki (2000) argues that the commodification of the death industry has mitigated such a perception against Japanese funeral workers. While the commodification of death seems like a positive development in the Japanese funeral industry, elsewhere, such commodification is viewed less positively. In the United States, one of the most common criticisms of the funeral industry is its profiteering, a perception that has dominated public opinion ever since journalist Jessica Mitford published *The American Way of Death* in 1963. As such, many developments in the new death in Euro-America have been based on a reaction against professionalization and capitalism, as exemplified by the home-death movements such as green burials and DIY funerals described by Olson in this volume and the trajectory of American funeral professionals from sanitation workers (undertakers and morticians) to service providers (funeral directors), as discussed by Dawdy. The first transition was associated with the popularization of embalming, and the second was linked to a critique against capitalism and the commodification of death.

However, pursuing profits in the contemporary Chinese funeral industry has a very different set of underpinnings due to the fact that China has been moving from a planned to a market economy. While the economic systems might have changed, however, the authoritarian nature of governance in China has not, even though there is more space now for private life. As such, many Chinese officials, industry leaders, and even the general public were ambivalent about the introduction of market-economy principles into the Chinese funeral industry. On the one hand, they (like Jessica Mitford) criticized its profit motive. On the other hand, they saw the movement toward a market economy as humanistic, in that marketization was meant to be about what the people, as consumers, wanted, in contrast to the state-only orientation of the planned economy.

It is with this contextualized understanding of professionalization and commodification of death in China that I now move to discuss the new kind of workers needed for this new era. Prior to introducing market economic principles in managing funeral parlors, whether a funeral parlor could financially sustain itself or needed to rely on state funding depended on whether the local government could successfully implement cremation. In Shanghai, since a near universal cremation rate was reached before the introduction of the market economy (it was reached during the Cultural Revolution), if state funeral parlors were to increase profits, they had to focus on changing the mindset of state workers. No longer should people have an "eat from the com-mon pot" mentality (meaning that people would get a share of food no matter how hard they worked). Now, state funeral workers were expected to transform themselves into entrepreneurs who were self-motivated and pursued their own self-interest (Liu 2015). Given the relative stability of the industry's association with pollution in China, a pollution-centered framework would be unable to grasp the emergence of this new kind of subject formation under China's now market-oriented governance of death.

It is with this specific process in mind that I explore in the following sections how Lin Wu, a Shanghai body cosmetician, became a successful death worker in a state funeral parlor. Chinese body cosmeticians were the closest equivalent to embalmers or morticians in the American funeral industry, albeit with a few significant differences. For one, arterial embalming—the defining characteris-tics of embalmers in the United States—was rare in China. The main tasks of Chinese body cosmeticians were limited to dressing the dead and applying a bit of makeup to their faces before funerals. Lin Wu was unique as a body cosmeti-cian because he sought new ways to actually repair and restore bodies, pushing back the line of damage over which the bereaved would have no choice but to host a closed-casket funeral. The next section, adapted from a series of inter-views I conducted with Lin Wu, presents Lin Wu's life story in his own words.

The Life Story of Lin Wu: A First-Person Narrative

I am Shanghainese, and I have always lived here. I was born in 1977. My mom worked in a funeral parlor throughout her life. When I was young, I rejected the idea of a career in a funeral parlor. I went to my first funeral parlor when I was four or five, because my mom was worried about leaving me at home alone during my summer vacation. I did not know what death was and had never seen any dead people. That day, I was roaming around in the parlor and had a lot of fun. After we went home, my mom told me what a funeral parlor was and how all those "people" I saw lying down on beds were dead; then I was very scared. I had always been a timid kid, so afterward I refused to allow my mom to take me there ever again. I told her that I would rather stay at home alone. When I was in school, whenever I needed to fill out a form that asked for my parents' occupation, I always wrote only my dad's occupation.

I started to learn art at a very young age. I studied art all the way through high school. I thought that I had some talent, and I always assumed that I would major in art in college and then do art-related work afterward. However, when I took the physical examination for the college entrance exam, I was diagnosed as color-blind. This resulted in my being disqualified outright from every art department. My parents later took me to see a doctor, and it turned out that I was just slower than other people in distinguishing yellow and green. For example, normal people might need only one second to distinguish the two, but I needed ten seconds. This meant that I could differentiate colors. However, because this physical exam was a one-time thing in the application process, my dream literally vanished overnight. All I wanted was to study art, and I felt that I had been handed the death penalty. As a result, I deliberately listed any department that was as far away from art as possible. I threw away all my brushes, paint, and equipment, and I ended up in a mechanical engineering department.

After I graduated from college, the state assigned me to work in a molding factory. I worked there for a total of a little bit over a year. At that time, there was an apprenticeship system. Whether or not you had professional skills, you had to work as an apprentice for three years. It took less than a year for me to pass my exams and to receive a professional certificate from the Labor Bureau. However, I was still an apprentice. In 1995, our factory had labor export [*laowu shuchu*] opportunities to work in Singapore. The annual salary would be RMB 70,000–80,000 [roughly US$11,000–13,000], which was considered a fortune. I was originally on the list to go, but for unknown reasons, they removed me later. This was the straw that broke the camel's back; I was so mad that I quit.

I did not want to work after I quit, and I spent time wandering around. My mom called me one day when I was out. She told me that a funeral parlor was having a large recruitment event and she asked me to take the recruitment exam. I negotiated with her. I told her that I would do my best to take the exam. If I got the job, I would work there for only five years. However, if I failed, she would give me RMB 50,000 [US$8,100] so I could buy a car. I wanted to be a taxi driver. There were not many cars on the road in Shanghai in 1995 and 1996, and I could feel that the taxi business was taking off. In addition, you could go around the city whenever you wanted!

The test subjects for the parlor's recruitment were language, math, and politics; they were basically the same kinds of tests as those for the college entrance exam. This recruitment was the last open recruitment for the parlors to recruit people using a nonprofit public sector staff contract [*shiye bianzhi*].[1] Three days after the exam, I received an interview notice. I heard that approximately sixteen or seventeen people had been offered interviews. Several leaders from the parlor conducted the interviews. Because I did not truly want to work there, I purposely did not give the best answers. However, three or four days after the interview, I was told to start my internship in the parlor. I therefore negotiated with my mom again; I told her that I did not want to work in the body cosmetic unit. My mom told me that it was traditional for all employees to start work in the cosmetic unit. "If you perform well, you can ask for a transfer to another unit," she said. I did not know at that time that my mom was lying.

All of us [new hires] started our internships in the body cosmetic unit. Each master [*shifu*] was responsible for two trainees. Every cosmetician was placed on one of six teams based on different tasks, such as changing the clothes of the deceased, applying makeup, verifying identities, and so on. We had to rotate our team tasks. I was afraid of working with dead bodies. However, I thought that if I could do my job well, I could ask for a transfer.

I saw the brushes the first day I worked on the cosmetic work. At that time, we still used oil paint to apply makeup on dead bodies, so the kinds of brushes used were exactly the same as those I had used in art class. Seeing the brushes was a painful reminder of the past, something that I wanted to put behind me. However, to do a good job so I could leave this unit, I still picked up the brushes to do my work. It did not take me too long to become good at applying makeup since I had learned drawing, oil painting, watercolor painting, and ink painting, and so on when I was a student. My desire to leave the cosmetic unit motivated me to improve my skills as quickly as possible. It took me only two or three minutes to apply basic makeup for a dead body.

There was a personnel transfer approximately three months later. I applied, but they rejected me because they thought that my performance in the body cosmetic unit was too good. I was truly upset, and to protest, I slowed down for two weeks. Some leaders came to talk to me. I also thought about things a lot during this time. I figured that because I could not get a transfer and I actually had talent at working in the cosmetic unit, I should probably just keep doing what I was doing. In any case, I finally came to terms with it.

In 2008, the parlor named a restorative art studio after me. My entrance into restorative art started in the summer of 1998. Before this, my master gave us some basic knowledge of human bones and muscles. I also used the books to understand what the master said, because many of them [the masters] were not good at explaining why things should be done in a certain way. I have always enjoyed reading. I have never cared too much about money. In fact, I handed my salary or any income to my mom as soon as I got it, without checking how much I got. I asked my mom to only give me an allowance every month to let me buy some books. Therefore, I sort of half learned from the masters and half from finding it out myself.

For some unknown reason, there was a rapid increase in the death rate from June through October 1998, and we handled as many as two hundred bodies per day. The cosmetic room was so busy that we could barely keep up. We used all the refrigerator space. Approximately 20 percent of the bodies began to decompose to a greater or lesser extent. My first restorative artwork was simply motivated by trying to fix bodies with makeup during my routine work during this time. My master saw me experimenting with new methods. He then called everyone in to see my work and asked people to think about how mine was different from other people's. I soon realized that applying makeup was not enough. I then performed more experiments with hypodermic embalming on necks or armpits and trying out some other possible recipes for the embalming solution. I often performed experiments at night after I finished my work at the parlor. I also volunteered to handle decomposed bodies. They actually came to me even before I asked, because other people had very little interest in doing this. There was no additional economic benefit to handling decomposed bodies at that time, so people had very little incentive to do restorative art. I am the kind of person who often questions and pushes the usual practice further. I gradually developed my own way of doing restorative art through self-improvement and self-learning.

In spring 2002, our work unit sent twelve people to a professional mortuary school in Canada, and I was one of them. This was a very important and eye-opening experience. I learned a lot during these four months. We learned embalming, restorative arts, and body molding. They also taught us several ways to do things. This helped me to clarify many puzzles I had before—like a cloudy sky suddenly opening up with sunlight. We had a final test at the end, in which the teacher asked us to choose one of many Asian people's pictures from a pile and "make a body" from scratch based on the picture. If you did not do it right, in the middle of the process, the teacher destroyed your clay, so you had to start again. My teacher did not destroy my clay once. Moreover, I was the only person who actually finished the assignment. I felt an inexpressible sense of achievement.

You heard about my big-character poster [*dazibao*] protest, right? There was a sudden increase in the income gap between cosmeticians and salespeople. I first made a poster to demand better pay for body cosmeticians. Before we posted the big-character poster, I asked all my fellow cosmeticians to sign their names on the poster. I told them that we were fighting for our collective interests, and if we succeeded, all of us could benefit from it. Everyone but one signed, including the then manager and vice manager of the cosmetic unit. Approximately fifteen minutes after we posted the poster, the vice chair of the parlor, someone from human resources [formerly known as the Political Work Department], and a third person came to talk to me. They asked me to take the poster down. That same afternoon, the party chief of the Shanghai funeral parlors, along with the chair of the parlor, came to talk to me. They said that they would consider our requests. I told them that we needed to have a deadline. They said two weeks. I said, "OK," and told them that if we did not receive a response after two weeks, our cosmetic unit would start slowing down work [*daigong*] for half of a day. If there was still no response, a half day of slowing down work would become a one-day strike or more. We did not want to paralyze the parlor, but we did know that if we went on strike, we *could* paralyze it. There was no alternative to the cosmetic units' work. Approximately four or five days after the poster, the officials announced new rules. All contractual laborers in the cosmetic units received raises. After the poster incident, many people came to say thank you when I visited other funeral parlors, since they also benefited from this incident.

Subject Formation: Ambiguity, Contingency, and Existential Crisis

Lin Wu's narrative reveals three major turning points in his personal journey toward becoming a body cosmetician. The first was when he was diagnosed as being color-blind. The second was when he quit his state-assigned job, becoming unemployed and eventually going to work in a funeral parlor. The third was his increasing frustration with income inequality between cosmeticians and salespeople, which reached a point where he decided to do something about it. There were smaller turning points in between, such as when he was turned down for job transfer requests. Some turning points constituted a clear break in the normal flow of life, such as his color-blindness diagnosis, while others were more gradual. These events where a life choice is made or a change is forced are what I call existential crises.

I interpret how Lin Wu reacted to each existential crisis by teasing out two types of motivational forces that propelled him to be an ethical person: pursuing self-realization and following social conventions. Moreover, I consider two different but related aspects of pursuing self-realization: self-interest and self-management. While these two aspects of self-realization are not exclusive to the market economy, they are emphasized under the market economy. From the perspective of the state, the combination of self-interest with self-management allows the state to govern the individual in the most cost-effective way. This idea of self (the combination of self-interest and self-management) is what some scholars describe as neoliberal subjects. As such, by singling out the pursuit of self-realization as a prime motivation in the following analysis, I intend to pay particular attention to the force of the market economy and how this force affects the cultivation of the person. Kneese, in this volume, delineates a very similar process happening when examining the historical record of insurance. She notices a growing imperative to take care of one's own funeral in order to be responsible for oneself.

Finally, I further divide social conventions into several types of moral discourses about the self and the person. Here, I am specifically referring to socialism (such as the socialist morality of equality or comradeship) and Confucianism (the relational self as embedded in hierarchical family relationships and reciprocity), as they were more prevalent in Lin Wu's narratives. To be clear, although I distinguish pursuing self-realization and following social conventions as two different types of motivational forces, these distinctions are analytical. The boundaries experienced are blurred, ambiguous, and uncertain. For example, there has been a long history of various types of social conventions that emphasize self-management, from qigong in popular culture to Confucian teachings in Sinophone societies that resonate with self-management. By the same token, in market-oriented societies, the pursuit of self-interest also often follows social conventions. While self-realization and social conventions do not need to be oppositional, in reality, the emergence of self-realization as the goal has become a major topic of public discourse on the changes that coincide with the introduction of the market economy. For this reason, I distinguish self-realization and social conventions as two different types of motivations, even though the boundary between them is blurred.

From Lin Wu's life story, we can see that when Lin Wu was diagnosed as color-blind and therefore disqualified from all arts-related college departments, he was forced to (re)articulate who he was and what he had wanted to be (an artist) into who else he could be (anything that was not an artist). Prior to this point, his artist self coexisted with his relational self, especially referring to being a son, a student, and a classmate. These different ideas of self coexisted without a clear demarcation of which was which or which was more important. Furthermore, among these different ideas of self, some were already in conflict. For example, being the son of a state funeral worker mother conflicted with his desire to be a normal classmate to other students and a normal student to his teachers, since his mother was "polluted." We see such conflict materialize when Lin Wu talked about how he was too embarrassed to let his teacher and classmates know that his mother worked in a funeral parlor. Meanwhile, his artist self was *not* in conflict with his being a son, a student, or a classmate. It is in this sense that I say subjectivity is ambiguous to begin with. All these different ideas of self (whether conflicting or not) coexisted under the surface until the color-blindness crisis forced Lin Wu to articulate his sense of self, an artist self, out of ambiguity. In fact, the color-blindness diagnosis *simultaneously* led him to articulate his sense of self as an artist and made him realize that he could be anything but an artist. There is a tragic irony here.

Lin Wu eventually pursued a mechanical engineering major because he wanted to choose a subject as remote from art as possible. He did not tell me whether his parents expressed any opinions on the matter. Did he make this decision by being a filial son or by being a socialist worker? The long tradition of workers being a prestigious class category and the new associations of engineering with modernity in urban China means that Lin Wu followed not only social conventions but also the conventions associated with a particular kind of socialist morality and modernity that upholds the value of manual labor. In fact, this manufacturing-related major might have matched the desire of his parents and allowed Lin Wu to act as a filial son as well. Meanwhile, however, by choosing something that was as far away as possible from art was itself a form of self-realization, even though Lin Wu was not clear about the degree to which this pursuit was based on maximizing self-interest, self-management, or both.

After Lin Wu graduated, he took the state-assigned job and officially became a part of a work unit. Being embedded in a work unit directly linked to the state without horizontal ties has been the quintessential image of a good socialist citizen in urban China since the revolution. During this process, we can see how pursuing self-realization and following social conventions coexisted without Lin Wu needing to articulate one over the other. For example, Lin Wu accepted and respected hierarchy in a work unit like a proper socialist person, yet at the same time, he was not happy with the three-year apprentice rule since it took him less than a year to obtain his professional license. His desire for merit-based evaluation shows that he wanted to pursue both self-interest, with its entailed material benefits, and self-management, with the hope that self-management would bring even more material benefits. Although being a conventional socialist worker was in conflict with his pursuit of self-realization, Lin Wu more or less followed social convention and left such conflicts unresolved. The ambiguity of subjectivity changed, however, when Lin Wu was removed from the labor export program to Singapore in 1995. At this moment, being a self-realizing person and a person who follows social conventions could no longer ambiguously coexist just below the surface. Instead, Lin reached another moment of articulation; by leaving his job, he chose self-interest as his path to self-realization.

However, we need to further contextualize Lin's choice of self-realization at this moment. Lin Wu entered the labor force at the tail end of the state's practice of assigning jobs. Only a few years afterward, there was no more universal job assignment (another result of China's market reforms). Even people with college degrees needed to fight for a job, including in the not-so-prestigious funeral profession, as described at the beginning of this chapter. The other side of disappearing job assignments was that in the 1990s, for the first time in the People's Republic of China, leaving a work unit and thinking about individual career choices became imaginable. In Shanghai in particular, the market economy was finally taking off at that time (Shanghai was slower than its rural counterparts for various political reasons). Lin's act of leaving the factory and his motivation for doing so were economically rational under this new ethos, which was a product of state collusion in the development of a market economy. Indeed, there may be no better picture of this newly formed ethos of being an autonomous self, bound by neither state nor family, than the picture of Lin Wu wandering around and staying unemployed. Wandering was itself an exploration of liminality. The thought of becoming a taxi driver, a self-employed entrepreneur, illustrates his wish to stop being a cog in a giant machine (working in the state molding factory) and to become the controller of a small and isolated personal space (a taxi driver with his own car).

However, it would be a mistake to assume that self-realization was the only motivation for Lin Wu's sense of self and actions at this moment. Lin Wu's mother called him while he was wandering around to ask him to work in a funeral parlor. His negotiation with his mother shows that while self-interest might have been important, family relationships, which have traditionally defined what it means to be a person in the Chinese context, had never ceased to play a powerful role. The importance of family responsibility eventually pushed him toward employment. A Confucian social convention regarding family obligation was articulated when Lin acted filially by accepting the job at the funeral parlor. We can also interpret this social convention based on how he spoke about his salary; he not only accepted the job for the sake of his mother but also gave all his salary to her without even calculating how much he earned (it was not uncommon for unmarried adult children to live at home with their parents in Shanghai, since housing was and remains highly expensive). In return, he received a very small amount of money as a book allowance. At a metalevel, he felt a desire to articulate this part of his story, and of his self, to me in the interview. This part of Lin Wu's story can be viewed as his attempt to carve out a personal and private corner while articulating and reconfiguring Confucian family ethics; it also indicates his disinterest in vulgar monetary affairs, even though his desire to be a taxi driver was conditioned by the reality of the market economy.

Finally, working in a funeral parlor (and in certain sectors of the Shanghai funeral industry) not only guarantees stability and relative prosperity to a person but also indicates that the person possesses privileged connections, or *guanxi* in Chinese, a kind of social capital that is crucial for navigating daily life, especially after the introduction of the market economy (Yang 1994). I found that many people who worked in funeral parlors often had connections to civil affairs bureaus (funeral parlors are public institutions managed by civil affair bureaus). In other words, becoming a funeral professional was itself the articulation and product of a relational self. All these different ideas of self existed ambiguously until a particular moment when Lin Wu felt the need (and the opportunity) to articulate and reorganize these different moral discourses regarding the meaning of being a person.

Lin Wu's account of how he became a body restorative artist reveals the tension of his multiple subjectivities. On the one hand, he emphasized how much he learned independently (from reading books and doing experiments) and by challenging existing practices. On the other hand, he could not deny that he learned from the older practitioners as well as through his work unit's support in the form of sending him to a Canadian mortuary school. The first (minor) step in resolving the abovementioned ambiguity was when Lin realized that he was "too talented" to achieve a job transfer. In this narrative, he implies that an artist self constituted an (imagined) essence of himself, such that even when working as a body cosmetician, he could not hide such a self. This idea of an authentic self, along with pride in one's craft (Weber [1904] 2009), is the major source of moral value in capitalism (in fact, the only source worthy of a person with integrity). Thus, Lin Wu reconfigured his socialist-Confucian subjectivity so that it became commensurable with his "authentic self." In other words, if we take his account of a more or less self-made hero as the only definition of self, we miss the complexity, plurality, and ambiguity of subjectivity that characterizes the self as an experienced and emergent subject.

Finally, these newly reconfigured subjectivities changed again, later, when Lin Wu experienced increased frustration with the income gap between cosmeticians and salespeople. The income disparities between cosmeticians and salespeople represented not only an economic penalty, but also a blow to his self-respect. For Lin Wu, such inequalities were not justifiable, since they did not result from merits. After all, funeral parlors were a state monopoly; how much could sales matter? This sense of injustice accumulated to the point that it eventually became another existential crisis for Lin, driving him to organize protests to fight for better treatment for all body cosmeticians. Instead of accepting the emphasis on self-interest and self-management (you should work for yourself, and the more you work, the more you will achieve), Lin Wu and his colleagues sought raises for *all* body cosmeticians. They were no longer individualized subjects pursuing self-realization but members of a collective working class. Lin's action in fighting against inequality articulated a socialist subjectivity out of ambiguity.

Conclusion

By providing one of the few in-depth accounts of Shanghai funeral professionals, I describe how the subjectivity of Chinese funeral professionals is constructed on the ground and in practice. From the above analysis, we might observe that people mostly do not consciously think about who they are, what motivates them, and which moral viewpoint is the most important in terms of what it means to be a person. Furthermore, these different ethical ideas of person coexist immediately under the surface (and sometimes on the surface) as people proceed through their daily lives. This observation echoes David Hume's idea of the multifaceted and ambiguous self ([1739] 1978, 252). For Lin Wu, such ambiguity in the ideas of the self began to change when he experienced existential crises and other challenges. Existential crises require people to pause in their taken-for-granted everyday life and consciously reflect upon who they are and how they should act accordingly at these moments.

Each existential crisis does not need to carry equal weight in a person's life. Dramatic and life-changing existential crises are important moments for people to work through the contradictions brought by different motivations, but they are by no means the only moments. Much less dramatic moments that merely require people to reflect on their existence, such as accepting an interview with an anthropologist or speaking to a friend or partner about who one is, was, and wants to be, are also moments of potential articulation and reconfiguration. Each reflection articulates and simultaneously reconfigures subjectivities out of ambiguity. Altogether, these three characteristics, ambiguous subjectivities, existential crisis, and contingent articulation are the elements momentarily generating subjectivity.

As a result, subjectivity is something that is always an articulation contingent on both a person's preexisting moral ideas of person and their contextualized decisions of what the self is and how the self acts (and should act). My approach to subjectivity not only allows us to gain ethnographic insight into how an ordinary Chinese person becomes a funeral professional but also provides an analytical framework that captures the complicated formation of the self even when marketization, economization, and neoliberalization have shaped the ideas of self in specific ways. It complements Laidlaw's (2014) ethical subjects by revealing how methodologically we could lay out the formation of ethical subjects. This bottom-up and person-centered view of subjectivity allows the study of contemporary funeral professionals in places where the concept of pollution continues to be strong to be shifted away from the perspective of symbolic pollution to one that takes into account both the structural "conduct of conduct" and the self-reflexivity of individuals in examining subject formation. Chinese state funeral workers represent a particularly good case for understanding subject formation, because the state consciously and purposefully shaped these individuals in specific ways. The goal of the anthropological exploration of subject formation is thus to identify when, how, and under what conditions the self is articulated and articulated in what ways.

Acknowledgments

The larger research project within which this research was conducted received funding from various sources at different stages. These sources include a Graduate Research Abroad Fellowship from Boston University, a National Study Abroad Scholarship from the Ministry of Education in Taiwan, a Mellon/ACLS

Dissertation Completion Fellowship, a Cora Du Bois Fellowship from Harvard University, an Early Career Scheme (ECS) Grant from The University Grants Committee in Hong Kong SAR, and support from the Hong Kong University of Science and Technology. Many people have helped me greatly in writing this piece at different stages: Kimberly Arkin, Robert Hefner, Charles Lindholm, Robert Weller, and Matthew West. Finally, I would like to give special thanks to the anonymous reviewers and the two book editors of our edited volume: Shannon Dawdy and Tamara Kneese. Any mistakes in this chapter are, of course, all mine.

Note

1. To simplify the complicated contract system in the PRC and its changes since the introduction of the market economy, we could take public-sector staff contracts as more or less guaranteed life-long employment with full benefits. This is in contrast to private sector staff contracts, which were generally a term-based contract with fewer benefits.

CHAPTER TWELVE

Grief Transformed

New Rituals in a Singaporean Chinese Funeral Parlor

RUTH E. TOULSON

In tiny Singapore, perhaps fifty people will die each day.[1] A small number, it seems, but in line with other wealthy countries with aging populations. What happens to those bodies? Where do they go? Far from Orchard Road's prestige malls, from the colonial grandeur of Raffles Hotel, and from the opulent casinos of Marina Bay Sands is the hidden world of the funeral parlor.

Singapore's funeral parlors line dead-end streets in out-of-the-way industrial estates, each street dedicated to a different dirty business: to laundry, to welding, to car repair, to death. Singapore's strict zoning laws restrict the business of death to these areas—each site a carefully measured minimum of four hundred meters away from housing—so that no one need look out their window and see a body arriving on a gurney or departing in a casket or be kept awake by the chanting of funeral prayers. The most populous, Lorong (Avenue) Thirty-Seven on Sin Ming Drive, is lined with funeral companies: Hock Heng Undertaker, Charity Casket, Ang Yew Seng Funeral Parlour, Singapore Casket Ltd, World Casket, An Lok Funeral Services, Fairprice Funeral, and One-Stop Buddhist. This is not a place most Singaporeans would choose to visit, but almost all Singaporean Chinese dead will pass through here or through the similar modest mortuaries and parlors on Lavender Street, Toa Payoh, and Geylang Bahru.[2] While the majority of Singaporeans still hold their funerals in the Housing Development Board (HDB) void deck or on the streets outside houses for those with landed property, their bodies come to these mortuaries first, to be embalmed and encoffined.[3] And an increasing number of Singaporeans avoid HDB or street funerals altogether, holding the entirety of their funerary rituals in parlors, to the extent that funerals are occasionally delayed because of the lack of an available space.

While Singaporean funeral parlors have existed since the 1970s, in this chapter I examine the emergence of a new kind of funeral parlor and of the rituals that happen within it. The services offered by the Life Celebrant (TLC), particularly the Showers of Love service that allows the bereaved to take part in a final, heavily ritualized washing of their dead, stand in contrast to "standard" practices in multiple ways. Where once, funeral workers were nearly entirely men, the staff of this business are mostly women, and only women conduct the Showers of Love rite. While standard funerals are nearly always religiously affiliated, regardless of the actual beliefs or practices of the dead, the rituals standardized and impersonal, TLC's rituals are seemingly secular and highly individualized. Most strikingly, the gentle attention paid to the corpse—the bereaved family members are guided to wash their relative's body, moving from feet to hands to face, and prompted to speak particular words of love, thanks, and apology—occurs in a societal context where the dead body has long been regarded as a thing to be feared.

Beyond the fact that it seems to upturn deeply entrenched Chinese beliefs in the polluted nature of the corpse, the Showers of Love service is a puzzle, too, because it is so different from the rituals that are emerging in other contexts, such as natural burial, tree, and sea burial, which largely downplay ritual elaboration and focus less on the corpse itself (see Clayden et al. 2014; Davis and Rumble 2012; Kawano 2010; Kelly 2015; Olson 2014, 2016c; Penmellen Boret 2014; Penmellen Boret, Long, and Kan 2017; Rowe 2011).[4] While the service is an anomaly—the vast majority of Singaporean Chinese funerals are not like this; even the proprietor's family and workers initially doubted her choice to introduce the service—it is, I argue, part of a wider revolution in attitudes to what funeral ritual should be and do.

This chapter, then, is an interrogation of the nature of ritual transformation. I ask, Why did this new ritual emerge, and in this particular form? More broadly, why are some ritual elements abandoned, seemingly without regret, while other ritual elements are clung to, becoming orthopraxy? My argument has two threads. First, I offer a careful examination of the ritual's details, revealing the complexity of seeming revolution. On deeper examination, the Showers of Love ritual, for all it seems at first glance to dismantle "traditional" values, also echoes and reinforces them. The ritual is inherently ambiguous—global in its borrowings but distinctly Singaporean in its values—in ways that reflect the ambiguity not only of dying, but of identity, religiosity, and familial love in Singapore. This is a ritual focused on the guided articulation of particular forms of relationality and of particular emotions that are expected to align with them.

Its emergence allows us to examine not only a ritual practice in transformation but also the transformation of grief itself. The need it meets is a need for new ways to grieve. Singapore, like many other places, is in a state of transition, the disquieting moment where ritual practice and grief no longer fit together, where standard ritual no longer adequately expresses grief. Second, then, this chapter is an examination of the emergence and attempted resolution of that discontinuity. Showers of Love makes visible multiple shifts—in what ritual should express and do, in what corpses mean and how they should be treated, and in the work of appropriate grieving.

As this chapter is a study of transformation, I begin with a brief description of "standard" Singaporean Chinese funeral practices and of the parlors in which they might be observed, and of the emergence of TLC.

"A Lifetime in a Day, Not a Day in a Lifetime"

While the Showers of Love service is a recent innovation, beginning in 2017, the Life Celebrant has a longer history. I first met its proprietor, Angjolie Mei, in 2012 on Sin Ming Drive, at Ang Yew Seng Funeral Parlour, the funeral business that bears her father's name. I had met Ang Yew Seng when I first conducted fieldwork in Singapore in 2003. A charismatic man, known as the "King of Caskets," he was a leader in the field and a philanthropist, known for his support of local religious institutions and generous in providing free funerals to the destitute. Ang Yew Seng was the first to supply caskets suitable for cremation. Initially, the imported lightweight caskets were available only with Christian iconography, but he arranged to have them decorated with Buddhist and Taoist imagery. More broadly, he helped Singaporean Chinese accept cremation, a necessity because of the shortage of land despite their strong preference for burial.

When her father died in 2004, with her mother worn down by the burden of the business, Angjolie left her job as a management trainee in a logistics company and began to work at Ang Yew Seng full time. It is an irony, perhaps, that Ang Yew Seng had always protected his children from the work of death, hoping that they would not be sullied by it. Only his untimely death led Angjolie to enter the industry. In a world dominated by men, once the preserve of the uneducated and regarded as the worst work one could do, Angjolie stood out; eloquent, dark hair to her waist, a roller-blading, salsa-dancing mortician, she was set on transforming the industry. At first there was resistance to women running the firm, particularly a young woman with new ideas. Some of the older men refused to work for her, telling her, "I've eaten more salt than you've eaten rice."[5]

In 2012, TLC shared a space with Ang Yew Seng. In the front office, Mrs. Ang ran the more "traditional" business. In a cramped backroom, separated from her mother by a wall of caskets, Angjolie worked to establish her own company, bringing new ideas to a field she saw as in desperate need of innovation.

Even then, Ang Yew Seng's parlors stood in contrast to other parlors in the street. They were newly renovated and far more luxurious, their walls lined with beige, silk-effect wallpaper, their floors tiled in marble, glass doors replacing the pull-down metal bars that secured the cheaper units. But the elegance of the upgraded parlors was rather different from the street itself, with its uneven sidewalks of cracked tile, lethally slippery after an afternoon storm, and the cheaper parlors owned by other businesses, their floors covered with patched linoleum, gouged from the dragging and stacking of rain-stained plastic chairs and tables, grime in the cracks from years of careless mopping. In some of the other parlors, air-conditioning units dripped and gurgled, whitewashed walls were pockmarked with black mold, and tables were left piled high with discarded polystyrene food containers, the remnants of congealed *char kway teo* bought from the hawker center on the corner, and crumpled paper napkins marked with grease-stained fingerprints.

All the parlors on Sin Ming Drive were modest. Each business had a small front office and one or two parlors, each large enough for just a casket and a circle of mourners. The parlor's front opened onto the street. Some had a makeshift mortuary in a back room. On many of the office desks, a miniature wooden coffin, its lid domed Chinese-style, held business cards, for a coffin can also bring luck. The street was hot and noisy. Throughout the night, recorded music played in each unit, a different CD for the Catholics or Protestants, for Taoists or Buddhists, the combined sounds becoming a jarring clamor. The hearse would pipe the same hymns or chants when the body left the next day; the music became so familiar that it provided the soundtrack to funeral workers' dreams. By sunset, when most mourners began to arrive, every parking space would be full, with cars struggling to turn in the narrow, dead-end street. One could predict that before the night was done, at least one turning vehicle would reverse into a metal garbage disposal unit overfilled with yesterday's flowers, tipping its contents onto the sidewalk. There would be the scrape of metal on metal, the sounding of horns, and then, perhaps, voices raised in argument, the beginnings of a scuffle atop the wilted chrysanthemums that covered the tiled walkway.

It was not merely Sin Ming's clamor that troubled Angjolie but the impersonal nature of the services offered there. Funeral workers were often brisk and ill-mannered, handling bodies with little care. The street was scruffy, undignified—well-worn sofas, foam escaping with sagging cushions, stood on the pavement to allow funeral workers to nap or watch television; chickens scratched in the dirt, and stray dogs stretched in the warmth of last night's ashes. Above all, the street was crowded with death and its ritual markers. Families were confronted by the painful reminder that their loss was merely one of many. During a funeral in the void deck or the street, the bereaved cannot forget that life goes on. Funerals are interrupted by neighbors taking their children to school, walking their dogs, or coming back and forth with bags of groceries, by laughter or arguments in the parking lot, and by the chime of the elevator bell. On Sin Ming Drive, in contrast, the bereaved were forced to face the ordinariness of death. For all it is hidden away in an isolated part of the island, spend an evening by the funeral parlors and one cannot help but see other bodies—bodies entering mortuaries, loosely covered, their draping doing little to disguise their form, a yellowed limb occasionally escaping its sheet, the gurney's metal wheels clanking loudly up and down the pavement edge; bodies lying in parlors and sliding into hearses—and other families in grief. In each funeral business office, the deceased's name is written in erasable marker on a whiteboard along with their departure times for cremation at Mandai or Bright Hill crematorium, scrawled over the traces of countless other names, a palimpsest reminder of death's ubiquity.[6]

Rituals, too, were largely impersonal. They weren't many real choices beyond Christian (Protestant or Catholic), Buddhist, or Taoist, no matter the degree of faithfulness of the deceased. Buddhist monks could be hired to attend each night to lead the family around the casket, prompting the family to repeat sutras that they did not understand. Angjolie's early innovations were to encourage family members to personalize funerals, to spend the evenings beside the casket selecting family photographs, folding paper cranes, and sharing stories rather than reciting prayers if praying held little meaning. She helped families create richly personal services, describing a funeral as "not a day in a life, but a life in a day." Angjolie also tried to foster a new attitude toward the corpse. She insisted on world-class embalming, importing Dodge Chemical, the most popular US brand, via New Zealand, and employing highly trained US, UK, or Australian qualified embalmers on staff rather than using the less-skilled peripatetic embalmers trained in less-rigorous courses in the Philippines.[7] The open casket has always been central to Chinese funerals, but viewing the body is still something that fills many visitors with fear. In contrast, Angjolie presented the viewing of the body—a body from which skillful embalming had erased all traces of sickness and created an appearance of peace—as a chance to spend valuable last moments with the dead. Still, even in this context, the decision to introduce Showers of Love was a controversial one.

Angjolie tells me that the ritual itself was inspired by the Japanese film *Departures*. The film, directed by Yōjirō Takita and released in 2008, tells the story of Daigo Kobayashi and his wife, Mika. When Daigo loses his job as a cellist, he is forced to leave Tokyo and return to his hometown. He sees a job advertisement for someone to assist with "departures" and presumes the position is at a travel agency. However, the job is actually that of a traditional mortician, or *nōkanshi*. Daigo takes the job and faces social ostracization; even his wife rejects him. However, when Mika observes the beauty and dignity with which Daigo performs ritualized encoffining, she is won over. The film ends when Daigo agrees to encoffin the body of his long-estranged father and, in the act of preparing his body, resolves their estrangement. Angjolie first thought of starting a similar business when in 2010 or 2011—she has forgotten the exact date—she was contacted by an elderly woman who asked if her team could provide the same service. The woman's son, a wealthy man, inspired by the film, had asked for eight Japanese *nōkanshi* to be brought to Singapore to await his father's death and then tend to his body, even importing a Japanese casket. The woman was Angjolie's first Showers of Love client, although many years passed before she made the service commercially available and obtained a funeral parlor and set it up for the ritual.

Parlor space is at a premium in Singapore, so Angjolie was taking a significant business risk when she set up one parlor devoted exclusively to Showers of Love services. The setup consists of some twenty-five seats that face a raised altar-like platform that contains a shallow depression to act as a bath. Initially, while the body is positioned and draped with towels to keep it modestly covered, curtains are drawn to separate the "altar" and the audience. Then, two female assistants—"Showers of Love Angels"—dressed in muted but elegant uniforms reminiscent of those worn by spa workers draw the curtains and begin to work in synchrony to wash the corpse. An "angel" begins by wiping the feet of the deceased and then asks a family member, generally the oldest child, to come forward to also wipe the feet. The angel prompts the family member to speak: "Let your mum know that it is time for her to rest, ask for her forgiveness. Say, 'Please forgive me . . . thank you, I forgive you, I am sorry, I love you." The washing of each body part prompts another recitation. When the hands are washed, the bereaved are prompted to say, "Thank you for feeding us when we were children. Now it is your time to rest"; on washing the face, "We are washing your face, preparing you for the next journey." As the family watches, one angel shampoos the hair, massages cream into the face, applies a face mask. Later in the ritual, after dressing and once the body is washed, the angels dry the body, again moving in synchrony, one on the left, one on the right, changing towels multiple times, always keeping the body covered. It is necessary to change the table, from the sloping bathing table to a flat table for dressing, during which time family members are instructed to step outside the room to take a break, a request that acknowledges the ritual's emotional intensity. Once the table is switched, the body is placed on a mattress and covered with a duvet, as if tucked in bed. Then, ensuring private body parts are covered, the bereaved help to dress the deceased. At the same time, an angel asks, "Did your Mum like nail polish? What was her favorite color?" before painting the finger- and toenails, while another attends to makeup and styles the hair.

Such actions are entirely unprecedented in the Chinese world of the dead. In a classic text on Chinese attitudes to death pollution, James L. Watson remarks, "One of the most puzzling aspects of Chinese mortuary ritual is the extreme ambivalence shown toward the physical remains of the deceased. . . . Few who have witnessed a funeral," he remarks, "can fail to be impressed by the fear and the apprehension that pervade the ritual. The general aversion to death, and anything associated with the corpse is so overpowering that ordinary villagers hesitate to become involved" (1982, 155). Watson describes "killing airs" that emanate from the corpse and "permeate the house of the deceased and cling to the mourners." So great is the polluting power of the corpse that "pregnant women and children are advised to stay well away. . . . Neighbors close their doors and find an excuse to be away for a few hours. Farmers make sure that sows with piglets are removed from sheds nearby and calves are taken out of the village" (1982, 158).

While Watson and Rawski's 1988 edited volume remains the standard work on Chinese death, it is now dated. Further, it draws largely from fieldwork in rural villages, very different from Singapore. And yet there is evidence that Singaporean Chinese people are still concerned about death pollution. Many visitors to a funeral still approach the coffin with caution, their hands behind their backs. At North American funerals, the upper body of the dead person is slightly raised so that the deceased's face can be seen from the side on approaching the casket. In Singapore, in contrast, dead bodies lay flat, so that viewing the body is a deliberate choice. Singaporean caskets also have an acrylic viewing panel, which covers the body but allows it to be viewed, something that American caskets lack. Showers of Love was also controversial, with other funeral directors remarking that few families would want such a service and that for reasons of health and hygiene, particularly the risk of coming into contact with embalming fluids, they discouraged family members from touching the body (Yeo Sijia 2017). And yet for all the controversy it garnered, the introduction of the Showers of Love service may not be as extreme a transformation as might first be imagined. In examining ritual transformation, there is a great deal to be read in both what is retained and what is discarded.

Of Flesh and Blood and Dirty Work

For all its seeming refutation of long-standing ideas about the danger of the corpse, the Showers of Love service can also be understood as a continuation of conventional Singaporean Chinese attitudes to the dead body. Far from suggesting the abandonment of pollution narratives, the ritual acknowledges their continued relevance. After all, there would be no controversy had pollution beliefs entirely lost their power. In explaining the ritual to families considering the service, Angjolie and her staff were clear to stress that the work of dealing with a corpse has three stages: sanitization, preservation, and presentation. The first two are dealt with in the mortuary; Showers of Love involves the family in the third stage only. Before the family engages with the body, much of what is perceived as the dirty work of death has already been done, particularly the removal of all that is bloody or fleshy, elements regarded as emitting the most serious forms of pollution (see Watson 1982, 182).

The continued existence of pollution beliefs is not surprising, as such beliefs do important cosmological work. The transformation from a loved living individual to an esteemed but distanced ancestor is a radical one, necessitating the rupture of existing relationships. It is for this reason that in Singaporean Chinese funeral rituals, an open casket is near obligatory. Even highly damaged bodies are viewed, their worst wounds perhaps covered with a napkin, in contrast to other contexts, where there has been a marked shift away from the open casket.[8] Viewing the corpse, seeing a loved person, familiar but also irreconcilably transformed and perhaps even frightening, emphasizes this painful but unavoidable transformation. It prompts the breaking of ties, necessary before their remaking in a very different form once the dead enter ancestorhood, which Charles Strafford (2000) suggests is the key element of Chinese funeral rites. It is worth noting that the beautifully embalmed bodies at TLC still bring this realization. If old rituals that focused on viewing the corpse were about being struck by undeniable difference, a once-familiar face grayed and sunken, it is not that a well-embalmed body gives the impression the dead still live. High-quality embalming, such as that offered at TLC, can wipe away evidence of illness, pain, and fatigue, but the state created is not one of being alive, but of a different state, a peaceful liminality. This state echoes the purposeful liminality of traditional Chinese funeral rites where, between physical death and burial, the dead in their caskets continue to socially live.

Touching the corpse and the casket is a necessary and gendered act of transformation. In older rituals, the purpose of funeral rites is to take on pollution, for only through the distribution of pollution can the dead to be transformed into ancestors. As Watson describes it:

> The decomposing flesh of a human is the ultimate form of disorder. . . . It interferes with the smooth transition from a proper state of life to a proper state of death. The object of funerary ritual is, in their view, to pass safely through the initial, polluting phase of decomposition to the point where the bones can be manipulated. What is interesting about the passive pollution of death . . . is that it has to be managed. It cannot just be left to pollute the cosmos, either in the world of the living or in the realm of ancestors. Death pollution has to be taken on, or incorporated, into the flesh of the living. (1982, 182)

Showers of Love focuses on similar gendered work. While frequently no longer necessarily understood as being about the distribution of pollution — few Singaporeans now view funeral rites as transformative, as acting to create ancestors from corpses with pollution distribution as necessary for that process, instead seeing funerals as commemorative — it still contains fear, which must be faced and worked through. Angjolie told me of a family whose members, particularly the dead woman's siblings, were initially opposed to the service. Only the daughter took part, with the father attending as an observer. While he did not touch the corpse, beyond finally placing his hands on his wife's calves, he watched as his daughter washed her mother's feet, hands, and face, while she wept. Afterward, his comment was that he was so very proud of her bravery, that he could not have done what she had done, but that he found the ritual deeply emotionally healing. Just as in older rituals, the Showers of Love ceremony allows the family to smooth their loved one's path to an afterlife.

Showers of Love also provides a key ritual element that has become increasingly rare in funeral rituals in Singapore. It gives grief time. Once funeral rites took many days, with families spending multiple nights in half sleep beside the casket. Bodies were buried in permanent graves which the family visited at Ching Ming. Now long funerals are rare. Few employers will grant much leave for a worker to sit beside a casket. And burial is now all but unheard of, with permanent graves replaced by cramped niches in columbaria.[9] In a context where death is denied both the space and time it was once granted, Showers of Love provides that anew, setting grief in necessary time.

Transforming Grief

In a recent conversation, I asked Angjolie whether she saw much evidence of fear of the corpse, whether she thought Singaporeans still commonly believe in death pollution. She suggested that what people have always feared was not the dead body but grief itself. When mourners kept their distance from the corpse, their real fear was that viewing the body might cause them to weep. Often, when families came to make funeral arrangements and Angjolie described the Showers of Love service to them, relatives would initially say that the service wasn't for them, as they were afraid it would make them cry. Angjolie would reassure them, stressing both that crying was good, a necessary step in the process of grieving, and that it was better to cry within the private space of the Showers of Love room than in front of all the guests at the void deck or funeral parlor. At Chinese funerals, crying has always been socially charged.

Synchronized crying of a particular sort was long a part of older Chinese funeral rites. Elizabeth Johnson, reflecting on fieldwork conducted in the 1960s and 1970s, notes:

> There are certain characteristics, unforgettable sounds associated with Chinese funerals: percussion instruments beating a solemn rhythm, the chanting of priests, the melodies of the *so-na*, and the lamenting of women. This

lamenting, high pitched and penetrating, conveys an intense expression of grief. It is both weeping and singing, repeating melodic phrases that end with calls to the dead and sobs. At certain points in the funeral process several women may wail together, but there may be times when a single woman will lament, entering the site alone and singing in a solitary out-pouring of grief. (1988, 135)

J. J. de Groot, the nineteenth-century Dutch Sinologist, writing on laments in an Amoy society, describes "a melancholy concert of death dirges, a concat-enation of complaints addressed to the dead, in accents of reproach for leaving them" (1972, 801). He labels this most distinctive expression of grief "the death howl." A woman was paid to lead the wailing because of the ritual work done by these particular tears; it was only through correct ritual performance, includ-ing appropriate crying, that the dead person could become an ancestor. These formalized paid-for tears were transformative. But public mourning also had its limits, with strict rules, dictated by family structure, on who should cry for whom. Stuart Thompson reflects on who should grieve: "Minimally, it seems, there must be a male chief mourner (ideally—typically a son) and a daughter (or niece or other substitute) to make offerings to the deceased" (1988, 74). Elizabeth Johnson notes that Hakka people would adopt daughters to partici-pate in funerals (1988, 149), while Susan Naquin concludes, "Funerals were intended to give formal expression not only to the feelings of grief and loss that a death generated but also to the ensuing rearrangement of relationships" (1988, 62). Centrally, expressions of grief within "traditional" ritual displayed that the social order took precedent over—and existed separate from—the emotional life of the individual. Sons, daughters, and daughters-in-law were required to perform in particular ways; during a father's funeral, for example, sons were expected to weep at the closing of the casket; women were compelled to throw themselves to the ground; daughters-in-law must show their abso-lute commitment to the dead man—who has, through marriage, become their father—by rubbing their hair on the casket, taking on his polluted substance as an act of love. Parents should not cry for a child, who in dying "out of turn" had behaved unfilially. While there hasn't been a paid wailer on Sin Ming Drive since the 1970s, private grief remains separated from the performativity of pub-lic mourning.

Crying during the Showers of Love service, then, is about more than griev-ing. It is about the articulation of relatedness, the acceptability of particular forms of familial love. And the ritual itself is therefore caught up in shifting attitudes to the family and to individual identity. When families choose a service like Showers of Love as opposed to more conventional funeral ritual, they frequently express dissatisfaction with older rituals that no longer fit the realities of their relationships, with older rites that suggest that dead parents are more important than living ones, that the greatest debt one owes to parents is to correctly perform their funeral rites, and that the creation of ancestors through the distribution of pollution, not the making of memories, is the purpose of funeral ritual. There is dissatisfaction, too, with ceremonies that the bereaved do not understand and with the expense and complexity of ritual paraphernalia. These shifts align with shifts in religious belief—the growing influence of Protestant Christianity and of Reformist Buddhism, which emphasizes ritual simplicity and doctrinal purity—discouraging the complex combination of Buddhist, Taoist, and animist beliefs that once constituted "Chinese religion" in Singapore—and places a focus on the individual and on belief, not practice.

Protestant Tears?

Services such as Showers of Love allow Singaporeans space to grieve in new ways, ways that reflect contemporary understandings of both familial relationships and individual subjectivity. This "newness"—of identity, belief, and love—requires careful analysis. I am not suggesting that via the Showers of Love Service, Angjolie is somehow prompting Singaporeans to cry in tears not their own. Yes, the ritual is filled with cultural borrowings and is global in its inspirations. While it was inspired initially by a Japanese film, the phrasings within it—"I love you, I thank you, I forgive you, I am sorry—for all that they echo key elements of filial piety, come from a supposed Hawaiian prayer. And Angjolie explained that she had designed the service to include each "love language"—words of affirmation, acts of service, receiving gifts, quality time, and physical touch—ideas drawn from an American popular psychology book. Yet despite this international bricolage, Angjolie's clients find these services deeply meaningful as the ritual presents a way of articulating grief, and love, that is not foreign to them. There is space for the Showers of Love service precisely because it emerges at a moment when the ways that people want to grieve and existing ritual practice no longer fit together, when older ways of imaging the family, ancestors, and the afterlife fail to reflect family life, and death, as it is lived.

Writing about the cultural particularity of grief is difficult. On the one hand, stressing cultural difference dehumanizes. I have never much been persuaded, for example, by historians who argue that in the past, due to high infant mortality rates, parents did not grieve for dead children, particularly when their evidence is merely the lack of elaborate grave markers.[10] Anthropologists are now troubled by Margaret Mead and Ruth Benedict's "Culture and Personality" school, which seemed to suggest that whole cultures share personality traits. In the Chinese context particularly, early work on the emotions of Chinese people seemed to render them emotionless automata (see Lee 2006 for a discussion of this). On the other hand, grief is socially particular. How could it not be? Crying doesn't happen in a cultural vacuum. To suggest as much would be to render particular kinds of crying "natural" in a way that actually naturalizes the ways only certain people cry.

An Anomaly?

The Showers of Love ritual might seem an anomaly. After all, it is a new ritual chosen by a small number of perhaps unusual families, themselves residents of a tiny island city-state. Singapore, as a nation, is difficult to read as an example of anything beyond itself; scholars interested in Chinese societies are far more likely to conduct research in mainland China, where, as can be noted from Huwy-min Lucia Liu's chapter in this volume, there are commonalities but also striking divergences. Researchers studying rapid economic transformations may discount Singapore because its developmental trajectory is highly unusual. Indeed, it is tempting to read Singapore as the product of the powerful vision of one man, Lee Kuan Yew, the nation's founding father, its first prime minister (from 1959 to 1990), then senior minister, then minister mentor until his retirement in 2011. In this, Singapore is incomparable with other relatively recent nations. Angjolie, too, is a one-off, a remarkable innovator whose vision differs significantly from other funeral directors who join her in the new guard of Singaporean death.

Beyond this, it is difficult to read the development of Showers of Love, or indeed any of the significant transformations in Singaporean Chinese funeral culture, as a standard story of transformation, for Singapore is not a "traditional" place being "made modern" but a project of modernity (colonial and postcolonial) in its own right. And yet Showers of Love matters because it provides a powerful lens through which to examine both ritual's purpose and how it is transformed, important questions in multiple contexts and ones that drive each of the chapters in this volume. In an essay in the seminal 1973 volume *The Interpretation of Cultures*, Clifford Geertz provides an analysis of a funeral from another, rather different, Southeast Asian context. Geertz gives a careful accounting of a funeral gone wrong, the funeral of a young man on Java that becomes fraught with difficulties when it becomes caught between traditional modes of funeral ritual—the *slametan*, a communal feast that is the central ritual form for all occasions of religious significance, which brought all neighbors together, emphasizing the interdependence of their lives in the rural village—and new political identities, shaped in the fiery cauldron of emergent nationalism. These new identities fragmented long-established religious syncretism, separating out Islam from the indigenous religious systems of which it had once been a part, emphasizing the religious system's Hinduist and animist elements instead and making each (Masjumi, Muslims, and Permai, the Hindu/animist/anti-Muslim) defining identities in their own right. The dead man is a Permai, but all are surprised when the traditional religious officiant, a Masjumi, gives the dead man's Permai identity as the reason he cannot assist with burying him. In this context, there seems no way forward.

Our understandings of death ritual's purpose, Geertz suggests, remain grounded in functionalism, whether Bronislaw Malinowski's psychological or A. R. Radcliffe-Brown's social-structural. This is the work that death ritual does: it heals the individual or heals the world, allowing the bereaved, and the society as a whole, to begin to restitch the social fabric in which death has rent a tear.[11] But functionalist explanations, focused as they are on ritual as a smoothly fitting cog in social systems understood as a machine, or a pumping organ in society imagined as a body, to borrow Herbert Spencer's organic analogy, as Geertz and others point out, do not deal well with conflict or transformation. "We functionalists," Edward Leach observes, "are not really 'ahistorical' by principle; it is simply that we do not know how to fit historical materials into our framework of concepts" (1954, 282).

Geertz suggests that the reason functional theory cannot cope with change "lies in its failure to treat sociological and cultural processes on equal terms" (1973, 143), presuming instead they are mirror images of each other. In the Javanese example, the traditional *slametan* funeral ritual is grounded in the social structure of the village. The cultural ideas at simultaneously play—the politicized religious identity of Muslim and Permai, prompting some individuals to imagine themselves not as village neighbors but as distinct and politically opposed—become impossible to reconcile with the sociological.

Showers of Love may also be analyzed in this way. Singaporean social structure has shifted. Many of the broader transformations in funeral rites are driven by demographic and economic transitions. It is the tendency toward smaller families, for example, that in large part explains the demand for parlor funerals. The demands of wage labor are central in driving the preference for shorter wakes, for few employers would tolerate multiple days away from work so the bereaved could sit beside a casket. These structural shifts occur simultaneously with shifts in ideas about identity, relationality, and subjectivity: What kind of person am I? How do I feel about love, relationships, loss? How should I grieve? Showers of Love brings together what we might label the structural and the cultural or symbolic in ways that more "traditional" funeral practices cannot. When I write of being at a moment where grief and ritual, in its traditional form, no longer fit together, what I am describing aligns with Geertz's analysis. Showers of Love, for the families who choose it, meaningfully brings together how their families are structured and how they imagine themselves.

This splitting of the structural and the cultural has its difficulties, for the categories are by no means as clear-cut as Geertz's writing suggests. Ritual carries the weight of social structure and yet is highly symbolically laden; structure and culture intertwine in relationships of causality and consequences far more than they diverge. But this analysis has power, because for all we are aware of the multiple critiques of functionalism, it does not discount functionalist explanations that illuminate that death ritual continues to do important social work. What strikes me most about Angjolie's accounts of the response to Showers of Love is the fact that families find deep healing in this new and unusual ritual.

This volume, more broadly, is part of a disciplinary return to the study of mortuary ritual. To understand the revitalization of death ritual as the subject of anthropological inquiry, it is necessary to understand why it was abandoned in the first place. The study of mortuary ritual fell out of disciplinary fashion when the theoretical perspectives within which it was grounded—the functionalist, the structuralist, the symbolic—also, rightly, fell out of theoretical favor. And yet to the degree that appropriately disposing the dead is one of few human universals, death ritual continues to be one of the very things that make us human. This volume, and the SAR seminar that inspired it, began with a question: How is the experience of death and mourning changing under conditions of growing religious plurality and secularization, technological mediation, and globalization? What this chapter suggests is that it is central to pay careful attention to the nature of each of these transformations, whether the transformation is to social structure or to "culture," as Geertz glosses it, and not to presume that transformations in different realms will occur in lockstep. It is often in the moment when transformations spiral away from each other that new rituals emerge to make sense of worlds that no longer neatly hang together. Beyond this, if Showers of Love teaches us anything, it is how much death ritual continues to matter, that it continues to have work to do.

There is a point when older ritual no longer fits easily with the form that grief takes and anthropological work must to be done to probe what causes that rupture. It is that point when new ritual forms emerge and are found to have value. It is this transformative point that is made visible by the emergence and growing popularity of Showers of Love. There is much to be examined, too, in what new rituals keep. For all that Showers of Love seems initially to reject pollution narratives and offer new perspectives on the corpse, it keeps many of the elements that justified belief in pollution, the idea that the living have work to do for the dead, and the idea that ritual, and grief, need space and time.

Notes

1. See Department of Statistics Singapore (2020).
2. My research focuses on the death practices of Singapore's ethnic Chinese majority, who constitute approximately 75 percent of the population, with the remaining population being approximately 15 percent Malay, 7 percent Indian, and 3 percent "Other." As in multiple other settings, the business of Singaporean death is nearly entirely segregated on lines of ethnicity.
3. Housing Development Board apartments are Singapore's iconic multistory public housing units in which some 90 percent of the population lives. The ground floor of these high-rise towers is left empty. Referred to as the "void deck," the space is used for funerals and other events such as weddings.
4. My use of Chinese throughout this article requires more discussion. The majority of Singaporean people of ethnic Chinese descent trace their origins to Guangdong and Fujian Provinces, from which their ancestors came, fleeing famine and conflict in the 1830s to 1850s. Since independence, the Singaporean state has done much to unify Singaporean Chinese so that they imagine themselves as Singaporeans first. Throughout this chapter, I draw on details of Chinese funeral practices from other places and times; indeed, many of the classic texts on Chinese death are based on now-dated fieldwork in rural Taiwan. While it is important to attend to differences, of which there will be many, such comparisons stand as rural Taiwanese share dialect (forms of Hokkien) and ancestral origins with many Singaporean Chinese. Further, one of the key arguments surrounding Chinese funeral ritual is that despite regional variation,

the key elements are the same, as such unification was a consequence of early political actions to unify the Chinese population. For this argument, see James Watson's introduction (1988b) to Watson and Rawski, *Death Ritual in Late Imperial and Early Modern China* (1988).

5. Angjolie Mei recently published *Dying to Meet You: Confessions of a Funeral Director* (2017), which documents her remarkable life story and her revolutionary attitude to Singaporean death practices. Her entrepreneurship has been widely noted, most recently as recipient of a Women Entrepreneur Award, Most Innovative category, 2019.

6. Angjolie is not the only person to have concerns about Singaporean funeral practices. See Sin (2019) for a recent example.

7. The current embalmer at Ang Yew Seng is from the Philippines, but he has more than ten years of experience.

8. There are variations in this. In the United States, viewing the body is more prevalent in the Midwest than on the East Coast, is common but declining among Roman Catholics but rare among Protestants, and remains the expectation for African American funerals throughout the nation.

9. Burial is permitted, but graves are exhumed after fifteen years. Almost all Singaporean Chinese are cremated, with the exception of those belonging to certain Christian denominations that insist on burial.

10. See the introduction to Newby and Toulson (2018) for a detailed discussion of this.

11. There are multiple other persuasive explanations of how ritual works. See, for example, Seligman et al. (2008).

.

On Endings

Commentary
The New Death

ELLEN BADONE

It was an honor and privilege for me to be asked to write a concluding commentary for this exciting and innovative collection of chapters. One feature that makes *The New Death* particularly valuable is its location at the intersections of multiple fields: the anthropology of death and dying; the anthropology of religion; science and technology studies; the new materialism; and media and cultural studies. I will start by reflecting on the contributions that the individual chapters and the volume as a whole make to the anthropological and interdisciplinary understanding of death in the contemporary world. Then, taking my lead from these chapters, I will reflexively address the broader issue of academic research about death, an area with which I have been engaged for over thirty years (Badone 1989, 1991, 2004, 2013, 2017, 2018).

In their introduction, Shannon Dawdy and Tamara Kneese set the agenda for the volume as a response to questions about how globalization, technological mediation, increased religious plurality, and secularization are impacting the experience of death and mourning in the twenty-first century. Recognizing that new practices associated with the disposition and memorialization of the dead are emerging around the globe, Dawdy and Kneese ask how these practices might represent either rupture or continuity with the past, how they might reflect new cosmologies and ideologies, and whether we are witnessing the development of a new relationship between the living and the dead. The chapters in *The New Death* explore these questions by focusing on two topics, mortality and death care. While the chapters in the section on mortality are concerned with discourses and imaginaries associated with death, and the chapters in the section on death care are more focused on the dynamics of the disposition of the body, the boundaries between these areas of concern are not rigidly adhered to in the chapters, which results in productive insights. In addition to these two main topical groupings, I would like to draw attention to the way in which the chapters in the volume also revolve around three intertwined themes: materiality, temporality, and personhood.

One of the refreshing aspects of this book is its grounding in the literature on the new materialism and its attention to death's materiality. This focus on materiality may be linked in part to Shannon Dawdy's background in archaeology, but it is also worth noting that several of the authors have embodied experience in death care. Toulson has worked as a mortician, Olson comes from a three-generation family of funeral directors, and Schiavenato is a birth doula who has accompanied many stillbirths. The emphasis on the materiality of death comes through especially strongly in Schwartz's discussion of touch in death care, Toulson's description of the physicality of newly created funerary rituals like the Showers of Love in Singapore, Schiavenato's accounts of physical interaction with the bodies of stillborn babies permitted through technological innovations like the CuddleCot, and Dawdy's and Liu's chapters on the materiality of interventions that care for the bodies of the deceased like cosmetic restoration and embalming.

The theme of temporality is highlighted in the chapters by Farman and Engelke, but it is also present in the chapters by Shiaveneto, Dawdy, and Toulson, which describe how innovations in funerary ritual expand the liminal period between death and disposition of the body, providing the bereaved with the time they need to interact with and mourn the deceased. Indeed, Engelke suggests that the conquest of time is a key element of funerary rituals in many places throughout the world, which reaffirm the continuity of life over death.

Finally, personhood emerges as an important concern in the chapters dealing with transhumanist projects by Farman and Huberman. The perpetuation of the self is precisely what transhumanists strive to ensure, by extending corporeal life through transfusions of "young blood," by uploading the contents of one's brain to a digital platform, like the BINA48 chatbot, or by preserving one's head or entire body cryogenically until medical science has overcome the conditions that caused one's demise. Personhood is also central to the chapters by Dawdy and Liu on the art and magic of embalming and cosmetic restoration. As Dawdy demonstrates, embalming perpetuates the "distilled essence" of the deceased, suspending them in a liminal state, not living, but equally not dead. In a different way, Liu also deals with personhood through her account of the way one funeral worker in Shanghai negotiates his subjectivity as he faces moments of existential crisis. I will turn now from these general observations about *The New Death* as a whole to a consideration of each chapter.[1]

Abou Farman's penetrating chapter, "Terminality: Technoscientific Eschatology in the Anthropocene," follows Timothy Leary's lead by extending the scope of reference of "terminality" from the state of a dying individual to that of the human species as a whole faced with the crises of the twenty-first century, including climate change, overpopulation, and the proliferation of nuclear warheads. Farman understands terminality as a "secular technoscientific eschatology" that involves an affective and intellectual orientation to the future—or more precisely, its nonexistence. He traces the genealogy of terminal thinking to nineteenth-century scientific developments like Cuvier's discovery of extinction and Kelvin's theory of the heat death of the universe and traces it through the work of twentieth-century figures like Max Weber and Freeman Dyson. Farman argues that in the twenty-first century, the transhumanist movement is seeking to escape terminality through strategies ranging from outer-space colonization to artificial intelligence and life-extension technologies that will augment human capacities, enabling superintelligent cyborgs to overcome the limitations of mortality and the threat of extinction. Far from being a bizarre aberration, this eclectic movement of "scientifically minded groups" is part of a continuum with "mainstream science and tech culture" that includes many influential Silicon Valley actors like Elon Musk and Ray Kurzweil, as well as figures like Stephen Hawking and Martine Rothblatt, inventor of Sirius satellite radio. Transhumanism is also intimately intertwined with economic power through its links to the expanding technology and biotech industries.

Farman shows how transhumanist discourses about saving "humanity" in the face of impending doom are actually concerned with saving a particular segment of humanity: the 1 percent and "white anxious class" of Europe and North America with its postcolonial legacy of civilization. As he puts it, "The issue here is not the survival of everyone but of some—and the question of 'who' is racially, structurally and geopolitically overdetermined." Although a different strand of transhumanism with different historical antecedents has emerged in Russia (Bernstein 2015, 2016, 2019), the movement Farman analyzes is primarily Anglo-American, white, and concerned not so much with the extinction of humans as with the extinction of the potential for the future creation of a "post-human cyborg technocivilization" that will outlast our current world, perhaps on another planet.

For Farman, the nihilism that emerges from Weber's picture of a disenchanted world is central to terminal eschatology.[2] In a universe that is strictly secular and material, the only avenue to a meaningful interpretation of existence is through belief in progress. Yet as we have come to realize, progress in science and human knowledge carries within it the seeds of our destruction; just as nuclear physics has enabled understanding of the workings of the cosmos, so too has it laid the basis for tools of global annihilation. Farman points out that secular humanists cannot believe in an afterlife, so "death is magically transformed into the meaning of life." Paradoxically, however, this "tragic" vision is also hopeless, since absolute extinction means that there will be no conscious agent to look back and recognize meaning, only "absolute nothingness." Thus, the question arises: "'What *was* it all for?'" Within the terminal eschatology, transhumanism circumvents this question by valorizing the ultimate achievements of civilization: museums, art, literature, and scientific knowledge. Pointing to the partial and Eurocentric character of this definition of civilization, at the end of the chapter Farman suggests that we need to rethink the future by devaluing these tokens of human accomplishment. The end of the Euro-American colonial world may in fact hold "radical potential" for the beginning of a new world, with new possibilities that draw on "other" ways of being.

Like Farman's chapter, Huberman's contribution explores the nexus between capitalism, whiteness, technology, and transhumanism in contemporary US society. Her masterful analysis draws on Marx's recognition of the vampire-like character of capital as "a form of accumulated dead labour that comes to dominate and oppress the living," sucking away their vitality. Focusing on the figure of Peter Thiel, infamous for his interest in parabiosis, a technique whereby blood from a young donor is transfused into an older person with the aim of reversing the aging process, Huberman argues that "contemporary biocapitalism has literalized Marx's metaphor, and in so doing, it has raised new questions and concerns about the contemporary extraction of surplus value and its effects on the American people." As she points out, the American transhumanist movement is dominated by older white men who have gained billions through Silicon Valley tech initiatives and who stand to gain, both financially and in terms of enhanced longevity, from the extraction of bodily substances from younger, less-privileged members of society. This situation leads Huberman to call for the formulation of a new counterpart to Mbembe's necropolitics, which she terms "vitapolitics." Instead of deploying the right to kill as a tool of human subjugation, vitapolitics involves the establishment of sovereignty through "the capacity to dictate who may escape death and live ever longer and more enhanced lives." As a case in point, Huberman points to Thiel's libertarian, anti-democratic political writings and to his support for Donald Trump. Presciently, she concludes that the transhumanist agenda of extracting life-enhancing bodily substances from some people for the benefit of others is entangled with politics, which is "becoming a life and death struggle for American democracy."[3]

Tamara Kneese's powerful analysis of the genealogy of surveillance and self-care in the US life insurance industry continues this volume's exploration of the interconnections among transhumanism, technologies of life extension, and white male privilege. Bringing together archival materials from the early twentieth-century Life Extension Institute (LEI), which had close ties to the insurance industry, and twenty-first-century algorithmic life insurance models, Kneese shows how care of the self is constructed as a morally responsible practice that increases worker productivity and decreases the chances of premature death, thus maximizing profits for life insurance companies. While the LEI promoted hygiene and healthy living through pamphlets and educational programs, present-day insurance companies employ strategies like providing their clients with Apple Watches and Fitbits. These devices both encourage self-optimization for the wearer and enable the company to access data about sleep and exercise patterns to be used in calculating insurance rates, together with other electronic sources of data like health records, lab data, prescription records, and information from social media. As Kneese argues, "Big data and predictive analytics" have allowed insurers to "dispense with physical exams and more obvious forms of surveillance." Nonetheless, as in the early twentieth century, life insurance one hundred years later continues to sort individuals and groups into "potentially valuable or inherently risky," based on ethnicity, race, demographic information, location data, and social media networks.

Kneese documents the historical connections between the life insurance industry and eugenics: several LEI members were prominent eugenicists. Likewise, the techniques of self-optimization that life insurance companies advocate promote life extension in the same way as transhumanist regimes of nutritional supplements and exercise. Significantly, it is now possible to buy insurance to cover the cost of cryogenic preservation after death, in the hope of eventual medical progress and reanimation (Cohen 2020). Moreover, as Kneese points out, there are parallels between the vampire imagery associated with capitalism that Huberman describes and the ways in which the insurance industry has enriched itself over the past century by exploiting the desire of working-class people for protection from impoverishment due to disability or death. Kneese advances the idea that life insurance itself is a strategy for controlling the contingency and uncertainty associated with death, part of the technology that American society uses to render death "manageable." Paradoxically, for over a century, Americans have willingly embraced life insurance along with its technologies of self-optimization and rhetoric of "responsible death," and in so doing, they have increased the profit margins of corporations. People buy life insurance to exert some degree of control beyond their own mortality, to thwart death by ensuring a good outcome for their loved ones after their own death. In this way, perhaps, we can interpret life insurance as another form of transhumanist technology.

Casey Golomski's self-reflexive chapter borrows the term *deathnography* from University of Toronto anthropology graduate student Henry Lee Heinonen (https://deathnography.libsyn.com) and uses it to describe writing ethnographically about death. Specifically, Golomski examines the dynamic process of crafting ethnographic knowledge about death with his interlocuters in the African kingdom of eSwatini (formerly Swaziland), where HIV prevalence is the highest in the world. After publishing his 2018 book *Funeral Culture: AIDS, Work, and Cultural Change in an African Kingdom*, Golomski returned to eSwatini and gifted copies of the book to the people he had encountered during fieldwork and whose stories he tells in the ethnography. Golomski describes reader response to the book in several contexts: in the home of a family with whom he had lived in eSwatini, with classes of university students in eSwatini and South Africa, at a conference with eSwatini and Zimbabwean academic colleagues, and with an eSwatini graduate student in the United States who was the teaching assistant for a course in which Golomski's book was used as a text. In presenting these conversations, Golomski highlights how deathnography can, at its best, be a practice of radical mourning that counters the dehumanization and devaluation of the lives of Indigenous and colonialized nonwhite peoples. Rather than othering, deathnography can challenge necropolitical regimes and reveal the shared mortality of ethnographers and the people whose stories they document. Together with our interlocuters, we gaze into the mirror of deathnography, seeking to elucidate "the origins of violence and structural pathways that condition death and knowledge about it in the communities with whom we work, as well as our own." Drawing on Ruth Behar (1996), Golomski offers this dialogical perspective as a path toward reimagining death and escaping the colonialist legacy of anthropology in which, at its worst, ethnographers resemble the vampire capitalists who suck the life out of other people to enhance their own.

Matthew Engelke's ethnographically rich and theoretically valuable chapter is one of the highlights of the volume. Engelke's analysis of time in British secular humanist funeral rites convincingly shows how these services are reflective of an immanent frame as opposed to a transcendent one. For secular humanists, death is the end of the self, and the concept of an afterlife is both implausible and morally suspect, since it is presumed that organizing existence around the promise of another world engenders neglect of one's ethical responsibilities in the current life. Like the transhumanists described in the chapters by Farman and Huberman, British secular humanists reject religion and embrace science and technology. Yet the transhumanists seek to use the latter to perpetuate subjectivity beyond death, while Engelke's interlocuters accept that "to die means the end of conscious personality" while "look[ing] death in the face with honesty, with dignity and with calm."

Time in the secular humanist perspective is exclusively secular, as opposed to Benjamin's "messianic time" or Taylor's "higher times," which are concerned "with the affairs of eternity." Nonetheless, Engelke finds that humanist ceremonies—like funerary ritual in other contexts around the globe—seek to reaffirm life's triumph over death and to conquer time. They do so through appeals to history and nostalgia, linking "personal and collective memory" and encompassing both deceased and mourners in an ongoing imagined community. Continuity is also evoked through reference to the genetic material the deceased have passed down to their children and grandchildren, and to the memories of the dead that the living cultivate. Engelke examines the way that time is controlled and managed within the ritual framework of humanist funerals, noting that although they almost always take place within a scheduled thirty-minute slot, time is slowed down in the ritual context, and celebrants invoke the liminality of the ceremony as a moment away from the busyness of everyday life when participants can reflect on life and death.

Humanist funerals are followed by cremation, and one ethnographic detail related to ritual temporality that Engelke mentions is that sometimes, due to a backlog at the crematorium, the body of the deceased may have to wait overnight after the service, since there is a queue for the oven. Engelke comments that this situation is "not hidden, but not exactly advertised either, since for many families, the idea of a loved one's remains waiting in a queue to be turned to ash is not a happy thought." In connection with this point, it is worth noting that in London, because of the high demand for crematorium facilities, bodies can be kept waiting three weeks or more between death and the funeral and cremation service, simply because there is a queue to use the chapel and the oven. I have personally experienced this situation when family members passed away in London, and I found that there is something very odd about how time is understood in this context. While waiting three weeks for a funeral, the body of the deceased is "gone," presumably in a morgue in the care of the funeral directors, and there is no interaction with the corpse over this period. The family seems to be expected to carry on with life, doing their normal activities before ritual closure has taken place and goodbyes have been said to the deceased. I found this extended period of liminality troubling, all the more so because it was not (at least in my experience) recognized as part of the *rite de passage* and hence is therefore in some senses not even liminal. It would be interesting to know more about how this prolonged interval between death and funeral ritual relates to the British secular humanist view of time. Given that there is no afterlife for secular humanists, I would imagine that they understand the "person" to have been extinguished at death, so perhaps it does not matter that the body is left waiting unaccompanied for weeks before its final disposition, which in any case does not involve a ritual transition to another state of existence. One also wonders how more traditionally religious people in the United Kingdom deal with this interval, but that is outside the scope of Engelke's chapter.

Another thought-provoking ethnographic detail connected to temporality in this chapter is Engelke's discussion with secular humanist funeral celebrant Janet about her references to "forever" and "eternity" in secular humanist funerals. While Engelke concludes that there is a certain degree of semantic looseness in the secular humanist ritual, and celebrants do not always mean everything they say in a literal sense, it seems to me that the concept of eternity is not incompatible with the secular humanist immanent frame. Time can be understood to continue, even though the individual consciousness is extinguished. Likewise, the universe may be understood as existing forever, despite the fact that people drop out of it and no longer exist except through their DNA or as atoms recycled in the environment. This is a secular understanding of time, but it is in direct contradiction to the terminality that Farman identifies as the secular eschatology characteristic of the Anthropocene. Referring to secular humanists in general terms, Farman suggests that "having eliminated the afterlife and made death final," they have "no option but to make death the very condition of a meaningful life." Significantly, all the British celebrants Engelke interviewed were passionate about "the meaning and sense of purpose they derived from their work." As he notes at the end of his chapter, the acknowledgment that time will eventually wipe away all subjectivity is in itself a way of conquering time and overcoming our fear of mortality.

LaShaya Howie presents the first of the two short ethnographic interludes that separate the sections of this volume on mortality and death care. Her thickly textured ethnographic account underscores the extent to which US society remains racially segregated, even in death. This chapter is a particularly significant contribution to the volume's assessment of what death looks like in the early twenty-first century, because it challenges assumptions by historians and social scientists that American funeral practices are homogenous and can be conflated with white funeral practices. Following in the footsteps of Karla Holloway (2002) and Suzanne Smith (2010), Howie shows how Black funeral homes are central sites of sociality in Black communities, and Black death care specialists address uniquely Black experiences of death. These experiences include the frequency of violent deaths, emanating from structural oppression and police brutality, that necessitate special skills in the arts of cosmetic restoration. Notably, the materiality of brutalized bodies at Black funerals has served to galvanize radical protest and demands for justice in the Black community; recall the significance of Emmett Till's open casket viewing as a catalyst for civil rights activism in the 1950s.[4]

Embalming and viewing remain a "cultural and spiritual practice that maintains social bonds" in twenty-first-century Black America. However, Black funeral directors fear that buyouts of family funeral homes by large, white-dominated corporations, the shifting of consumer preferences toward cremation, and the gentrification of formerly Black neighborhoods threaten their role and the unique character of Black death care.[5] Vampire capitalism resurfaces in this chapter, as funeral corporations target Black funeral homes for takeovers because the Black community still spends "good money" on funerals. For Black family funeral businesses, such corporate buyouts are particularly poignant tragedies, since they undermine generational succession, a form of continuity that transcends mortality and as Engelke's humanists would say, conquers time.

Like their communities, African American funeral homes have been disproportionately impacted by COVID-19. In the words of Claudia Rankine (2015), "The condition of black life is one of mourning." Yet in the face of mourning, as the world witnessed in May 2020 after the murder of George Floyd, Black funeral ritual and death care continue to humanize bodies and persons who have been desecrated by injustice and oppression. The shining, white horse–drawn carriage that carried Floyd's golden casket to the Houston Memorial Gardens and the formality of the procession reaffirmed Floyd's dignity and valorized his life.

The second ethnographic interlude, by Stephanie Schiavenato, is a moving, visceral account that captures the physicality of pregnancy, birth, and pregnancy loss and highlights the themes of temporality and materiality. Here, material technology—the CuddleCot, a refrigerated bassinet for dead babies—expands time, allowing bereaved parents to spend longer periods with their child. Schiavenato reflexively draws on her own experience of pregnancy loss and her work as a birth doula to draw attention to the interconnection between body and mind—*bodymind*—in the experience of reproductive death. I would like to suggest that this concept, drawn from feminist disability studies, is relevant to several of the other chapters in this collection, and may in fact be important to consider in work on death and dying more generally.

Brazilian scholar Francisco Ortega (2009) has coined the term *cerebral subject* to describe "brain-centered approaches to the human person" that privilege neuroscientific theories and technologies in the interpretation of social and individual behavior and affect (see also Rose and Abi-Rached 2013). More recently, together with Fernando Vidal, Ortega traces the genealogy of the cerebral subject to seventeenth-century debates about the location of the soul, which led to the development in the eighteenth and nineteenth centuries of the assumption that the brain is the "only part of the body we need in order to be ourselves" (Vidal and Ortega 2017:7). This "neurocentrism" seems to underlie much of the transhumanist agenda. Certainly, it is evident in cryonics, where frequently only the head (read brain) of a patient is cryogenically preserved, and in proposals to upload the contents of one's brain to a digital platform to perpetuate one's existence beyond the body's death (see Farman 2013, 74). While the "neural turn" (Vidal and Ortega 2017) may have materialized the brain through imaging such as fMRIs, it is also the heir of mind-body dualism. Schiavenato's bodymind calls this contemporary focus on the brain into question and raises the possibility of a more integrated approach to both bereavement and death itself, one that is materially rooted in bodily experience.

Moving into the section of the book focused on death care, Schwartz's chapter is important for connecting the volume to scholarship in cultural and media studies and for drawing attention to touch in care for the dead. As Schwartz notes, with its origins in funeral photography, embalming has created an emphasis on the visual in the relationship between the living and the corpse. By contrast, she calls for a "haptics of death" that takes into account "*all* modes of touch involved in death care, including those that some might consider cold, medical, or opportunistic." Schwartz rejects the nostalgic rhetoric of the death-positive movement that represents death care in some past golden age as female, noncommercial, and non-professionalized and asserts that over history, such treatment of the dead has devolved into its opposite. Schwartz starts from the assumptions that technological mediation, like death, is a human constant, and that the hand is an instrument of mediation in death care that separates the ritual object of the corpse from human society. As she argues, "The hand as *device* denaturalizes the distinction between the technological and the natural, a binary often deployed in contemporary death cultures to hierarchize modes of death care." Offering a taxonomy of different kinds of touch in contemporary treatment of the dead, the instrumental and the caring, she seeks to overcome the "naturalness" of taken-for-granted ideas about gender and care. Schwartz also pays attention to settings in which touch and care are absent, observing that the privilege of receiving death care "that feels meaningful is unequally distributed," especially during crisis situations like the COVID-19 pandemic.

The key example of the connection between touch and death care that Schwartz analyzes involves embalming: the preservation of the body of Evita Perón for public display in Argentina during the 1950s. This focus provides a segue into the next chapter in the volume, Shannon Dawdy's highly original interpretation of the characteristically American practice of embalming. The cases of "extreme embalming" that Dawdy describes are primarily concerned with the *visual* impact created by a tableau in which the deceased is presented as engaged in activities they enjoyed during life.[6] However, she also references the importance of touch in mediating the relationship between the living and the dead, recounting how embalming enabled a bereaved young man to engage with the only remaining recognizable part of his father's body, his left foot, following a plane accident.

Dawdy convincingly claims that embalming is a meaningful act that does cultural work, not simply the product of a superficial American refusal to confront the reality of death. As in the case of the young man who found solace in stroking his father's foot, the work that embalming does is therapeutic. Like medieval saints' relics, embalmed bodies in twenty-first-century America have power to heal the living. Tracing its roots in part to nineteenth-century spiritualism and Egyptomania, Dawdy claims that embalming is a magical act of transformation that requires a willing suspension of disbelief on the part of the living, so that the deceased appears to be "undead," either sleeping, or in the case of newer practices of extreme embalming, engaged in ordinary daily occupations.

The twin themes of temporality and personhood reemerge in Dawdy's analysis. As she shows, the cultural work of embalming involves conquering time, transcending death by erasing the traces of illness and aging from the deceased's body and extending the liminal time when the person remains in the world of the living. Whether presented as sleeping in an open casket or engaged in lifelike activities as in the extreme embalming tableaux, the deceased is both "there" and "not there," no longer a speaking individual with agency but "an intensified if distilled *presence* of their personhood." Dawdy actually uses the term *spirit* here, which fittingly reflects the ambiguity about the after-life associated with embalming. In the liminal time and space created through the embalmer's magic, the question of where the person goes after death is deferred. In fact, Dawdy argues that the American practice of embalming cre-ates the "undead"—"a nonbreathing but sleeping human," whose integrity is protected even after the funeral through burial in a sealed metal casket and concrete vault.

While this vision of the departed may be comforting to Americans, Peter Metcalf's classic article about death ritual among the Berawan of Indonesia in the 1970s shows that such preservation of the material body is not universally perceived in a positive light. Following Hertz's ([1907] 1960) insights and like the Greek villagers described by Danforth (1982), the Berawan understood disinte-gration of the body to be necessary for the smooth transition of the deceased to the world of the dead. Metcalf's interlocuters feared that undecomposed bodies risked reanimation through possession by an evil nonhuman spirit that would turn the body into a hideous monster that could never be vanquished, since it is already dead. Berawan people reacted with horror to Metcalf's description of American funeral practices, envisioning America as "a land carpeted with potential zombies" (Metcalf 2010). Perhaps the difference between the horrify-ing and the comforting perspectives on embalming has something to do with different understandings of the afterlife. According to Metcalf, the Berawan in the 1970s shared a consensus that ultimately, the spirits of their dead would be welcomed into a radiant land where they would continue to exist. In contrast, Dawdy observes that the majority of Americans she interviewed say "death is a mystery." As one of her interlocuters says, "The truth is, once you gone, you don't know *where* those people are at." Instead of fearing the undead, according to Dawdy, Americans "worship" them, engaging in a kind of "pagan magic."

Dawdy's discussion of magic innovatively integrates entertainment magic with consideration of magic as an anthropological category. Significantly, her examples of extreme embalming come from Black communities in New Orleans, arguably a place where death has always been very much present in the world of the living. As Howie outlines in her chapter, embalming remains central to Black practices of death care, even though its popularity is declining among white Americans. One question that Dawdy's analysis does not explore is, What does it mean for American deathways if embalming is losing its magic and giving way to what funeral directors refer to as "direct cremation"?[7]

If embalming, as Dawdy and many funeral directors claim, is therapeutic for the bereaved, the home-funeral movement, skillfully portrayed in Olson's chapter, also offers therapy, but in a different mode. Part of the "death-positive" community, home-funeral advocates reject specialized, industrial, and bureaucratized death care in favor of "an alternate ontology of the corpse—one that is grounded not in a conception of the corpse as an aberrant public-health concern warranting the intervention of state-regulated experts but rather as a natural, normal body that calls for continued care from intimates." Like Schwartz, who considers the discourse of death doulas about preindustrial treatment of the dead to be nostalgic rhetoric rather than historical fact, Olson argues that the home-funeral movement is not reviving the death-care practices of earlier periods but rather creating something new. Another key insight of this chapter is that the "bureaucratized death culture" that home-funeral advocates reject can in fact be "richly affect laden." Both the home-funeral movement and the funeral industry are culturally constructed strategies for dealing with death.

Tracing the connections between the home-funeral movement and the earlier home birth and home hospice movements, all of which have been led by women and have rejected the medicalization of biological processes, Olson deftly depicts the ambivalence that home-funeral practitioners express toward credentialization and professionalization. While rejecting the funeral industry, many home-funeral advocates are in favor of establishing "core competencies" and credentials for their sector, partly so that they can be viewed as valid "death professionals" and partly to ease bureaucratic obstacles like hospitals' insistence on releasing bodies only to certified morticians. Olson describes the debates within the National Home Funeral Alliance about establishing core competencies for home-funeral officiants, an example of the standardization and bureaucratization that Victor Turner (1969) identified as the "routinization of communitas" that takes place as social movements evolve.

Significantly, part of the justification for blocking the home-funeral movement in America rests on an appeal to public health: embalming and disposal of the body by regulated methods is perceived to safeguard society from "unclean and dangerous corpses." While not ritually elaborated as in traditional Chinese funerary rituals, death pollution is arguably an unspoken source of uneasiness for Americans. Concern with the transgressive, polluting character of the dead body provides a bridge between Olson's chapter and the final two contributions to the volume, both of which portray changing patterns of death care and attitudes toward pollution in Sinophone settings. The first of these chapters, by Huwy-min Lucia Liu, recounts the life story of Lin Wu, a state funeral-parlor worker in contemporary Shanghai. In its focus on a single individual, this chapter connects to the theme of personhood that runs through the volume. Lin Wu's fascinating narrative shows how he defines his subjectivity from multiple possibilities in the face of existential crises over the life course. His "authentic self" as an artist is expressed through his work as a cosmetic restorer of bodies and his pride in his skill. Here, the volume's theme of materiality intersects with personhood, since Lin Wu's subjectivity is constructed "on the ground" through material practices using material substances and tools like oil paints and brushes. Liu's chapter also provides important ethnographic insights into the changing landscape of death in twenty-first-century Shanghai. While ideas about death pollution continue to remain important in contemporary China, Liu seeks to avoid essentializing funeral workers like Lin Wu by interpreting them solely through the lens of their marginalized status. As she points out, people now recognize that the funeral industry provides well-paid and stable employment.

Liu provides a nuanced and detailed analysis of change and continuity in funeral practices in Shanghai. Prior to 1949, "Chinese deathways . . . were based on the concepts of spirits, afterlife, pollution, and Confucian social hierarchy. Traditionally, properly performed funerals transformed dead bodies into ancestors who were situated in a reciprocal relationship with the living." As Liu documents, subsequently, especially during the Cultural Revolution, the Chinese Communist Party sought to reorient loyalty away from kinship units to the state, by modernizing funeral practices and purging them of "superstitious" elements such as the burning of paper money and siting of graves according to principles of feng shui.[8] In this period, funeral workers took on a disciplinary role, ensuring that citizens followed the state's funerary directives. More recently, with the introduction of the socialist market economy, funeral parlors have become financially independent units offering an array of services with the goal of making a profit. This marketization of death care has been interpreted by people in Shanghai as a humanistic trend rather than a form of profiteering, as in the case of the American funeral industry (see, for example, Mitford [1963]). It is viewed as humanistic, because instead of enforcing a state-mandated set of practices, funeral "salespeople" now encourage their clients to exercise choice in requesting services.

Globalization has also contributed to developments in death care in contemporary Shanghai; Lin Wu spent four months at a mortician's college in Canada, where he learned new techniques related to embalming and restorative arts. As in the American contexts described by Dawdy, in Shanghai, Lin Wu works magic through his art to transform the corpse from biological material into a cultural product that has been aesthetically embellished. Through the magic of aesthetic elaboration, the pollution associated with the "uncanny" corpse as "matter out of place" (Douglas 1966), a dead body in the social world of the living, is removed.

The final chapter in the volume, by Ruth Toulson, deals with innovation in funeral practices in the Chinese community of Singapore, where zoning laws restrict the funeral business to marginalized industrial areas and "dead-end streets." Once again, the issue of death pollution in a Sinophone context arises, but significantly, while Liu seeks to broaden anthropological analysis beyond concerns about pollution, Toulson draws attention to the enduring significance of ideas about the corpse as polluting and the need for the living to do ritual work for the dead. Toulson describes the Showers of Love ritual created by a pioneering woman entrepreneur who took over her family's funeral business after the death of her father in 2004. In Showers of Love, women funerary workers guide family members through a process of washing the embalmed body of their loved one and caring for the deceased through gestures such as painting a mother's nails. At the same time, the family is encouraged to talk to the deceased, to express their feelings of love and regret, and to cry. With respect to the latter, Toulson documents how crying reveals both continuity and change between "traditional" Chinese funerals and innovative rites like Showers of Love. In different ways, crying in both contexts indexes relatedness and ideas about appropriate familial love. Moreover, like older Singaporean Chinese rituals, Showers of Love allows family members to do work for the dead that eases their path to the afterlife, but now this work involves washing and caring for the body rather than taking on death pollution. The new ritual also provides time and space for grief, linking it to the broader theme of temporality and death explored throughout this volume.

One of the most important contributions of Toulson's chapter is that it provides an intriguing glimpse into the dynamics of how funerary rituals are invented in the globalized world. Showers of Love is a unique creation that brings together elements from various sources including the Japanese film *Departures* and American pop psychology. As with the innovations in American deathways described by Olson and Howie, Showers of Love is marked by the predominance of women, and as in Dawdy's chapter, families find profound healing through interacting with the embalmed body in Showers of Love.

At the end of her chapter, which is also the final ethnographic chapter of the book, Toulson fittingly returns to one of the central questions explored in the volume: "How is the experience of death and mourning changing under conditions of growing religious plurality and secularization, technological mediation, and globalization?" Seeking theoretical frameworks through which to analyze these processes, Toulson draws on Geertz's (1973) classic account of a failed funeral in Java during the 1950s, where newly politicized religious identities clashed with older ritual forms based on collective village solidarity. Toulson claims that in contemporary Singapore as in much of the world in the early twenty-first century, we can see a parallel lack of fit between simultaneous "transformations in different realms (technological, religious, social)." In the face of such developments, new rites like Showers of Love are generated, to respond to ongoing concerns for meaning. Thus, she concludes, "death ritual continues to matter" and merits anthropological attention, since "appropriately disposing the dead is, one might argue, one of few human universals, one of the very things that makes us human."

While I agree with Toulson that anthropologists and others who do research on death must pay attention to ritual, I am equally cognizant of Renato Rosaldo's (1989) admonition that we must not neglect the power of emotion in the face of death. In a passionate appeal born out of his own bereavement, Rosaldo cautions that ritual is a busy intersection to which all participants bring their situated personal histories and perspectives. This intersection is not always equally healing or generative of meaning for everyone who passes through it. I am particularly reminded of Rosaldo's caution when considering the healing potential of embalming. While its magic may be therapeutic for some, not all mourners are able to suspend disbelief. I have encountered people who have experienced the embalmed body of a loved one as distasteful or grotesque and who find they are unable to reconnect through the materiality of the cosmetically restored corpse to the person as known during life. Toulson is correct to point to the limits of functionalist interpretations of ritual: sometimes it simply leaves the bereaved angry, alienated, and hopelessly fractured.

Inspired by the chapters in this volume, I would like to suggest that the three interconnected concerns I have traced through its chapters—materiality, temporality, and personhood—encapsulate the crux of the dilemma posed by death. It is the failure of the material body to withstand time and the vexed relationship between the body and personhood that make death so poignant a rupture, so awe-inspiring in its finality, and ultimately so impossible to imagine. As Schwartz so eloquently puts it, death, like technological mediation, is "inextricable from the human condition." While there may be a myriad of ways that death has been mediated culturally and technologically throughout human history, we all bleed the same color, as Black Lives Matter protesters remind us. Blood is part of the materiality of death, flowing outside the skin that marks the boundary of the body. In the same way, dying is precipitated by the loss of breath—again, to reference Black Lives Matter, death comes when "I can't breathe." The relationship between breath and blood provides an apt metaphor for the interpenetration of body and subjectivity, bodymind. Breath itself is invisible, immaterial, but it enables the animation of the material body. Death occurs when that material body loses its agency, its power to breathe, move, and speak independently.

Even as we recognize the interweaving of bodymind, it is easy to imagine that personhood persists in some fashion after the body decays. That sense of persistence is shared by many people in the contemporary world, in both the global North and the global South, *pace* the British secular humanists whom Engelke encountered. In my own discussions with Americans at the annual Afterlife Awareness Conference, I encountered the view that those who die enter a realm of unconditional love and that consciousness is a form of energy that can never disappear according to the laws of physics, only change its form. Similarly, I was told, quantum physics has proven the possibility of "retrocausality," establishing that time moves both backward and forward, not unidirectionally (Badone 2018). What implications does that temporal perspective have for terminality, or for the need of rituals that conquer time?

Writing during COVID-19, death seems more of an imminent possibility than in "normal" times. Yet even so, it is difficult to imagine what it would be like to die—searing pain, choking for breath, cessation of sensation, blackness? The experience, paradoxically, can only be known by living it. Try as we might to project ourselves into the space of death, it is hard to encompass. Like La

Rochefoucauld, we find that "death and the sun are not to be looked at steadily" (quoted in Enright 1983, 39).⁹ We might well ask whether the chapters in this collection — or indeed any academic research — can truly engage with death? Or is the academic study of death and its associated practices like buying life insurance, a way to "manage" the fundamentally unknown and unknowable character of death? Death presents such an overwhelming mystery, and it is so difficult to conceive of the extinction of one's personhood — or the transformation of the self into something radically different and unknown — that it is almost impossible to conceptualize. Whether we realize it or not, perhaps as anthropologists and others who study death, we are not in fact confronting it but rather (paradoxically) engaged in distancing ourselves from our own mortality. Moreover, like Engelke's humanist celebrants, we deathnographers are passionately engaged with the people we encounter, and we find our vocation profoundly meaningful. In this way, we too conquer time.

Notes

1. Significantly, although definitely relevant to medical anthropology, *The New Death* does not directly address some of the twenty-first-century processes of "remaking death" that medical anthropologists have been concerned with, namely medical assistance in dying (Buchbinder 2018; Hannig 2019) or brain death and organ transplantation (Lock 2001; Sharp 2006, 2007). I would argue that the latter procedures can be placed on a continuum linking mainstream medicine with the transhumanist project.

2. I wonder if Farman's focus on the terminal might have prevented him from recognizing the extent to which the world remains enchanted or has become reenchanted. For many groups of people, those who are part of organized religious movements like Pentecostalism that are experiencing a revitalization worldwide — as well as others who may not be attached to formal religious institutions but nonetheless see themselves as "spiritual" — the afterlife and supernatural entities continue to have currency (Csordas 2009, 2020; Heelas 1996; Hefner 2013; Luhrmann 2012; Wallis 2003). Indeed, Jon Bialecki's work with Mormon transhumanists suggests that this movement is itself not incompatible with religious understandings of the world (Bialecki 2019, 2020, forthcoming).

3. As a number of medical anthropologists have revealed, similar "vampirish" practices exist in multiple global contexts, notably connected to organ transplantation. For example, Sherine Hamdy (2012) outlines how in Egypt, elites exploit individuals from precarious backgrounds, offering to pay them for kidneys or parts of liver lobes. Once these body parts have been extracted, the "donors" are left vulnerable to the hazards of life under marginal conditions,

including an underfunded healthcare system and environmental pollution caused by the industrial activities that enabled the wealthy organ buyers to amass their capital in the first place. See also Scheper-Hughes and Wacquant (2003) and Cohen (1999).

4. Nyle Fort, a doctoral candidate at Princeton who grew up in the Black funeral industry, highlights the significance of funerals as sites of political mobilization in the US Black community in his forthcoming dissertation, "Amazing Grief: The Politics of African American Mourning"; see https://www.ircpl.columbia. edu/videos, "Life after Death in Black America."

5. The growing feminization of death care is also a development that Black America shares with white America and other global contexts, as the later chapters in this volume by Olson and Toulson indicate.

6. The cases of extreme embalming that Dawdy describes evoked parallels for me with the *Body Worlds* exhibitions facilitated by Gunther von Hagens's technology of plastination. However, unlike the tableaux Dawdy describes, where embalming perpetuates the essence of a known individual cherished by the living who engage with them, the *Body Worlds* tableaux present the dead engaged in lifelike activities but as anonymous bodies with all anatomical structures visible (see Walter 2004).

7. One innovative alternative to both burial and cremation is being pioneered by Columbia University's DeathLAB (http://deathlab.org). It involves the creation of public memorial spaces where bodies would be sealed in anaerobic containers with microorganisms that would reduce the corpses to light-generating energy. The containers would be suspended from architectural features built into the urban landscape that would include open space and public walkways illuminated by the recycled bodies.

8. See also Whyte (1988).

9. I have quoted this maxim in another essay on similar themes (Badone 2013). See also Lambek (2016) for a related discussion.

Afterword

Atoms, Star Dust, and Fungi
Death and Secular Eschatologies

ANYA BERNSTEIN

In early fall of 2018, I attended an unusual week-long gathering in Santa Fe, New Mexico. I had just returned from the Siberian Arctic, a postapocalyptic landscape of thawing permafrost slumps, fierce mosquitos, and methane-filled lakes that are prone to catching fire. My purpose was to explore a utopian project currently under way there that aims to reverse death, "resurrect" extinct species, and reengineer the landscape of bubbling, squelching mud (which nearly swallowed one of my indispensable knee-high rubber waders) into a verdant new Eden as part of a scheme to slow down global warming. When I stepped off the plane in the cozy Santa Fe regional airport, I got whiffs of smoke from nearby forest fires, but even so, New Mexico's colorful high desert and striking red rocks provided a welcome change of scenery. The seminar was housed in the School for Advanced Research (SAR), and I had been invited as a discussant for about a dozen pre-circulated papers about contemporary death cultures. We spent our days at the likewise utopian SAR listening to papers at the leisurely pace of two per day—a genuine luxury in our era of rapid-fire fifteen-minute presentations at conferences—and touring the campus of stunning adobe architecture, Native American art, and a dog cemetery. The seminar was immediately and lovingly nicknamed the "death camp" by the participants, and it did indeed resemble a quirky summer camp, where along with the shared meals, we traded ideas about what it means to live and die in the twenty-first century. Aside from the seminar's substantive focus, all there was in this idyllic setting to remind us of the ultimate fragility of life were the faint gusts of smoky wind. In fact, given our necropolitical obsessions, it might have been we who seemed slightly out of place amid the paradisiacal rustic charm.

Now, as I recraft my remarks as a seminar discussant into this afterword, life has been brought to a virtual halt by the COVID-19 pandemic, and death feels literally ubiquitous. The Siberian Arctic and the idyllic SAR campus, in contrast — not to mention life outside my apartment window beneath the low gray New England winter sky — seem but distant utopian dreams. The necro-political, the terminal, and the eschatological, as this volume demonstrates, remain as relevant now as during those long-gone warm autumnal days in Santa Fe. In what follows, I bring together some themes addressed in the volume that go beyond the obvious focus on death and mortality, including time and tempo-rality and technology and biopolitics, in addition to the more classic topics of funerary ritual, religion, and secularism. I also offer reflections on whether my own experience studying death and immortality in post-Soviet contexts, ranging from the Buddhist to the technofuturist, might be drawn on to shift not only the ethnographic but also the epistemic lens through which we read the issues raised in the preceding chapters.

"We Conquer Time"

One theme that immediately stood out was the concern with time and temporal-ity. A recurrent interest throughout the chapters is in the relationship between concepts of time and death. As Matthew Engelke notes, for a funeral, timing is everything. Funerals have their own particular temporality. Like all rituals, they take us out of time, creating a break in our ordinary routines. This stepping out of time is a necessary part of the ritual transformation that has to take place if we are to emerge renewed. Humanist cremation rites, while carefully timed, are not rushed. To cremate a body takes exactly ninety minutes. Indeed, nothing is ever rushed in a cemetery, where even speed limits are capped at a modest five miles an hour. Are funeral rituals then about conquering time? If in religious conceptions death is conquered by the affirmation of rebirth and regeneration, in humanist funeral ceremonies death signifies the end to the one and only life one has. For humanists, the idea of an afterlife, as Engelke writes, is a "challenge to the truth of time." The humanist says, "We conquer time by recognizing that we cannot conquer time." Yet we see in these chapters that the language of continuation nonetheless persists, whether by way of memory, genetics, or cosmological musings about atoms, star dust, and nature. This same language appears in the green burial movement. According to a recent popular media piece, "Everything on this planet is made up of atoms. . . . In theory, we are all made of stardust" (Rehagen 2016).

    The question of time emerges prominently in Stephanie Schiavenato's piece on reproductive mourning and loss, as well as in Ruth Toulson's exploration of a new ritual of body washing in Singapore. As Toulson notes, time emerges as something essential for the grief process to take place; the Shower of Love ritual she examines "gives grief time." Similarly, the CuddleCot, a technologically striking innovation amounting to a refrigerated bassinet for dead babies "buys parents time to get to know the baby and to say goodbye." Time, it has been shown, is inextricably linked to temperature (Radin and Kowal 2017), and death-related innovations from cryonics to therapeutic hypothermia to the CuddleCot rely on the simple fact that cooling slows time and thus the passing of life—in some cases indefinitely. The CuddleCot, by slowing processes of physiological decomposition, provides grieving parents "time to get to know the baby they are meeting for the first time, albeit postmortem. Time to make memories. Time to say goodbye."

Yet even in this technoscientifically enabled and prolonged goodbye we see glimpses of hope and of a continuation beyond the finality of death. The quintessential question asked by most religions about death also troubles the secular discourse on mortality: If there was a person that inhabited the now-cold body, where did it go? Moving from the cold body of the baby to the postpartum body of the grieving mother, Schiavenato discusses "fetal microchimerism," a fascinating phenomenon in which fetal cells remain in the maternal blood and tissues for years after the pregnancy is over. The hopeful language of continuation invoked by secular humanists in metaphors of the dead transforming into trees or star dust reemerges here in the guise of science itself: What if the dead babies persist in the mother's breast milk or in her frontal lobe? To atoms, trees, and star dust are thus added the mother's milk and her brain as potential places to house the secular dead.

Are secular humanists then invoking types of symbolic immortality, as identified long ago by psychologists Robert J. Lifton and Eric Olson as a universal response, a reconciliation between the finality of biological death and the striving for some kind of continuation? Lifton and Olson ([1974] 2004) classified these symbolizing modes according to five ideal types. First, biological immortality envisions extending life through one's children, family, or even nation. Second, creative immortality conceives the overcoming of death in the form of art, literature, and knowledge that survive the individual. Third are religious beliefs in resurrection, reincarnation, and rebirth. A fourth such symbolic strategy appears in the idea that we return to nature as our bodies decompose, a major part of the ideologies behind both humanist death rituals and green funerals. And the fifth comprises a variety of experiential states—trance, collective effervescence, psychedelic-induced ecstasy—in all of which there is no death.

Yet what happens under the condition of "terminality," as proposed by Abou Farman to denote a new awareness of the *end* that is "collective, scientific, and secular"? As Farman argues, this emerging sense of doom is to be thought of as an affective regime specifically propagated through "science and scientific symbolic language." Science is both the culprit and the savior in this story, a technoscientific eschatology that might be unique to this specific historical moment in the West. Importantly, by this definition, terminality is not a distant end but an outcome that might be just around the corner. If complete extinction is the future, not only of humanity but of all life on earth and perhaps the universe itself so that there is no continuation of life through children, memory, works of art, or even life as such, what kinds of politics, ethics, and metaphysics emerge in the process? If culture, in the broadest Tylorian sense, is at least in part about the transcendence of time and collective survival in the face of individual death, what happens once, as a collective, we become terminal?

Who Lives and Who Dies?

The volume's second major unifying theme concerns technology and the biopolitical shifts it engenders. Whatever the authors describe—people rejecting received technologies in the postmortem care of the body, technology threatening to drive humanity and possibly all life on earth to utter extinction, the self-tracking technologies being used by new life insurance companies, technologies bearing the troubling promise to reverse aging but only for the very affluent, or technology that suspends beings between life and death, it is clear that technology has already redefined what it means to be alive, dead, or in a state of protracted liminality between the two.

Take parabiosis, for example, the exchange of blood between organisms. Originally pioneered in early Soviet Russia, it was conceived as a utopian practice of "mutual" blood exchanges for purposes of rejuvenation, bearing benefits to both giver and receiver (see Bernstein 2019). Jenny Huberman looks at the practice in the contemporary American context referred to as "young blood transfusion," considering the anxieties that arise when only the superrich like Peter Thiel would ever benefit. Parabiosis, as currently developed in the United States, raises new questions not only about biopolitics but also about new forms of "biocapital" and growing social inequalities. Not only are the time and resources of the less economically well-off available for the more affluent to use to their advantage, but now also their very body substances are there to be alienated and transferred.

For several decades now, various technological developments have been redefining life and death, changing the notions of the normal and the pathological, of illness and health, and bringing into being new forms of life and new forms of death (Franklin and Lock 2003). The acceptance of brain death as the contemporary legal criterion made death into a problem to be managed and timed to work with the emerging transplantation technology, enabling commodification of the body and its parts. Most recently, the digital death industry has promised eternal life in cyberspace through the creation of digital avatars and industries of digital estate planning, which commodify what they consider the very essence of the person defined as information.

Similarly, as Kneese shows, new life insurance industries use algorithms that reduce the person to data obtained via tracking devices, such as "counted steps, heart rate, hydration status, weight, and oxygen levels." As she so persuasively argues, with all their radical novelty, these new industries seem to follow surprisingly old corporate logics of death management. Life insurance, she argues, is a "way of managing death, but it's also a means of categorizing individuals and populations as potentially valuable or inherently risky." And estate planning and life insurance are perfect examples of old-fashioned industries poised for what Silicon Valley calls "disruption." As Farman notes regarding transhumanist survivalism (itself a kind of insurance), notions of risk and securitization are profitable, and capitalization of risk drives the digital estate planning industry as well. The idea that some individuals or entire populations are riskier than others goes hand in hand with the notion that some are more worthy of survival. As biological matter is reimagined as information and notions of well-being and health are remade through technological biomedical enhancement, personhood is increasingly tied to notions of self-optimization and productivity.

To Mourn Together

Mortuary rituals have always been of interest to anthropologists, from the early days of the discipline through to present-day explorations of home funerals, humanist funerals, embalming, and online mourning. Anthropologists since Durkheim have noted that while grieving involves individual emotions, mourning is about our collective ways of coping with loss. Put differently, individual emotion, or grief, comes to expression collectively through culturally prescribed ways of mourning. What, then, do recent shifts in collective ways of mourning tell us about the contemporary moment? In a reflexive piece on his work on HIV/AIDS in eSwatini, Casey Golomski points to necropolitics as the "nocturnal" side of biopolitics, which, along with racialization and other abuses of power, is often expressed in the funereal. He proposes that an ethnography of death—a *deathnography*—can itself be a technology, in that it has the potential to become anti-necropolitical, a form of "radical mourning" undertaken together with the communities we write about, foregrounding our shared mortality. How do we write about mourning? And how do we mourn together with our interlocutors?

In the United States, cremations have been increasingly replacing traditional burials, engendering a variety of innovative ways to deal with the remains, from making memorial art of the ashes to sending them into space or blending them into artificial coral reefs. We are used to such novelties being hyped in the media, but less frequently do we hear about the effects that the shift from burials to cremations can have on marginalized communities for which burials have long been a site of sociality and family continuity. LaShaya Howie shows how the change provokes anxiety among Black funeral professionals, who simultaneously rely on burials for their livelihood and feel a deep cultural loss as Black funeral practices appear to be "slipping away" from them. Funeral services, as Howie points out, remain an extremely racially segregated sector of the American economy, and now Black funerary practices are being increasingly transformed by such other social forces as gentrification and the change in familial, gender, and intergenerational dynamics. Howie is concerned that Black funerals will follow the fate of the Black press, Black banks, and historically Black colleges, all of which have been engulfed by white consumer markets.

This general shift from burials to cremations in the United States, however, is counterbalanced by a growing rejection of cremation by some consumers, not least for its carbon footprint and effect on the environment. One of the most striking recent transformations of funerary rituals in the American context is the growing popularity of home funerals and green burials, as described by Philip Olson (this volume) and Shannon Dawdy (forthcoming). Home-funeral advocates want to care for their own dead without the mediation of licensed funeral professionals and with minimal technological intervention in the management of dead bodies. As Olson notes, the home-funeral trend is intimately

tied up with women's, anticorporate, New Age, and environmentalist movements all at once, and there are many parallels to be found between the trends
toward home funerals and their green counterparts. Both home funerals and
green burials are examples of what anthropologists have long called "invented
traditions," in which knowledge that is recent in origin is constituted as being
old, often tinged with a great deal of nostalgia. As with all funerary rituals,
home funerals result from negotiations between home-funeral professionals
(with their ambiguous legal status), relatives, and the general public, as they
reflect current subjectivities and larger social trends. The questions here have
to do with what is being gained, and what abandoned, by this shift to green and
home funerals. Why is this happening? Why now?

As Margaret Schwartz notes, movements like these see themselves as resisting the dominant practices of death care. Home funerals place a lot of rhetorical
emphasis on a certain notion of touch, which is viewed as intimate, as being
equivalent to having an emotional connection with the body and is something
that the proponents view as missing from corporate funereal practices. Yet
touch is certainly present in embalming, which involves washing and cleaning
the body, dressing it, and applying makeup. Other types of touch in embalming,
such as making incisions in the body to fill it with embalming liquid, are more
invasive. Embalming touch can certainly be intimate, but proper boundaries
must constantly be maintained to avoid "the danger of too much intimacy" or
even charge of necrophilia, as was faced by the embalmer of the Argentinian
first lady Eva Perón. Or to take another example, body cosmeticians in China, as
described by Lucia Liu, may be the closest equivalent to an American embalmer.
As cosmeticians, they dress the dead, apply makeup, and occasionally perform
hypodermic embalming. In more extreme cases involving the disfigurement of
the deceased, they work as restorative artists preparing the body for viewing,
since in China, a closed-casket funeral is considered a "bad death." This they do
with the utmost care and personal touch.

Despite certain types of embalming being used by cosmeticians in China,
in no country is the practice as widespread as it is in the United States. Taking
issue with the idea that the popularity of embalmment in the United States
is the result of secularization, Shannon Dawdy proposes instead that it came
about as a transformation of a religious into a magical practice. Embalmers are
the neo-Egyptian magicians of our time, equipped with their own kind of tricks
to make dead bodies appear alive. The mystery that embalmers produce, Dawdy
argues, is the illusion that there is no death, only a deep sleep. The reference

to Egyptology is a striking one, and it may resonate cross-culturally, as there is some evidence that Vladimir Lenin's embalmers in the Soviet Union were inspired equally by their belief in the powers of science and the 1925 discovery of King Tut's mummy in Egypt. As for Lenin, their first impulse was to freeze the body, but with electricity so unreliable in war-torn postrevolutionary Russia, they decided on embalmment, and Egyptomania could have been one of the factors in the decision. Also striking is the metaphorical similarity. The idea was for Lenin's body to be read as sleeping, the task being to make the dead leader appear not to be dead. Embalming practices create an illusion of liminality between life and death, but they can also reverse time. Just as the effect of cooling the body is to slow down time, so the therapeutic aspect of viewing the embalmed corpse lies in the way it enables not denial, but a certain postponement of death. In the case of Lenin, the government wanted to give workers and peasants arriving from all over the enormous country time to say goodbye to their leader. As the lines of viewers grew and eventually seemed endless, the decision was made to embalm the body and keep it permanently on display.

Whether working for the state or for private funeral homes, Dawdy argues, contemporary embalmers, like other death-ritual professionals, are modern magicians. And it is not only the body but also time that is the very substance of their magic. Indeed, as we have already seen, the manipulation of time is a common theme in funerary rituals. Like the humanist officiants described by Engelke, embalmers can also speed up time—and by doing so speed up grief. What does the shift to home and green funerals signify at this point? Do they represent acceptance of a finality that embalming postpones, a finality that humanists accept and celebrate but transhumanists deny and strive to overcome?

Extinction and Eternity

If technologies such as organ transplantation, anti-aging medicine, biogerontology, and cryonic suspension—all technoscientific means of deferring death—are peculiar to the "secular modern's" denial of the finality of death, what do we make of humanist, green, and home-funeral movements? Are they not also secular moderns? As Dawdy and Kneese note in their introduction, a broader movement of death acceptance has recently emerged in the form of "death salons," where one can have conversations about death, dying, and grief. Leaders of the movement present the new practice as a reaction to our death-denying culture. So on the one hand, we have death acceptance, or the "death-positive" movement. On the other, there is transhumanism, understood here in the broadest sense as the desire to overcome death by technoscientific means, which is not limited to a group of libertarians and activists but part of a wider trend consistent with medical logics, where death is viewed as a certain kind of failure. These two tendencies exist side by side in contemporary society and, moreover, seem to be both intensifying and gaining adherents. If the death-acceptance movement rests on the claim that we have overmedicalized death and become excessively engaged in its denial, transhumanism argues that death is not medicalized enough—accepting mortality too quickly is simply defeatist.

Yet *death-denying* is perhaps not quite the right term to describe the transhumanist ethos, which is rather a rebellion against death and the human condition in general. Death, according to transhumanists, should be seen as a curable disease, and any inability on our part to mobilize as a species to defeat it is a sign of collective weakness and lack of vision. Thus, the cryonic corpse suspended in liquid nitrogen and a green corpse being happily devoured by flesh-eating fungi represent a specific dialectic of our times. Both are tropes of hope—one hoping for continuity in the imminent overcoming of death and the other for continuity in the cycle of life and eternity of the natural order. At the same time, fears of imminent species extinction unsettle both sorts of hopes in a powerful way. What if continuity were suddenly off the table? The question brings us back to the problem of "radical futurelessness," proposed by Abou Farman as a particular imaginary organizing discourse and practice today. Farman's terminality goes beyond the way the specter of death is confronted by the secular humanist, producing along with radical futurelessness something like radical meaninglessness as well.

Similar bursts of terminality have been met with historically, likewise producing powerful feelings of secular meaninglessness. Using my own work as a touchstone, the scientific discovery that perhaps caused more metaphysical despair than any other is the second law of thermodynamics and the notion of entropy (Bernstein 2019). Formulated independently in 1850 and 1851 by the German physicist Rudolph Clausius and Scottish mathematician and physicist William Thompson (later Lord Kelvin), the second law states that entropy in a closed system never decreases. The law was immediately subjected to cosmological and metaphysical readings, especially after Clausius extended its implications beyond physical closed systems, consistent with the controversial theory of the "heat death of the universe." As entropy increases, the argument went, energy will dissipate, and the universe will cool off until it ultimately becomes too cold to sustain life (Kragh 2008).

This secular eschatology, in suggesting a hollow and finite universe, created a crisis of meaning in intellectual circles around Europe, perhaps best captured by the Russian writer Fyodor Dostoyevsky in the lament of his title character in the novel *The Adolescent*. Anastasia Gacheva, one of the central interlocutors in my own fieldwork on Russian immortalism and a person from whom I was humbled to learn so much, quoted the passage so often that I have it memorized almost entirely in Russian. The English translation is as follows:

> Why should I unequivocally love my neighbor or your future mankind, which I'll never get to see, which won't know about me and which in turn will turn into dust, leaving not a single trace or memory behind (time counts for nothing here), when the Earth will in turn become an icy rock and will fly off into the void with an infinite number of similar icy rocks? In short, you cannot imagine anything more pointless! . . . Tell me, why should I be noble, especially if nothing lasts beyond a moment?" (Dostoyevsky [1875] 2016, 60)

Gacheva's interest related back to a trope in Russian literature of Dostoyesky's time, of the so-called logical suiciders (*logicheskii samoubiitsa*), or people attempting to deduce in strict logical terms that life has no meaning and that it is therefore not worth continuing. Such pessimism was characteristic of a more general malaise and crisis of meaning in the mid- to late 1800s. Not only had the universe been declared finite by physics, but Darwinian evolution had dislodged humans from the pedestal of creation, just as Copernicus earlier had displaced the earth from the center of the universe. If, prior to the heat death theory, humans could count on at least symbolic immortality, as in the continuation of the self through children and creative works, the cooling off of the universe left no such hope. Even Darwin was dismayed; he wrote in his autobiography that he found the thought of "complete annihilation after such long-continued slow process [of evolution] . . . intolerable" (Darwin 1897, 282).[1]

Russia comes up not only because I work there but also because what happened in Russia in response to the implications of the second law of thermodynamics is a canonical story that can put some of the ideas in this volume—focused as they are on contemporary death—in historical perspective and highlight common genealogies. Perhaps it can also help us generate theory from a less likely place. This is not "theory from the South" (Comaroff and Comaroff 2012) but "theory from the Second World."

Made distraught by the radical futurelessness signaled by science, a charismatic Russian thinker named Nikolai Fedorov, writing in the second half of the nineteenth century, suggested that the proper use of science and technology would be to modify humans to be immortal, while at the same time resurrecting the dead and dispatching the resurrected generations to populate other planets. Some of his ideas impressed Konstantin Tsiolkovsky, a self-taught scientist credited with calculating the first formula for a liquid-propellant rocket, which later led to the creation of the Soviet space program. As with our present-day advocates of outer space "relocation" like Stephen Hawking or Elon Musk, the lost future is to be reclaimed in outer space. But alongside the century and a half separating the two visions is another crucial difference. The earlier idea posited a collective future—with life-extending benefits of mutual blood transfusions, resurrection, and immortality to be regarded as basic rights for all, not just for a select few wealthy survivalists headed to Mars or New Zealand.

In the meantime, a philosophical trend known as the "redemption of history" (*opravdanie istorii*) has emerged in Russia to deal with what Farman calls the "ultimate unredeemable event." Extinction, because of its nature as unredeemable, pushes the limits of secular humanism and its idea of the tragic, leading to nihilism. But this nihilism, Farman provocatively suggests, could be productively used to bring about radical positive change. And this is exactly what happened in Russia. Before nihilism became a bad word, there appeared in Russia in the nineteenth century a loose group of thinkers who called themselves nihilists. They formed a radically secularist political movement concerned with social justice, and some of the later revolutionary socialists came out of these circles. Russian transhumanist and immortalist movements are also inextricably linked to these nineteenth-century roots. "Russians are either apocalyptics or nihilists," wrote the famous émigré philosopher Nikolai Berdyaev later in his book *The Russian Idea* ([1946] 1948, 193). While other cultures are often concerned with origins, Russians are "people of the end," as he put it, eschatological nihilists.

The notion of the heat death of the universe thus created Russian immortalism, which in turn created the Soviet space program, which later turned into the space race between the United States and the Soviet Union, defining, together with the nuclear arms race, the essence of the Cold War and driving the world to near extinction. With the end of the Soviet Union, we no longer have the "second," that is, socialist, world. Instead, we are all now postsocialist (Buck-Morss 2008). Is it possible, then, that the prospect of nuclear holocaust did for the American idea of futurelessness what the second law of thermodynamics did for its Russian counterpart in the mid-nineteenth century? Or, at least since the second law, have we always been futureless? If it turns out, after all, that secular humanism is neither intellectually nor emotionally equipped to deal with the reality of imminent anthropogenic extinction caused by climate change or nuclear catastrophe, will the talk of atoms and star dust at secular and green funerals eventually be found lacking? Will there be a new turn to transhumanism as a way to ensure some sort of continuity, either literal or symbolic? And if so, what can we do to provincialize American technofuturism and technoutopianism? Can it be dissociated from its libertarian roots and made to serve some collective good?

To pose one final question, is this technoutopianism a new religion, a substitute for one, or an expression of underlying Judeo-Christian ideas? Despite some parallels, I would agree with Farman that it is none of these. Rather, both transhumanist technoprogressivism and its accompanying fears of extinction are quintessentially secular phenomena. The secular eschatology and striving for immortality are not in contradiction but go hand in hand. To me, it is this conflation of apocalyptic anticipation with the desire for immortality, paired with the rapid technological change that reconfigures the boundaries between life and death, that best tells the story of our times (Bernstein 2019, 231). The secular and the religious, immortality and extinction, cryonics and green funerals are mutually constituted and exist in dialectical tension. It is by starting to consider both how this dialectic came to be and what it does, as well as what social and material effects it produces, that we will advance the understanding of death in the twenty-first century.

Note

1.   This passage is cited from the conclusion in Bernstein (2019, 223–24).

Adams, Kim, Char Barrett, Linda Bergh, Zalene Corey, Amy Cunningham, Lucinda Herring, Sandra LaGrega, Claire Turnham, Lee Webster, and Sara Williams. 2020. *Home Funeral Guides and Pandemic Care* (webinar). National Home Funeral Association, March 24, 2020. https://vimeo.com/400666632?fbclid=IwAR3kxD7D-RERFnKxxqlw-D-B59v5s0cml-wH08mTLFeus-GTaQFA3ohHbz3Y.

Adams, Vincanne, Michelle Murphy, and Adele Clarke. 2009. "Anticipation: Technoscience, Life, Affect, Temporality." *Subjectivities* 28 (1): 246–65.

Alsever, Jennifer. 2013. "5 Billionaires Who Want to Live Forever." *Fortune*, April 4. http://fortune.com/2013/04/04/5-billionaires-who-want-to-live-forever.

Amanik, Allan, and Kami Fletcher, eds. 2020. *Till Death Do Us Part: American Ethnic Cemeteries as Borders Uncrossed*. Jackson: University of Mississippi Press.

Anderson, Benedict. 1991. *Imagined Communities: Reflections on the Origins and Spread of Nationalism*. 2nd ed. London: Verso.

Ara, Pedro. 1996. *Eva Perón: La verdadera historia contada por el médico que preservó su cuerpo* [Eva Perón: The true story as told by the doctor who preserved her body]. Buenos Aires: Editorial Sudamericana.

Ariès, Philippe. 1974a. *Western Attitudes toward Death*. Baltimore: Johns Hopkins University Press.

———. 1974b. "The Reversal of Death: Changes in Attitudes toward Death in Western Societies." *American Quarterly* 26 (5): 536–60.

———. 1981. "Invisible Death." *Wilson Quarterly* 5 (1): 105–15.

Armstrong, David. 1987. "Silence and Truth in Death and Dying." *Social Science and Medicine* 24 (8): 651–57.

Arnold, Michael, Martin Gibbs, Tamara Kohn, James Meese, and Bjorn Nansen. 2018. *Death and Digital Media*. London: Routledge.

Auchter, Jessica. 2016. "Paying Attention to Dead Bodies: The Future of Security Studies." *Journal of Global Security Studies* 1 (1): 36–50.

Aulino, Felicity. 2016. "Rituals of Care for the Elderly in Northern Thailand: Merit, Morality, and the Everyday of Long-Term Care." *American Ethnologist* 43 (1): 91–102.

Badone, Ellen. 1989. "The Appointed Hour: Death, Worldview and Social Change in Brittany." Berkeley: University of California Press.

———. 1991. "Memories of Marie-Thérèse." In *Coping with the Final Tragedy: Cultural*

Variation in Dying and Grieving, edited by David R. Counts and Dorothy A. Counts, 213–30. Amityville, NY: Baywood.

———. 2004. Death Omens in a Breton Memorate. In *Death, Mourning and Burial: A Cross-Cultural Reader*, edited by Antonius C. G. M. Robben, 65–70. Oxford: Blackwell.

———. 2013. "Reflections on Death, Religion, Identity and the Anthropology of Religion." In *A Companion to the Anthropology of Religion*, edited by Janice Boddy and Michael Lambek, 425–43. Hoboken, NJ: Wiley.

———. 2017. "The Rosary as a Meditation on Death at a Marian Apparition Shrine." In *The Anthropology of Catholicism: A Reader*, edited by Kristin Norget, Valentina Napolitano, and Maya Mayblin, 201–10. Berkeley: University of California Press.

———. 2018. "After-Death Communications: Signs from the Otherworld in Contemporary North America." In *A Companion to the Anthropology of Death*, edited by Antonius C. G. M. Robben, 293–305. Hoboken, NJ: Wiley.

Bainbridge, William Sims. 2017. *Dynamic Secularization: Information Technology and the Tension between Religion and Science*. Arlington, VA: Springer Press.

Barnes, Jessica, Michael R. Dove, Myanna Lahsen, Andrew Mathews, Pamela McElwee, Roderick McIntosh, Frances Moore, Jessica O'Reilly, Ben Orlove, Rajendra Puri, Harbey Weiss, and Karina Yager. 2013. "Contribution of Anthropology to the Study of Climate Change." *Nature Climate Change* 3: 541–44.

Barrow, Mark V., Jr. 2009. *Nature's Ghosts: Confronting Extinction from the Age of Jefferson to the Age of Ecology*. Chicago: University of Chicago Press.

Barthes, Roland. 2009. *The Grain of the Voice*. Evanston, IL: Northwestern University Press.

Batty, Mike, Arun Tripathi, Alice Kroll, Cheng-Sheng Peter Wu, David Moore, Chris Stehno, Lucas Lau, Jim Guszcza, and Mitch Katcher. 2010. *Predictive Modeling for Life Insurance: Ways Life Insurers Can Participate in the Business Analytics Revolution*. Deloitte Consulting. www.soa.org/globalassets/assets/files/research/projects/research-pred-mod-life-batty.pdf.

BBC News. 2017. "Ancient Chinese Tomb-Sweeping Festival Goes Hi-tech. April 4. www.bbc.com/news/world-asia-39487437.

———. 2019. "Extinction Rebellion: Climate Change Protesters at Natural History Museum." April 22. www.bbc.com/news/uk-england-london-48011838.

Becker, Ernest. 1973. *The Denial of Death*. New York: Free Press.

Becker, Gaylene. 2000. *The Elusive Embryo: How Women and Men Approach New Reproductive Technologies*. Berkeley: University of California Press.

Behar, Ruth. 1996. *The Vulnerable Observer: Anthropology That Breaks Your Heart*. Boston: Beacon.

———. (2015) 2020. "Read More, Write Less." In *Writing Anthropology: Essays on Craft and Commitment*, edited by Carole McGranahan, 45–53. Reprint, Durham, NC: Duke University Press.

Belk, Donna, Margaret Eden, Wendy Lyons, and Holly Stevens. 2009. *Undertaken with Love: A Home Funeral Guide for Congregations and Communities*. Austin, TX: Home Funeral Committee Manual Publishing Group.

Benjamin, Ruha. 2019. *Race after Technology*. New York: Polity.

Bercovici, Jeff. 2016. "Peter Thiel Is Very, Very Interested in Young People's Blood." *Inc.*, August 1. www.inc.com/jeff-bercovici/peter-thiel-young-blood.html.

———. 2018 "Silicon Valley's Latest Lifehack: Death." *OneZero*, July 18, 2018. https://medium.com/s/futurehuman/game-over-bf20324ba420.

Berdyaev, Nikolay. (1946) 1948. *The Russian Idea*. Translated by R. M. French. New York: Macmillan.

Berliner, Lauren, and Nora Kenworthy. 2017. "Producing a Worthy Illness: Personal Crowdfunding amidst Financial Crisis." *Social Science and Medicine* 187:233–42.

Berman, Marshall. (1983) 1988. *All That Is Solid Melts into Air: The Experience of Modernity*. Reprint, London: Penguin.

Bernard, Jessie. 1949. "Sociological Mirror for Cultural Anthropologists." *American Anthropologist* 51 (4): 671–77.

Bernard, Tara Siegel. 2015. "Giving Out Private Data for Discount in Insurance." *New York Times*, April 8. http://www.nytimes.com/2015/04/08/your-money/giving-out-private-data-for-discount-in-insurance.html?_r=0.

Bernstein, Anya. 2015. "Freeze, Die, Come to Life: The Many Paths to Immortality in Post-Soviet Russia." *American Ethnologist* 42 (4): 766–81.

———. 2016. "Love and Resurrection: Remaking Life and Death in Contemporary Russia." *American Anthropologist* 118 (1): 12–23.

———. 2019. *The Future of Immortality: Remaking Life and Death in Contemporary Russia*. Princeton, NJ: Princeton University Press.

Berry, Daina Ramey. 2017. *The Price for Their Pound of Flesh: The Value of the Enslaved, from Womb to Grave, in the Building of a Nation*. New York: Penguin.

Bever, Lindsay. 2017. "This Terminally Ill Infant Will Be Allowed to Die. But First, His Parents Will Say Goodbye." *Washington Post*, June 30. www.washingtonpost.com/news/worldviews/wp/2017/06/29/against-his-parents-wishes-this-terminally-ill-infant-will-be-allowed-to-die/.

Bialecki, Jon. 2019. "Gods, Ais, and Mormon Transhumanism." *Platypus* blog, February 14, 2019. http://blog.castac.org/2019/02/gods-ais-mormon-transhumanism/.

———. 2020. "Kolob Runs on Domo: Mormon Secrets and Transhumanist Code." *Ethnos*. https://doi.org/10.1080/00141844.2020.1770311.

———. Forthcoming. "A Machine for Making Gods: Mormonism, Transhumanism, and Speculative Thought." New York: Fordham University Press.

Biehl, João. 2005. *Vita: Life in a Zone of Social Abandonment*. Berkeley: University of California Press.

Blankholm, Joseph. 2014. "The Political Advantages of a Polysemous Secular." *Journal for the Scientific Study of Religion* 53 (4): 775–90.

Blauner, Robert. 1966. "Death and Social Structure." *Psychiatry* 24:378–94.

Bloch, Maurice. 1989. "Symbols, Song, Dance, and Features of Articulation: Is Religion an Extreme Form of Traditional Authority?" In *Ritual, History, and Power: Selected Papers in Anthropology*, 19–45. London: Athlone.

Bloch, Maurice, and Jonathan Parry. 1982. Introduction to *Death and the Regeneration of Life*, edited by Maurice Bloch and Jonathan Parry, 1–44. Cambridge, UK: Cambridge University Press.

Blow, Charles. 2018. "White Extinction Anxiety." *New York Times*, June 24. www.nytimes.com/2018/06/24/opinion/america-white-extinction.html.

Boelderl, Artur, and Daniela Mayr. 1995. "The Undead and the Living Dead: Images of Vampires and Zombies in Contemporary Culture." *Journal of Psychohistory* 23 (1): 51–65.

Boret, Sébastien Penmellen, Susan Orpett Long, and Sergei Kan. 2017. *Death in the Early Twenty-First Century: Authority, Innovation, and Mortuary Rites*. London: Palgrave McMillan.

Bostrom, Nick. 2002. "Existential Risks: Analyzing Human Extinction Scenarios." *Journal of Evolution and Technology* 9 (1): 1–30.

———. 2005. "A History of Transhumanist Thought." *Journal of Evolution and Technology* 1 (1): 1–25.

Bouk, Dan. 2015. *How Our Days Became Numbered: Risk and the Rise of the Statistical Individual*. Chicago: University of Chicago Press.

Bourdieu, Pierre. 1977. *Outline of a Theory of Practice*, translated by Richard Nice. Cambridge, UK: Cambridge University Press.

Boym, Svetlana. 2001. *The Future of Nostalgia*. New York: Basic Books.

Brantlinger, Patrick. 2003. *Dark Vanishings: Discourse on the Extinction of Primitive Races, 1800–1930*. Kindle. Ithaca, NY: Cornell University Press.

Brassier, Ray. 2007. "The Truth of Extinction." In *Nihil Unbound: Enlightenment and Extinction*, 205–39. New York: Palgrave MacMillan.

Brier, Bob. 1980. *Ancient Egyptian Magic*. New York: Quill.

Brody, Jane. 1983. "Influential Theory on 'Bonding' at Birth Is Now Questioned." *New York Times*, March 29. www.nytimes.com/1983/03/29/science/influential-theory-on-bonding-at-birth-is-now-questioned.html.

——. 2019. "A Device That Gives Parents of Stillborn Babies Time to Say Goodbye." *New York Times*, January 14. www.nytimes.com/2019/01/14/well/family/a-device-that-gives-parents-of-stillborn-babies-time-to-say-goodbye.html.

Brown, Brittany. 2018. "Ancestral Landscapes: A Study of Historical Black Cemeteries and Contemporary Practices of Commemoration among African Americans in Duval County, Jacksonville, FL." PhD diss., College of William & Mary. http://dx.doi.org/10.21220/s2-hnxh-6968.

Brown, Vincent. 2008. *The Reaper's Garden: Death and Power in the World of Atlantic Slavery*. Cambridge, MA: Harvard University Press.

Buchbinder, Mara. 2018. "Choreographing Death: A Social Phenomenology of Medical Aid-in-Dying in the United States." *Medical Anthropology Quarterly* 32 (4): 481–97.

Buck-Morss, Susan. 2008. "Theorizing Today: The Post-Soviet Condition." *Log* 11 (Winter): 23–31.

Burnham, John. 1964. *Suicide of the West: An Essay on the Meaning and Destiny of Liberalism*. New York: John Day.

Byers, Dylan. 2018. "Why Peter Thiel Is Leaving Silicon Valley." *CNNBusiness*, February 15. https://money.cnn.com/2018/02/15/technology/peter-thiel-leaving-silicon-valley/index.html.

Cann, Candi K., ed. 2018. *The Routledge Handbook of Death and the Afterlife*. New York: Routledge.

Carlson, Lisa. 1987. *Caring for Your Own Dead*. Hinesburg, VT: Upper Access.

Carsten, Janet. 2011. "Substance and Relationality: Blood in Contexts." *Annual Review of Anthropology* 40:19–35.

Carver, Terrell. 1998. *The Postmodern Marx*. University Park: Pennsylvania State University Press.

Casey, Tina. 2016. "'Worst Three Days' for Donald Trump and a Weird Week for Peter Thiel." *Triple Pundit*, August 4. www.triplepundit.com/2016/08/worst-3-days-donald-trump-weird-week-peter-thiel.

Casper, Monica, and Lisa Jean Moore. 2009. *Missing Bodies: The Politics of Visibility*. New York: New York University Press.

Castoriadis, Cornelius. 1987. *The Imaginary Institution of Society*. Translated by Kathleen Blamey. Cambridge, MA: MIT Press.

Cazdyn, Eric 2012. *The Already Dead*. Durham, NC: Duke University Press.

Césaire, Aimé. 2013 [1939]. *Return to My Native Land*. Translated by John Berger and Anna Bostock. Brooklyn, NY: Archipelago.

Chakrabarty, Dipesh. 2017. "The Politics of Climate Change Is More Than the Politics of Capitalism." *Theory, Culture & Society* 34 (2–3): 34.

Chang, Cilo. 2016. "Is Peter Thiel a Vampire?" *New Republic*, August 1. https://newrepublic.com/minutes/135706/peter-thiel-vampire.

Chapman, Ben. 2016. Facebook Blocks Admiral from Reading Posts to Judge If Customers Are Safe Drivers. *Independent*, November 2. http://www.independent.co.uk/news/business/news/admiral-car-insurance-premiums-read-facebook-posts-privacy-a7392981.html.

Chiappelli, Jeremiah. 2008. "The Problem of Embalming." *Journal of Environmental Health* 75 (5): 25–28.

Chodorkoff, Rebecca. 2016. "Peter Thiel Wants to Suck Your Blood." Op Ed. *BTR Today*, September 4. http://www.btrtoday.com/read/themeweek/nostalgia/94-article.

Ciccariello-Maher, George. 2018. My Best Friend Lost His Life to the Gig Economy. *Nation*, July 10. www.thenation.com/article/archive/best-friend-lost-life-gig-economy/.

Clark, John P. 2016. *The Tragedy of Common Sense*. Regina: Changing Suns.

Clayden, Andy, Trish Green, Jenny Hockey, and Mark Powell. 2014. *Natural Burial: Landscape, Practice and Experience*. London: Routledge.

Cockburn, Cynthia. 1985. *Machineries of Dominance: Women, Men and Technical Know-How*. London: Pluto.

Cohen, Jeremy. 2020. "Frozen Bodies and Future Imaginaries: Assisted Dying, Cryonics, and a Good Death." *Religions* 11 (11): 584. https://doi.org/10.3390/rel11110584.

Cohen, Lawrence. 1999. "Where It Hurts: Indian Material for an Ethics of Organ Transplantation." *Daedalus* 128 (4): 135–65.

———. 2001. "The Other Kidney: Biopolitics beyond Recognition." *Body & Society* 7 (2–3): 9–29.

Comaroff, Jean, and John Comaroff. 1999. "Occult Economies and the Violence of Abstraction: Notes from the South African Postcolony." *American Ethnologist* 26 (2): 279–303.

———. 2002. "Alien-Nation: Zombies, Immigrants, and Millennial Capitalism." *South Atlantic Quarterly* 101 (4): 779–805.

———. 2012. *Theory from the South: Or, How Euro-America is Evolving toward Africa.* Boulder, CO: Paradigm Publishers.

Conklin, Beth A., and Lynn Morgan. 1996. "Babies, Bodies and the Personhood in North America and a Native Amazonian Society." *Ethos* 24 (4): 657–94.

Coole, Diana, and Samantha Frost, eds. 2010. *New Materialisms: Ontology, Agency, and Politics.* Durham, NC: Duke University Press.

Corbett, Jessica. 2019. "In Just One Decade, Corporations Destroyed 50 Million Hectares of Forest—An Area the Size of Spain." *Common Dreams*, June 11. www.commondreams.org/news/2019/06/11/just-one-decade-corporations-destroyed-50-million-hectares-forest-area-size-spain.

Costa Vargas, João, and Jaime Amparo Alves. 2010. "Geographies of Death: An Intersectional Analysis of Police Lethality and the Racialized Regimes of Citizenship in São Paulo." *Ethnic and Racial Studies* 33 (4): 611–36.

Couliano, Ioan P. 1987. *Eros and Magic in the Renaissance*, translated by Margaret Cook. Chicago: University of Chicago Press.

Cox, Rachel. 2005. "A Movement to Bring Grief Back Home." *Washington Post*, June 6. www.washingtonpost.com/archive/politics/2005/06/05/a-movement-to-bring-grief-back-home/547f13e0-4c6f-4e68-b5dc-1cbf01e0d7a5/.

Crawford, Kate, Jessica Lingel, and Tero Karppi. 2015. Our Metrics, Ourselves: A Hundred Years of Self-Tracking from the Weight Scale to the Wrist Wearable Device. *European Journal of Cultural Studies* 18 (4–5): 479–96.

Csordas, Thomas, ed. 2009. *Transnational Transcendence: Essays on Religion and Globalization.* Berkeley: University of California Press.

———. 2020. "Specter, Phantom, Demon." *Ethos* 47 (4): 519–29.

Danforth, Loring M. 1982. *The Death Rituals of Rural Greece.* Princeton, NJ: Princeton University Press.

Das, Venna, and Clara Han. 2016. *Living and Dying in the Contemporary World: A Compendium.* Berkeley: University of California Press.

Davidson, Megan. 2019. *Your Birth Plan: A Guide to Navigating All of Your Choices in Childbirth.* London: Rowman & Littlefield.

Davies, Douglas J., and Hannah Rumble. 2012. *Natural Burial: Secular Spiritualities and Funeral Innovation.* London: Continuum.

Dawdy, Shannon Lee. 2013. "Archeology of Modern American Death: Grave Goods and Blithe Mementos." In *The Oxford Handbook of the Archaeology of the*

Contemporary World, edited by Paul Graves-Brown and Rodney Harrison, 451–65. Oxford: Oxford University Press.

———. 2019. "Zombies and a Decaying American Ontology." *Journal of Historical Sociology* 32: 17–25.

———. Forthcoming. *American Afterlives: Reinventing Death in the Twenty-First Century*. Princeton, NJ: Princeton University Press.

Dawdy, Shannon Lee, and Daniel Zox, dirs. Forthcoming. *I Like Dirt*. http://ilikedirtfilm.com/.

DeBord-Snyder Funeral Home. 2015. "Metal Caskets versus Wood Caskets—What You Should Consider." Blog post, July 2015. www.debordsnyder.com/metal-caskets-versus-wood-caskets-what-you-should-consider/.

De León, Jason. 2015. *Land of Open Graves: Living and Dying on the Migrant Trail*. Berkeley: University of California Press.

Dendle, Peter. 2007. "The Zombie as Barometer of Cultural Anxiety." In *Monsters and the Monstrous: Myths and Metaphors of Enduring Evil*, edited by Niall Scott, 45–57. New York: Rodopi.

Department of Statistics Singapore. 2020. "Death and Life Expectancy." www.singstat.gov.sg/find-data/search-by-theme/population/death-and-life-expectancy/latest-data.

Diamond, Jared. 2005. *Collapse: How Societies Choose to Fail or Succeed*. New York: Viking.

Díaz, Sandra, Josef Settele, Eduardo S. Brondízio, Hien T. Ngo, Maximilien Guèze, John Agard, Almust Arneth, Patricia Balvanera, Kate A. Brauman, Stuart H. M. Butchart, Kai M. A. Chan, Lucas A. Garibaldi, Kazuhito Ichii, Jianguo Liu, Suneetha M. Subramanian, Guy F. Midgley, Patricia Miloslavich, Zsolt Molnár, David Obura, Alexander Pfaff, Stephen Polasky, Andy Purvis, Jona Razzaque, Belinda Reyers, Rinku Roy Chowdhury, Yunne-Jai Shin, Ingrid J. Visseren-Hamakers, Katherine J. Willis, and Cynthia N. Zayas, eds. 2019. "Summary for Policymakers of the Global Assessment Report on Biodiversity and Ecosystem Services of the Intergovernmental Science-Policy Platform on Biodiversity and Ecosystem Services. Bonn: Intergovernmental Science-Policy Platform on Biodiversity and Ecosystem Services Secretariat." https://doi.org/10.5281/zenodo.3553579.

Doherty, Thomas J., and Susan Clayton. 2011. "The Psychological Impacts of Global Climate Change." *American Psychologist* 66 (4): 265–76.

Dostoyevsky, Fyodor. (1875) 2016. *The Adolescent*. Translated by Dora O'Brien. London: Alma Classics.

Doughty, Caitlin. 2014. *Smoke Gets in Your Eyes and Other Lessons from the Crematory*. New York: W. W. Norton.

———. 2017. *From Here to Eternity: Traveling the World to Find the Good Death*. New York: W. W. Norton.

Douglas, Mary. [1966] 2002. *Purity and Danger: An Analysis of Concepts of Pollution and Taboo*. New York: Routledge.

Drabold, Will. 2016. "Read Peter Thiel's Speech at the Republican National Convention." *Time Magazine*, July 21. http://time.com/4417679/republican-convention-peter-thiel-transcript.

Dubow, Sara. 2011. *Ourselves Unborn: A History of the Fetus in Modern America*. New York: Oxford University Press.

During, Simon. 2002. *Modern Enchantments: The Cultural Power of Secular Magic*. Cambridge, MA: Harvard University Press. Kindle.

Duymazlar, Khan. 2016. "Modest Proposal: Let's Sell Our Blood to Peter Thiel and Redistribute Wealth in America." *Startup Grind*, August 3. https://medium.com/startup-grind/lets-sell-our-blood-to-peter-thiel-and-redistribute-wealth-in-america-80f29683f621.

Dyson, Freeman J. 1979. "Time without End: Physics and Biology in an Open Universe." *Reviews of Modern Physics* 51 (3): 447–60.

Eagleton, Terry. 2009. *Sweet Violence: The Idea of the Tragic*. New York: Wiley.

———. 2011. *Why Marx Was Right*. New Haven, CT: Yale University Press.

Ehrlich, Paul, and Mary Ehrlich. 1968. *Population Bomb*. New York: Ballantine.

Engelke, Matthew. 2014. Christianity and the Anthropology of Secular Humanism. *Current Anthropology* 55, S10: S292–S301.

———. 2015a. "The Coffin Question: Death and Materiality in Humanist Funerals." *Material Religion* 11 (1): 26–49.

———. 2015b. "'Good without God:' Happiness and Pleasure among the Humanists." *Hau: Journal of Ethnographic Theory* 5 (3): 69–91.

———. 2015c. "Humanist Ceremonies: The Case of Non-Religious Funerals in Britain." In *The Wiley Blackwell Handbook of Humanism*, edited by Andrew Copson and A. C. Grayling, 216–33. Oxford: Wiley Blackwell.

———. 2019. "The Anthropology of Death Revisited." *Annual Review of Anthropology* 48:29–44.

Enright, D. J., ed. 1983. *The Oxford Book of Death*. Oxford: Oxford University Press.

Eubanks, Virginia. 2018. *Automating Inequality*. New York: St. Martin's.

Fabian, Johannes. (1973) 2004. "How Others Die: Reflections on the Anthropology of Death." In *Death, Mourning, and Burial: A Cross-Cultural Reader*, edited by Antonius G. C. M. Robben, 49–61. Reprint, New York: Blackwell.

Farman, Abou. 2012. "Secular Immortal." PhD diss., City University of New York.

———. 2013. "Speculative Matter: Secular Bodies, Minds, and Persons." *Cultural Anthropology* 28 (4): 737–59.

———. 2017. "Terminality." *Social Text* 35, no. 2 (131): 93–118.

———. 2020. *On Not Dying: Secular Immortality in the Age of Technoscience*. Minneapolis: University of Minnesota Press.

Farman, Abou, and Richard Rottenburg. 2019. "Introduction: Measures of Future Health: Planetary and Non-human Health: from the Nonhuman to the Planetary: An Introductory Essay." *Medical Anthropology Theory* [special issue] 6 (3): 1–28.

Farrell, James J.1980. *Inventing the American Way of Death, 1830–1920*. Philadelphia: Temple University Press.

Farrell, Joseph. 2017. "Down on the Plantation with Vampires and Ghouls." *Giza Death Star*, June 3. https://gizadeathstar.com/2017/06/plantation-vampires-ghouls-inc.

Faust, Drew Gilpin. 2009. *This Republic of Suffering: Death and the American Civil War*. New York: Knopf.

Feldman, Brian. 2016. "Peter Thiel Is Poised to Become a National Villain." *New York*, November 10. http://nymag.com/intelligencer/2016/11/peter-thiel-is-poised-to-become-a-national-villain.html.

Ferguson, David. 2016. "Billionaire Peter Thiel Thinks Young People's Blood Can Keep Him Young Forever." *Raw Story*, August 1. www.rawstory.com/2016/08/billionaire-peter-thiel-thinks-young-peoples-blood-can-keep-him-young-forever/.

Feuer, Alan, and Jasmine Kim. 2020. "It's 'Unconscionable' that a New York City Funeral Home Left Corpses in Vans, Mayor Bill de Blasio Says." *CNBC*, April 30. www.cnbc.com/2020/04/30/coronavirus-it-is-unconscionable-that-a-new-york-city-funeral-home-left-corpses-in-vans-mayor-bill-de-blasio-says.html.

Feuer, Alan, Ashley Southall, and Michael Gold. 2020. "Dozens of Decomposing Bodies Found in Trucks at Brooklyn Funeral Home." *New York Times*, April 29. www.nytimes.com/2020/04/29/nyregion/bodies-brooklyn-funeral-home-coronavirus.html.

Fiegerman, Seth. 2016. "Peter Thiel Joins Trump's Transition Team." *CNNBusiness*, November 11. https://money.cnn.com/2016/11/11/technology/peter-thiel-trump-team/index.html.

Fisk, Eugene Lyman. 1913. *Linking the Life Insurance Companies to the Public Health Movement*. Postal Life Insurance Company. Accessed at Reed College Archives and Special Collections and New York Academy of Medicine library, pamphlet collection. Pamphlet.

———. 1922. *Fatigue in Industry*. Life Extension Institute. New York Academy of Medicine library, pamphlet collection. Pamphlet.

Fisk, Eugene Lyman, and Irving Fisher. 1916. *How to Live: Rules for Healthful Living Based on Modern Science*. New York: Funk & Wagnalls.

Fletcher, Kami. 2020. *Till Death Do Us Part: American Ethnic Cemeteries and Boarders Uncrossed*. Jackson: University Press of Mississippi.

Fort, Nyle. "Amazing Grief: African American Mourning and Contemporary Black Activism." PhD diss., Princeton University.

Fortuna, Harry. 2017. "Seeking Eternal Life, Silicon Valley Is Solving for Death." *Quartz*, November 8. https://qz.com/1123164/seeking-eternal-life-silicon-valley-is-solving-for-death.

Foucault, Michel. 1978. "We 'Other Victorians.'" In *History of Sexuality*. Vol. 1, *An Introduction*, translated by Robert Hurley, 2–13. New York: Pantheon.

———. 1988. *Technologies of the Self: A Seminar with Michel Foucault*. Boston: University of Massachusetts Press.

Franklin, Sarah. 2013. *Biological Relatives: IVF, Stem Cells, and the Future of Kinship*. Durham, NC: Duke University Press.

Franklin, Sarah, and Margaret Lock, eds. 2003. *Remaking Life and Death: Toward an Anthropology of the Biosciences*. Santa Fe, NM: SAR Press.

Frazer, James George. (1890) 1976. *The Golden Bough: A Study in Magic and Religion*. Reprint, London: Macmillan Press.

Freud, Sigmund. (1899) 2003. *The Uncanny*. Translated by David McLintock. Reprint, New York: Penguin.

———. (1913) 1919. *Totem and Taboo*. Translated by Abraham A. Brill. Reprint, New York: Moffatt and Yard.

———. 1916. *Wit and Its Relation to the Unconscious*. Translated by Abraham A. Brill. New York: Moffatt and Yard.

———. (1920) 2009. *Beyond the Pleasure Principle*. Translated by Caroline J. M. Hubback. Reprint, Lawrence, KS: Neeland Media.

Friend, Tad. 2017. "Silicon Valley's Quest to Live Forever." *New Yorker*, April 3. www.newyorker.com/magazine/2017/04/03/silicon-valleys-quest-to-live-forever/.

Frymorgen, Tomasz. 2017. "The Super Rich Are Injecting Blood from Teenagers to Gain 'Immortality.'" *BBC News*, August 25. www.bbc.co.uk/bbcthree/article/347828f8-6e7f-4a9b-92ab-95f637a9dc2e.

Funchess, Dan. 2019. "How to Build Relationships with Hospices." *GoToStage*, February 22. www.gotostage.com/channel/6b3ac92118be452d97580300f1c5c5ad/recording/.

Fustel De Coulanges, Numa Denis. 2001. *The Ancient City: A Study on the Religion, Laws, and Institutions of Greece and Rome*. Kitchener: Batoche.

Garces-Foley, Kathleen, ed. 2006. *Death and Religion in a Changing World*. New York: Routledge.

Geertz, Clifford. 1973. "Ritual and Social Change: A Javanese Example." In *The Interpretation of Cultures*, 142–69. New York: Basic Books.

Geraci, Robert. 2010. *Apocalyptic AI: Visions of Heaven in Robotics, Artificial Intelligence and Virtual Reality*. Oxford: Oxford University Press.

Gilligan, T. Scott, and Thomas F. H. Stueve. 2011. *Mortuary Law*. Cincinnati, OH: The Cincinnati Foundation for Mortuary Education

Gilmore, Ruth Wilson. 2002. "Fatal Couplings of Power and Difference: Notes on Racism and Geography." *Professional Geographer* 54 (1): 15–24.

Ginsburg, Faye. 1998. *Contested Lives: The Abortion Debate in an American Community*. Berkeley: University of California Press.

Gittlitz, A. M. 2016. "Let Them Drink Blood." *New Inquiry*, December 27. https://thenewinquiry.com/let-them-drink-blood/.

Giuffrida, Angela. 2020. "'A Proper Funeral:' Families Try to Claim Covid-19 Victims from a Milan Cemetery." *Guardian*, June 10.

Gnostic Warrior. 2016. "Blood Magick: The Elites Are Pursuing Immortality Using the Blood of Younger People." *Gnostic Warrior*, August 1. https://gnosticwarrior.com/elites-immortality-childrens-blood.html.

Goldberg, Jonah. 2018. *Suicide of the West: How the Rebirth of Tribalism, Populism, Nationalism, and Identity Politics Is Destroying American Democracy*. New York: Crown Forum.

Gollner, Adam L. 2013. "The Immortality Financiers: The Billionaires Who Want to Live Forever." *Daily Beast*. www.thedailybeast.com/the-immortality-inanciers-the-billionaires-who-want-to-live-forever.

Golomski, Casey. 2018. *Funeral Culture: AIDS, Work, and Cultural Change in an African Kingdom*. Bloomington: Indiana University Press.

Gorer, Geoffrey. 1955a. "The Pornography of Death." In *Death, Grief, and Mourning*, edited by Geoffrey Gorer, 192–99. New York: Doubleday.

———. 1955b. "The Pornography of Death." *Encounter* (October): 49–52.

Gray, John. 2011. *The Immortalization Commission: Science and the Strange Quest to Cheat Death*. New York: Farrar, Straus and Giroux.

Green, Emma. 2016. "State Mandated Mourning for Aborted Fetuses." *Atlantic*, May 14. www.theatlantic.com/politics/archive/2016/05/state-mandated-mourning-for-aborted-fetuses/482688/.

Greene, Richard, and K. Silem Mohammad, eds. 2010. *Zombies, Vampires, and Philosophy: New Life for the Undead*. Chicago: Open Court.

Greenpeace. 2019. "Countdown to Extinction: What Will It Take to Get Companies to Act?" www.greenpeace.org/international/publication/22247/countdown-extinction-report-deforestation-commodities-soya-palm-oil/.

Gregg, Melissa. 2018. *Counterproductive: Time Management in the Knowledge Economy*. Durham, NC: Duke University Press.

Groot, Jan Jakob Maria de. (1910) 1972. *The Religious Systems of China: Its Ancient Forms, Evolution, History and Present Aspect, Manners, Customs and Social Institutions Connected Therewith*. Reprint, Taipei: Ch'eng-wen.

Grossman, Lev. 2011. "2045: The Year Man Becomes Immortal." *Time*, February 10. http://content.time.com/time/magazine/article/0,9171,2048299,00.html.

Hagerty, Alexa. 2014. "Speak Softly to the Dead: The Uses of Enchantment in American Home Funerals." *Social Anthropology* 22 (4): 428–42.

Halfon, Saul. 2015. "Contesting Human Security Expertise: Technical Practices in Reconfiguring International Security." In *Security Expertise: Practice, Power, Responsibility*, edited by Trine V. Berling and Christian Bueger, 141–57. London: Routledge.

Hallam, Elizabeth, and Jenny Hockey. 2001. *Death, Memory and Material Culture*. London: Routledge.

Halvorson, Hans and Helge Kragh. 2019. "Cosmology and Theology." In *Stanford Encyclopedia of Philosophy*, edited by Edward N. Zalta. https://plato.stanford.edu/archives/spr2019/entries/cosmology-theology/.

Hamdy, Sherine. 2012. *Our Bodies Belong to God: Organ Transplants, Islam, and the Struggle for Human Dignity in Egypt*. Berkeley: University of California Press.

Hankin, Laura. 2016. "Is Peter Thiel a Vampire? Twitter Thinks So." *Romper*, August 1. www.romper.com/p/is-peter-thiel-a-vampire-twitter-thinks-so-15467.

Hannig, Anita. 2019. "Author(iz)ing Death: Medical Aid-in-Dying and the Morality of Suicide." *Cultural Anthropology* 34 (1): 53–77.

Hansen, James. 2009. *Storms of My Children: The Truth about the Coming Climate Catastrophe and Our Last Chance to Save Humanity*. New York: Bloomsbury.

Haraway, Donna. 2015. "Anthropocene, Capitalocene, Plantationocene, Chthulucene: Making Kin." *Environmental Humanities* 6 (1): 159–65.

Hardin, Garett. 1974. "Living on a Lifeboat." *Bioscience* 24 (10): 561–68.

Harding, Susan, and Kathleen Stewart. 1999. "Bad Endings: American Apocalypsis." *Annual Review of Anthropology* 28:285–310.

Hardy, Quentin. 2016. "Technology Transforms How Insurers Calculate Risk." *New York Times*, April 6. http://www.nytimes.com/2016/04/07/business/deal-book/technology-transforms-how-insurers-calculate-risk.html.

Harrington, Rebecca. 2016. "Here's What Happens When You Take the 'Anti-aging' Supplement Peter Thiel Swears By." *Business Insider*, February 17. www.businessinsider.com/human-growth-hormone-health-effects-2016–2.

Harris, Ainsley. 2017. "4 Life Insurance Startups Asking Millennials to Face Their Mortality." *Fast Company*, July 21. www.fastcompany.com/40442090/these-life-insurance-startups-asking-millennials-to-face-their-mortality.

Harris, Mark. 2007. *Grave Matters: A Journey through the Modern Funeral Industry to a Natural Way of Burial.* New York: Scribner.

Hartman, Saidiya. 2007. *Lose Your Mother: A Journey along the Atlantic Slave Route.* New York: Farrar, Straus, and Giroux.

Hartmann, Betsy. 2017. *The American Syndrome: Apocalypse, War and Our Call to Greatness.* New York: Seven Stories.

Harvey, Fiona. 2018. "'Tipping Points' Could Exacerbate Climate Crisis, Scientists Fear." *Guardian*, October 9. www.theguardian.com/environment/2018/oct/09/tipping-points-could-exacerbate-climate-crisis-scientists-fear.

Hawking, Stephen W., and Thomas Hertog. 2018. "A Smooth Exit from Eternal Inflation?" *Journal of High-Energy Physics* 147. doi: 10.1007/jhep04(2018)147.

Hayasaki, Erika, 2013. "Death Is Having a Moment." *Atlantic*, October 25. www.theatlantic.com/health/archive/2013/10/death-is-having-a-moment/280777/.

Haynes, Gavin. 2017. "Ambrosia: The Startup Harvesting the Blood of the Young." *Guardian*, August 21. www.theguardian.com/society/shortcuts/2017/aug/21/ambrosia-the-startup-harvesting-the-blood-of-the-young.

Heelas, Paul. 1996. *The New Age Movement.* Oxford: Blackwell.

Hefner, Robert W., ed. 2013. *Global Pentecostalism in the 21st Century.* Bloomington: University of Indiana Press.

Heidegger, Martin. (1927) 1962. *Being and Time.* Translated by John Macquarrie and Edward Robinson. Reprint, Oxford: Basil Blackwell.

———. 1981. *The Question Concerning Technology and Other Essays.* Translated by William Lovitt. New York: Harper.

Helmreich, Stefan. 2008. Species of Biocapital. *Science as Culture* 17 (4): 463–78.

Herrick, James. 2017. *Visions of Technological Transcendence: Human Enhancement and the Rhetoric of the Future.* Anderson, SC: Parlor Press.

Hertz, Robert. (1900) 1960. *Death and the Right Hand*, translated by Rodney and Claudia Needham. Reprint, New York: Free Press.

Hicks, Nolan. 2020. "NYC Storing Bodies inside Refrigerated Trucks in Brooklyn Parking Lot." *New York Post*, May 4. https://nypost.com/2020/05/04/nyc-storing-bodies-inside-refrigerated-trucks-in-brooklyn-parking-lot/.

Hirshbein, Laura D. 1999. "Masculinity, Work, and the Fountain of Youth: Irving Fisher and the Life Extension Institute, 1914–31." *Canadian Bulletin of Medical History* 16 (1): 89–124.

Hobart, Hi'ilei, and Tamara Kneese. 2020. "Radical Care: Survival Strategies for Uncertain Times." *Social Text* 38, no. 1 (142), 1–16.

Hockey, Jenny, Carol Komaromy, and Kate Woodthorpe, eds. 2010. *The Matter of Death: Space, Place and Materiality*. Basingstoke: Palgrave Macmillan.

Holloway, Karla F. C. 2002. *Passed On: African American Mourning Stories*. Durham, NC: Duke University Press.

Horn, Dara. 2018. "The Men Who Want to Live Forever." *New York Times*, January 25. www.nytimes.com/2018/01/25/opinion/sunday/silicon-valley-immortality.html.

Howarth, Glenys. 1996. *Last Rites: The Work of the Modern Funeral Director*. Amityville, NY: Baywood.

Howie, LaShaya. 2017. "What the Bones at the Proposed Topgolf Site Ask of Us." *Charlotte Observer*, July 5. http://www.charlotteobserver.com/opinion/op-ed/article159695569.html.

Huberman, Jenny. 2012. "Forever a Fan: Reflections on the Branding of Death and the Production of Value." *Anthropological Theory* 12 (4): 467–85.

Hughes, James. 2004. *Citizen Cyborg: Why Democratic Societies Must Respond to the Redesigned Human of the Future*. Nashville, TN: Westview Press.

———. 2012. "The Politics of Transhumanism and the Techno-Millennial Imagination, 1626–2030." *Zygon* 47 (4): 757–76.

———. 2019. "Cyborg Buddha, Transhuman Enlightenment, and Basic Income: Interview with James Hughes." By Euvie Ivanova and Mike Gilliland. *FutureThinkers* podcast. https://futurethinkers.org/cyborg-buddha-james-hughes-transhuman-enlightenment.

Hull, Gordon, and Frank Pasquale. 2018. "Toward a Critical Theory of Corporate Wellness." *BioSocieties* 13 (1): 190–212. https://doi.org/10.1057/s41292-017-0064-1.

Hume, David. (1739) 1978. *A Treatise of Human Nature*. Reprint, New York: Oxford University Press.

Hunleth, Jean. 2017. *Children as Caregivers: The Global Fight against Tuberculosis and HIV in Zambia*. New Brunswick, NJ: Rutgers University Press.

Hunn, David, and Kim Bell. 2014. "Why Was Michael Brown's Body Left There for

Hours?" *St. Louis Post Dispatch*, September 14. www.stltoday.com/news/
local/crime-and-courts/why-was-michael-browns-body-left-there-for-
hours/article_0b73ec58-c6a1–516e-882f-74d18a4246e0.html.

Hustead, Edwin C. 1988. "The History of Actuarial Mortality Tables in the United
States." *Journal of Insurance Medicine* 20 (4): 12–16.

Ingram, Mathew. 2016. "Billionaire Who Helped Bankrupt Gawker Says He
Would Do It Again." *Fortune*, August 15. http://fortune.com/2016/08/15/
thiel-essay-gawker.

IPBES (Intergovernmental Platform on Biodiversity and Ecosystem Services). 2018.
"Not Just Commodities: World Needs Broader Appreciation of Nature's
Contributions to People." January 18. https://www.eurekalert.org/pub_
releases/2018-01/tca-njc011218.php.

IPCC (Intergovernmental Panel on Climate Change). 2018. *Global Warming of 1.5°C.
An IPCC Special Report on the Impacts of Global Warming of 1.5°C above
Pre-industrial Levels and Related Global Greenhouse Gas Emission Path-
ways, in the Context of Strengthening the Global Response to the Threat of
Climate Change, Sustainable Development, and Efforts to Eradicate Poverty*,
edited by Valérie Masson-Delmotte, Panmao Zhai, Hans-Otto Pörtner,
Debra C. Roberts, James Skea, Priyadarshi R. Shukla, Anna Pirani, Wilfran
Moufouma-Okia, Clotilde Péan, Roz Pidcock, Sarah Connors, J. B. Robin
Matthews, Yang Chen, Xiao Zhou, Melissa I. Gomis, Elisabeth Lonnoy, Tom
Maycock, Melinda Tignor, and Tim Waterfield. Geneva: World Meteorologi-
cal Organization. www.ipcc.ch/sr15/chapter/summary-for-policy-makers/.

Isaacson, Betsy. 2015. "Silicon Valley Is Trying to Make Humans Immortal—And Finding Some Success." *Newsweek*, March 5. www.newsweek.com/2015/03/13/
silicon-valley-trying-make-humans-immortal-and-finding-some-
success-311402.html.

Jackson, Charles O. 1977. "American Attitudes to Death." *Journal of American Studies* 11
(3): 297–312.

Jacobsen, Michael Hviid, ed. 2017. *Postmortal Society: Towards a Sociology of Immortality*. London: Routledge.

Jain, S. Lochlann. 2013. *Malignant: How Cancer becomes Us*. Berkeley: University of
California Press.

Jameson, Fredric. 2003. The End of Temporality. *Critical Inquiry* 29 (4): 695–718.

Janazah Project. 2020. https://www.thejanazahproject.org/#about.

Jasanoff, Sheila, and Sang-Hyun Kim. 2015. *Dreamscapes of Modernity: Sociotechnical
Imaginaries and the Fabrication of Power*. Chicago: University of Chicago
Press.

Johnson, Elizabeth. 1988. "Grieving for the Dead, Grieving for the Living: Funeral

Laments of Hakka Women." In *Death Ritual in Late Imperial and Early Modern China*, edited by James L. Watson and Evelyn Rawski, 135–63. Berkeley: University of California Press.

Kalusa, Walima T., and Megan Vaughan. 2013. *Death, Belief, and Politics in Central African History*. Lusaka: Lembani Trust.

Kavod v'Nichum and Gamliel Institute. 2020a. *Handbook for Hevra Kadisha Members*. www.jewish-funerals.org/handbook-for-hevra-kadisha-members/.

———. 2020b. "More about Kavod v'Nichum." www.jewish-funerals.org/more-about-kavod-vnichum.

Kawano, Satsuki. 2010. *Nature's Embrace: Japan's Aging Urbanites and New Death Rites*. Honolulu: University of Hawai'i Press.

Kelly, Suzanne. 2015. *Greening Death: Reclaiming Burial Practices and Restoring Our Tie to the Earth*. London: Rowman and Littlefield.

Kennell, John H., and Marshall H. Klaus. 1976. *Mother-Infant Bonding*. St. Louis: C. V. Mosby.

Klerkx, Greg. 2006. "The Transhumanists as Tribe." In *Better Humans? The Politics of Human Enhancement and Life Extension*, edited by Paul Miller and James Wilsdon, 59–66. London: Demos.

Kluckhohn, Clyde. 1949. *Mirror for Man: The Relation of Anthropology to Modern Life*. New York: Whittlesey House.

Kneese, Tamara. 2014. "QR Codes for the Dead." *Atlantic*, May 21. www.theatlantic.com/technology/archive/2014/05/qr-codes-for-the-dead/370901/.

———. 2016. "Digital Afterlives: From the Electronic Village to the Networked Estate." PhD diss., New York University.

———. 2018. "Mourning the Commons: Circulating Affect in Crowdfunded Funeral Campaigns." *Social Media + Society* 4 (1). https://doi.org/10.1177/2056305117743350.

———. 2020. "Pay It Forward." *Real Life*, June 22. https://reallifemag.com/pay-it-forward/.

Knorr Cetina, Karin. 1999. *Epistemic Cultures: How the Sciences Make Knowledge*. Cambridge, MA: Harvard University Press.

Knox, Elizabeth. n.d. "Crossings: A New Vision of Death Care." *Crossings*, http://www.crossings.net/story.html.

Kokalitcheva, Kia. 2016. "Silicon Valley Investor Peter Thiel Will Join Trump's Transition Team." *Fortune*, November 11. https://fortune.com/2016/11/11/thiel-trump-transition team/.

Kolbert, Elizabeth. 2014. *The Sixth Extinction: An Unnatural History*. New York: Henry Holt.

Kopp, Emily. 2020. "National Body Bag Shortage Exacerbates Funeral Homes' Problems." *Roll Call*, May 14. www.rollcall.com/2020/05/14/ national-body-bag-shortage-exacerbates-funeral-homes-problems/.

Kosoff, Maya. 2016a. "Peter Thiel Wants to Inject Himself with Young People's Blood." *Vanity Fair*, August 1. www.vanityfair.com/news/2016/08/ peter-thiel-wants-to-inject-himself-with-young-peoples-blood.

———. 2016b. "Donald Trump Reportedly Wants Peter Thiel on the Supreme Court." *Vanity Fair*, September 15. www.vanityfair.com/news/2016/09/ peter-thiel-supreme-court.

———. 2017 "This Anti-Aging Start-Up Is Charging Thousands of Dollars for Teen Blood." *Vanity Fair*, June 1. www.vanityfair.com/news/2017/06/ this-anti-aging-start-up-is-paying-thousands-of-dollars-for-teen-blood.

Kragh, Helge. 2008. *Entropic Creation: Religious Contexts of Thermodynamics and Cosmology*. Burlington, VT: Routledge.

Krämer, Sybille. 2006. "The Cultural Techniques of Time Axis Manipulation: On Friedrich Kittler's Conception of Media." *Theory, Culture & Society* 28 (7–8): 93–109.

Krauss, Lawrence. 2012. *A Universe from Nothing*. New York: Simon & Schuster.

Laderman, Gary. 1996. *The Sacred Remains: American Attitudes toward Death, 1799–1883*. New Haven, CT: Yale University Press.

———. 2005. *Rest in Peace: A Cultural History of Death and the Funeral Home in Twentieth-Century America*. Oxford: Oxford University Press.

Lagerkvist, Amanda. 2016. "Existential Media: Toward a Theorization of Digital Thrownness." *New Media and Society* 19 (1): 96–110.

Laidlaw, James. 2014. *The Subject of Virtue: An Anthropology of Ethics and Freedom*. Cambridge, UK: Cambridge University Press.

Lambek, Michael. 2016. "After Life." In *Living and Dying in the Contemporary World: A Compendium*, edited by Veena Das and Clara Han, 629–47. Berkeley: University of California Press.

Laqueur, Thomas. 2015. *The Work of the Dead: A Cultural History of Mortal Remains*. Princeton, NJ: Princeton University Press.

Lasch, Christopher. 1991. *The True and Only Heaven: Progress and Its Critics*. W. W. Norton. Kindle.

Latour, Bruno. 2017. *Facing Gaia: Eight Lectures on the New Climate Regime*. Translated by Catherine Porter. Cambridge, UK: Polity.

Law, Rob. 2019. "I Have Felt Hopelessness over Climate Change. Here Is How We
    Move past the Immense Grief." *Guardian*, May 9. www.theguardian.com/
    commentisfree/2019/may/09/i-have-felt-hopelessness-over-climate-
    change-here-is-how-we-move-past-the-immense-grief.

Layne, Linda. 2003. *Motherhood Lost: A Feminist Account of Pregnancy Loss in
    America*. New York: Routledge.

Leach, Edmund. 1954. *Political Systems of Highland Burma*. Cambridge, MA: Harvard
    University Press.

Leahy, Stephen. 2018. "Climate Change Impacts Worse than Expected,
    Global Report Warns." *National Geographic*, October 7,
    2018. www.nationalgeographic.com/environment/2018/10/
    ipcc-report-climate-change-impacts-forests-emissions/.

Leary, Timothy. 1997. *Designs for Dying*. New York: HarperEdge.

Lecher, Colin. 2016. "Peter Thiel Is Joining Donald Trump's Transition Team."
    Verge, November 11. www.theverge.com/2016/11/11/13602026/
    peter-thiel-trump-transition-team-facebook.

Lee, Haiyan. 2006. *Revolution of the Heart: A Genealogy of Love in China, 1900–1950*.
    Berkeley: University of California Press.

Lee, Lois. 2015. *Recognizing the Non-religious: Reimagining the Secular*. Oxford: Oxford
    University Press.

Lee, Rebekah. 2011. "Death 'On the Move': Funerals, Entrepreneurs and the Rural-
    Urban Nexus in South Africa." *Journal of the International African Institute*
    81 (2): 226–47.

Lee, Rebekah, and Megan Vaughan. 2008. "Death and Dying in the History of Africa
    since 1800." *Journal of African History* 49 (3): 341–59.

Leon, Irving. 1992. "Perinatal Loss: A Critiqué of Current Hospital Practices." *Clinical
    Pediatrics* 31 (6): 366–74.

Levack, Brian P., ed. 1992. *Anthropological Studies of Witchcraft, Magic, and Religion*.
    Vol 1. New York: Garland.

Lifton, Robert Jay. 1987. *The Future of Immortality and Other Essays for a Nuclear Age*.
    New York: Basic Books.

Lifton, Robert Jay, and Eric Olson. (1974) 2004. "Symbolic Immortality." In *Death,
    Mourning, and Burial: A Cross-Cultural Reader*, edited by Antonius C. G. M.
    Robben, 32–40. Reprint, Malden, MA: Blackwell.

Liu, Huwy-min Lucia. 2015. "Dying Socialist in Capitalist Shanghai: Memorial Meet-
    ings, Death Ritual, and Perceptions of Self in Urban Chinese Funerals." PhD
    diss., Boston University.

———. 2019. "Market Economy Lives, Socialist Death: Contemporary Commemorations in Urban China." *Modern China* 47 (2): 178–203.

———. 2020a. "Ritual and Pluralism: Religious Variations on Socialist Death Rituals in Urban China." *Critique of Anthropology* 40 (1): 102–24.

———. 2020b. "The Civil Governance of Death: The Making of Chinese Political Subjects at the End of Life." *Journal of Asian Studies* 80 (1): 49–71.

Livingston, Julie. 2020. *Self-Devouring Growth: A Planetary Parable as Told from Southern Africa.* Durham, NC: Duke University Press.

Lock, Margaret. 2001. *Twice Dead: Organ Transplants and the Reinvention of Death.* Berkeley: University of California Press.

Lofland, Lyn. (1978) 2019. *The Craft of Dying: The Modern Face of Death.* Cambridge, MA: The MIT Press.

Luciano, Dana. 2007. *Arranging Grief: Sacred Time and the Body in Nineteenth-Century America.* New York: New York University Press.

Luhrmann, Tanya M. 2012. *When God Talks Back: Understanding the American Evangelical Relationship with God.* New York: Vintage.

Lukhele, Francis. 2016. "Tears of the Rainbow: Mourning in South African Culture." *Critical Arts* 30 (1): 31–44.

MacLellan, Matthew. 2013. "Marx's Vampires: An Althusserian Critique." *Rethinking Marxism: A Journal of Economics, Culture & Society* 25 (4): 549–65.

Madson, Diana. 2018. "Why Feedback Loops Are One of the Most Troubling Parts of Global Warming." *YaleClimateConnections*, February 7. www.yaleclimate connections.org/2018/02/why-feedback-loops-are-troubling/.

Malinowski, Bronislaw. 1948. *Magic, Science, and Religion and Other Essays.* Boston: Beacon Press.

Marcus, George, ed. 1995. *Technoscientific Imaginaries: Conversations, Profiles, and Memoirs.* Chicago: University of Chicago Press.

Masco, Joseph. 2008. "Target Audience." *Bulletin of the Atomic Scientists* 64 (3): 22–31.

———. 2010. "Bad Weather: On Planetary Crisis." *Social Studies of Science* 40 (1): 7–40.

———. 2012. "The End of Ends." *Anthropological Quarterly* 85 (4): 1107–24.

———. 2015. "The Age of Fallout." *History of the Present: A Journal of Critical History* 5 (2): 137–66.

Mauss, Marcel. 1972. *A General Theory of Magic.* Translated by Robert Brain. New York: Routledge.

Mayer, Robert G. 2011. *Embalming: History, Theory, and Practice.* 5th ed. New York: McGraw Hill.

Maxman, Amy. 2017. "Questionable 'Young Blood' Transfusions Offered in U. S. as Anti-Aging Remedy." *MIT Technology Review*, January 13. www.technologyreview.com/s/603242/questionable-young-blood-transfusions-offered-in-us-as-anti-aging-remedy.

Mbembe, Achille. 2003. Necropolitics. *Public Culture* 15 (1): 11–40.

———. (2001) 2015. *On the Postcolony*. Reprint, Johannesburg: Wits University Press.

McCarthy, Kieren. 2016. "VC Vampire: Peter Thiel Wants to Live Forever." *Register*, August 1. www.theregister.co.uk/2016/08/01/peter_thiel_wants_young_blood_for_longevit.

McGauely, Joe. 2017. "Amazon's CEO Is on a Quest to Stop Aging." *Thrillist*, January 27. www.thrillist.com/tech/nation/amazon-jeff-bezos-anti-aging-unity-biotechnology.

McIntyre, Douglas A. 2011. "The Ten Companies that Control the Death Industry." *247wallst* (blog), January 13. https://247wallst.com/investing/2011/01/13/the-ten-companies-that-control-the-death-industry/.

McKie, Robin. 2017. "Biologists Think 50% of Species Will Be Facing Extinction by the End of the Century." *Guardian*, February 25. www.theguardian.com/environment/2017/feb/25/half-all-species-extinct-end-century-vatican-conference.

McLeod, Ken. 2012. "The Ends of Humanity." *Aeon*, November 12.

McLuhan, Marshall. 1964. *Understanding Media: The Extensions of Man*. New York: McGraw Hill.

Mecklin, John, ed. 2018. "It Is Now Two Minutes to Midnight: 2018 Doomsday Clock Statement." *Bulletin of Atomic Scientists*, Science and Security Board, January 25. https://thebulletin.org/2018-doomsday-clock-statement/.

Mei, Angjolie. 2017. *Dying to Meet You: Confessions of a Funeral Director*. Singapore: Epigram Books.

Meier, Allison. 2013. "The Cast Iron Coffin That Was Too Creepy Even for the Victorians." *Atlas Obscura*, December 30. www.atlasobscura.com/.

Meredith, Sam. 2018. "Two Weeks before His Death, Stephen Hawking Predicted 'The End of the Universe.'" *CNBC*, March 19. www.cnbc.com/2018/03/19/stephen-hawking-physicist-predicted-end-of-the-universe-two-weeks-before-his-death.html.

Merid, Beza. 2019. "Fight for Our Health: Activism in the Face of Health Insurance Precarity." *BioSocieties* 15 (2): 159–81.

Metcalf, Peter. 2010. "Death Be Not Strange." In *Magic, Witchcraft and Religion: A Reader in the Anthropology of Religion*, edited by Pamela A. Moro and James E. Myers, 345–48. 8th ed. New York: McGraw Hill.

Metcalf, Peter, and Richard Huntington. 1991. *Celebrations of Death: The Anthropology of Mortuary Ritual*. 2nd ed. Cambridge, UK: Cambridge University Press.

Metzinger, Thomas. 2017. "Silicon Valley Is Selling an Ancient Dream of Immortality." *Financial Times*, August 18. www.ft.com/content/7a89c998–828d-11e7–94e2-c5b903247afd.

Milstein, Cindy. 2017. "Prologue: Cracks in the Wall." In *Rebellious Mourning: The Collective Work of Grief*, edited by Cindy Milstein, 1–12. Chico, CA: AK Press.

Mitford, Jessica. (1963) 2000. *The American Way of Death Revisited*. Rev. ed. New York: Vintage.

Money Morning. 2020. "Top Biotech Companies Race to Unlock the "Immortality Gene." https://moneymorning.com/how-to-live-rich-and-live-forever/top-biotech-companies-race-to-unlock-the-immortality-gene.

Montgomery, Philip, and Maggie Jones. 2020. "How Do You Maintain Dignity for the Dead in a Pandemic?" *New York Times*, May 14. www.nytimes.com/2020/05/14/magazine/funeral-home-covid.html.

Moreman, Christopher M., and A. David Lewis. 2014. *Digital Death: Mortality and Beyond in the Online Ages*. Santa Barbara, CA: Praeger.

Moretti, Franco. 1983. *Signs Taken for Wonders: Essays in the Sociology of Literary Forms*. New York: Verso.

Morgan, Lynn M. 2009. *Icons of Life: A Cultural History of Human Embryos*. Berkeley: University of California Press.

Morgan, Lynn M., and M. W. Michaels. 1999. *Fetal Subjects, Feminist Positions*. Philadelphia: University of Pennsylvania Press.

Morris, Chris. 2018. "Why Peter Thiel Is Leaving Silicon Valley for L. A." *Fortune*, February 15. http://fortune.com/2018/02/15/peter-thiel-leaving-silicon-valley.

Morris, David Z. 2016. "Peter Thiel Pledges $1.25 Million to Support Donald Trump." *Fortune*, October 16. http://fortune.com/2016/10/16/peter-thiel-donald-trump-support.

Morse, Jack. 2016. "Billionaire Trump Supporter Peter Thiel Wants the Blood of Young People." *SFist*, August 1. http://sfist.com/2016/08/01/billionaire_trump_supporter_peter_t.php.

Morton, Timothy. 2013. *Hyperobjects: Philosophy and Ecology after the End of the World*. Minneapolis: University of Minnesota Press.

Murphy, Sharon Ann. 2010. *Investing in Life: Insurance in Antebellum America*. Baltimore, MD: Johns Hopkins University Press.

Naquin, Susan. 1988. "Funerals in North China: Uniformity and Variation." In *Death Ritual in Late Imperial and Early Modern China*, edited by James L. Watson and Evelyn Rawski, 37–70. Berkeley: University of California Press.

National End-of-Life Doula Alliance (NEDA). 2019. http://www.nedalliance.org/.

National Funeral Directors Association (NFDA). 2015. "NFDA Cremation and Burial Report Released: Rate of Cremation Surpasses That of Burial in 2015." NFDA, June 30, 2016. www.nfda.org/news/media-center/nfda-news-releases/ id/1310/2016-nfda-cremation-and-burial-report-released-rate-of-cremation-surpasses-that-of-burial-in-2015.

———. 2018. *NFDA Cremation and Burial Report: Research, Statistics, and Projects (July 2018)*. Brookfield, WI: NFDA.

———. n.d. "Embalming and COVID-19." NFDA.org. www.nfda.org/news/ in-the-news/nfda-news/id/4974/embalming-covid-19.

National Home Funeral Alliance (NHFA). 2019a. "Core Competencies." www. homefuneralalliance.org/core-competencies.html.

———. 2019b. "The NHFA Position on Licensure, Standards, and Certification." www. homefuneralalliance.org/certification—licensure.html.

———. 2019c "Who We Are and How We Got Here." www.homefuneralalliance.org/ history-of-the-nhfa.html.

Naughton, John. 2016. "The Only Living Trump Supporter in Silicon Valley." *Guardian*, May 22. www.theguardian.com/commentisfree/2016/may/22/ peter-thiel-paypal-donald-trump-silicon-valley-libertarian.

Navarro, Marysa, and Nicholas Fraser. 1996. *Evita: The Real Life of Eva Perón*. New York: W. W. Norton.

Neocleous, Mark. 2003. "The Political Economy of the Dead: Marx's Vampires." *History of Political Thought* 24 (4): 668–84.

New York Times. 1913. "National Society to Conserve Life: Life Extension Institute to Teach Hygiene and Prevention of Disease." *New York Times*, December 30.

———. 2020. "Covid World Map: Tracking the Global Outbreak." *New York Times*. www.nytimes.com/interactive/2020/world/coronavirus-maps.html.

Newby, Zahra, and Ruth Toulson, eds. 2018. *The Materiality of Mourning: Cross-Disciplinary Perspectives*. London: Routledge.

Newton, Casey. 2017. "Speak, Memory." *Verge*. www.theverge.com/a/luka-artificial-intelligence-memorial-roman-mazurenko-bot.

Niehaus, Isak. 2005. "Witches and Zombies of the South African Lowveld: Discourse, Accusations and Subjective Reality." *Journal of the Royal Anthropological Institute* 11 (2): 191–210.

Nietzsche, Friedrich. 1989 (1873). "On Truth and Lying in an Extra-Moral Sense." In *Friedrich Nietzsche on Rhetoric and Language*, edited and translated byBlair Gilman and David Parent, 246–57. Oxford: Oxford University Press.

Noble, Safiya U. 2018. *Algorithms of Oppression*. New York: New York University Press.

Nyawo, Sonene. 2018. "Socio-cultural Religious Constructions of Women and Fertility and their Implications in the Context of HIV and AIDS in Swaziland." *BOLESWA Journal of Theology and Religious Studies* 5 (1): 101–12

O'Gieblyn, Meghan. 2017. "Ghost in the Cloud: Transhumanism's Simulation Theology." *N+1* 28 (Spring). https://nplusonemag.com/issue-28/essays/ghost-in-the-cloud/.

O'Gorman, Marcel. 2015. *Necromedia*. Minneapolis: University of Minnesota Press.

Ohlheiser, Abby. 2020. "The Lonely Reality of Zoom Funerals." *MIT Technology Review*, April 13. www.technologyreview.com/2020/04/13/999348/covid-19-grief-zoom-funerals/.

Olson, Philip R. 2014. "Flush and Bone: Funeralizing Alkaline Hydrolysis in the United States." *Science, Technology, and Human Values* 39 (5): 666–93.

———. 2016a. "Domesticating Deathcare: The Women of the U. S. Natural Deathcare Movement." *Journal of Medical Humanities* 39 (2): 195–215.

———. 2016b. "Custody of the Corpse: Controlling Alkaline Hydrolysis in U.S. Deathcare Markets." In *Death in a Consumer Culture*, edited by Susan Dobscha, 75–88. New York: Routledge.

———. 2016c. "Knowing 'Necro-Waste.'" *Social Epistemology* 30 (3): 1–20.

Ong, Aihwa. 1988. "The Production of Possession: Spirits and the Multinational Corporation in Malaysia." *American Ethnologist* 15 (1): 28–42.

Oppel, Richard A. Jr., Robert Gebeloff, K. K. Rebecca Lai, Will Wright, and Mitch Smith. 2020. "The Fullest Look Yet at the Racial Inequality of Coronavirus." *New York Times*, July 5, 2020. www.nytimes.com/interactive/2020/07/05/us/coronavirus-latinos-african-americans-cdc-data.html.

Order of the Good Death. 2020a. *Death Positive Movement* (blog). http://www.orderofthegooddeath.com/resources/death-positive-movement.

———. 2020b. *Home Funerals* (blog). http://www.orderofthegooddeath.com/resources/home-funerals#1.

Ortega, Francisco. 2009. "The Cerebral Subject and the Challenge of Neurodiversity." *BioSocieties* 4 (4): 425–45.

Osnos, Evan. 2017. "Doomsday Prep for the Super-Rich." *New Yorker*. January 30. www.newyorker.com/magazine/2017/01/30/doomsday-prep-for-the-super-rich

Panichas, George. 1981. "Vampires, Werewolves, and Economic Exploitation." *Social Theory and Practice* 7 (2): 223–42.

Parveen, Nazia. 2020. "The Muslim Bereaved Cruelly Deprived of Closure by Coronavirus." *Guardian*, July 7.

Patel, Geeta. 2006. "Risky Subjects: Insurance, Sexuality, and Capital." *Social Text* 24, no. 4 (89): 25–65.

Peck, Dennis L., and Clifton D. Bryant, eds. 2009 *Encyclopedia of Death and the Human Experience*. Thousand Oaks, CA: Sage.

Penmellen Boret, Sébastien. 2014. *Japanese Tree Burial: Ecology, Kinship and the Culture of Death*. London: Routledge.

Penmellen Boret, Sébastien, Susan Orpett Long, and Sergei Kan. 2017. *Death in the Early Twenty-first Century: Authority, Innovation, and Mortuary Rites*. London: Palgrave MacMillan.

Peters, Benjamin. 2016. "Digital." In *Digital Keywords: A Vocabulary of Information Science & Culture*, edited by B. Peters, 93–108. Princeton, NJ: Princeton University Press.

Plater, Michael. 1996. *African American Entrepreneurship in Richmond, 1890–1940*: The Story of R. C. Scott. New York: Garland.

Plotnick, Rachel. 2015. "What Happens When You Push This?: Toward a History of the Not-So-Easy Button." *Information & Culture* 50 (3): 315–38.

Porges, Stephen. n.d. "Home of Dr. Stephen Porges." www.stephenporges.com/.

Prendergast, David, Jenny Hockey, and Leonie Kellaher. 2006. "Blowing in the Wind? Identity, Materiality, and the Destination of Human Ashes." *Journal of the Royal Anthropological Institute* 12 (4): 881–98.

Povinelli, Elizabeth. 2011. *Economies of Abandonment*. Durham, NC: Duke University Press.

Powell, Miles A. 2016. *Vanishing America: Species Extinction, Racial Peril, and the Origins of Conservation*. Cambridge, MA: Harvard University Press.

Price, Margaret. 2015. "The Bodymind Problem and the Possibilities of Pain." *Hypatia* 20 (1): 268–84.

Prince, Russ Alan. 2018. "Who Wants to Live Forever? . . . The Super-Rich That's Who (And Most Everyone Else)." *Forbes*, January 2. www.forbes.com/sites/russalanprince/2018/01/02/who-wants-to-live-forever-the-super-rich-thats-who-and-most-everyone-else/#7d1319c44ab2.

Pringle, Heather. 2001. *The Mummy Congress: Science, Obsession, and the Everlasting Dead*. New York: Hyperion.

Prudential Insurance Company. "Five Minutes Talk with the Prudential on Industrial Life Insurance." 1918. Pamphlet. Newark, NJ.

Purdy, Jedediah. 2016. "The Anti-Democratic Worldview of Steve Bannon and Peter Thiel." *Politico*, November 30. www.politico.com/magazine/story/2016/11/donald-trump-steve-bannon-peter-thiel-214490.

Quack, Johannes. 2012. *Disenchanting India: Organized Rationalism and the Criticism of Religion in India*. Oxford: Oxford University Press.

Quirk, Vanessa. 2017. "The Urban Death Project: Bringing Death Back into the Urban Realm." *Metropolis*, February 24. www.metropolismag.com/cities/the-urban-death-project-bringing-death-back-into-the-urban-realm/.

Radin, Joanna, and Emma Kowal. 2017. *Cryopolitics: Frozen Life in a Melting World*. Cambridge, MA: MIT Press.

Ragone, Helene. 1994. *Surrogate Motherhood: Conception in the Heart*. Boulder, CO: Westview Press.

Rahman, Khaleda. 2020. "What Is a Home Funeral? How to Care for Sick or Deceased Ones at Home during Coronavirus Pandemic." *Newsweek*, March 26. www.newsweek.com/home-funeral-coronavirus-1494396.

Ralph, Michael. 2012. "Life . . . in the Midst of Death: Notes on the Relationship between Slave Insurance, Life Insurance and Disability." *Disability Studies Quarterly* 32 (3).

Rana, Saqib. 2020. "5 Startups That Want to Help You Live Forever." *Future of Everything*. www.futureofeverything.io/5-startups-want-help-live-forever.

Rankine, Claudia. 2015. "The Condition of Black Life Is One of Mourning." *New York Times Magazine*, June 22. www.nytimes.com/2015/06/22/magazine/the-condition-of-black-life-is-one-of-mourning.html.

Rappaport, Roy. 1999. *Ritual and Religion in the Making of Humanity*. Cambridge, UK: Cambridge University Press.

Regis, Ed. 1994. "Meet the Extropians." *Wired*, October 1. www.wired.com/1994/10/extropians.

Rehagen, Tony. 2016. "Green Burials Are Forcing the Funeral Industry to Rethink Death." *Bloomberg*, October 27. www.bloomberg.com/features/2016-green-burial/.

Rhine, Kathryn. 2016. *The Unseen Things: Women, Secrecy, and HIV in Northern Nigeria*. Bloomington: Indiana University Press.

Richardson, Benjamin Ward. 1878. "Some Original Researches on Putrefactive Changes and of the Preservation of Animal Substances." *The Journal of the Society of Arts* 26 (1349): 911–24.

Ricoveri, Giovanna. 2013. *Nature for Sale: The Commons versus Commodities*. London: Pluto.

Riley, Tonya. 2016. "The Many Rich Men Who Have Tried to Live Forever." *MEL*. https://melmagazine.com/en-us/story/the-many-rich-men-who-have-tried-to-live-forever.

Robben, Antonius C. G. M. 2004. "Death and Anthropology: An Introduction." In

Death, Mourning, and Burial: A Cross-Cultural Reader, edited by Antonius C. G. M. Robben, 1–16. New York: Blackwell.

———. 2018. *A Companion to the Anthropology of Death*. Hoboken, NJ: Wiley Blackwell.

Roberts, Dorothy. 1997. *Killing the Black Body: Race, Reproduction, and the Meaning of Liberty*. New York: Vintage.

Roberts, Sophie. 2017. "'I Completely Broke Down': Heartbreaking Photos Show How a Mum Spent 16 Days with Her Dead Baby Girl—Even Took Her Tragic Daughters for Walks in Pram. *Sun*, February 1. www.thesun.co.uk/living/2756669/heartbreaking-photos-show-how-a-mum-spent-16-days-with-her-dead-baby-girl-and-even-took-her-tragic-daughter-for-walks-in-a-pram/.

Root, Tik. 2020. "Three Days in a Detroit Funeral Home Ravaged by the Coronavirus." *Time*, May 1. https://time.com/5830477/funeral-home-coronavirus/.

Rosaldo, Renato. 1989. "Grief and a Headhunter's Rage." In *Culture and Truth: The Remaking of Social Analysis*, 121. Boston: Beacon.

Rose, Nikolas. 2007. *The Politics of Life Itself: Biomedicine, Power, and Subjectivity in the Twenty-First Century*. Princeton, NJ: Princeton University Press.

Rose, Nikolas, and Joelle M. Abi-Rached. 2013. *Neuro: The New Brain Sciences and the Management of the Mind*. Princeton, NJ: Princeton University Press.

Rowe, Mark Michael. 2011. *Bonds of the Dead: Temples, Burial, and the Transformation of Contemporary Japanese Buddhism*. Chicago: University of Chicago Press.

Royle, Edward. 1974. *Victorian Infidels: The Origins of the British Secularist Movement, 1791–1866*. Manchester: Manchester University Press.

Ruby, Jay. 1995. *Secure the Shadow: Death and Photography in America*. Cambridge, MA: MIT Press.

Rundblad, Georganne. 1995. "Exhuming Women's Premarket Duties in the Care of the Dead." *Gender and Society* 9 (2): 173–92.

Rush, Merilynne. 2015. *Home Funeral Guides: Illuminating the Path*. http://afterdeathhomecare.com/ebook/.

Rushkoff, Douglas. 2018. "Survival of the Richest: The Wealthy are Planning to Leave Us Behind." *Medium*, July 5, 2018. https://medium.com/s/futurehuman/survival-of-the-richest-9ef6cdddocc1.

Sanburn, Josh. 2020. "'The Last of the First Responders': Inside One Funeral Home's COVID-19 Crisis." *Vanity Fair*, June 25. www.vanityfair.com/news/2020/06/inside-the-coronavirus-crisis-at-a-queens-funeral-home.

Schalk, Sami. 2018. *Bodyminds Reimagined: (Dis)ability, Race, and Gender in Black Women's Speculative Fiction*. Durham, NC: Duke University Press.

Schantz, Mark S. 2008. *Awaiting the Heavenly Country: The Civil War and America's Culture of Death*. Ithaca, NY: Cornell Press.

Scharping, Nathaniel. 2018. "What Stephen Hawking's Final Paper Says (and Doesn't Say)." *Discover*, March 20. http://blogs.discovermagazine.com/d-brief/2018/03/20/stephen-hawking-final-paper/#.XPZlYSOZPOQ.

Scheper-Hughes, Nancy. 1993. *Death without Weeping: The Violence of Everyday Life in Brazil*. Berkeley: University of California Press.

Scheper-Hughes, Nancy, and Loic Wacquant, eds. 2003. *Commodifying Bodies*. London: Sage.

Schieber, Jonathan. 2018. "The Jay-Z Backed Life Insurance Startup, Ethos, Has Raised $35 Million." *TechCrunch*, October 30. https://techcrunch.com/2018/10/30/the-jay-z-backed-life-insurance-startup-ethos-has-raised-35-million/.

Schneider, David. (1968) 1980. *American Kinship: A Cultural Account*. Chicago: University of Chicago Press.

Schüll, Natasha Dow. 2016. "Data for Life: Wearable Technology and the Design of Self-Care." *BioSocieties* 11 (3): 1–17.

Schwartz, Margaret. 2015. *Dead Matter: The Meaning of Iconic Corpses*. Minneapolis: University of Minnesota Press.

———. 2016. "Mourning What Matters: On David Bowie and Laquan McDonald." *University of Minnesota Press Blog*, January 21, 2016. https://uminnpressblog.com/2016/01/21/mourning-what-matters-on-david-bowie-and-laquan-mcdonald/.

Schwartz, Peter, and Doug Randall. 2003. *An Abrupt Climate Change Scenario and Its Implications for National Security October 2003*. Washington, DC: Institute for Agricultural and Trade Policy. www.iatp.org/documents/abrupt-climate-change-scenario-and-its-implications-united-states-national-security.

Schwartzman, Peter. 2019. "When a Black-Owned Funeral Home in a Gentrifying City Has No One Left to Bury." *Washington Post*, September 5. www.washingtonpost.com/local/dc-politics/at-center-of-changing-dc-requiem-for-a-funeral-home-that-catered-to-blacks/2019/09/05/c03767ca-8614–11e9-a870-b9c411dc4312_story.html?fbclid=IwAR30_BnatbCdisvULF7VkDM4mSkk-NX3GZS70gsFvdd2hwyksQNP3ut8brI.

Seaver, Nick. 2017. "Algorithms as Culture: Some Tactics for the Ethnography of Algorithmic Systems." *Big Data & Society* (December 2017). https://doi.org/10.1177/2053951717738104.

Seligman, Adam, Robert Weller, Michael Puett, and Bennett Simon. 2008. *Ritual and its Consequences: The Limits of Sincerity*. Oxford: Oxford University Press.

Shaffrey, Ted. 2018. "Death Becomes Her: Women Make Inroads in Funeral Industry."

Associated Press, November 27, 2018. https://apnews.com/80d5b988f9ac4f27
9ee60b4fb51a79f4.

Sharma, Sarah. 2014. *In the Meantime: Temporality and Cultural Politics*. Durham, NC:
Duke University Press.

Sharp, Lesley. 2006. *Strange Harvest: Organ Transplants, Denatured Bodies, and the
Transformed Self*. Berkeley: University of California Press.

———. 2007. *Bodies, Commodities, and Biotechnologies: Death, Mourning and Scientific Desire in the Realm of Human Organ Transfer*. New York: Columbia
University Press.

Sharpe, Christina. 2016. *In the Wake: On Blackness and Being*. Durham, NC: Duke
University Press.

Shepherd, Andrew, Lin Gilbert, Alan S. Muir, Hannes Konrad, Malcolm McMillan,
Thomas Slater, Kate H. Briggs, Aud V. Sundal, Anna E. Hogg, and Marcus E.
Engdahl. 2019. "Trends in Antarctic Ice Sheet Elevation and Mass." *Geophysi-
cal Research Letters* 46 (14): 8174–83. https://doi.org/10.1029/2019GL082182.

Shukman, David. 2016. "Hawking: Humans at Risk of Lethal 'Own Goal.'" *BBC News*,
January 19. www.bbc.com/news/science-environment-35344664.

Sessa, Ben. 2017. *The Psychedelic Renaissance: Reassessing the Role of Psychedelic Drugs
in 21st Century Psychiatry and Society*. Albany: State University of New York
Press.

Sin, Yuen. 2019. "Was Body Left Uncovered at Funeral Parlour?"
Straits Times, June 9. www.straitstimes.com/singapore/
was-body-left-uncovered-at-funeral-parlour.

Siner, Emily. 2019. "Called to Be a Funeral Director: Most Mortuary School
Grads Are First in the Family." *NPR*, September 23. www.npr.
org/2019/09/23/752557052/called-to-be-a-funeral-director-most-
mortuary-school-grads-are-first-in-the-fami.

Sloane, David Charles. 2018. *Is the Cemetery Dead?* Chicago: University of Chicago
Press.

Smith, Andrew. 2001. "Reading Wealth in Nigeria: Occult Capitalism and Marx's
Vampires." *Historical Materialism* 9: 39–59.

Smith, Suzanne E. 2010. *To Serve the Living: Funeral Directors and the African American Way of Death*. Cambridge, MA: Harvard University Press.

Somatic Experiencing Trauma Institute. n.d. https://traumahealing.org/.

Spera, Keith. 2012. "'Uncle' Lionel Batiste Gets Send Off as Unique as the Man Himself." *Times Picayune*, July 20. www.nola.com/entertainment_life/music/
article_78f7b478-e4e6-5490-ac61-1cd8da6cdc76.html.

Spillers, Hortense. 2003. "Mama's Baby, Papa's Maybe: An American Grammar Book."

In *Black and White and in Color: Essays on American Literature and Culture*, 203–29. Chicago: University of Chicago Press.

Stafford, Charles. 2000. *Separation and Reunion in Modern China*. Cambridge, UK: Cambridge University Press.

Stanley, Tiffany. 2016. "The Disappearance of a Distinctively Black Way to Mourn." *Atlantic*, January 26. www.theatlantic.com/business/archive/2016/01/black-funeral-homes-mourning/426807/.

Star, Susan Leigh, ed. 1995. *Ecologies of Knowledge: Work and Politics in Science and Technology*. Albany: SUNY Press.

Steinbuch, Yaron. 2020. "Italian Actor Luca Franzese Pleads for Help in Video Showing Dead Sister." *New York Post*, March 12. https://nypost.com/2020/03/12/italian-actor-luca-franzese-pleads-for-help-in-video-showing-dead-sister/.

Stoknes, Per Espen. 2015. "The Great Grief: How to Cope with Losing Our World." *Common Dreams*, May 14. www.commondreams.org/views/2015/05/14/great-grief-how-cope-losing-our-world.

Strathern, Marilyn. 1992. *Reproducing the Future: Essays on Anthropology, Kinship, and the New Reproductive Technologies*. New York: Routledge.

Suzuki, Hikaru. 2000. *The Price of Death: The Funeral Industry in Contemporary Japan*. Stanford, CA: Stanford University Press.

Swenson, Kyle. 2019. "More Than a Thousand Arrested in 'Extinction Rebellion' Protests against Climate Change." *Washington Post*, April 23. www.washingtonpost.com/nation/2019/04/23/hundreds-arrested-extinction-rebellion-protests-against-climate-change/?noredirect=on&utm_term=.c508ea9ee7fe.

Takita, Yōjirō, dir. *Departures*. 2008. Tokyo, Japan: Tokyo Broadcasting.

Tammilehto, Olli. 1985. "The Blind Spots of Eco-fascist Linkola." *Suomi* 6/7. http://www.tammilehto.info/english/linkolablind.php.

Tarnoff, Ben. 2016. "Donald Trump, Peter Thiel and the Death of Democracy." *Guardian*, July 21. www.theguardian.com/technology/2016/jul/21/peter-thiel-republican-convention-speech.

Taylor, Charles. 2003. *Modern Social Imaginaries*. Durham, NC: Duke University Press.

———. 2007. *A Secular Age*. Cambridge, MA: The Belknap Press of Harvard University Press.

Taylor, Michael L. 2014. "The Civil War Experiences of a New Orleans Undertaker." *Louisiana History: The Journal of the Louisiana Historical Association* 55 (3): 261–81.

Teman, Ellie. 2010. *Birthing a Mother: The Surrogate Body and the Pregnant Self*. Berkeley: University of California Press.

Tessler, Itzchak. 2014. "New Procedure Allows Parents to Bury Stillborn Babies." *Ynetnews*, August 10. www.ynetnews.com/articles/0,7340,L-4557158,00.html.

Thiel, Peter. 2009. "The Education of a Libertarian." *Cato Unbound*, April 13. www.cato-unbound.org/2009/04/13/peter-thiel/education-libertarian.

Thompson, Cadie. 2015. "6 Billionaires Who Want to Live Forever." *Business Insider*, September 2. www.businessinsider.com/billionaires-who-want-to-live-forever-2015-9.

Thompson, Charis. 2005. *Making Parents: The Ontological Choreography of Reproductive Technologies*. Cambridge, MA: MIT Press.

Thompson, E. P. 1967. "Time, Work-Discipline, and Industrial Capitalism." *Past & Present* 38: 56–97.

Thompson, Stuart E. 1988. "Death, Food, and Fertility." In *Death Ritual in Late Imperial and Early Modern China*, edited by James L. Watson and Evelyn Rawski, 71–108. Berkeley: University of California Press.

Thompson, William E. 1991. "Handling the Stigma of Handling the Dead: Morticians and Funeral Directors." *Deviant Behavior: An Interdisciplinary Journal* 12 (4): 403–29.

Thwala, Phumelele. 1999. "Sexual Abuse, HIV/AIDS, and the Legal Rights of Women in Swaziland." In *AIDS and Development in Africa*, edited by Kempe Ronald Hope, Sr., 69–82. Binghamton, NY: Haworth Press.

Tollefson, Jeff. 2015. "Is the 2 °C World a Fantasy?" *Nature* 527 (7579): 436–38.

———. 2018. "IPCC Says Limiting Global Warming to 1.5 °C Will Require Drastic Action." *Nature* 562: 172–73.

Toulson, Ruth. 2013. "A Funeral Director Looks for Love: Dating and the Dirty Business of Death in Singapore." Paper presented at Americana Anthropological Association Annual Conference, Chicago, November 20–24.

Trafton, Scott. 2004. *Egypt Land: Race and Nineteenth-Century Egyptomania*. Durham, NC: Duke University Press.

Trompette, Pascale, and Mélanie Lemonnier. 2009. "Funeral Embalming: The Transformation of a Medical Innovation." *Science Studies* 22 (2): 9–30.

Trotter, J. K. 2016. "Peter Thiel Is Interested in Harvesting the Blood of the Young." *Gawker*, August 1. https://gawker.com/peter-thiel-is-interested-in-harvesting-the-blood-of-th-1784649830.

Turner, Christine, dir. 2013. *Homegoing*. P.O.V/American Documentary. Peralta Pictures.

Turner, Victor. 1967. *The Forest of Symbols: Aspects of Ndembu Ritual*. Ithaca, NY: Cornell University Press.

———. 1969. *The Ritual Process: Structure and Anti-Structure*. Ithaca, NY: Cornell University Press.

Ucko, Peter J. 1969. "Ethnography and Archaeological Interpretation of Funerary Remains." *World Archaeology* 1 (2): 262–80.

Vaad Harabonim of Queens. 2020. "About the Chevra Kadisha." https://queensvaad. org/chevra-kadisha/about-the-chevra-kadisha/.

Vanacore, Andrew. 2014. "Socialite Easterling Goes Out as She Wanted—With a Party." *New Orleans Advocate*, April 26. www.theadvocate.com/new_orleans/news/ article_acc7f238–57c5–531f-a5c1-d35d21f44df0.html.

Verdery, Katherine. 1999. *The Political Lives of Dead Bodies*. New York: Columbia University Press.

Vespa, Jonathan. 2018. "The Graying of America: More Older Adults than Kids by 2035." United States Census Bureau, March 13, 2018. www.census.gov/library/ stories/2018/03/graying-america.html.

Vidal, Fernando, and Francisco Ortega. 2017. *Being Brains: Making the Cerebral Subject*. New York: Fordham University Press.

Virilio, Paul. 1997. *Open Sky*. Translated by Julie Rose. New York: Verso.

Vitello Paul. 2013. "John Kennell, Advocate of Infant Bonding, Dies at 91." *New York Times*, September 21. www.nytimes.com/2013/09/22/health/john-kennell-advocate-of-infant-bonding-dies-at-91.html.

Waddell, Braeden. 2019. "Locals Protest to Protect Historically Black Cemetery, Three Arrested." *AWOL*, February 21. https://awolau.org/3249/slider/ locals-protest-to-protect-historically-black-cemetery-three-arrested/.

Wajcman, Judy. 1991. *Feminism Confronts Technology*. Cambridge, UK: Polity.

Waldby, Catherine, and Robert Mitchell. 2006. *Tissue Economies: Blood, Organs, and Cell Lines in Late Capitalism*. Durham, NC: Duke University Press.

Wall, Mike. 2016. "Stephen Hawking Wants to Ride Virgin Galactic's New Passenger Spaceship." *Space*, February 20. www.space.com/31993-stephen-hawking-virgin-galactic-spaceshiptwo-unity.html?jwsource=em.

Wallis, Robert J. 2003. *Shamans/Neo-Shamans*. London: Routledge.

Walls, Jerry, ed. 2010. Introduction to *Oxford Handbook of Eschatology*, 3–18. Oxford: Oxford University Press.

Walsh, Brian. 2017. "When You Die, You'll Probably Be Embalmed. Thank Abraham Lincoln for That." *Conversation*, October 30. https://theconversation.com/ how-lincolns-embrace-of-embalming-birthed-the-american-funeral-industry-86196?xid=PS_smithsonian.

Walter, Tony. 1994. *The Revival of Death*. London: Routledge.

————. 2004. "Plastination for Display: A New Way to Dispose of the Dead." *Journal of the Royal Anthropological Institute* 10 (3): 603–27.

————. 2020. *Death in the Modern World*. Newbury Park, CA: Sage.

Watson, James L. 1982. "Of Flesh and Bones: The Management of Death Pollution in Cantonese Society." In *Death and the Regeneration of Life*, edited by Maurice Bloch and Jonathan Parry, 155–86. Cambridge, UK: Cambridge University Press.

————. 1988a. "Funeral Specialists in Cantonese Society: Pollution, Performance, and Social Hierarchy." In *Death Ritual in Late Imperial and Early Modern China*, edited by James L. Watson and Evelyn Rawski, 108–34. Berkeley: University of California Press.

————. 1988b. "The Structure of Chinese Funeral Rites: Elementary Forms, Ritual Sequence and the Primacy of Performance." In *Death Ritual in Late Imperial and Early Modern China*, edited by James L. Watson and Evelyn Rawski, 3–19. Berkeley: University of California Press.

Watson, James L., and Evelyn Rawski. 1988. *Death Ritual in Late Imperial and Early Modern China*. Berkeley: University of California Press.

Watts, Jonathan. 2018. "Stop Biodiversity Loss or We Could Face Our Own Extinction, Warns UN." *Guardian*, November 6. www.theguardian.com/environment/2018/nov/03/stop-biodiversity-loss-or-we-could-face-our-own-extinction-warns-un.

————. 2019. "Human Society under Urgent Threat from Loss of Earth's Natural Life." *Guardian*, May 6. www.theguardian.com/environment/2019/may/06/human-society-under-urgent-threat-loss-earth-natural-life-un-report.

Waugh, Evelyn. 1948. *The Loved One: An Anglo-American Tragedy*. Boston: Little, Brown.

Waweru, Nduta. 2018. "King Mswati's Eighth Wife, Senteni Masango, Laid to Rest Today." *Face2Face Africa*, April 8. https://face2faceafrica.com/article/king-mswatis-eighth-wife-senteni-masango-laid-rest-today.

Weber, Max. 1946. "Science as a Vocation." In *From Max Weber: Essays in Sociology*, translated and edited by Hans H. Gerth and Charles Wright Mills, 129–56. New York: Oxford University Press.

————. (1904) 2009. *The Protestant Ethic and the Spirit of Capitalism with Other Writings on the Rise of the West*. Translated by Stephen Kalberg. Reprint, New York: Oxford University Press.

Weinberg, Abigail. 2019. "A New Study Found That 15,000 People Died Because Their State Didn't Expand Medicaid." *Mother Jones*, July 24. www.motherjones.com/politics/2019/07/a-new-study-found-that-15000-people-died-because-their-state-didnt-expand-medicaid/.

Weisman, Alans. 2007. "Hot Legacy." In *The World Without Us*, 256–78. New York: St. Martin's.

Wells, Amos R. (1921) 2016. *The Collected Poems of Amos R. Wells*. Charleston, SC: Bibliolife. Facsimile copy of book originally published by Christian Endeavor World, Boston, MA.

Wernimont, Jacqueline. 2019. *Numbered Lives: Life and Death in Quantum Media*. Cambridge, MA: MIT Press.

Wescott, Daniel J., Kelly Brinsko, Marina Faerman, Stephanie D. Golda, Jeff Nichols, Mark Spigelman, Bob Stewart, Margaret Streeter, Robert H. Tykot, and Ljuba Zamstein. 2010. "Fisk Patent Metallic Burial Case from Western Missouri: An Interdisciplinary and Comprehensive Effort to Reconstruct the History of an Early Settler of Lexington, Missouri." *Archaeological and Anthropological Sciences* 2 (4): 283–305.

Westrate, Elizabeth, dir. 2003. *A Family Undertaking*, 2003. New York, Five Spot Films for Independent Television Service. Brooklyn, NY: Icarus Films.

White, Luise. 2000 *Speaking with Vampires: Rumor and History in Colonial Africa*. Berkeley: University of California Press.

Whittaker, G. Clay. 2016. "Trump Might Nominate Peter Thiel for Supreme Court: Rumor Has It." *Popular Science*, September 15. www.popsci.com/trump-might-nominate-peter-thiel-for-supreme-court.

Whyte, Angus. 2013. *After-Dinner Tales*. Bloomington, IN: Xlibris Corporation.

Whyte, Martin K. 1988. "Death in the People's Republic of China." In *Death Ritual in Late Imperial and Modern China*, edited by James L. Watson and Evelyn S. Rawski, 289–316. Berkeley: University of California Press.

Williams, Pete. 2019. "Supreme Court Upholds Indiana Abortion Law Requiring Fetal Remains Be Buried or Cremated." *NBC News*, May 28. www.nbcnews.com/politics/supreme-court/supreme-court-upholds-indiana-abortion-law-requiring-fetal-remains-be-n1010736.

Williams, Timothy. 2014. "The Graying of America Is Speeding." *New York Times*, May 6. www.nytimes.com/2014/05/07/us/graying-of-america-is-speeding-report-says.html.

Wolfe, S. J. 2009. *Mummies in Nineteenth-Century America: Ancient Egyptians as Artifacts*. Jefferson, NC: McFarland.

Wolff, Robert Paul. 1988. *Moneybags Must Be So Lucky: On the Literary Structure of Capital*. Amherst: University of Massachusetts Press.

Wynne Willson, Jane. 1990. *Funerals without God*. London: British Humanist Association.

Yang, Mayfair. 1994. *Gifts, Favors, and Banquets: The Art of Social Relationships in China*. Ithaca, NY: Cornell University Press.

Yates, JoAnne. 2005. *Structuring the Information Age: Life Insurance and Technology in the Twentieth Century*. Baltimore, MD: The Johns Hopkins University Press.

Yeo Sijia, Sonia. 2017. Preparing Departed Loved Ones for Their Final Journey. *Todayonline*, July 8, 2017. www.todayonline.com/lifestyle/preparing-departed-loved-ones-their-final-journey?fbclid=IwAR1_I-vzVZFVSVhSBVoO-jOgTueSYBefNuFUTAawgvpJHr4SxmT3jj0RvBM.

Yurchak, Alexei. 2015. "Bodies of Lenin: The Hidden Science of Communist Sovereignty." *Representations* 129 (1): 116–57.

Yusoff, Kathryn. 2018. *A Billion Black Anthropocenes or None*. Minneapolis: University of Minnesota Press.

Zelizer, Viviana. 1978. "Human Values and the Market: The Case of Life Insurance and Death in 19th-Century America." *American Journal of Sociology* 84 (3): 591–610.

———. 1979. *Morals and Markets: The Development of Life Insurance in the United States*. Livingston, NJ: Transaction Books.

———. 2009. *The Purchase of Intimacy*. Princeton, NJ: Princeton University Press.

Zhavoronkov, Alex. 2018. "We Are an Industry Now: The Emergence of AI-powered Longevity Biotechnology Industry." *Startup*, June 28. https://medium.com/swlh/we-are-an-industry-now-the-emergence-of-ai-powered-longevity-biotechnology-industry-1508a0596d3c.

Zimmer, Carl. 2015. "A Pregnancy Souvenir: Cells That Are Not Your Own. *New York Times*, September 10. www.nytimes.com/2015/09/15/science/a-pregnancy-souvenir-cells-that-are-not-your-own.html.

Zwane, Nokuthula. 2019. "Royal Swazi Rites for Mswati's Wife." *Sowetan LIVE: Sunday World*, March 12. www.sowetanlive.co.za/sundayworld/news/2019-03-12-royal-swazi-rites-for-mswatis-wife/.

Participants in the School for Advanced Research Advanced Seminar "21st-Century Death Cultures," co-chaired by Shannon Lee Dawdy and Tamara Kneese, September 23–27, 2018. Left to right: Shannon Lee Dawdy, Anya Bernstein, Rebekah Lee, Matthew Engelke, Abou Farman, Tim Hutchings, Tamara Kneese, Philip Olson, Jenny Huberman, and Margaret Schwartz. Photograph by Garret Vreeland. © School for Advanced Research.

ELLEN BADONE
Departments of Anthropology and Religious Studies, McMaster University

ANYA BERNSTEIN
Department of Anthropology, Harvard University

SHANNON LEE DAWDY
Department of Anthropology, University of Chicago

MATTHEW ENGELKE
Department of Religion, Columbia University

ABOU FARMAN
Department of Anthropology, The New School

CASEY GOLOMSKI
Department of Anthropology, University of New Hampshire

LASHAYA HOWIE
Department of Anthropology, University of Chicago

JENNY HUBERMAN
Department of Sociology, University of Missouri-Kansas City

TAMARA KNEESE
Media Studies Department, University of San Francisco

HUWY-MIN LUCIA LIU
Department of Sociology and Anthropology, George Mason University

PHILIP R. OLSON
Department of Science, Technology, and Society

STEPHANIE SCHIAVENATO
Department of Anthropology, New York University

MARGARET SCHWARTZ
Fordham University, Department of Communication and Media Studies

RUTH E. TOULSON
Maryland Institute College of Art

Page numbers in italic text indicate illustrations.

feminism: and death, 10, 11, 115, 182; feminist disability studies, 172n7, 288; and medical self-knowledge, 80

Fisher, Irving, 88, 89, 99. *See also* Life Extension Institute

Fisk, Almond Dunbar, 200

Fisk, Eugene Lyman, 97, 99, 100, 101. *See also* Life Extension Institute

FlexMort, 168, 171; Cuddlecot, 168–71

Floyd, George, 238, 287

Foucault, Michel, 89, 178

Franzese family: Luca, 236; Theresa, 236

Freud, Sigmund, 1–2, 10, 180, 196

Funchess, Dan, 225–26

Funeral Consumers Alliance, 227

funeral homes/parlors, 10, 16, 186, 187, 191; Black/African American ownership of, 159n5; COVID-19 pandemic and, 199; in the People's Republic of China, 241, 242, 243, 245–46, 247–48, 250, 254; in Singapore, 259, 261–62; in the US, 6, 160n9, 164, 178, 198

funerals, 113, 125; British Humanist Association and, 126–32, 136; as jobsites, 130; protests associated with, 118

Future of Humanity Institute (Oxford University), 28, 32

Future of Life Institute (MIT), 39

futurists, 23, 57, 61, 99. *See also* transhumanism

futurity, 40–41

Gard, Charlie, 171

gay persons, 114. *See also* queerness

Geertz, Clifford, 272, 273, 274

gender, 113–14, 116; death-care industry in the US and, 152, 155, 178, 190; death practices and, 12, 192, 228, 239n8, 261–62, 267–68, 269; trans persons, 78. *See also* doulas; midwives; women

ghosts, 54, 66, 215

gig economy, 76–77

globalization, 7, 9, 12, 209, 279, 293, 294

GoFundMe, 76, 79

Gorer, Geoffrey, 1

gossip/rumor, 53, 54, 55, 64, 188

gravestones, 135

graveyards. *See* cemeteries

green burials/death practices, 11, 12, 245, 300, 304–5

grief/grieving 19, 139, 179, 268, 273, 274, 303; crying as expression of, 21, 268–71; cultural particularity of, 270–71; DIY/home-funeral/home death movement and, 234; reproductive grief, 161, 167; sonic expression of and Sinophone funerals, 268–70

Hallam, Elizabeth, 6

haptics: boundaries of, 188–89; touch/hand in death care, 177–78, 181–82, 184, 190–91; touch/hand as mediating, 183, 185–86; social inequality and, 179, 184–85

Hardin, Garrett, 43

Hawking, Stephen, 27–28, 32, 33, 34, 49–50n1

Hayasaki, Erika, 9–10

health: public health, 75, 92, 97, 98, 100, 219, 291; sanitation, 21, 199, 213, 224. *See also* COVID-19 pandemic; HIV/AIDS

health-care providers/institutions, 166, 167, 188, 222, 223–26, 236, 296n1; release of human remains by, 229–30

Heidegger, Martin, 15, 180–81

Heinonen, Henry Lee, 106, 284

Hertz, Robert, 5, 125

HIV/AIDS, 106, 108, 109–10, 113, 114, 120; ethnography of, 117, 124n1

Hobart, Hi'ilei, 79

Hockey, Jenny, 6

Schwartz, Margaret, 179–80
science, 15, 214, 295, 307–8; British
    Humanist Association funerals
    and, 140, 142, 143, 301; DIY/home-
    funeral/home death movement
    and, 234; futurelessness and, 31,
    309, 310; neuroscience, 288; nucle-
    ar testing and, 40; technoscience,
    3, 31, 306, 307; terminality and, 33,
    34–36, 302
Seaver, Nick, 75
secular humanism, 22, 126; despair as
    result of, 34, 41, 46–48, 307–8,
    310. *See also* British Humanist
    Association
secularization, 7, 242
self-care practices, 74, 75, 79–80, 86; data
    collection and, 81, 82; life industry
    and, 86, 87, 93–94, 100; morality
    and, 89, 97; neoliberalism and,
    89–90; worker productivity and,
    93–94, 101
self-optimization practices, 15, 73, 90;
    worker productivity and, 81, 84,
    88–89, 93
Showers of Love service, 271; origin
    of, 264; procedure of, 264–65;
    traditional beliefs/practices and,
    266–67, 268–69; as reflecting
    changing beliefs, 267–68, 270 273
Silicon Valley, 14, 53, 59, 60, 61, 64, 73,
    74, 282; transhumanists and, 32,
    57–58, 70n6
Singapore, 114, 244, 271; Chinese popu-
    lation of, 259, 265–66, 270, 274n2,
    274n4; cremation, as practice in,
    261, 275n9; death rituals in, 259,
    263, 266–68, 270, 273; embalming,
    as practice in, 259, 263–64, 266,
    267; funeral parlors in, 259–63,
    264
Singularity Institute for Artificial
    Intelligence (SIAI)/Machine

Intelligence Research Institute
    (MIRI), 38–39
Sinophone cultures: death-care profes-
    sionals in, 243–4; death pollution,
    244–45, 260, 265, 266, 292; death
    practices/rituals, 242, 261, 264,
    266–67, 270, 274–75n44
Sloane, David Charles, 8
Smith, Christen, 116–17
social inequality, 63, 69, 107; death-care
    industry in the US and, 150,
    159n7; death practices and, 7, 8–9,
    12, 80, 115, 179, 237; insurance
    companies in the US and, 74, 75,
    81, 88–89, 90, 92–93, 94, 96–97,
    98; racialization and, 118–19, 121,
    151, 179, 287; transhumanism and,
    54, 55; in the US, 202, 238, 302–3;
    vampires/vampirism and, 54, 55,
    59, 60–61, 67
socialism, 70n6, 243, 251, 252–53, 255
social media: and death practices, 9, 12,
    13, 17; Facebook, 9, 84, 236; insur-
    ance companies' use of data from,
    84. *See also* technology
social reform movements, in the US, 97,
    98, 99, 100
South Africa, 54, 117–18
Soviet Union, 306, 309. *See also* Russia
Spillers, Hortense, 43
spirit, 111, 128, 183, 204, 212, 290; spirit
    possession, 54–55, 290
Spiritualism, 201, 215
subjectivity, 250–56, 270, 273, 285, 286;
    brain as central to, 288
Sullivan, F. A., 202
Suvalescu, Julian, 44
Swaziland. *See* eSwatini
Swazi people, 106, 114, 115, 120. *See also*
    eSwatini

taboos: the corpse and, 1–2; related to
    death, 1, 20, 114, 119, 197

www.ingramcontent.com/pod-product-compliance
Lightning Source LLC
Chambersburg PA
CBHW030916270326
41929CB00008B/724